EMPIRE'S NURSERY

# Empire's Nursery

*Children's Literature and the Origins of the American Century*

Brian Rouleau

NEW YORK UNIVERSITY PRESS
New York

NEW YORK UNIVERSITY PRESS
New York
www.nyupress.org

© 2021 by New York University
All rights reserved

References to Internet websites (URLs) were accurate at the time of writing. Neither the author nor New York University Press is responsible for URLs that may have expired or changed since the manuscript was prepared.

Library of Congress Cataloging-in-Publication Data
Names: Rouleau, Brian, author.
Title: Empire's nursery : children's literature and the origins of the American century / Brian Rouleau.
Description: New York : New York University Press, [2021] | Includes bibliographical references and index.
Identifiers: LCCN 2021003070 | ISBN 9781479804474 (hardback) | ISBN 9781479804504 (ebook) | ISBN 9781479804481 (ebook other)
Subjects: LCSH: Children's literature, American—History and criticism. | Young adult literature, American—History and criticism. | Internationalism in literature.
Classification: LCC PS490 .R68 2021 | DDC 810.9/9282—dc23
LC record available at https://lccn.loc.gov/2021003070

New York University Press books are printed on acid-free paper, and their binding materials are chosen for strength and durability. We strive to use environmentally responsible suppliers and materials to the greatest extent possible in publishing our books.

Manufactured in the United States of America

10 9 8 7 6 5 4 3 2 1

Also available as an ebook

*For Katherine*

CONTENTS

Introduction: Juvenile Foreign Relations; or, Policy at the Level of Popular Fiction   1

1. How the West Was Fun   21

2. Serialized Imperialism   55

3. Empire's Amateurs   89

4. Internationalist Impulses   119

5. Dollar Diplomacy for the Price of a Few Nickels   154

6. Comic Book Cold War   188

Epilogue: The Empire Writes Back   225

*Acknowledgments*   233

*Notes*   235

*Index*   299

*About the Author*   311

# Introduction

*Juvenile Foreign Relations; or, Policy at the Level of Popular Fiction*

In February 1941, Henry Luce, publisher of *Time* magazine, circulated a now-famous editorial announcing the so-called American Century's birth. Luce urged his fellow citizens to dispense with their isolationist instincts and embrace a strengthened role for the United States abroad. This new era should begin, he suggested, with the country's entry into World War II. But after America's inevitable triumph, he believed the nation could then proceed to redeem the remainder of the world for democracy. The United States was to become an international missionary, spreading the gospel of freedom and uplifting foreign peoples. Luce's call to arms eventually came to fruition in the form of a more muscular foreign policy that deepened America's engagement with global affairs.[1]

Perhaps less familiar, however, was a competing claim made by sociologist Ellen Key, who in 1900 conjectured an upcoming epoch known as the Century of the Child. In a book popular among influential academics and policymakers in the United States, Key pressed people to devote more time and resources to the welfare of youths. It was her hope that the next hundred years might see child labor eradicated. In its place would arise a concomitant commitment to the promotion of childhood as a sheltered stage in life reserved exclusively for education and play. The Century of the Child, Key believed, could revolutionize international relations once the world's countries reorganized themselves around the interests of their littlest citizens.[2]

Luce and Key never spoke directly. But *Empire's Nursery* suggests that we place their respective conceptualizations of the global order—the American Century and the Century of the Child—into productive conversation. For although Luce's term became shorthand for postwar America's imperial aspirations, and Key's inspired child-centered reforms both in the United States and beyond, they are not so disparate

1

as it may initially appear. In fact, children's literature acted as one of the principal forums through which adults attempted to articulate and amplify their sense of America's rightful role as a global hegemony. Once the concept of childhood as a developmental phase distinct from all others gained greater cultural and legal currency in the United States, young people were approached as a crucial audience whose consent could help legitimize the country's increasing involvement in international affairs. The origins of the American Century can be traced in part to a series of children's authors who had sought, since the 1860s at least, to educate young people regarding their nation's hemispheric and global obligations. The success of these writers in doing so must be measured in the growing popular embrace of an activist American state overseas.[3]

Therefore, we should reimagine children's literature published between the Civil War and the Vietnam War as a species of diplomatic discourse. Expansionist policies, after all, did not simply need to be promulgated; they needed to be made generationally durable. Empire is not simply the exercise of power across territorial space or a coercive control over subject peoples. Instead, empires entail investment across time. The next generation of junior imperialists must always have hegemonic habits of thought introduced to them if international agendas are to be replicated. The young had to be made ideological allies for the ethic of empire to endure. This was the assumption that undergirded what we might call juvenile foreign relations. Children's literature seeded among young people a conviction that their country's command of a continent (and later the world) was essential to the maintenance of international order. It perpetuated across several generations the sense that America's supervisory authority over "inferior" nations and peoples made the United States a great and powerful polity. Authors attempted to acculturate their young audience into an ongoing imperial project.[4]

Empires more generally require stories to justify their existence. Geopolitical gendarmes like the United States rely upon conceptual frameworks that explain their claims to power. As a result, "representational machines" in the metropole busily churn out cultural products that glorify the redemptive influence of America's capital, technology, and armed forces. This book, however, challenges the implicit assumption among many scholars that the fictions sustaining expansionist policymaking were for "adults only." Kids, it turns out, acted as an important audience as well. And, in the United States, children's literature has been one of the most important forums by which adults sought to instill in young people an imperial consciousness. Presumptions about America's inherent right to govern a continent did not materialize out of thin air. The country's assumption of its role as the leader of the free world was hardly *sui generis*. Rather, these expectations represent fruit borne of patient cultural work among young people. Since the 1860s at least, children in the United States were raised in a climate that often celebrated the exercise of national power over others deemed unfit for self-government. Their books and periodicals invited youths to rehearse justifications for America's pretensions to global preeminence.[5]

Children's literature, in fact, provided an ideal venue through which to promote America's sovereign authority abroad. The genre allowed ardent imperialists to conceal their aggressive agendas with a veneer of virtuousness. Authors exploited perceptions of childhood as a stage in life characterized by innocence and wonder in order to sanitize the more brutal dimensions of US colonialism on the North American continent and beyond. The supposedly nonthreatening nature of the child and children's literature thereby helped to disguise dominion's unsavory nature. A country born in the throes of anti-colonial struggle, after all, could not help but harbor ambivalent sentiments regarding empire. By transforming territorial and commercial expansion into a wholesome sort of "child's play," juvenile literature reduced popular resistance to policies and practices that might otherwise have been harder to swallow. Youth reading provided a key venue wherein Americans portrayed themselves as the selfless heroes of their own international scheming. Potent mythologies regarding the inherent beneficence of Uncle Sam's ministrations were imparted by those speaking to the nation's rising generations. Here, in its conversion into harmless "kids' stuff," lay one of the crucial mechanisms by which American empire managed to remain "hidden" for so many years.[6]

The literature written specifically for children, when considered collectively, should therefore be perceived as an important component of the larger history of the United States in the world. Recent scholarship has sought to highlight the multiple ways in which America's past has intersected with foreign peoples and external influences. Various forces contributed to the country's globalization. Immigration, capitalist development, and religion, among other factors, have recently received attention for the parts they played in internationalizing the American experience. So too have new cohorts of people been depicted as some of the principal drivers of the nation's foreign relations. Informal imperialists and nonstate actors now occupy pivotal positions in our histories of the United States and its connections to the wider world.[7]

And yet, diverse as this cast of characters has become, notice one thing they share in common: their adulthood. It is as if human experience with foreign relations only begins with the age of majority. What might be gained once we appreciate the influence of young people, as both spectators and agent, in the long history of America's association with the world? Children and adolescents, after all, are more present in the history of international affairs than might be suspected at first glance. They are hiding in plain sight. Imaginative scholars have recently begun to arrive at new and important insights by considering, in a more sustained manner, young people as an omnipresent audience for, object of, and even contributor to American foreign relations. This book is an effort to contribute something to that still-burgeoning conversation between historians of childhood and diplomacy.[8]

The discourse of juvenile foreign relations asks us to reconceive American empire as, at least in part, a youth project. Though not the country's only imperial agents (or even its most powerful), children were indispensable to the cultural process by which America's right to administer the affairs of "lesser" peoples gained widespread acceptance. If we think of empire as one nation's assertion of its responsibility to rule another—even if cloaked in the rhetoric of charitability—then kids must be viewed as actors who duplicated that presumption across time. American empire expanded because young people, for their own reasons, experienced it as a good and fun part of their lives, something worth feeling invested in.

## Juvenile Jingoes

Interpretive dividends start to pay once we cease to treat young people as a silent minority and instead recognize that, for significant stretches of American history, people under the age of 20 have comprised a plurality—and before 1890 a majority—of the population. Many of the books and magazines for youths discussed here, meanwhile, had some of the highest circulation numbers among all printed matter in the United States. Focusing on young people is therefore hardly an act of generational tokenism but rather a recognition of the crucial role played by a sizeable slice of America's demographic pie. Authors at the time rarely failed to acknowledge as much. The editors of the *American Boy* magazine only joined a chorus of voices when they remarked that, while "we are now a prosperous and happy people," the "task of keeping us so rests with the boy of today." If "the surest way to make good citizens [was] to make good boys," then "the future of this country" could only be "assured when the spirit of American patriotism is implanted in the young and buoyant hearts of our American boys." Inspiring a love of country necessary to national survival, as it turned out, often coincided with the ennoblement of imperial achievement. Efforts to determine political outcomes—including the embrace of empire—meant winning the hearts and minds of youths.[9]

Children's literature thus helps us to understand the mechanisms by which America's offspring were socialized into an increasingly global outlook. But, as the above quote illustrates, sensationalist fiction for youth often purported to speak with boys specifically. The protagonists of these tales were almost always young men, and the authors who directly addressed their audiences assumed they possessed a predominantly male composition. Such storytelling, therefore, was not simply about educating generations of American youth regarding their imperial responsibilities. Empire was also portrayed as a means to coach boys in the art of manhood. It was meant to model masculine duty for their emulation. Books and periodicals marketed to young men during the long nineteenth century's protracted crisis of manliness found in juvenile foreign relations an opportunity to revivify rugged martial virtues. Yet for as much as publishers intended for empire's nursery to be a boys' club, the evidence suggests that girls regularly crashed the gates. The history of US empire must make room for young people—both boys and girls—as an important constituency in its construction. We should also acknowledge, however, that the boys who eagerly read violent colonial narratives were raised to believe in their sex's particular entitlement to imperial power.[10]

Moreover, that imperial power intersected with racial power. The two ideologies—imperialism and racism—often reinforced one another.

Popular fiction for young people almost always spoke to white children specifically. It justified empire as a rightful enactment of the white race's responsibility to "lesser" peoples deemed incapable of self-rule. The discourse of juvenile foreign relations was therefore also intended as an education in the necessity of America's own racial hierarchy. The Black and Brown bodies marked for subjugation "out there," in the West and beyond, had to be kept under control at home as well. Some of white America's first exposure to systematized racism—a kind of folk racial taxonomy—occurred within the pages of juvenile literature. When covered with a coating of imperial adventurism, this ideology was able to take firmer root. White dominance could be difficult to disentangle from fun. Children's literature became an important delivery vehicle for the racial thinking that made imperialism possible, even as empire abroad further legitimated the country's domestic color hierarchy—a dynamic that has been called Jim Crow colonialism.[11]

Of course, the regularity with which female readers infiltrated a genre "meant" for their brothers gestures to a larger disjuncture between authorial intentions and lived experience. No perfect correlation between the reading one does as a child and the politics they develop as an adult can be postulated. Youths who read rabidly imperialistic rhetoric early in life were not necessarily fated to embrace those ideas as they aged. People are not automatons whose initial programming later results in specific sensibilities. Publishers could not guarantee foreign policy outcomes. The issue of reader response is subtler and more speculative. What many children's authors committed themselves to instead was arguing for audiences the virtues of imperialism.

Children's literature should be considered one field among many that generated desire and provided justification for American empire. Media firms helped advance expansionist ideologies by naturalizing the West and other global frontiers as ripe for US exploitation. Publishing houses mitigated the violence and dispossession that attended America's growing global footprint by dehumanizing those who resisted their generous Uncle Sam. Children's literature made it that much harder for many young people to understand North America and the world beyond as anything other than an extension of their own nation's dominion. As such, the genre deserves more attention as a critical component of the larger edifice scholars call the "culture of United States imperialism." As

Figure I.1. As their reading increasingly diverged from that of adults, children gathered in separate spaces to discuss the content of their books. Many of those arenas became imperial nurseries, suffused with rhetoric and imagery championing American expansion. Library of Congress Prints and Photographs Division.

the country colonized the West and its insular possessions, children's authors simultaneously sought to exercise a quasi-colonial authority over young readers asked to embrace the idea of imperial altruism. America's ability to apply hard power overseas, often without significant domestic opposition, depended on the persuasive capabilities of writers speaking to youthful audiences.[12]

The children whom editors targeted, however, were neither passive participants in their own politicization nor the docile "subjects" that imperious cultural authorities expected to address. We cannot presume that authors held sway over a virtually captive youth audience. If publications are to succeed, children must *choose* to find them palatable. If messaging is to perpetuate across generational lines, junior citizens must find it worthy of perpetuation. Therefore, *Empire's Nursery* seeks to locate, wherever possible, the voices of children and adolescents themselves. It will delve into the international perspective of young people and demonstrate their contributions to ongoing conversations about the proper relationship of the United States to colonized or dependent peoples in North America and elsewhere. This is no easy task. The child's relationship to fiction is difficult to discern, and young people rarely read literature in any straightforward or literal manner. Authorial intentions can be distorted within the crucible of youthful imagination while a text's "meaning" depends upon when it is read, where it is read, and how a reader has been trained to read. Prose is "polyvocal," its messaging heterogeneous and inconsistent. Any adult who revisits cherished childhood books is often astonished to discover how certain themes and meanings utterly evaded their younger selves.[13]

But even with these caveats, it is still the case that kids exercised a certain degree of influence over the content of their reading material, thereby contributing to broader national dialogues about US empire. Indeed, many authors and editors of children's literature promoted a sense of possessive investment in expansion by fostering a cooperative dynamic between creators and consumers. Ultimately, this book posits that youth culture acted as an important but understudied battleground for competing ideas regarding the propriety of directing American power toward imperial ends. Furthermore, *Empire's Nursery* treats young people as important (if unequal) co-producers of the broader discourse of American aggrandizement. In so doing, it locates politics in hitherto unexpected places, and among an age cohort usually considered apolitical or pre-political. What limited evidence we have points to lively debate about diplomacy among a segment of the population we are ordinarily content to overlook. Children may not have been policymakers, but the cultural construction of imperialism did at least partly reflect their demands. Empire did not simply work "on" junior citizens but "through" them as well.[14]

Yet all that discussion did not often produce significant challenges to adult authority. Juveniles frequently expressed enthusiasm for expansionistic agendas and sought to replicate the language used to justify the dispossession of others considered unlike themselves. And in so doing, they reveal the interpretive mistake we often make in conflating agency with resistance. There is a tendency among scholars to find young people as fully realized historical actors only in those moments where they actively subvert or contest dominant social structures. We remain most fascinated with those individuals who, for whatever set of reasons or motives, defy prescribed social relations. The problem with this particular paradigm, however, is that it can overlook the crucial roles of consent and conformity in the replication of cultural norms, including those that govern understandings of the United States in the wider world. While historians rightly tend to emphasize the importance of change over time, the significance of stasis should not be ignored. Children are often a critical force for philosophical continuity.

Minors, therefore, did not passively mirror prevailing attitudes, but instead played an active part in the reproduction of imperial values. It is uncommon, after all, for young people to offer anything like a full-throated challenge to the status quo and its grownup gatekeepers. Most youths ultimately aim to please their superiors in what is an age-based hierarchy; they are almost always rewarded for doing so and punished for any failure to obey. This results in what has been called the child's instinct toward compliance. But compliance should not be confused with unthinking obedience. Children's assent is its own form of agency. Rather than fixating exclusively on youthful challenges to authority, we should work to understand how young people's choices to affirm and replicate particular power structures is itself a phenomenon worthy of study. Many of the basic assumptions governing American foreign relations, broadly defined, represent the legacy of lessons learned (and willingly embraced) by young people operating under their own auspices and toward their own ends. Children most often exercise power and shape the cultures in which they live largely by agreeing to ally themselves with adult desires. We therefore should not fail to deny them a say in their own history, even if they do not say what we might like to hear.[15]

And one of the key avenues by which young people spoke up, and voiced a sense of national belonging, was to express their commitment to the republic's international agenda. Children connected themselves to the state through their investment in imperial politics. Meanwhile, conscious appeals to young people and an immersion in youth culture helped authors to articulate the meaning, purpose, and stakes of American foreign policy. Whether publications meant to introduce America's children to the country's Indian population or offer capsule ethnographies of foreign countries, ideologues sought to manage the outlooks of young people and promote consensus surrounding federal foreign policymaking. Empire's children became a crucial (if underappreciated) sector helping to bolster an expansionist vision for the wider world.

Yet the obverse is equally true. Systems can break down when the rising generation no longer finds validation in imperial narratives. The study of youths—and youth culture more generally—aids our ability to comprehend how various assumptions regarding the role of the United States in global affairs are either reproduced or altered across time. And though stasis is more common, young people have sometimes developed new ways of seeing and engaging with the world that better reflected their own priorities. In so doing, they have subtly changed the nation's subsequent approach to foreign relations. "It is within children's cultures," we are reminded, "that new sensibilities evolve." At moments when elders fail to satisfactorily explain to their successors the application of American power in an international arena, major shifts in policy have become possible. Thus, this book also traces undercurrents of imperial skepticism within children's literature (and children's outlooks) that helped to deconstruct empire's nursery toward the twentieth century's tail end.[16]

In ways we are only beginning to appreciate, generational distinctions, often cultivated by youths themselves, act as an important driver for fresh forms of diplomacy. When scholars of foreign relations, broadly construed, pay closer attention to the history of childhood, they begin to find new types of transnational networks, discover varieties of international association they had not yet considered, and locate the growth of imperial sensibilities in hitherto unfamiliar spaces. To the extent that empire became "a way of life" among Americans between the Civil War and Vietnam, we must see young people's embrace of expansionist ideology as a contributing factor. Imperial habits of thought were not simply handed down from on high. Many neophyte nationalists, expecting to achieve their own objectives, clamored to participate in the enactment of US hegemony. Others, meanwhile, sought to dismantle those power structures.[17]

## Embracing Sensation

Historians have repeatedly emphasized that the growing omnipresence of children's literature in the nineteenth-century United States helped legitimate (and sacralize) childhood as a distinct stage in life. A history of children's literature, however, is also inescapably a history of children's reading. The chronological contours of this study reflect that fact. Beginning the monograph in the middle of the nineteenth century should not imply that youths lacked their own books prior to the Civil War, but it does recognize that the postbellum literary marketplace became far more "age-segmented" than its precursor. Ending with the Vietnam conflict, meanwhile, is not meant to suggest that children's literature ceased to impact the lives of juvenile Americans at that point.[18]

The start and the finish for *Empire's Nursery* instead reflect the roughly hundred-year period when adult writers made their most vigorous attempts to instill in young readers a belief in the benevolence of their country's foreign relations agenda *and* the culture writ large worked hardest to create what has been termed the "priceless child." Thus, even as the authors of juvenile literature imbued childhood with its increasingly rich social significance, they likewise more fully entrenched expansionist approaches to American foreign relations. The processes of sanctifying children and enacting empire not only occurred in concert but were in fact mutually reinforcing. That colonization was itself justified by the "child-like" qualities of "barbarian" peoples only strengthened the connection. So too did the fact that then (as now), interventionist foreign policy programs could be rationalized as necessary for the protection of either the nation's children or imperiled innocents elsewhere.[19]

Prior to the 1850s, most youth literature was either didactic or religious in nature. Global or transcontinental themes were harder to find. Authors instead sought to replicate the habits and manners that made a person respectable, at least by the standards of an emerging bourgeoise. Antebellum books possessed a politics, of course, but that politics was less avowedly imperial. Early juvenile literature built character rather than empire; it was meant to engender the virtue considered essential to a healthy republic's citizenry. After the 1960s, on the other hand, countercultural forces regularly challenged previously mainstream pieties regarding America's inherent magnanimity. As television's popularization altered the means by which political messaging reached most children, juvenile literature changed its tune. US empire no longer appeared as a legitimate aspiration. Authors more commonly treated it as an embarrassment, something from which youths should be sheltered.[20]

But the roughly 100 years between those two poles—from the Civil War to Vietnam—saw systematic efforts on the part of writers to promote among their young audience members an enthusiastic embrace of America's international influence. Part of that story has to do with the development of a national market for juvenile publications during the postbellum period. Previously, youth reading had been far more regionally oriented. Northerners and Midwesterners learned about the virtues of free labor, while white Southern children were raised to become "masters of small worlds." After the slaveholders' rebellion concluded, however, and a more nationally integrated system of transportation infrastructure arose, kids in disparate corners of the country began to share reading material like never before. This posed a problem for publishers. How could a newly national children's literature circumvent regional or parochial concerns? One method for doing so was to focus on imperial subject matter. Issues like the subjugation of the West or the War of 1898 seemed to possess a transcendent quality. No matter what their background, prospective readers (always imagined at the time as white American boys) were thought amenable to American empire.[21]

Moreover, these were years when the child's position within the family shifted, albeit gradually and unevenly, from one of economic to affective value. The "work" kids could be asked to perform became tied less and less to the marketplace. Instead, they were meant to be educated. New laws and shifting mores pulled many young people out of the labor pool and urged them to train as citizens, and that at a time when the nation itself embarked upon the paths of empire in North America and beyond. Citizenship, then, was itself an increasingly imperial proposition, and young people were invited to reckon with that reality. The historic confluence of these events—an American society more publicly committed to both its children *and* an expansionist foreign policy—therefore demands recognition. The sensationalistic stories of savage Indians, supplicating Cubans, and inhuman communists populating juvenile bookstores invited the nation's youth to imagine US interventionism as a necessary civilizational bulwark. Children's literature sought to mold an American youth better prepared to accept and endorse their country's newfound obligations, first as a transcontinental and later a world power.

But youths more eagerly "bought in" to the imperial frame because it was sold to them at precisely the moment when their daily lives became vastly more circumscribed. Empire was exciting. It was "out there," a freer space beyond the monotony and routine of schoolwork and chores. The culture of imperialism, in other words, was not haughtily imposed by adult authorities. There was an intergenerational dynamic at play, wherein kids, responding to changes in their own lives, demanded the compensatory relief that expansionist antics afforded. Infamous censorship crusader Anthony Comstock actually acknowledged as much when, in his campaign to kill the dime novel, he complained that "the hero of each story is a boy who has escaped the restraints of home." Or, as another reader more fondly remembered, "the American boy's soul soared and sang" as he read of "battles with Indians and 'Greasers.'" "Out of his surroundings, however sordid, the boy was lifted," thanks to "the producer of dime fiction." The appeal of empire to American youths, in other words, was exactly its association with escape. As tedium quieted adolescent lives, the country's culture industries churned out an antidote in the form of copious stories detailing imperial adventurism.[22]

So widespread was this discourse of juvenile foreign relations that it presents problems of evidentiary density. Put simply, there is too much to read. In an effort to make analysis feasible, some source material had to be set aside. As a result, this cannot be a study of schoolbooks. Nor, for that matter, will this volume deal with more timeless, standalone texts considered "canon." Unfortunately, my interest in the forest necessitates missing more than a few trees along the way. Instead, the principal archives consulted were those of the popular press. Critics may have spurned cheap fiction as vile, but circulation figures suggest that young Americans much preferred thrilling tales of territorial conquest and overseas adventure to the high-minded and domestically oriented stories characterizing the antebellum era.[23]

The argument begins in the 1860s largely because this was the decade when a national market for mass-produced and inexpensive children's media arose. Previously, parents selected texts for their children. These

Figure 1.2. As this satiric cartoon suggests, adults were well aware of the violent imperial fantasies permeating the pages of postbellum children's literature. Library of Congress Prints and Photographs Division.

were books meant to be read as a family unit and intended to impart a moral. Cheap fiction's widespread appearance—largely as novels sold to youths during the Civil War—changed the landscape of juvenile literacy. Much to the chagrin of their mothers and fathers, many young people could now afford to purchase and peruse reading material independent of adult supervision. And those books and magazines exchanged their previously prescriptive function for a more adventure-oriented ethos. Fearing the overstimulation of young minds, adult censors denounced the new stress placed on excitement in children's literature as "sensationalism." They worried over plots that had precocious junior protagonists venturing beyond the fireside. But youths themselves embraced these changes wholeheartedly. Therefore, from the postbellum era's dime novels and the Gilded Age's youth magazines to turn-of-the-century series fiction, from early twentieth-century pulps to the comics of postwar America, the focus here is on what *many* (but by no means all) youths themselves most often *chose* to read rather than what they were told to read. Excluded are *some* young people who did not or could not partake of popular culture.[24]

Shortcomings inevitably result. For one, "children's literature" encompasses an astonishing array of sources, only the tiniest fraction of which is addressed here. Problematic, too, is the way in which talk of a generic "youth culture" or "juvenile readership" inherently flattens the diversity of each during the century under consideration. Examining mass-market children's reading almost automatically reduces the sample size of historical actors to literate and leisured individuals. Many millions of unschooled persons would not have engaged with the efforts at imperialist indoctrination discussed here. Moreover, those same children, even if they possessed a rudimentary literacy, found less time to read once they became wage laborers. Populations of working-class and immigrant youths (and their specific subcultures) are therefore heavily underrepresented in this study.[25]

So too are nonwhite children. With rare exceptions, Black, Indian, and Asian juveniles (among others) did not find much children's literature that spoke to their specific experiences. Only gradually would peoples of color find themselves depicted as anything other than antagonists in mainstream youth media. This has been one of the genre's slowest but most significant transformations. As colonized populations rose up to chronicle the crimes committed against them, children's literature had a harder time sustaining the supposed virtues of US empire. A decidedly leftward drift among authors for young people became more and more pronounced across the twentieth century, particularly as nonwhite writers for children garnered notoriety. For much of the time period and in most of the texts considered here, however, authors addressed an implied reader who was white, a boy, and of the middling classes. Children of color, on the other hand, were themselves "the colonized" in imperial fiction. When writers permitted them to speak, it was usually to provide some justification for their own subjugation. Many of this book's conclusions are therefore similarly bounded. It is hoped that *Empire's Nursery* can help chronicle the power dynamics within youth publishing that long made mainstream children's culture deeply monochromatic, while avoiding the reinscription of those same racial disparities.[26]

## The Nursery's Architecture

*Empire's Nursery* follows a roughly linear but somewhat broken timeline toward its denouement in Vietnam. Each chapter covers a particular moment in the history of the United States in the world and explores how that era's most popular children's literature structured those events for young readers. The book's various parts, however, also tend to focus on specific genres. Because those genres often possessed staying power, or slowly evolved into new forms of children's media, some mild chronological confusion became unavoidable. Neat periodization is not possible when wrestling with a literary world where texts take on a life of their own, continually resurfacing, intermixing, or transforming to meet a new generation's needs.

Chapter 1 deals with dime novels, "cheap fiction," and the valorization of America's postbellum territorial expansion. Quantitatively speaking, no single subgenre of children's literature proved more popular than the Western. Even more remarkable than the amount of material printed, however, has been the comparative lack of interest shown by scholars. But if we view US-Indian relations and the long "War for the West" as the most important driver of mid-nineteenth-century diplomacy, it suddenly makes sense to approach children's Westerns as core texts in the legitimization of settler colonial aims. Authors justified America's expansionist impulses by portraying geographic growth as a gift to posterity, denounced Indians as impediments to national progress, and enlisted young people as the future stewards of territorial empire.

The second chapter deals with the War of 1898, the US-Philippine War, and other "small-scale" conflicts at the turn of the twentieth century. To do so, it focuses on Edward Stratemeyer's so-called literary syndicate. Stratemeyer may be best known as either "Franklin W. Dixon" or "Carolyn Keene," pseudonymous authors of the Hardy Boys and Nancy Drew mysteries. But he first attained fame in 1898 as a purveyor of imperially inflected adventure stories for boys. His self-proclaimed authorial mission was to promote among American children a patriotic devotion to the country's recently won overseas empire. Tales set in Cuba and the Philippines were supposed to educate American youths regarding their country's (and their own) newfound commitments abroad. Yet the fan mail adolescents sent to Stratemeyer reveals a more complicated picture, one in which young people expressed their own thoughts on the subject.

The third chapter looks almost exclusively at the voices of minors themselves. It examines the vast archive of late nineteenth- and early twentieth-century amateur newspapers. These were tiny broadsheets published by juveniles at home using one of the era's most popular toys, the tabletop printing press. Children and adolescents (typically aged 10 to 20) wrote news articles and editorials on the topics of the day, and then circulated these pint-sized papers locally, regionally, and nationally. This chapter, therefore, is devoted to excavating and explicating perhaps the single largest public sphere historians have yet to explore. The fact that young people controlled the content of these newspapers makes them particularly intriguing sources. As it turns out, youths frequently wished to weigh in on diplomatic questions. Adolescents offered an array of opinions on territorial expansion in North America, Indian affairs, immigration, the war with Spain, and other issues. Amateur newspapers demonstrate the willingness of children to contribute to debates about topics scholars typically depict as implicitly "adult" in their orientation.

It is true that, as one historian has noted, "finding a critique of empire in a children's text is rare." The fourth chapter, however, argues that while imperialists were often dominant among the voices speaking to young people, jingoes did not entirely control the conversation. Imperialism's other, anti-imperialism, also found a home in certain segments of the youth literary market. Contrary impulses toward multilateralism, cosmopolitanism, and pacifism competed for children's attention, particularly during the interwar years. Writing in opposition to the senseless slaughter of trench warfare, the rise of fascism in Europe, and the naked nativism that fueled the effort to restrict immigration, authors who subscribed to the "cultural gifts" movement sought to build a better world by altering the attitudes of America's youth. Convinced by a professionalized class of Progressive-era child studies experts that the prejudices that produced conflict were largely a result of youthful habits, activists and missionaries sought a solution by attempting to inculcate very different values in juvenile audiences. Childhood, as a concept, and children, as a cohort, were thus placed at the center of conversations meant to promote cultural internationalism and remake relations between states.[27]

Chapter 5 explores pulp periodicals (so-called because of the cheap paper they were printed on) marketed to American teenagers during the first third of the twentieth century. The stories were diverse, but many dealt, in particular, with dollar diplomacy and the slew of US military deployments meant to "stabilize" Latin American and Caribbean countries. In their racism and pugnaciousness, however, they acted as a foil to the more pacifistic Progressive literature of the post–World War I era.

Ultimately, this chapter argues that the period's muscular interpretation of the Monroe Doctrine was partly a product of pulp fiction's proselytizing about US police powers in the Western Hemisphere and beyond.

Comic books, the focus of chapter 6, also provide one of the more fascinating glimpses into how foreign policy programs were made palatable for young readers. Their wild popularity makes the genre essential to any understanding of children's engagement with international affairs. Emerging out of early twentieth-century newspaper cartoons and pulp fiction, comic books attained complete dominance of the youth literary market by 1950. The storylines of those assorted publications—from superhero epics to high school romance—were rarely divorced from broader conversations about American commitments around the world. Indeed, the comic industry often promoted a militaristic agenda to burnish its patriotic credentials. But such plots were no mere cynical ploy. Big firms like Marvel and DC, as well as more niche outfits like EC and Quality, collected reams of market research as a means to know their audience, and, at least through the Vietnam War, kids found fun in the country's enhanced strategic obligations. Among children, the case for an interventionist "American Century" was most commonly made by brightly colored comics.

Finally, a brief epilogue discusses the transition to an era dominated by television. Young people now had foreign relations dramatized for them by their Saturday morning cartoons. Children's literature after the Vietnam War, meanwhile, became the province of self-professed liberals. Many were white college graduates who had seen adventurism abroad discredited by the era's anti-war and civil rights protests. Others were authors of color—hailing from the country's internal and external colonies—who began to publish children's literature documenting the struggles of those most affected by US expansionism. But in a curious irony, the openly imperialistic children's literature of an earlier era has recently been resuscitated by niche presses marketing their wares to conservative homeschoolers. Rebranded as an antidote to the "PC poison" printed by contemporary left-leaning authors, the nativism, xenophobia, and belligerence of earlier generations has found a new home among those most dissatisfied with modernity.

When combined, all of this literature acted as a nursery for American empire. It helped lay the broader cultural foundation upon which differential power relations between the United States and its dependencies could be normalized. Expansionist foreign policies cannot take shape (and cannot solidify over time) without an imperially minded public receptive to the idea of Uncle Sam's benevolent interventionism. A whole host of factors contributed to the widespread acknowledgment of America's rightful role as an arbiter of international affairs. Historians have reimagined numerous texts—from novels and films to Wild West shows and the midway displays at World's Fairs—as integral to the popular culture that satisfied an increasing public appetite for overseas entanglements. Yet young people were also very much a part of this unfolding process. Some of the most important architects of US global authority were juvenile authors and their junior audiences. Together, they helped lay a foundation for Americans' broad-based acceptance of their country as a superpower with important international responsibilities. Though excluded from the tables at which formal foreign policy was made, writers for children and their young fans still socialized large parts of the country into an ethic of American supremacy.[28]

Henry Luce may have coined the term "American Century," but he misspoke when calling out his countrymen for their failure "to accommodate themselves spiritually and practically to [the] fact" that the United States "became in the twentieth century the most powerful and the most vital nation in the world." Many American citizens did not need, as Luce implored, to "seek and bring forth a vision of America as a world power." Rather, by the 1940s, he addressed several generations well prepared to receive his words. Children's literature had strived to implant ideas about America's multiplying diplomatic obligations long ago. Belief in the indispensability and exceptionalism of the United States could not have rooted so firmly in the national imagination without the complicity of books and periodicals meant to mold young minds. It is to the history of those influential children's publications that we now turn.[29]

# 1

## How the West Was Fun

After the Civil War, Harry Harrison found himself stationed at a stockade along the Northern Plains. His mission was, as he put it, "to protect the hardy pioneers from the attacks of the Indians." Preparing to perform some reconnaissance at a nearby village one day, Harrison loaded up on firearms and saddled his horse. He expected trouble. The guns were meant as a deterrent, but the scout admitted that heavy weaponry "will not prevent the stratagem of the indians from trying to procure your scalp." As if on cue, he "heard a cry which made [the] blood run cold, so to speak, through [his] veins. It was the terrible war cry of the indians." Soon finding himself "bound hand and foot and tied to a tree" by "blood thirsty savages," the situation seemed dire. And yet, improbably, a bear ambled into the Native American encampment. The animal proved enough of a distraction for Harrison to make his escape. He "reached the fort without any further adventures."[1]

It was an eventful day, or, at least, it would have been were any of the above story true. Harry Harrison was certainly real enough. But in the 1870s, he was a still a young boy living in New Jersey with his parents. He was not old enough to serve as a soldier in the army and had not been tasked with the defense of American settlers. It is highly doubtful that he ever traveled west of the Appalachian Mountains, let alone the Mississippi River. Instead, he merely fantasized about frontier escapades; he could only dream about butchering Indians in service of civilization. Harry Harrison expressed those aspirations through his creative writing.

The resulting story, entitled "An Adventure with the Indians," possessed very little polish. It was comprised of two short sheets of paper. Misspellings and run-on sentences plagued every paragraph. The *deus ex machina* of the bear's appearance signaled a young, inexperienced writer's attempt to rapidly wrap up an account that had not been carefully plotted. But the significance of young Harry Harrison's tall tale does not lie in its relative lack of literary merit. Rather, the narrative gestures to the deeply imperial nature of children's imaginations during the postbellum period. For many young people, to act on an inventive impulse was to contemplate the era's expansionist policies and politics. Harry was hardly the only boy (or girl) who found a way to insinuate themselves into the conquest of the American West.

This chapter utilizes the archives of Gilded Age and Progressive Era youth culture—including juvenile literature, pubescent periodicals, "cheap fiction," and children's storytelling—in order to explore the means by which calls for genocidal violence spread across generational lines. Young people throughout the United States, it turns out, played a crucial (if underappreciated) part in the construction and normalization of what we might call "settler colonial sentiments." These habits of thought included the assent to and legitimization of the violent seizure of Native American land and the displacement or slaughter of Indians themselves; the articulation (and thus solidification of) broader understandings regarding the region's racial hierarchy; and eventual expressions of support for a reservation system supposedly geared toward the material and spiritual elevation of subjugated indigenous people. Adult-authored children's books and the literary creations of kids themselves, therefore, show us how and why young people "bought into" America's long-running settler colonial project. Adolescent novels helped to structure a forgotten demographic's reception of multipronged imperial policymaking in the US West. This media universe also embedded celebratory commemoration of Western conquests more deeply into the country's culture.[2]

But youths did not always unanimously and unthinkingly embrace what they read. Rather, they accepted or reshaped it based on their own desires and needs. In some cases, the continuous evolution of ideas about and conceptualizations of the West depended upon the challenges to orthodoxy that children offered. At other times, certain ideas about America's "pioneer heritage" were reified (one is tempted to say ossified) in large part because young people, working with their own agendas, actively chose to proliferate them. Historical agency, in other words, is not always expressed as dissent. The valorization of the West—as a region but more importantly as a space that embodied a particular set of ideals—only makes sense if we can appreciate the ways in which children acceded to the reproduction of those attitudes and values. Young people were, therefore, a critical constituency in the rhetorical reaffirmation of US settler colonialism.[3]

This is, ultimately, an approach to Western history that asks scholars to, in Karen Sánchez-Eppler's words, "take age seriously as a meaningful category of analysis" and embrace children as "significant and varied participants in the making of social meaning." From parents to their offspring and publishers to juvenile audiences, within schoolrooms and libraries, and among clubs, playhouses, and youth organizations, America's "rightful" role in the West was debated and discussed. Territorial expansion was a proposition made to young people in a variety of venues, one they consented to (and at times rejected or at least amended) for reasons of their own, reasons that they occasionally took time to articulate. When a New Jersey boy bragged of his Indian-fighting acumen, he unwittingly demonstrated the ways in which imperialistic thinking about the West was perpetuated across time. Looking at how and why such sentiments became popular among the later nineteenth century's children can help us better understand the pervasiveness, power, and longevity of America's frontier fixation. It also provides part of the answer to one historian's recent query regarding the West: "how might [the region's] historical traumas and resentments, myths and symbols, be passed down the centuries from one generation to another?" It turns out that young people *themselves* actively took up pen, paper, and press to propagate, for their own purposes, the frontier's mythologization.[4]

## Settler Colonial Storytelling

The Gilded Age and Progressive Era remain particularly significant in the history of American childhood because they were periods characterized by the development of the first truly national market for juvenile mass culture. Before the turn to radio and television, interlinked railroads and roads, when combined with improved printing and paper-making processes, allowed for distributors to saturate young audiences with widely available and inexpensive books, magazines, and newspapers. Here was the rise of what has been called the "industrial book." All of this affordably priced literature was usually lumped together and labeled "dime novels," even if actual prices and formats ranged more widely. The Civil War—as both an event and a subject for storytellers—did a great deal to popularize the genre. Initially, hundreds of thousands of oftentimes bored Union soldiers provided publishers with their readiest customers, but, by the postbellum years, the medium's audience was overwhelmingly young.[5]

Soon after their introduction in the 1860s, dime publications were advertised and sold to adolescents as an independent demographic with its own tastes and desires. As a contemporary assessment noted, cheap fiction attracted an array of customers, "but with them, before them, and after them come boys. The most ardent class of patrons . . . are boys." Their particular appetite for Western-themed material, meanwhile, meant that a large percentage of what American children were reading from roughly 1870 to 1900 was set along the frontier. Firms founded by individuals such as Erastus and Irwin Beadle, Frank Tousey, and George Munro made millions satisfying that demand. Popular imprints dramatizing transcontinental expansion were, of course, not the only books available to young readers. But they were clearly the most widely read, so much so that the authors of self-consciously "respectable" children's publications were themselves forced to adopt sensationalist tropes. Meanwhile, attempts to suppress, outlaw, or burn what some educators branded as "printed poison" proved futile in the face of children's unquenchable thirst for frontier romance. Later reminiscences marveled at "how the boys swarmed to buy copies as they came hot from the press." Around the country, groups of youths were said to gather within "trysting-places" and pore over the "wild deeds of forest, prairie, and mountain!"[6]

These settler colonial stories, which circulated among young readers in the later nineteenth century, sought to instill a few key lessons. The first of these refrains reminded juvenile citizens to take responsibility for the upkeep and continuation of the transcontinental empire they had inherited. Magazines and novels connected past deeds with present circumstance. Readers might import richer significance into their own lives were they linked, in some way, with the struggles and sacrifices of an original cohort of settler colonial strivers and the country's "terrible history of relentless war waged between pioneers and the treacherous red man." Or, as the multivolume *Frontier Series* lectured, "many a young American" should extol "those brave men and women who drove out the savage from the Great West, and laid the foundations of that

Figure 1.1. Sensationalistic imagery littered the pages of Western juvenile fiction. So that adolescent readers would purchase and could better relate to the material, both the stories and their crudely drawn pictures ordinarily emphasized the youthfulness of the settler protagonists. Col. Prentiss Ingraham, *The Boy Guide* (New York: Beadle and Company, 1872, repr. 1908).

mighty empire, of which we Americans of to-day are so justly proud." Kids ought to appreciate that it was "your grandfathers, not the men to be frightened," who fought to ensure that "the Indians are gone, civilization and the arts of peace have taken their places, and the cities of white men occupy the ground where stood their miserable huts." Assurances were also made that "they will burn our villages no more, nor will they murder women and children." It was the white settler, in other words, to whom young people owed their current contentment. Savvy publishers, for their part, increasingly sought to gratify their mostly juvenile fan base by emphasizing the youthfulness of these pioneer heroes and dedicating books "To Young America." More paternalistically minded publications that refused to grant kids a meaningful role in the "civilizing" of the West, meanwhile, recorded slumping sales and bankruptcies. In real ways, the dollars, cents, and consumer choices of America's youth helped to entrench and exalt a particularly violent and triumphalist version of the nation's past.[7]

It was rare, after all, for Indians to appear in this literature as anything other than miscreants motivated by bloodlust, or, as one publication described them, "grim, swarthy figures . . . on the trail for blood!" "What shadowy form is that," another asked, "which glides from tree to tree, with stealthy footsteps that awake no echo?" It was, the answer came, "like a human being—but in nature's most wild and terrible aspect—an Indian on the war path." "It is not customary for the conscience of an Indian to give him any trouble," yet another story began, "unless it smites him for not having done some act of cruelty which he had neglected." Some tales took the sanguinary semantics to their logical end, depicting Native Americans as "those human foes to the white race, those vampyres of the West." What passed for character development in juvenile literature set along the frontier usually consisted of a protagonist coming to the realization that one could not trust an Indian.[8]

Those who spoke of Western indigenes as victims eventually acquired, through trial and misfortune, the wisdom to recognize the folly of their earlier empathy. "Harry Hardskull," for one, had been a "peaceable, hard-working man" who often "[sided] with the Indians in many of their disputes with the whites, believing that they were unjustly treated." Soon enough, however, the murder of his wife and child sobered Harry considerably, "and he became their most inveterate enemy, resolving to devote his whole life in doing what he could to effect their entire extermination." William Harper, witness to his son's kidnapping by the Sioux, remarked that though "I have been the best of friends to them," now "I will be the Nemesis of the redmen who did this thing." He promised that "the Indians shall perish from the face of the earth!" In another story, a boy named Ben Rogers survives the massacre of his entire family and dedicates the remainder of his life to revenge. "He has had the lifeblood of more of the red devils than any man I know," and, the narrator asked his readers, "can you blame him?" Once again, Native Americans were not allowed to appear as anything other than, in the protagonist's words, "the incarnation of savagery, treachery and ferocity" who "shoot unarmed men, tomahawk women and brain little children." Accounts of malicious Indians, meanwhile, were often offset by a concomitant emphasis on the professionalism and restraint of American militias sent in pursuit. White violence played a purely redemptive role in the West. "Sturdy pioneers" who innocently "cried for peace" were contrasted with "the Indian of the western world" and their reveling in a "crimson carnival of blood."[9]

On those rare occasions when wanton violence did not motivate Native depredations, authors usually attributed their actions to an "unnatural" urge to seduce and sexually violate white women. This was, of course, a staple in the broader discourse of Indian-hating, but it is interesting to note the regularity with which the threat of rape pervades reading material meant for young audiences. Whether Jenny, "carried into captivity to share the wigwam of some haughty chief," or Lena, "who shall be [the Apache] Wishawan's squaw," or any other number of women threatened with oblique references to "revolting tortures fifty times more terrible than death to a true woman," the story's contours remained mostly unchanged. The role of women in these yarns was to thwart such advances and await rescue. Honor, a crucial concept within settlerist juvenile literature, was something men earned or preserved in combat with "savage" foes. Women, on the other hand, mostly worked to guard against the threat of miscegenation; for them, integrity possessed sexual overtones and stressed dependency. As a Mrs. Felton, one fictive white captive of the Comanche, pleaded, "spare me the terrible doom of becoming the wife of an Indian!" Inevitably abducted by her unwelcome suitor, it was up to a white settler to redeem the "damsel in distress."

Vowing that he "would rather see her dead than united to an Indian," the man secured both the captive's release and her hand in marriage. Female resistance in the face of such "barbaric" sexual overtures usually became the extent of women's "active" role along the fictional frontier. Boys were having rehearsed for them, in admittedly extreme ways, their manly duties as future guardians and protectors of the "gentler sex."[10]

Considerable condemnation, meanwhile, was reserved for federal agents and civilian bureaucrats who preached pacifism in the West. These were figures lampooned as comically incompetent and hopelessly deluded in their commitment to the diplomatic resolution of what readers were assured was the military problem of inveterate Indian hostility. "He is going to 'reason' with the Indians," sneered one such skeptic of a Bureau of Indian Affairs agent. "Reason with them!" the man scoffed again. "Reason with a rock, a rattlesnake, a coyote, or anything else senseless and cruel but don't reason with an Indian. You are mad to attempt it!" In another story, a settler, asked by a missionary to care for a wounded Indian, swears that "I wouldn't give one of the red skins a glass of water to save his life!" "There isn't a particle of gratitude in one of 'em," the harangue continued. "Give any of them all you have and ten to one, he'll steal upon you out of a bush, and take your scalp." The evangelical's epiphany came when he later acknowledged that Native Americans "seem to me the lowest, meanest, most treacherous, and hardened of the human race. I do not wonder that it is so difficult to civilize or Christianize them." Meanwhile, Cowboy Chris and Round-up Rube, regular characters in the boys' magazine *Western Weekly*, repeatedly complain that "ef 'tadn't bin fer ther derned fool [Indian] agents, ther red whelps'd never bin half so bad ter handle." Faith in force and the folly of negotiation, therefore, were governing principles in the West as it appeared in the pages of periodicals printed for adolescent consumption.[11]

Sporadic sympathy for the plight of Native Americans and appeals to the "noble savage" did sometimes appear within these texts. For example, William Barrows's *Twelve Nights in the Hunter's Camp*, written to provide "a healthful stimulus to every young reader," expressed "deep feeling and sorrow" that Indians, like "prints on the sands of the Pacific," would "soon be washed out and forgotten." Or, as another juvenile periodical, the *Golden Argosy*, put it, "as westward the course of empire takes its way, the poor Indian is forced backward . . . as certainly as the hand of the clock travels its slow circuit." But such stock forms of grief were only another part of the settler colonial script. Pro forma professions of sadness regarding the so-called vanishing Indian had become a literary trope since the 1830s removals. These thoughts did little to curtail a concomitant sense that whatever losses indigenous people had sustained, the benefits vastly outweighed the costs. As Barrows himself observed, "the wilderness has become a garden, and barbarism has given place to civilization." Indian extirpation was the "sacrifice of one race for the elevation and glory of another," and reflected only the necessary outlays meant to ensure "imperial success in the founding of new states." Indians had "withered from the land," a different writer observed, but "who will say it was not for the best?" Rhetorical questions such as these clearly hoped to short-circuit children's compassion for Native Americans. If, in the words of another essayist, the "untutored savage" was actuated only by "implacable hatred"—his "hands often literally bathed in blood"—no one should mourn their passing. Young readers were instead invited to lament "the sacrifice of our own race in this gigantic march of western progress." They were asked to more fully consider that "it costs something of white toil and hardship and sorrow to turn a wilderness into the fruitful field." Paeans to progress dwarfed imperialist nostalgia for an evaporating Indian.[12]

And, as the above quote illustrates, emphasis was indeed placed on whiteness. Settler colonial fiction was a key vehicle through which racialist and white supremacist ideology was presented to many young Americans—indeed, such literature was probably their first exposure to such ideas in any systematized way. And so, even as *The Argosy* chronicled feats of Indian strength and cunning, its editors could not help but insert the observation that while Native peoples "held their own well against the pioneers," the "Caucasian race, under similar surroundings and environments, surpasses all others in physical as well as in mental attainments." "Read the lives of Boone, Kenton, the Zanes and their compeers," another such story went, "and you will be impressed that they were raised up by Providence to subdue and conquer the land for the white man—for civilization." And still another author observed that the Indian appeared "to have subsisted in substantially their present position from a very early age, while the Caucasian race has been constantly progressive, having built up in succession a number of great empires." Young readers were asked to "suppose that there is a great and permanent difference in the physical and intellectual constitution of the different races" which "cannot be changed." The conclusion to this line of thinking seemed obvious: "[U]nder these circumstances it was as inevitable, and as much in fulfillment of the designs of divine Providence, that the old races should be supplanted by the new." A "higher and nobler" people, in other words, was in the midst of clearing the continent of barbarians. Children inheriting the fruits of that process, meanwhile, were assured that their consciences could remain clean. Indians would embrace their rightful removal by a worthier race of people.[13]

Territorial expansion was therefore presented as a fait accompli. Questions were rarely asked about westering, past or present, because the benefits seemed so readily apparent. With the logic that, as one publisher phrased it, "insects take the color of the bark on which they feed," so too would child consumers of settler colonial kids' literature come to "sympathize with, and emulate, the virtues they find here so portrayed." Reading habits reproduced important traits and built within boys the same "character which has transformed a wilderness into a land of liberty and wealth." Transcontinentalism, in other words, was not simply an accomplished geopolitical fact. It was, instead, conceived of as an ennobling set of merits—manliness, fortitude, and bravery among others—that ought to help structure the means by which young people in the United States were raised. A healthy literary diet of imperialistically themed literature would enshrine an earlier generation's courageous deeds while ensuring a proper upbringing in the present. Empire in the West, this reasoning went, might build character in the suburbs. For, as one children's author stated, the "stormy scenes of the frontier" inculcated both a "spirit of self-sacrifice and neighborly kindness" and an "unflinching courage and endurance . . . full as necessary to success in life now as then." Or, echoed another story, "there are wholesome lessons . . . in the examples of stern endurance" pioneers learned "while experiencing the horrors of Indian invasion" and overcoming "those dark and bloody days."[14]

In an era before television (let alone syndicated television), these novellas, story papers, and periodicals consisted of manifest destiny's reruns. Themes and concepts—from savage cruelty and wilderness as a form of wastefulness to the benevolent extension of Christian religious principles—that had fueled the first generations of American expansionists were reintroduced for their heirs. Children born in the late nineteenth century and growing up as Frederick Jackson Turner worried over the frontier's closure, were asked to imagine the horrors of a near-empty continent populated by so-called wandering barbarians and to contrast that nightmare scenario with the many blessings of civilization they currently enjoyed. To ensure that such a scene never came to pass, some youth periodicals even sought to stimulate settlement by providing instructions on how to file land claims and survive the first years on a new farm.[15]

Nor did advertisements peppering children's periodicals provide respite from the relentless messaging. The purveyors of the "Daniel Boone Cabin" promised their product would whisk consumers into the West, where they might spend an afternoon "wandering free in the wild woods" and listening to the "distant wolves howl and the blood-curdling yell of the painted savage." And "is it strange that the log cabin is dear to the hearts of American boys," the ad asked. After all, it "saw the birth of our nation," and "its rude interior sheltered our great men." "Any boy," they therefore promised, "can build a log house large enough to form a comfortable camp for vacation days," and in so doing, lay claim to a proud tradition of colonization. Because, to put it in the plain English of a fictionalized Buffalo Bill, "there is no more brilliant page in American history than the winning of the West," and no better "example of manliness, courage, and devotion to duty" than the nation's "pioneers, old scouts, and plainsmen."[16]

## Boys and Girls Write Back

Such settlerist panegyrics were common enough. They could be repeated ad infinitum. Or, perhaps more appropriately, ad nauseam. Yet reiteration on the part of publishers is not the same as inculcation on the part of their youthful readers. The questions that loom large over the vast archive of children's literature are, of course, the extent to which the audience absorbed any of this and the ends to which kids might have put such didactic imperial discourse. The *Army and Navy Weekly*, for example, explicitly stated that their paper was designed to provide "a knowledge of the history of our country," recount "[the] glorious deeds of brave and patriotic men," and "inspire [the boys of America] with a love of country and give them examples they should emulate." But, to the extent that we can assess, were publishers successful in meeting such clearly articulated goals? Answering this question is not easy—gauging reader response never is—but there are a few sources to which we might turn.[17]

One such avenue for exploration lies in the vast number of "letters to the editor" these publications inspired. Most adventure-oriented periodicals contained sections toward their back pages—variously termed the "mail bag," "trading post," or "watering hole"—that contained communications received from readers and the responses those missives inspired. Young people often wrote in to express their adulation for Western heroes, suggesting that in many instances, these publications accomplished their hagiographical mission. A boy named Frank Booth, for example, wrote the editors of *Buffalo Bill's Stories* to share a poem he had composed: "Early in the Wild West Days/When men in buckskin were making fame/I will gladly mention their names, Buffalo Bill and Texas Jack/They did the work that did not fail/To drive Injun and outlaw off the trail/Now those men are resting from labors/And enjoy the glories they have gained." And how surprising was the tone of this boy's poem—glorying as it did in "the Injun's" annihilation—given that the magazine sold itself as a compilation of "pioneer heroes and daring deeds" comprising "the adventurous history of our country" and "how our land was won from the wild beasts, outlaws, and savages"?[18]

When boys like young S. G. Reid said, "the pleasure I've known in reading your writing is unexpressable," or when little Robert McIntyre claimed to have "learned very much" about the West, including information about "snakes, reptiles, and indian customs," we can reasonably speculate that many young readers often imbibed these books' intended lessons. Why else would kids write to purveyors of juvenile Westerns like "Old Pard," "delighted to say that we shall continue to read them, for they are very interesting as well as instructive." That is, youths not only derived great enjoyment from this literature, but felt more knowledgeable for having read it. Some audacious kids even insisted that they were in fact authoritative sources of information, as when "Emily L.C." saluted *Young America* from San Francisco and asked "if you would like me to write something about the Chinese, for there are lots of them out here, and I think I can tell some very interesting things." Seven-year-old

Anna Alice also displayed some daring when she wrote from the Kansas frontier to "correct the record" and tell of the "Indians [who] took me off with them." Because "they look ugly," she said, and "make you laugh to see them when they come to our house all painted and with such a funny dress . . . I would not like to be an Indian baby." But, she also conceded that, on the whole, "they like us and we like them." There was, therefore, something that to her rang untrue in the magazine's one-dimensional rendering of Natives.[19]

Even more indicative of the impact Western adventure fiction had on adolescent lives was young readers' insistence that stories of past frontier feats inspired them in the present. Children, in other words, actively embraced the creative and imaginative spaces opened up by Western novels. They seem to have read works set in the West and featuring young protagonists as scripts or cues by which they might model their own behavior. The results of such conscious emulative effort could be peculiar, as readers residing in suburbs and cities sought to reenact forms of bravery and bravado better suited to heavily fictionalized borderlands. A boy from New York City named William Roth, for example, wrote to publishers Street and Smith to advertise his devotion as a "pledged pard" of Buffalo Bill, but also to tell of his own "adventures" and "narrow escapes" after he was "attacked by tramps" attempting to rob him. The courage to stand his ground came from reading. It was a theme boy-readers often returned to in their correspondence with corporate officers addressed as confidants. Pliny Thurston from St. Louis spoke of a run-in with wolves, but, "thanks to reading Buffalo Bill stories, I knew how to handle them, for I used my gun for all it was worth." Paul McShane, another aficionado, wrote to tell of his escape from an accident on the family farm, an obstacle overcome because "I had been reading the Buffalo Bill stories, and I thought how brave Buffalo Bill was and I thought I would be brave too." Memoirists also remembered "long afternoons" of boyhood play featuring the "war-cries of encountering tribes." "We had a book in those days called 'Western Adventure,'" another reminiscence went, "which was made up of tales of pioneer and frontier life, and we were constantly reading ourselves back into that life." "We read of [Indians] at night till we were afraid to go up the ladder to the ambuscade of savages in our loft, but we fought them over again by day with undaunted spirits." In innumerable contexts, kids rehearsed settlerist conquest.[20]

But beyond the specifics of any one case, it seems as though many young readers found genuine inspiration in tales of the "Wild West," and actively utilized those narratives to provide structure and meaning to their own lives, distant as they may have been, in both time and location, from frontier protagonists. Not that this instinct should be particularly surprising or inexplicable, given the regularity with which this media insisted that while the West "was a terrible schooling for a boy, it taught him how to look out for himself, and made a man of him long before his years of manhood were reached." Juvenile protagonists in these stories, after some sort of heroic display (usually connected to the murder of an Indian), were regularly approached by individuals twice their age who would remark that "boy as you are, you are the best man in the fort." Such plot points surely gratified readers anxious to hear that youth was no impediment to bravery or worth on the frontier. American adolescents eager to cross the threshold into maturity had at least one model of masculinity readily available to them within the pages of such adventure literature.[21]

Other audience segments, however, seemed less prepared to entirely embrace what they read about the West. One of the more interesting examples of this can be found in the regular correspondence that girls composed to both commend and complain about settlerist stories. No matter how often tales emphasized the primacy of men in US empire-making across the West, and no matter how clearly—in their editorial voice, in their storytelling choices, even in their advertisements—such publications were marketed toward a male audience, they attracted a sizeable cohort of female fans. That might explain why so many women wrote in with an almost apologetic tone, as did Jane Harris, who remarked that she "really love[d] Western stories, even if I am a girl." The almost too-perfectly-named 12-year-old Mary Wolstencroft also wrote, noting that "even if I am a girl I enjoy boys' books a lot." To another editor it was remarked, "for if I am a girl, I like stories of boys better than I do stories of girls; there is so much more excitement in boys' stories." Yet another young woman wrote in to the author "Old Pard" to thank him for sending her a badge signaling membership in his readers' club; she noted that some thought she should "not wear it because she was a girl," but, she defiantly declared, "it does not make any difference with me." There was, in other words, an awareness on the part of young women who read about westward expansion in the pages of these books and magazines that they were not the intended audience. The impression was not mistaken, if we take seriously (as these girls must have) commentary which claimed, as did one periodical, that westward expansion was "a job that called for men, men of strength and courage who were willing to fight and die for a cause." But whatever the gendered intentions or masculine messaging of these texts, girls regularly wrote in to comment upon their avid consumption of the genre. Some went so far as to demand changes that would better reflect their own devotion to Western literature.[22]

"I wonder if there is room in your column for a girl," Anna Newman, another correspondent, mused. At once bowing to the restrictions and limitations of the domestically oriented female world of early twentieth-century America—"I haven't really done much adventuring 'cause I am, as I say, only a girl"—Newman still scolded the editors for their overemphasis on manliness in the "winning of the West." After all, she reasoned, "ages n' ages ago, a relative of mother's crossed the continent in a covered wagon . . . so I must surely be endowed with the same spirit of adventure." Another young woman, named Louise, began her letter to *The Boys' Best Weekly* by stating that "even though I am a girl, I like your weekly all the same." It turns out she had been stealing copies from her brother. But rather than make excuses for herself, she got right down to business in her second sentence: "the complaint I have is that you don't give enough of the girls in the stories." So, she asked, "could not you induce the author to bring [a woman] more prominently into one or more of the stories, so that we can really see her as she is, and not at a distance?" Unable to relate to females rendered as caricatures, girls like these wrote fan mail devoted to denying one of the basic premises of the frontier's juvenile print culture: that men had been the only people who mattered in the history of the US West.[23]

At once both deferential and defiant, the more conversationally oriented back pages of these settlerist story papers allowed many readers (and a surprising number of girls) to inject themselves into the narratives, past and present, then under construction and thus subject to revision. Publishers for their part never quite seemed to know what to do with such demands: As the curt reply to one such plea for better coverage of feminine characters stated, "this publication makes no pretense of filling the wants of the girls." But for as much as authors aspired to present a clearly defined (and deeply gendered) narrative of conquest and colonization in the West, the audience seemed to resist those boundaries. They took no particular issue with the bombastic messaging and racialized politics embedded within these stories' deep structures. Rather, girls' complaints hinged on their own desire for inclusivity. The mixed sense of personal and national validation expansionist narratives offered to American boys ought to be, they reasoned, similarly available to the country's girls. Histories of the frontier and fictions of empire felt incomplete when they failed to recognize the contributions of pioneer women.[24]

That consideration must have weighed heavily as more and more middle-class children at the turn of the century were segregated from adult society and shunted through assiduously age-graded educational institutions. Given those circumstances, they may have looked to Western fantasies of consequential juvenile achievement as freeing. People who were increasingly disconnected from their elders—an earlier era of more raucous age-mixing demonstrably came to a close by the end of the nineteenth century—probably enjoyed reading about youthful protagonists who made meaningful contributions to the country's political and military history. The reality is, many young people were less often making those contributions in their own lives as a result of institutions and cultural norms that insisted upon delaying their maturation. Indeed, it is instructive to observe that this pioneer literature emphasizing the capacities of teenaged protagonists arose at almost the same cultural moment that adolescence, as a sociological construct, also came into vogue. As new establishments like secondary schools appeared in order to contain and corral the free expression of this cohort's supposedly inveterate impulses toward delinquency, Western literature attained popularity by painting the frontier as a place which predated the structural changes to their lives that many adolescents—and boys in particular—found stultifying. For in the West, people led "lives so free and easy that many a repining white boy must sigh with regret and envy" as he "thinks of the number of times he has to wash his face and hands weekly, the boots he is made to keep tidy, the hair he must comb," and his many other responsibilities.[25]

Therefore, when no less a cultural critic than Louisa May Alcott denounced dime "sensation stories," she missed the mark. The problem with "such trash," she chided, was its reliance upon "optical delusions," absurd contrivances of plot that placed mere boys in positions of power. But what Alcott called the "evil and vulgarity" of precocious juvenile protagonists was instead embraced by young readers as pluck. Middle-class children leading ever more routinized and predictable lives loved to enter imaginative worlds of greater possibility. Empire in the West provided one such setting for ephebic empowerment—so much so, in fact, that widely circulated youth periodicals like *The Argosy* felt compelled to run editorials urging boys to think carefully before following in the footsteps of their frontier idols. J. L. Harbour's "A Sermon for Boys" expressed the exasperation of a Westerner witness to an endless parade of "Eastern boys" seduced across the Rocky Mountains by "the glaring falsehoods that come to you in the shape of dime novels and other cheap literature." The author knew that "many of you are dissatisfied with the dull monotony of the homes in which you have lived all your lives." He understood that "the restraints" imposed by parents and school "may be a little irksome." But Harbour counseled patience before "the delusions that have brought disappointment to many young fellows who have come West" claimed another victim. Inverting Horace Greeley's famous exhortation, the editorial urged adolescents to remain home and "leave well enough alone." As for the "wonderful things"—tales of adventure and easy money—boys read about the region? "Don't you believe half of it" and "have nothing to do with such books." Jack Crawford, a similarly concerned citizen, wrote a column for the *American Boy Magazine* weeping over the "poor little innocent dupes ... who have abandoned their homes to exterminate Indians." "Not one in a thousand ever reached the Missouri River, and those who did get beyond that stream inevitably went to work in the kitchens of hotels washing dishes until their parents could send for them."[26]

Such warnings often fell on deaf ears, however, so long as the reading of cheap frontier stories appealed to youths seeking to carve out some sovereignty for themselves. Adult reminiscences of their childhood reading habits often emphasized the giddy thrill of "hiding [dime novels] in the big geographies and other books which we were supposed to be studying" or "ke[eping] them carefully concealed in the attic." Equally revealing were the comments of another memoirist who claimed never to have read such literature: "had I ever been forbidden to read dime novels, doubtless I should have read many." The taboo nature of the genre enhanced its appeal for those seeking to defy disapproving adults. Such transgression was itself a peer-bonding mechanism among young people. As one man noted, "dime novels were forbidden, but I have a distinct recollection of disobeying my orders and reading at least a few. They were passed about, more or less, among us boys." Or, as another confession conceded, youths wanted reading to "suit themselves," not their parents. Consequently, they would always disregard their elders, "seek out the stalls where trash is peddled," "slink into sly corners," imaginatively "organize scalping parties, and set out for the Rockies in search of Indians." Reading about and reaffirming the conquest of the West became bound up in the titillation of petty teenage rebellion.[27]

But what we should also notice in these reflections is the changed (and changing) circumstances within which youths read and related to these publications. The basic contours and content of magazine material did not shift much over the course of 30 years, but the ways in which readers made it relevant to their lives surely did. In this way, even with the concerns of the West as a military or political problem—very real in the 1870s and 1880s, perhaps less so by the 1890s and 1900s following the region's "territorialization" and "pacification"—disappearing, young people simply cast new or developing issues with "older" characters and extant plotlines derived from frontier parables. Boys attempting to navigate urban centers ravaged by the petty crime that years of financial panic and untrammeled industrialization helped breed or survive increasingly standardized school years in the suburbs found in Western-themed media similar solutions to the disparate problems their lives posed. This helps explain the region's resilience as a cultural phenomenon even as integrative forces made it less visibly distinct from the East.

### Amateur Stories

A sizeable archive of amateur stories written by young people themselves also hints at the continued relevance of the frontier, even as more "official" channels like the Census Bureau pronounced it dead. Some of it was submitted for publication in the periodicals printed for juvenile audiences. Other adolescents self-published using small slips of paper and the so-called toy or tabletop press. This compact printing device was a postbellum invention that allowed junior authors to produce their own fiction. Many then traded those stories with likeminded enthusiasts through the US mail. Sadly, few archives have preserved such material. The little that survives, however, hints at a youthful infatuation with the West.

Indians made their obligatory appearance in these amateur stories as "painted devils" or "imps and devils" uttering "demoniac screeches" as they "tore the gory scalp from the cranium" of an unlucky victim. Adolescents repeated (and thus affirmed) the sort of wisdom offered by dime novel dramas, such as one boy's remark that "an Indian, like a rattlesnake, may be trusted only when his fangs are removed. He will shake your hand all day and at nightfall will take your scalp." They understood the West as "a war to the death between white and red man." Given such anti-aborigine sentiments, it should come as no surprise that boys drafted stories to celebrate, in their words, the "mighty migrations" of the "American pioneer" who "crossed a great continent . . . in his headlong pursuit of the Star of Empire." True, they admitted, heroic settlers had "almost annihilate[d] the race of men that threatened [them] with distruction." But this was cause for celebration, not lamentation. America's frontiersmen, one boy argued, "present examples of determination, energy, and bravery that all history cannot match." "White men," another boomed, had only "endeavored to aid the advance of civilization into an unsettled wilderness."[28]

If anything, amateur authors, in their expansionist encomiums, were even more hyperbolic than "professional" publications. Boyish scouts were said to be "noted for [their] many deeds of reckless daring." Their "death dealing rifles sent many a Red to the happy hunting grounds." They "vowed eternal hate toward the entire race of Indians." Heroes "not old" were portrayed as both "a veritable Hercules in muscular endowments" and "a formidable antagonist for wild Indians to grapple with." "Infuriated and blood thirsty savages" met their match in the form of conspicuously young rangers, and the adults in these stories were usually effusive in their praise for superhuman minors whose fearlessness and ingenuity "checked the audacity of the Indians." Erastus Beadle, the founder of one of the larger nineteenth-century dime novel publishers, once quipped that the high body counts of his books represented a kind of brinksmanship within the industry. When rival firms sold more violent stories, his company felt pressured to "kill a few more Indians than we used to" in order to keep up. A different dynamic, however, played out among juvenile authors. The bloody deeds of their adolescent protagonists seemed fixated on proving the capabilities of young people loosed from parental oversight. The fictive butchery of Native Americans became one method by which youths publicized their own maturity. Revolting against certain strains of thinking that increasingly depicted children as helpless innocents in need of prolonged supervision, juvenile authors churned out stories that emphasized what one boy called the "dauntless bravery" of particularly childlike characters.[29]

Other stories featured young protagonists ordering around their elders and exposing older companions as fools or cowards. The figurative frontier, in youthful imagination, inverted power relations between real-life parents and children. Novice novellas depicted deferential adults indebted to their Indian-killing kids. "Dashing Dick," described as a "daring boy," was relied upon by his parents to transform his "particular hate against the treacherous Camanches" into "death-dealing shots." And in a different story where a much older man swears of his adolescent companion that "I'll follow him to the gates of Hades," one gets an even greater sense of this dynamic. The duo bonded, of course, by using firearms to "satisfy their hatred of the red race." Youths, in their own minds, exhibited an irresistible aura of expertise and intellect. Numerous amateur stories, in fact, focused on boys who found themselves in the company of men sent to slaughter Indians and who, after participating in the butchery, "won the admiration of all."[30]

There were other dynamics at play though. Boys like Geoffrey Randolph from Fostoria, Ohio seemed to enjoy the rehearsal of their manly obligations to women within the short stories they wrote. His "Old Tim's Leap," clocking in at around one page in length, managed to compress for his friends' consumption several of the gendered conventions of the dime genre. The story itself involved "a party of Indians" who "came down upon [Tim's] home" and "massacred his wife and every one of his children." The "rough borderer, a man of daring courage" and "a splendid athlete, swore by all that was sacred he would 'get square' with the wretches who had made his life so desolate." Carnage ensued. "Old Tim" spent the remainder of his years "wiping out every red-skin possible . . . with as pitiless a persistency as they had shown in slaughtering his wife and children."[31]

A different literary creation named "Buffalo Ned" pursued similar ends. Introduced as "a boy about the age of fifteen," Ned noted that "the Sioux Indians was on the war path and making raids on Emigrant trains." Seeing "something on the plains, as if persued by some foe," the fearless trapper "broke forth saying if that is not a girl you may shoot me dead. Ha! If I know my self I will rescue the girl." The roughly paragraph-long tale ends abruptly with a simple declarative: "he rode out to the rescue." The hasty ending was a common convention. One very young boy's story, no more than a few sentences long, simply had a "maiden in distress" cry out the name of her redeemer, "Squint-Eye, the Squatter." And then, "instantly the sharp crack of a rifle is heard, and the Red Man begins to eat dust." This was the West stripped down to what young people saw as its essential elements. Imperiled women, righteous white vengeance, and dead Indians. Kids who managed to misspell even the titles of their tales, such as the author of "A Luckey Escape," still got this basic narrative architecture correct. It was essential to their intelligibility. Of course, some amateur authors, as inexperienced but enthusiastic writers, could not help but strain the bounds of credulity. One story even transformed two boys, seeking "SPORT and ADVENTURE now," into the "magicians of the plains," wizards who conjured flames from their fingertips to destroy "terrible red men" and "blood-thirsty savages."[32]

Most of the alter egos boys assumed, however, took on similar characteristics. They were repeatedly and explicitly depicted as handsome, athletic, brave, and dutiful toward distressed damsels. The West became the perfect screen upon which to project teenaged dreams of desirability and notoriety. It was a space that seemed ideally suited to the freest possible expression of violent impulses directed toward chivalric ends. Some boys were clearly using these stories to work through pubescent problems with the opposite sex. One such author, for example, imagined a meeting between his boy pioneer, John Steele, and Olive, the beautiful daughter of a nearby settler. In a passage dripping with scorn for girls the author seemed to know in real life, an aside remarked that the pioneer girl "shook hands with him, although he was a stranger, in a manner that would do some of our 'fine,' 'educated,' 'stylish' young ladies in the east some good to see." Always fraught teenaged romantic relations could be smoothed over in stories nominally set in the West but clearly speaking to situations much closer to home. Part of the explanation for the frontier's durability in the national imagination lay in its capacity to encompass (sometimes generationally specific) issues far removed from the purely political.[33]

Many magazines also encouraged these sorts of creative exercises which helped continuously revivify the West as an emblem of totemic significance to kids. Thomas Elliott, who identified himself as a student at the Washington Grammar School, submitted a story to the *Boys' and Girls' Journal* that told of the frontiersman "Camelli." Almost as if filling in the blanks of a template, the tale told of the "dead and charred remains of [a] sister and aged mother," a boy "maddened by rage" whose "blood boiled for revenge" against "the red man," "steel sunk into the throat" of a "savage Indian," and a boastful aside that "by way of digression, I may say that American arms are always victorious, and their battles achieved with most triumphant success." *The Boys' Own*, meanwhile, contained a section called "Stories by Boy Contributors," and a disproportionate number of those accounts fixated on the West. Carlos Vane, from the small New York town of Port Chester, offered one titled "My First Adventure," which detailed a run-in with a "party of wild Indians on the war-path" who "amused themselves by thrusting sharp-pointed sticks at us." Only a daring escape "put an end to these tortures." Another boy-contributor, Francis Mackey from Cincinnati, adopted for himself the moniker "Scouting Tom," and told the paper a tall tale of his "sledge-hammer fist" cracking the skulls of countless "yelling, blood-thirsty Crows." His fantasy was a murderous one of plunging knives and repeating rifles, of several "savages sent to the happy hunting grounds," all meant to save a community of settlers who "attributed their success" to the young narrator. Edgar Slade, of Washington, DC, took up the life of Kit Carson, recounting an entirely fabricated anecdote about "the best guide, scout, and Indian-fighter" that "I can truthfully say has never been told before." His account spoke of an ambush foiled, "leaden bullets sped on their errands of death," and "shrieks of agony" as "red[s] fell upon their face[s] dead." Just as important as the content, though, was the addendum the author added, stating that he "would be pleased to exchange copies of this book for other amateur publications."[34]

Most of this "do-it-yourself" literature stated as much, suggesting a lively network connecting juvenile authors across the country. The leading archive of this material has items printed in large cities and small towns from San Francisco to Rockland, Maine. And, significantly, the lingua franca which linked adolescents living in disparate corners of the country was dominated by Western imagery. The settlerist spin on American history was further reinforced because it became a crucial intranational communicative tool among the postbellum republic's rising generation. As Walter Mott gushed to his favorite author, the pseudonymous "Old Pard," his Western stories were "bringing boys all over America to know each other" in their shared love for frontier literature. "Any of my boy pards," as fans of the series called themselves, "may write to me and I'll be very much pleased [to] give their letters immediate attention." Other boys wrote "Pard" to announce that their devotion to his stories inspired them to form "correspondence committees" exchanging letters, as one fan boasted, "between young fellows in different parts of our grand United States." And in various communities around the country, boys and girls clearly forged peer bonds with one another by founding reading clubs rooted in a shared love of Western idiom. Seeking official sanction, they sometimes wrote simply to ask "your opinion of naming a club we have formed," one "we have called 'The Chums.'" Many adolescents, therefore, utilized settler colonial storytelling as the basis for regional and national community-making among their own specific age cohort. A shared appreciation for "frontier heroics" helped to define what it meant to be a "real American boy."[35]

These mostly white and mostly middle-class child-authors, then, did not form any sort of oppositional counterpublic to the colonial discourse then prominent in their literature. Rather, it was something closer to a parallel public. Young people's writing, when compared to the universe of juvenile literature within which they were immersed, evidenced a broadly similar thematic thrust. Their storytelling was put toward ends more specific to an adolescent demographic, but it was, content-wise, mostly an act of mimicry. As a result, there is an irony on display. Young people often wrote their own Western fiction as means to reaffirm bonds between themselves and other boys. Adolescents aspired to demonstrate the literary abilities particular to their own generation, one defined in opposition to the older individuals who surrounded them. And yet, the vast majority of their creative output involved the replication, in miniature, of adult-authored texts. In cementing ties between one another, youths by and large solidified imperial structures of thinking and feeling. They helped disseminate and normalize an insensitivity to indigenes (and others) who absorbed the impact of American power.[36]

Most notable about all this juvenile "blood and thunder," however, was the fact that it flowed forth unprompted. In some cases, publishers simply asked their readers to create, and promised to circulate what they received. In other cases, young people simply printed and exchanged such stories between one another. Either way, what young people *chose* to invent, the overwhelming thrust of their imaginative exercises, involved Indian extirpation and settler colonial heroics. With their own particular corner of the literary market steeped in the noble deeds of pioneer generations, many kids seemed to believe that to think artistically was to recite the same sorts of violent fantasies that were regularly presented to them. Their output tended to read as variations on a similar brutal refrain meant to validate the violent dispossession of Native Americans. The process we witness, as a result, is that by which the virtues of empire were reified. Children's assent, in other words, should be construed as its own form of agency. Western juvenilia reveals how—contra the historian's bias toward youthful challenges to authority—young people's choices often reproduced particular power structures.[37]

Other constituencies, however, used their fictionalizations of the frontier to defy certain conventions of the Western genre. Some female amateur story authors seemed particularly determined to rectify gender imbalances within the pages of adult-authored stories. Their own micro-novels, drafted for publication and circulation among the same youth networks that disseminated material written by boys, positioned girls closer to the center of the action. Due to its cheap manufacture and ephemeral nature, little enough of the amateur literature as a whole has survived in the archive. Even less written by women remains available. But what there is suggests the desire of some girls to challenge male storytelling convention. Their efforts might best be characterized as an act of reclamation. The first few dime novels after all—such as Ann S. Stephens's *Malaeska*—were written by women and featured female protagonists. This was a bid for respectability on the part of publishers. They imagined that the reading public would perceive stories authored by women as somehow more suitable for family consumption. Though the pretense was quickly abandoned by editors, many girl readers seem to have cherished the West as a place that promised something approaching gender parity. When, during the 1870s and 1880s, firms slashed the number of stories written by women and attempted to steer girls toward romance fiction, some female fans seem to have revolted. As "authoresses" disappeared from the covers of mass-produced sensational frontier fiction, girls rushed in to fill the breach.[38]

For example, in one amateur tale titled "Fred's Adventure," the more "traditional" arc of the damsel in distress rescued from Indian captivity was reversed. Instead, a young man on the verge of death at the hands of "savages" is saved by the timely intervention of a "maiden." Rather than the woman being instantly smitten with her savior, roles reversed. "Bowing to the young lady," the man "poured out his whole heart in thanks to the one who had saved his life." Another story, titled "Mad Betsy," announced that the protagonist was the "scourge of the Apaches." Rather than serve as a sacrificial victim or object of affection, Betsy became "a terror to the Apaches," and, as it is stated, "their bravest warriors tremble at the sound of her wild laugh." She scalps, dismembers, and brutalizes the tribesmen who, we learn, had slaughtered her family. In the process, a fascinating transposition takes place wherein the type of character— a wife and mother—whose death ordinarily drove male revenge fantasies instead becomes herself the avenger of lost loved ones. Even as boys' stories featured sentences that spoke admiringly of "bands of white men fighting for their lives and the lives of their wives and sisters against hordes of howling Indians," figures like "Mad Betsy" unsubtly undermined stereotypes regarding the passive or silent frontier-dwelling female.[39]

Some girls also seemed willing to rehearse the strange sexual politics of settler colonial fiction. A Pennsylvania teenager named Alice Lane circulated among her peers a short story titled "The Old Cabin." In it, she showed her broad familiarity with the trope of the Indian's obsession with white beauty. The tale, set along some undisclosed frontier, featured as its protagonist a 14-year-old girl, the sole daughter of a settler. She complained of the local Native American tribe's tendency to "admire, more than she approved, the face and form of the beautiful white squaw." They "often would ask her if she would not go with them to their wigwams." After their amorous overtures were rebuffed, the Indians' anger became uncontrollable. "There is no fox more sly, there is no tiger more blood thirsty," the young author proclaimed, "than an enraged savage of the woods when there is an injury to resent." In a nod to the Western genre's obsession with white women's sexual slavery as a fate worse than death, the tribe's "council of war decided that every pale face must die except those females whom some of the young chiefs might save as prisoners." The entire affair, however, clears up quite conventionally and quickly. A white male savior rescues the girl and kills her would-be rapists. What makes the story remarkable is both the way it centers the experience of a young woman and prioritizes the fulfillment of her desires as opposed to that of the male avenger. It is much harder to find similar themes in stories drafted by boys.[40]

Yet another tale told of "Patty, the Girl Rifle Shot," who saved a prospecting party of imperiled men by "dealing out death shots" and "emptying saddles" of their Indian occupants "like a winged spirit of destruction." This kind of inversion of the then-dominant gender hierarchy by no means prevailed among those who prepared stories for local audiences, but it appears to have been more common than in "professional" publications, and suggests the ways in which younger women struggled to promote worlds where their abilities and social position were not so heavily delineated. Some girls, it seems clear, did not entirely embrace the ideology of manifest domesticity. Mass culture may have depicted homemaking as the white woman's essential contribution to American empire in the West, but these amateur stories rejected stereotypes suggesting the pacifying power of passive wives and daughters.[41]

War and conquest, in girls' own fiction, were not exclusively masculine pursuits. This flew in the face of contemporary assessments, which claimed to see a strict gender bifurcation in adolescent reading habits. One observer, for example, thought that, given women's "slight experience with fire-arms and rough riding, it can hardly be supposed that the Girl Dead-Shot" and other frontier figures "appeals to them with the fascination that might be exercised by something more nearly within the ordinary possibilities of imitation." Female readers "must even be puzzled," the appraisal continued, "at such ideals, and wonder at the boys' admiration of them." Even a cursory review of the archive of amateur authors, however, suggests the purely wishful nature of such thinking. What actually seemed to "puzzle" some of the "gentler sex" was the absence of pioneer protagonists who looked like them. But they compensated for those silences by drafting their own tales of women's achievements. Settler colonial storytelling as a whole may have been fairly conservative in its gender politics, but the genre could be seized upon and reformulated by those critical of the limited range offered to female protagonists. In doing so, some of the era's "new girls"—precursors to the liberated New Women of a later date—lodged a subtle but striking critique of their culture's circumscribed gender roles. Still, it is telling that in these stories, the principal manner by which empowered women demonstrate their worth is by killing Indians, and their primary reward for doing so is white male affection. Girl writers blunted the transgressive possibilities of their prose by ideologically allying themselves with settlerist triumphalism. Adolescent protest was built atop Native American suffering.[42]

## From Conquest to Commiseration

By the early twentieth century, however, we can see an emerging rift within the settlerist literature disseminated for juvenile consumption. The mid- to late nineteenth century had barely blinked in the face of westward expansion and Indian dispossession. Nearly every narrative exploration of that process had described it as a positive good. An occasional paragraph halted to reflect on demographic decline among Native Americans, but quickly waved away white culpability through relentless (and racialist) appeals to fate or inevitability. So too, as we have seen, did the words of young people largely restate that rhetoric, even if it was framed in ways more relevant to the specific demands for respectability made by adolescents. And while children's cheap fiction itself, as a genre, had always inspired its fair share of consternation, many saw no inherent problem with such literature. As one cultural authority asserted in 1879, "it is not a bad impulse but a good one that makes the child seek the kind of reading you call sensational." In his revealing assessment, young people's obsession with settlerist storytelling was only a healthful expression of "that love of adventure which has made the Anglo-American race spread itself across a continent." Reading habits usefully recapitulated imperial urges.[43]

But after the Wounded Knee Massacre, and as US sovereignty in the West coalesced, Progressives came to control the political levers of America's internal colonialism. Once the overwhelming majority of indigenous peoples were stripped of their fighting capacity, remanded to reservations, and subjected to various experiments in cultural uplift, new perspectives started to appear in the youth media market. This juvenile literature reassessed indigenous communities as important contributors to the nation's multiracial history and instructive contrasts to the worst excesses of a materialistic and superficial modernity. It asked America's youth to wrestle with what were described as the gross injustices perpetrated against aboriginal people. The "victims" in these stories were no longer graphically butchered pioneer women and children but rather the same Native Americans who an earlier generation had been content to characterize as bloodthirsty brutes. Some authors, in other words, began to construe the country's settler colonial history not as a heroic achievement but as something more like a criminal record.[44]

Francis Rolt-Wheeler's 1913 young adult novel, *The Boy with the U.S. Indians*, is emblematic of this broader shift toward broadmindedness. In the preface, the author asserted unequivocally that Native Americans have been the "most misunderstood of all races" thanks largely to their demonization within a prejudiced popular literature. He asked white children to wipe the slate clean and reconsider what they had previously heard or read so that "the Indian [might] at last win the recognition that is his due." In an about-face from preceding publications, Rolt-Wheeler insisted that Indians command the respect of young readers exactly because they embodied the "bravery, manliness, courtesy, [and] obedience to ideals" that ought to guide the lives of all Americans. He then recited a litany of abuses inflicted upon Native Americans: "banished from the home of his forefathers, hounded to restricted reservations, tricked and exploited by politicians, and deliberately shot or starved to death," Indians had been thoroughly mistreated by both the government and its citizens.[45]

The book did not mince words. Kids were told that the previous hundred years had been an "evil time" in the country's history. They were urged not to recoil in fear at the thought of the "savage," but rather to bridge cultural divides so as to see the "kinship of brave spirits between the redskin and the white." Rolt-Wheeler also broke with settler colonial storytelling convention by allowing Native Americans themselves to speak. Individual chapters fictionalized interviews with Indian subjects, who gave voice to their misfortunes and suffering. The resulting tale looked almost nothing like most of the previous half-century's juvenile literature, fixated as it had been on legitimating the nation's territorial claims to the West, exalting white pioneers as the land's rightful claimants and vilifying as massacres moments of indigenous resistance.[46]

Books such as *The Boy with the U.S. Indians* were not entirely new, of course. They represented the distillation of long-standing objections—made most often by evangelical activists—to cruelty toward Native peoples. Skepticism about settlerism had been articulated in the United States since the 1830s debate over Removal at least. More recently, Peace Policy advocates such as Helen Hunt Jackson and her deeply influential *Century of Dishonor* (1881) popularized a systemic critique of federal Indian affairs which read a great deal like Rolt-Wheeler's account. But what made the early twentieth-century rhetoric important was its more regular appearance in books written for and marketed to children. There was some precedent for such sensibilities in the pages of mid-nineteenth-century periodicals printed for youths by missionary organizations. But those publications occupied a marginal corner of the juvenile public sphere. The youth demographic had been dominated mostly by acclamatory accounts that depicted American expansion as a divinely ordained process productive of all that had made the United States great.[47]

Now, at the turn of the twentieth century, and in increasing numbers, reading material began to appear which called those orthodoxies into question. Settler colonialism developed, for some, an unsavory reputation. Part of the concern revolved around the question of children's discipline, a sense among educators that "every third boy reads such literature, and that he is the hardest to deal with." As one anxious parent phrased it, young people "prevented from engaging in hand-to-hand conflicts with howling savages" might instead "break [their] teacher's watch-chain." After all, "the Boy Scout or the Boy Phoenix" or any other such Western desperado "would never have thought of doing less." But beyond stamping out the petty delinquency supposedly bred by settlerist literature, reformers appealed to more idealistic ends. A new class of cosmopolitan children's books would become, in the words of one writer, "an entering wedge of affection that could mature into largeness of heart." Encouraging young people's empathy for Native Americans might help "improve race relations" and make amends for past exploitation.[48]

Even these baby steps toward revisionism, of course, still dealt in stereotype and dripped with condescension. When, in an attempt to humanize Natives, middlebrow publications like *St. Nicholas* circulated items like their *Indian Stories* for boys and girls, they sometimes managed only to discover new ways of demeaning their subject matter. The changes in content and tone, however, proved instructive. In "A Fourth of July Among the Indians," three boys, who "like all boys, wanted to see real live Indians," hop aboard a train and visit the local reservation. But rather than risk their throats being cut like the protagonists of old, these young Americans traded tobacco for Native knives brandished as mere curiosities. And when "the most blood-curdling yells that ever pierced the ears of three white boys" awakened them, terror turned to relief when the hearers remembered that "the Indian war-whoop" was "simply the beginning of the day's celebration," a dance performed for customers. The excursion ended not with Indians killed in righteous combat but an uneventful "return trip toward the railroad and civilization." Another story doted over "A Boy's Visit to Chief Joseph," wherein a 13-year-old traveler declared the Nez Perce warrior "in every way most kind and hospitable to his young guest." "Fun Among the Red Boys," meanwhile, catalogued a joyous few hours spent coming to the realization that "red children are very like white children." In each instance, Native peoples were now described as a touristic spectacle. Rather than evading skulking savages, youthful characters sought the pleasure of an Indian's company and paid for the enactment of rituals that once signaled imminent danger. Readers of this new class of settler colonial children's literature were urged to feel forlorn and nostalgic for an era of primitive simplicity forever lost. They were asked to read reprints of old "Indian legends" for the wholesome lessons therein located. Tellingly, and unlike dime novels, these tales were told almost entirely by women, the vanguard of a Progressive Era push among educators to abolish war and remake relations between states by instilling greater empathy in the rising generation (see chapter 4).[49]

We should not, of course, imagine that such publications—which counseled compassion for Native Americans and a more relativistic understanding of the Indians' plight—immediately displaced what had come before. Old habits die hard. A great deal of the juvenile literature and youth periodicals printed well into the 1920s and 1930s continued to traffic in the same swaggering commitment to ethnic cleansing present during the postbellum period. At almost the same moment *St. Nicholas* encouraged cross-racial conversation, other imprints persisted in branding Indians as "the incarnation of savagery, treachery and ferocity," filling their readers' ears with "their infernal howls in scenes of sickening butchery," and denouncing cowards "who come out here gushing about the 'red men's wrongs.'" Bad poetry written for American boys by counterfeit Indians, meanwhile, begged forgiveness for the sins of their fathers. "Where once I harried wagon-trains," confessed "Pablo, chief of the Southern Utes," the "White Man grows his corn." "So you," his sons, "shall live and die in peace and nevermore shall kill/And turn the sod and pray to God and do the White Man's will/And eat his meat and grow his wheat and keep your conscience still." Defeat alone, not anti-racism, had rendered "savage" foes tractable.[50]

But, with the physical threat of Native American uprising not nearly as real then as it had been for those living at an earlier point in time, there was more rhetorical space within which a child's compassion for indigenous people might be allowed to flourish. Those openings were quickly exploited by individuals and authors seeking to reimagine settler colonialism as something that had been done *to* Native Americans rather than *for* the country. By the middle of the twentieth century, and with population decline reversed, indigenous people themselves used their boarding school educations to author—as part of a broader Native American literary movement one scholar has termed "talking back to civilization"—nationally distributed children's stories detailing reservation life and their struggles for acceptance within society. Indian images in youth literature, as in the broader culture, became more heavily contested.[51]

It is much harder, however, to gauge the reception of these changes. We must, in the end, accept that any attempt to measure the precise influence of popular media on children's development will be more speculative than definitive. The question itself has been a staple of adult discourse about childhood for centuries. Contemporary hand-wringing over the malign impact of the Internet or violent video games on youth culture does not seem appreciably different from fin-de-siècle frustration—perfectly encapsulated by Anthony Comstock and his censorship crusaders—with the "immoral" and "overstimulating" content

Figure 1.2. Though satirizing the unquenchable thirst of young readers for "exterminationist" literature and worrying about the pernicious influence of cheap and tawdry dime novels on impressionable kids, *Puck*'s "Food of Our Youth" still recognized the immense influence of imperially minded series fiction and story papers on children coming of age. "The Food of Our Youth," *Puck* 10, no. 237 (September 21, 1881). Library of Congress Prints and Photographs Division.

contained within the pages of sensationalistic juvenile fiction. Today, we decry an online teenaged subculture of viciousness and bullying with real-world ramifications. The late nineteenth century saw its own frenzies emerge with episodes like that of 14-year-old Jesse Pomeroy, the "Boston Boy Fiend." When charged with the murder of several other children, his lawyer portrayed him as a victim of the flash papers he devotedly devoured. But in attempting to measure the impact of popular culture on youthful behavior at its most transgressive, we may miss the importance of the ordinary.[52]

The small moments where a young person composed a bit of settlerist poetry or wrote a short story praising the Indian-fighting expertise of Buffalo Bill can, when aggregated, probably tell us more about the ways in which the West spoke to Americans across time. Such ephemera never made headlines, but it did the often-unseen work required to perpetuate a frontier mythos which asked that young people consider themselves rightful heirs to an act of righteous conquest. We are still struggling with the ramifications of the rhetorical sleights of hand—the blind eye turned to so much suffering—required to make the West fun for white children. But neither should we forget that the same archives that seem to chronicle the ennoblement of cultural eradication also contain evidence regarding the efforts of children themselves, in ways large and small, to literally change the narrative. Young women, for example, sought to restructure some of the masculine excesses of the genre. And some others saw the West as an increasingly stale setting for storytelling. They asked for something new, and even professed sympathy for Indians.

That sense of disenchantment was most capably expressed by an adolescent author's parody piece entitled "Plots." A sarcastic send-up of his fellow amateur writers, the page-long essay mocked their pretensions to originality. Referring to other junior novelists, he commenced by observing that "they begin to write without the least forethought whatever." But planning was never necessary, he continued, when scripting "a story of the western wilds." Instead, one needed only to follow a simple recipe. "The plot," the wag waxed, "invariably is, as follows: a wagon train is crossing the plains" and "is set upon by a band of howling savages." In turn, "the emigrants, with three exceptions, are killed." A boy hero and an old trapper flee, "while the heroine, who is a rare beauty, is borne into captivity." Finally, "after the slaying of countless indians," the prisoner is rescued. It "all winds up with the happy marriage of the couple while the honest old fellow who helps in the escape leans on his rifle and blesses the nuptials."[53]

It was a devastating indictment of most amateur stories circulating Gilded Age America. And his observations, it might be added, were largely accurate. This humorous skewering of the "stories of the western wilds" accurately summarizes the vast majority of juvenile literary output. It also resembles, for that matter, the plots of most adult-authored novels. The junior satirist's observations signal some recognition on the part of young people themselves that the West looked increasingly drained of originality and excitement. Miners, loggers, and homesteaders had stripped the region's resources bare by the turn of the century; some kids seemed to believe the same could be said about its artistic potency. The sentiment, of course, was hardly universally shared. Amateur stories set in the region still appeared in large numbers well into the 1880s and early 1890s. So too did settlerist dime novels written for young readers.[54]

But the tediousness of the frontier parodied in "Plots" proved somewhat prescient. Several factors combined to push the region from the forefront of public consciousness. For one, the pacification of the West, complete by 1890 at the latest, seemed to denude it of the incident and excitement that attracted the attention of youths. Changes in US postal policy, meanwhile, made dime novels and magazines more expensive to distribute. So too did cutthroat competition among several of the largest children's publishing firms help restructure the industry in ways unfavorable to settler-colonial-themed sensationalism. Finally, the War of 1898 and new forms of foreign policy adventurism overseas directed America's attention, at least for a time, away from the West. The sum total of these disparate transformations was quickly felt among the country's juvenile demographic. Whereas the dime novel had once disseminated expansionist sentiment heralding the conquest of a continent, now the series book arose to sing of Uncle Sam's growing global empire.

# 2

## Serialized Imperialism

One day ten-year-old Harry Morris picked up a pen to draft a fan letter. Yet the missive's famous recipient, "Arthur Winfield," did not exist. Winfield, author of Harry's favorite juvenile series books, the "Rover Boys," was a pseudonym created by American book publisher Edward Stratemeyer as part of a larger literary syndicate populated by titans including the Hardy Boys and Nancy Drew. Morris's praiseful note gushed that Winfield "wrote the best books ever" and knew "how to put that touch in them that gets boys." Revealingly, Harry even claimed to "imitate the Rovers as much as I can." Conscious emulative effort meant that young people could become dynamic participants in their own politicization. The opportunities for imaginative play opened by children's literature enabled such self-fashioning. But the content of these stories matters too. The Rover series, with its exotic settings, was one part of a larger effort to instill in young people an imperial consciousness—to spur, as Stratemeyer said in a 1906 interview, "a deeper interest in the affairs of the world" on the part of the rising generation.[1]

Edward Stratemeyer is an important historical figure precisely because of his enormous influence over millions of American boys and girls at the turn of the twentieth century. He personally wrote hundreds of books for young people and oversaw the production of many more. They were released as individual hardcovers cheaply fashioned and then marketed to juvenile audiences. Typically, each edition formed an installment in one of several different series running concurrently. The volumes themselves tackled a variety of subjects, including travel, technology, war, or athletics. Soon enough, sales figures soared and the size of his endeavor grew exponentially. In order to handle so many demands on his time, Stratemeyer founded his own literary syndicate. He outlined stories and sent them to ghost writers. These individuals remained anonymous, were paid a flat rate per novel, and did not retain the copyright to or receive royalties for their work. For Stratemeyer,

55

publishing became an industrial operation, something he himself called a "fiction factory." Eventually, the business yielded titles numbering into the thousands. By the time he died in 1930, Edward Stratemeyer was arguably the most prolific writer and publisher in American history. He became so by talking to children.[2]

What makes Stratemeyer's life particularly useful to think about here is the near-perfect overlap between his career and the history of America's overseas empire. From its inception, the Stratemeyer Syndicate, unlike settlerist dime fiction, focused on the nation's foreign relations beyond North America. As such, the writer and editor extraordinaire helped transition children's literature from the exterminationist ethos of the 1870s and 1880s to an imperial model rooted in the prolonged US management of "brown brothers" abroad. His first successful foray into mass-produced fiction was the "Old Glory Series," which followed the adventures of three brothers during the War of 1898 and Philippine-American War. Later volumes, meanwhile, tackled US involvement in the Mexican Revolution, the Boxer Rebellion, and several hemispheric "police actions" authorized by the Roosevelt Corollary's muscular reading of the Monroe Doctrine. As the frontier formally "closed" and policymakers built the military and diplomatic scaffolding meant to support America's expanded role in international affairs, Stratemeyer took it upon himself to integrate juvenile citizens into the shift away from the continent and toward something larger. His major contribution to the history of US empire was to facilitate for the nation's young people a kind of cultural globalism. He asked them to see the wider world as a new field for enterprise. He attempted to naturalize the pacification and incorporation of millions of new subjects (residing in the Philippines, Puerto Rico, and elsewhere) into the body politic. In Stratemeyer's eyes, a "Greater United States" comprising much of North America and interspersed with overseas colonies had now, as he put it, been catapulted to "the front rank of the nations of the world." "Our Flag is respected as it was never respected before," the "future is large with possibilities, and it remains for the generation I am addressing to rise up and embrace those opportunities and make the most of them."[3]

Stratemeyer was always explicit about his goal of actuating adolescent interest in US empire. Postbellum dime novels had emphasized the conquest of North America. After 1898, Stratemeyer led juvenile literature in a pivot toward more internationally oriented subject matter. "The modern boy grows up more quickly," he thought. "He is likely to be a manlier fellow, with a deeper interest in the affairs of the world than the youth of a generation ago." Stratemeyer knew that the adolescent "appetite for information is whetted by what he reads." Therefore, he looked upon it as a duty to stimulate within kids "a desire to know what is going on in the world," as "knowledge of these subjects is necessary to an understanding of world affairs." "History and geography are not in themselves interesting to the average boy," he admitted, but that had to be rectified for America to assume its rightful role as a global power. The best means to accomplish this, Stratemeyer concluded, was to paint pertinent information with a veneer of what he called "incident and escapade." "Cuba and the Philippines," along with "South and Central America, are now fields which are attracting much attention in the United States." His books helped channel that broader excitement down the age scale and into the ranks of the young. For, as Stratemeyer's publisher swore, "youth feeds on adventure and sensation."[4]

Collectively, Stratemeyer Syndicate series books (along with literature produced by their many imitators and competitors) shed light on the multigenerational durability of imperial ideology and how a wider acceptance of the United States as an arbiter in international affairs arose. It is telling that Stratemeyer explicitly claimed that his books imparted "much the same message" as had been publicly outlined by the State Department in 1895: that "the mission of this country is not merely to pose but to act [and] to forego no fitting opportunity to further the progress of civilization." Out of the mouths of the characters he created came repeated reaffirmation of the basic point that the United States now possessed responsibilities extending beyond its immediate borders. At such a seemingly auspicious moment, series fiction could step in and supplement a school system that rarely seemed to stimulate student interest. As Stratemeyer envisioned it, the genre would serve to make the American scramble for colonies and resources abroad interesting, even vital, to those who would inherit that vast apparatus.[5]

Judging by the fan mail Stratemeyer accumulated, it was a very successful messaging campaign. As he later boasted, "I receive a great many letters from boys and girls who read my books," which "shows their hearts are with you." Kids like Harry Morris regularly wrote their favorite syndicate

Figure 2.1. Edward Stratemeyer became one of the most prolific authors in US history, and did so by making imperial appeals to young readers. Manuscripts and Archives Division, New York Public Library. *Portrait of Edward Stratemeyer*. New York Public Library Digital Collections.

authors and storybook characters to lavish them with praise. Children's letters were often explicit in extolling the books for their educational value. Series fiction sparked an interest, junior enthusiasts claimed, in charting America's increasing entanglement with corners of the world rarely mentioned in earlier juvenile literature. Even more important, however, was Stratemeyer's regular insistence that fan mail helped generate content for syndicate stories. As young people wrote in to request more militarized or interventionist plotlines, corporate officers circulated memos enjoining empire in the company's output. In this sense, Stratemeyer was no puppet master pulling the strings of the compliant masses. Rather, the demands of adolescents themselves helped to create a colonially inflected youth culture in the United States. Authors and audience united to mutually valorize empire after the War of 1898. The outward or externally oriented American state was built, in part, atop youthful ebullience.[6]

## The Series Book Arises

Commentators in the late nineteenth century were quick to recognize the importance of youth to the "newly" imperialistic United States. Children represented a potentially lucrative market as well as a group to be incorporated into the expansionistic aims of the nation. William C. Sprague lent his voice to a chorus when he wrote, in an 1899 issue of the *American Boy*, that "there is enough literature for men and women—enough for children; but is there quite enough for the wide-awake, aspiring American boy who is just turning the corner into manhood?"[7]

The era found many writers answering Sprague's call to arms. They enlisted their literary talents, such as they were, in the service of American empire. Adolescents "turning the corner into manhood" seemed the perfect audience to address at a time when many in the press and in politics likened American acquisition of overseas colonies to a confirmation of national maturity. A typically bombastic speech by enthusiastic expansionist Senator Albert Beveridge articulated that very idea. "When a people reach its young manhood as the American people has reached its young manhood," he noted, "they naturally look beyond their boundaries for their energy and enterprise [and] the world becomes their field." The primacy of youth was a particular obsession of his. "Our nation is young. Our country is young. Our flag is young. Our destiny is the destiny of the young among nations." Author Frank Norris reiterated the correlation between youth and national ambition when he likened the country's frantic search for new frontiers beyond the West to "the boy shut indoors who finds his scope circumscribed and fills the whole place with the racket of his activity," while Jack London concurred by proclaiming: "What a playball has this planet of ours become." Such imperial rhetoric politicized boyhood and linked young men and the nation. No one embodied this fact better than Theodore Roosevelt, the man thought most representative of the era. Not only was he the youngest person ever to become president, but he was also written about and depicted as exuding a boyish exuberance.[8]

An infant republic had seemingly grown up overnight and would require the zeal of those who, when old enough, were to assume the responsibilities of an imperial future—hence, the call for a literature to take up that task. As one editor assumed, "the influence of reading on character is one of the most powerful [and] is granted by every high-minded person." In short, he summarized, "we are what we read." Connecting the widespread belief in the influence of reading habits with the quest to incorporate the nation's boys into the imperial project, children's book authors sought to tie America's international ambitions to those of the rising generation. There is a great deal to learn about American imperialism from studying the works of writers who endeavored to narrate, explain, and justify the republic's use of military force in service of colonialism. Juvenile series fiction reveals a literary culture fixated on transforming boys and young men into political allies of the project to enhance US influence overseas.[9]

Series fiction's dominance, by the early 1900s, of the youth market derived from structural changes within the publishing industry itself. Dime novel distributors became, to some extent, victims of their own success. As more and more ten-cent firms attempted to crowd newsstands, profits for any one establishment diminished. Literacy rates and thus the size of the juvenile reading public actually grew during the Gilded Age, but with so much competition, it became difficult for businesses to prosper. Almost inevitably, given the era's impulse toward industrial consolidation, one of the larger publishers, the United States Book Company (USBC), attempted to corner the market by forming a "cheap literature trust." The USBC endeavored to destroy its rivals by buying up nearly every printing plate used in the book production process. It also began to purchase (and hoard) the copyrights for innumerable stories. Other companies soon did the same. These were the first shots of the so-called Fiction Wars of the early 1890s. By the time the Panic of 1893 struck, the USBC and its competitors had drained their capital reserves and proved unable to weather the economic downturn. Their vaults were full of unpublished manuscripts, but cash-strapped customers had stopped spending on literature. Contemporaneous changes in postal law, meanwhile, reclassified dime novels, denying them the discounted freight rates they had previously enjoyed. Increased shipping costs cut further into profit margins. Collapse ensued.[10]

Out of the wreckage, however, arose new opportunities for a different kind of publisher. Dime novel firms fell apart. But the dime novel itself had also been dragged into disrepute. Moral crusaders vowed to clean up the American children's literature market, and cheap publications bore the brunt of their efforts. Respectable-looking series fiction books, attractively bound with hard covers, and guaranteeing "wholesome" content to parents, now stepped into the breach. Edward Stratemeyer was by far the most influential contributor to this new wave of children's reading. In 1905 he formed his publishing syndicate, which revolutionized the production of juvenile literature in the United States. But for all his influence, Stratemeyer remained a shadowy figure. Hoping to corner the juvenile fiction market, he became the architect of his own anonymity. He brought together and supervised a team of writers to produce under numerous pen names an array of books, thereby creating the *illusion* of competition. Best known today as the creator of the Hardy Boys and Nancy Drew detective stories, Stratemeyer also wrote tales of baseball, technology (Tom Swift, most famously), and globetrotting. Perhaps the first American author to fully recognize children as a legitimate consumer group with purchasing power and discriminating tastes, Stratemeyer built his syndicate around the idea of juvenile agency in book selection.[11]

But his success was hardly unprecedented. Aspects of Stratemeyer's eventual business model and method of writing owed a great deal to an earlier cohort of serial novelists like Horatio Alger, as well as nineteenth-century household names like William Taylor Adams (pseudonym Oliver Optic) and Captain Mayne Reid. Several British writers were also progenitors, including G. A. Henty, H. Rider Haggard (author of the Allan Quatermain tales), and others who composed installments centered on the adventures of boys within the British empire. The United States' victory in 1898 signaled to Stratemeyer the need for a series that introduced America's youth to their new empire in the same way that Henty's stories inculcated an imperialistic pride within his Victorian audience. Henty and Stratemeyer were both savvy enough to recognize that child-readers hungered to feel included in broader political currents. What set Stratemeyer apart, however, was his willingness to rid syndicate books of influential adults. Rather than rely on kindly adult benefactors to push the plot forward, as had Alger and his generation, Stratemeyer's characters were universally young and depended entirely upon their own resourcefulness and ingenuity to resolve conflicts. Juvenile readers now, in effect, saw *themselves* take precedence in the projection of American power abroad. The broad circulation of these books suggests that it was a winning formula.[12]

Until now, scholars have studied Stratemeyer and his factory-like operation almost solely out of an interest in the intersection of literature and mass production. His books, however, deserve serious consideration for the themes that appear in them and what they reveal about American attitudes toward both their own country and the world. Typically scorned by critics as cheap and sensationalistic drivel, juvenile series fiction occupies a minor place in the study of popular culture. The wide dissemination of Stratemeyer's work and the legions of young admirers who flooded his office with fan mail, however, hint at the value of deeper analysis of the themes and ramifications of such mass-produced culture. By his death in 1930, Stratemeyer's syndicate had distributed more than 200 million series books throughout the United States. Such numbers alone suggest some degree of ideological influence over American youth.[13]

From the start, Stratemeyer used US overseas empire as a setting for and theme of his youth fiction. The six books in his first successful publication, the Old Glory Series, which began production in 1898, follow the "haps and mishaps" of the Russell brothers (Larry, Ben, and Walter) across both Cuba and the Philippines. Incomplete circulation figures point to first-month's sales of 6,000 or more, making them blockbusters by the standards of the time. Surveys of libraries, public school officials, and students confirmed the wild popularity of Stratemeyer's work as compared to the "classics" favored by educators. The Old Glory Series catapulted the relatively obscure author into national prominence. The formulas and themes that made these books a sensation would be used again and again by Stratemeyer and his peers. As the genre's most widely read author, Stratemeyer exemplifies how the War of 1898 and the Philippine-American War were stripped down and repackaged for American boys at the turn of the twentieth century.[14]

In the world as portrayed in these books, the colonized are almost always subordinate and supplicant, suited for and even requiring rule by the very white American men into whom the books' target audience would grow. Edward Stratemeyer and the other authors of juvenile series fiction typically eschewed nuance in favor of moral and political absolutes. Complex problems pertaining to the acquisition and administering of overseas territory disappeared within the pages of these stories. Unlike the adult domain, there was no contrary, anti-imperialist discourse among syndicate series fiction authors. Juvenile stories depicted American aims in the Caribbean and Pacific as inherently benevolent. As writers argued for their adolescent audiences, newly acquired territory would be regenerative of national boyhood. It would also come without cost. Deprived of its ambiguities, contradictions, and overall messiness, aggression abroad became literal child's play. Altogether, Stratemeyer and other youth authors avoided asking readers to contemplate real conditions in the Philippines, Cuba, and beyond. Boys instead encountered a palatable series of romanticized and exoticized images standing in for US foreign policy. Addressed as the future inheritors of a nascent "American century," the nation's children once again became a target audience for imperialist discourse.

## Strenuous Lives and the Stratemeyer Hero

In a rare interview, Stratemeyer provided a Newark newspaper with a brief but revealing look at the philosophy his books espoused. He declared that he had "no toleration for that which is namby-pamby or wishy-washy in juvenile literature." The present, he reasoned, was a "strenuous age . . . and the boys of to-day are clever and up-to-date and appreciate that which is true to life quite as much as their elders." Part of a generation of thinkers who fretted that the nation's "magazines are getting so lady-like that naturally they will soon menstruate," Stratemeyer concluded that the duty of any boys' author was to restore national vitality by giving young readers "the incident and adventure" they desired. Echoing Theodore Roosevelt's advocacy for the "strenuous life," Stratemeyer's comments suggest his embeddedness in the era's discourse. The author's diction ("namby-pamby") and rhetoric reflect exasperation on the part of Americans indignant over the rampant luxury and idleness thought to be corrupting national boyhood. "The boy needs good literature," an essayist in the *American Boy* philosophized. "He is growing restless under restraint, dreams dreams, gets aspirations, and begins to do things." A contributor to *Boy's Life* also worried about degeneration. "The boys of this country," he began, "are not namby-pamby youths, devoid of imagination, and who know nothing and care nothing about the greater world awaiting them. They want to read and know something beyond the dull level of their own street and town."[15]

Academics, meanwhile, analyzed the country's alleged "boy problem." A new pseudoscience—"Boyology"—arose to study the conditions under which sons might flourish. Taken together, commentaries and developments such as these envisioned the domestic environment as an enervating space of entrapment. Young men desperately needed vigorous exercise and time outdoors. They needed to experience the world beyond the coddling embrace of their mothers. Authors who rhapsodized about the importance of aspiration and the "greater world awaiting" America's boys often saw overseas empire as the means to that end. And if not every one of them had the good fortune to be building character abroad, then he might figuratively do so by turning the pages of an adventure novel. The indirect imperialism offered to young readers of series fiction was imagined as the antidote to an overcivilized age. Such books might help salvage America's boys, and thus, in a larger sense, the country's ability to compete in what many depicted as a Darwinian struggle among rival states. In some sense, Stratemeyer's series fiction anticipated the admonitions of G. Stanley Hall. The influential theorist of adolescence, concerned about "feminized boys," urged parents to let your sons "read stories with bloodshed in them." Empire's mayhem, even if only experienced vicariously, might provide an answer to incipient national emasculation. It was time for the pampered Little Lord Fauntleroys of the world to cast off their "mama's" apron strings.[16]

As a result, in Stratemeyer's depictions of the War of 1898 and the Philippine War, the adolescent reader was more than a spectator. Grammatical constructions, such as the frequent use of inclusive pronouns ("we" and "our"), introduced readers into the action, while incessant patriotic overtures integrated them into the sense of national triumph following American victories in both conflicts. "Nothing can stand up," a common chorus rang, "against the Stars and Stripes, our glorious flag of freedom." Stratemeyer and other series fiction writers provided a space for youngsters to perform patriotism and share in the prognostications of national destiny that swept the country following the War of 1898. The author made this manifest in the prefaces to his war stories. "Though the adventures may seem overdrawn," Stratemeyer wrote, "[we] must remember that Young America is full of pluck and daring, and never comes to the front more conspicuously than when fighting for the honor of Old Glory." Comments such as these reassured boys not old enough to enlist that they too possessed the stuff of dashing heroes.[17]

In speaking directly to his audience, Stratemeyer's intentions were manifold. In one sense this was a business strategy designed to create a loyal following. The author attempted to evoke a sense of personal investment in characters whom he portrayed as "average American boys"—or, in other words, just like "you," the juvenile reader. Perceiving oneself as a participant in the action might enhance the desire to see an adventure through to the end, and, just as important, purchase the next book in the series. But, in a much broader rhetorical ploy, Stratemeyer tinkered with the author-reader relationship by tailoring his stories to what he thought were the specific needs of American boys. In doing so, he widened the growing gulf between child and adult reading habits at the end of the nineteenth century. Stratemeyer offered boys a sense of self-importance that stemmed from his insistence that these were their books, their adventures. He encouraged adolescents to see themselves as a distinct demographic. They could do so, in part, through their choice of reading material.[18]

Stratemeyer, along with other juvenile series fiction authors, portrayed the nation's boys as the inheritors of the flag's triumph. He allotted them an imagined place in the act of conquest itself. Formula stories, according to theorists, became hugely popular due to the "basic emotional security they offer the reader." Mimetic literature portrays "the world as we know it," but series fiction offers the convenience of "an ideal world, without the disorder, the ambiguity, and the limitations of . . . our existence." A form of escapism, such works stress action and plot over complex characterization in order to "take us out of ourselves . . . by confirming an idealized self-image." But, in addition to this generalized form of literary escape, Stratemeyer's Old Glory Series addressed a specific period in time. Juvenile literature shaped the shared mental images of overseas empire entertained by the nation's boys. As newspapers and magazines assured parents of their place at an auspicious moment in American history, the popular culture of youth included children in nominally adult affairs. Stratemeyer even jubilantly declared, at the end of the series, that "the last of the Filipinos were utterly routed, and Malolos was *ours!*" Boys could now insert themselves into the new national narrative of overseas expansion.[19]

But if the Stratemeyer series allowed for the ritual enactment of boyish patriotism, through whom did the juvenile reader see and speak? The series' heroes represented an amalgamation of "strenuous life" dogma and "muscular Christian" doctrine stuffed into the uniform of a US soldier. In the Old Glory Series, these Stratemeyer archetypes were known collectively as the Russell brothers. The Russells (Larry, Walter, and Ben) embodied what Anthony Rotundo calls the "passionate manhood" of the late nineteenth century. Contemporary fears of the "overcivilization" and "feminization" of American men prompted pundits and parents to push for a youth culture that valued the strength of boys' bodies as much as their minds. Stratemeyer's young heroes, therefore, insisted upon the importance of "action" and "struggle" in molding their respective characters. The savagery of the battlefield, as was found in 1898, provided an opportunity for men to recapture for themselves a certain primordial essence that modernity and its many comforts had conspired against.[20]

Stratemeyer chiseled his characters from the most rugged rocks of masculinity. Portrayed as "tall, well-built, and with a make-up that was thoroughly manly," the Russell brothers displayed the physical prowess so important to ideas of manhood at the time. Of equal importance was their unwillingness to sacrifice their honor no matter the circumstances. Thus Larry Russell, having lost his wallet and confronted with the emasculating prospect of accepting charity from a kindly stranger, claimed that he was "not of that kind." "Setting to work manfully," he preserved his dignity by laboring to erase the debt. The implication of Stratemeyer's diction, of course, was that women possessed the luxury of dependence while men ought to bear the burden of self-reliance without complaint.[21]

The Stratemeyer hero, while "patriotic to the core," also scrupulously adhered to a set of ethical principles that emphasized the primacy of personal responsibility. Whether slogging through mud, burning under a tropical sun, or struggling against some merciless foe, the Russell brothers sing out in unison, "We're working for Uncle Sam, so let's make the best of it!" Repeatedly contrasted with those in his midst who would loaf about, the Stratemeyer hero steps onto the first few pages of every novel to exclaim that he is "aching to get back to [his] duty." Surely, the boy-dynamo reasons to a comrade, we have "both been idle long enough." The language suggests a nearly pathological imperative for purposeful activity. Even after being severely wounded on the battlefield, the Stratemeyer hero "took his medicine like a man," never "letting his bravery desert him" and always expressing a desire for further opportunities to "show his mettle." All of these traits were emphasized as part of Stratemeyer's attempt to strategically distinguish his series fiction from the dime novels that ignited a critical backlash in the 1880s. While periodicals complained that frontier fiction had caused young people to "become dissatisfied with the prosaic duties of every-day life and long to become cow-boys," Stratemeyer stressed that *his* protagonists cheerfully embraced work and obligation as moral imperatives.[22]

Stratemeyer used these traits to guide his readers through potentially thorny policy questions. Empire's ambiguities and ambivalences evaporated in the face of such single-minded devotion to country. Discussing an upcoming campaign against Filipino insurgents, Larry and Ben avoided any mention of arguably problematic war aims with a shrug of the shoulders. We are "not politicians," they declared, "only one of Uncle Sam's soldier boys." Accordingly, they decided to "leave these big questions of statesmanship alone and do [their] duty as [they found] it." Their deference was rewarded with the praiseful reply of a commanding officer: "That's the kind of talk I like to hear, Russell. The man who is willing to do his whole duty—to do exactly as he is told to do—is the man we are after." One did not, in other words, need to question the obligations imposed by empire. Young readers were told that obedience was its own reward. Anything that supposedly served national interests overseas could be construed as legitimate.[23]

Throughout these books, Stratemeyer posed a series of facile binaries. The plucky, compliant, sober-minded, strenuously living lads of the Russell clan encountered and eventually triumphed over those characters possessing the contrary traits of duplicity, dishonor, and intemperance. Reduced to a skeleton of itself, the Stratemeyer story presented an easy-to-follow set of instructions, the result of which was the transformation of boy into man. Stratemeyer swiftly carried his reader through a series of clear-cut ethical quandaries. Yet moral victories over fops and dandies were not the only sources of affirmation for the series fiction hero. For if Stratemeyer spent large portions of his books establishing the criteria for a model boyhood, there still awaited the larger task of integrating America's youth into the wider world opened up by American victory in the War of 1898. In their encounters with the country's new clients abroad, the Russell brothers made good their vow to show readers what American boys could do.

### "Furiners," "Haythins," and Those "Clever Yankee Lads"

After the United States went to war with Spain, many cultural outlets ennobled the struggle. Anthropomorphizing the nation as a knight-errant, Americans justified their intervention by conceptualizing the enemy's oppressed colonies as damsels in distress. Visual and literary media legitimated the use of force with a language of chivalry. Contained within all of these fictions lay the gendered dichotomy of savior and saved. Oppressed Cubans and Filipinos were feminized as a way to underscore their relative weakness. By soundly "whipping the Dons"—as Spaniards were derided—the United States would do the world a splendid service. It was, moreover, conceived as an act of republican anti-colonial selflessness. The Teller Amendment attached to Congress's war resolution, which disavowed annexationist aims for postwar Cuba, demonstrated America's noblesse oblige.[24]

If this fanciful tale helped bring the United States onto the battlefield in 1898, quick victory brought with it a representational about-face. Soldiers, officers, and observers in Cuba and the Philippines stood aghast at what they termed the "savagery" of the peoples they encountered abroad. Popular writing about the war soon depicted occupied peoples as less the feminized damsel and more the infantilized child-barbarian. Referred to alternately as "impudent," "ruthless," "dirty," and "ignorant," insular inhabitants became objects of scorn rather than the recipients of rescue. As Theodore Roosevelt averred, "if there is no self-control and self-mastery" among such people, "the control and the mastery will ultimately be imposed from without." US authorities moved to deny recently liberated nations their sovereignty. Never mind that indigenous independence movements had been fighting for years in those places. Instead, in highly racialized terms, Americans rejected Cuban and Filipino capacities for self-government. President McKinley and much of the country's political establishment articulated a vision of friendly American hegemony referred to as "benevolent assimilation." US forces would occupy and "civilize" territory seized during the war until such time as its residents were deemed fit to manage their own affairs.²⁵

These same shifts in policy and attitude played out in Edward Stratemeyer's Old Glory Series. By looking at his books, works that he promised were "accurate, historically," we can locate not only one man's understanding of American imperialism but also the lessons the author deemed worthy of passing on to young readers. The first of these centers around the inherent deviousness of nonwhite racial groups. Suspicion, bordering on paranoia, appears in the encounters the Russells have with foreign peoples. Characters remind one another constantly that Natives cannot be counted upon for anything except ill will and treachery. Stratemeyer wrote during a period of widespread nativism and racism, and such rhetoric repeats itself throughout his novels. In numerous situations, the brothers' misgivings about the credibility of indigenous intentions are amply rewarded. In one particularly dramatic scene, Ben displays charity to a wounded Filipino soldier by offering him water, but the man returned that kindness by trying to kill his American savior. Ben, possessing only gallant intentions, "could barely speak, the scene had so unnerved him."²⁶

"Such treachery," Stratemeyer tells us, "was almost beyond his comprehension." Apparently, the boy-soldier had yet to learn that "the Filipinos, of a pure Malayan blood . . . are full of cunning and trickery, and have absolutely no conscience." The last gasp of bravery that in an American warrior might have been considered "pluckiness to the end" was, in a Filipino, nothing more than perfidy. It served only to instruct readers regarding the racial characteristics of the Philippines. Regular reprise of similar scenes, wherein the honest intentions of noble-minded American boys are met with duplicity, eventually finds the brothers going into battle under the cry of a compatriot: "Down wid the haythins that don't know the meanin' of honor!" The contrast between the two groups became another binary that distinguished the main characters (and the readers meant to identify with them) from the new empire's savage inhabitants.²⁷

If the average Native was not working to destroy a Yankee hero, there was a good chance that individual was not working at all. In Stratemeyer's books, peoples overseas exhibited little inclination to labor. Authorial asides, made for the educational benefit of readers, often chided them for their supposed lack of a Protestant work ethic. In contrast to the Stratemeyer hero's search for fulfilling labor, the colonized only toiled "to obtain a little cash with which to buy liquor." Not only was the sloth of these "dusky, fat, ill-smelling" Natives repulsive to the protagonists, it was also frustrating. As Ben remarks to his friend Gilbert, local farmers could raise crops for profit if they so desired, but unfortunately, "the average Cuban, it must be confessed, is rather lazy." Such talk reveals the leveling effect of the discourse of savagery. In applying the same admonition to each racial group they encounter, these fictional observers tended to homogenize myriad cultures into a uniform inferiority. Subalterns overseas were reduced to a series of types, each displaying characteristics deemed deficient and thereby inviting US rule. Stratemeyer urged his vast juvenile audience to see recent acquisitions abroad as being in deep need of assistance from their rightful overlords, who would inject into stagnant societies a "vigor that only the Anglo-Saxon race knows." He repackaged for junior citizens then-contemporary rhetoric exalting white Americans as "master organizers" meant to "establish system where chaos reigns" and "lead in the regeneration of the world." Often the highest compliment a story's character could be paid was the declaration that "he's a white man through and through, none whiter anywhere."[28]

In Stratemeyer's imperialist youth adventures, Cubans or Filipinos rarely speak with their own voice. They appear as little more than fixtures in the landscape. So easily did the colonized disappear into the tropical background that they were often equated with animals. The Natives who "glided away noiselessly like some beast of the forest" or "crashed through the jungle like so many wild cattle" blend in because of their obvious inhumanity. Understood to behave like "brutes," they became suitable objects for subjugation. Yet as portrayed by Stratemeyer, local individuals often cheerfully accepted their subordination to Americans. One Cuban woman is "proud to think she was serving 'un Americano,'" while others stand by wondering what those "'clever Yankees' would do next." Many express gratitude toward their liberators. In one scene, rebel Cuban guerrillas sight the intrepid Russell brothers and cry in unison: "Our deliverers have come at last!" As for revolutionaries who

"Drop it or I'll fire." — *Page* 161.

Figure 2.2. Series book illustrations often emphasized the power that Anglo-Saxon youths could wield over America's new subjects overseas. Edward Stratemeyer, *Under Otis in the Philippines or, A Young Officer in the Tropics* (Boston: Lee and Shepard, 1899), 161.

displayed displeasure over Yankee meddling, such ingrates "had yet to learn that the trained soldiers of Spain could be conquered only by the equally, or better, trained soldiers of the United States." Surrounded by a dedicated band of Cuban *insurrectos* who had been fighting for their independence long before Uncle Sam's arrival in 1898, the best the Russells can offer is condemnation of their filthy faces, disgust over the state of their uniforms, and a prophetic whisper among themselves: "They mean well . . . but we won't get much assistance from these chaps." Reduced from soldiers to supplicants by Stratemeyer, Cuban and Filipino patriots quickly handed their cause over to their Anglo-Saxon superiors. It was, in the author's words, simply a "true story" of how "our own glorious United States stepped in and gave to Cuba the precious boon of liberty."

And if Cuban independence "belonged" to their Yankee benefactors, then young readers could be made to understand that the island should remain "under the guiding hand of Uncle Sam." American kids were told to prepare for a long haul: "to bring these people to genuine civilization will take many years of patient labor and encouragement." Exterminationism, however, was off the table.[29]

In Stratemeyer's tales, moreover, Native women are defeminized by right of their race. Referred to as "fat, grim-looking wenches," or simply females, "for [they] cannot call such immodest creatures ladies," the damsels in distress were stripped of their womanhood and instead derided for their supposed lack of homemaking skill. Their houses seemed unkept, they could not cook decent food, and their children appeared undisciplined. Throughout the course of their adventures, the Russells lament the rancid cuisine and domiciles "overrun with vermin—a not uncommon thing, even in the dwellings of the middle classes." Universalizing Victorian ideas about proper domesticity, Stratemeyer offered readers the opportunity to contrast their own surroundings with the rampant squalor of the imagined empire. The cleanliness and order that idealized American mothers enforced within their own homes, unattainable to the barbaric or degraded women of the Caribbean or Philippines, reaffirmed the superiority of the readers' own social system. Gender thus became another binary axis along which Stratemeyer dramatized the necessity of US empire as an engine for uplift abroad. This was the youth-oriented dimension of a broader discourse fixated upon the domestic "deficiencies" of the colonized as a means to legitimate imperial interventions. It had worked in the West, and now found wider applicability after 1898.[30]

The only other moments where women appeared in these stories dealt with chivalric roleplay. White boy-soldiers could prove their heroic qualities by stepping forward to protect a member of the "weaker sex." Such gallantry also confirmed the savagery of Native men unable to treat women with the respect and delicacy they deserved. Ben Russell, for example, became indignant at the thought of "two men . . . misusing some woman." Hearing a "cry for aid [that] appealed to his heart," he rescued his Filipino damsel moments before her ruthless captors were to kill her. Before fainting, the suffering girl composes herself long enough to express undying gratitude in "a sweet voice that went straight to Ben's heart." But, having done his duty manfully, the lad quickly foreclosed on the possibility of any sort of romantic entanglement. Only "an American girl will be good enough," he swore. Distressed Native women provided a means for heroes to demonstrate courageousness, but as objects of affection, they could not surpass their white counterparts. Stratemeyer makes it clear that while the valor of American boys would inevitably win hearts abroad, miscegenation was unthinkable. Hence, as Ben's maiden "came close to embracing him . . . he backed out and shifted the subject." A boy's patriotic duty was to his country; his romantic duty was to his own race.[31]

Stratemeyer used his protagonists to propagate expansionist policies. From the outset of hostilities in the Philippines, the Russell brothers engage in unwieldy paraphrasings of Theodore Roosevelt and other imperialists. Stratemeyer echoed a standard defense of America's instrumentality in insular affairs by forcing his characters to remark that "we've got to bring them into submission. If we don't, they'll be fighting amongst themselves all the time." Dismissing the Philippine Declaration of Independence, Ben reasons that the "natives are very ignorant, and willing to do anything that their educated and wily leaders wanted of them." The "rebels" may have been "strapping fellows," but they were, at heart, "hot-headed" people "as ignorant as so many children" and easily manipulated by "crafty" rulers who could "make the masses believe almost anything." "Even if they do throw off the yoke of Spain," another story averred, "I don't believe they are capable of governing themselves." Not once were young readers asked to question either the legitimacy (or efficacy) of US policies overseas or the absolute necessity of the country's continued involvement in other people's affairs. The power of Stratemeyer's storytelling was in its repetitive reassertions regarding the inherent incompetence of alien peoples recently brought under the aegis of American administrators.[32]

## Series Fiction beyond Stratemeyer

Edward Stratemeyer, however, was not the only author to speak with youthful audiences. Influenced by the genre's paterfamilias, his competitors produced series that exhibited the same obsession with white supremacy, the beneficence of American foreign policy, and the importance of inculcating patriotism among boys. The identities of the protagonists and location of the action sometimes shifted. What remained constant was an unwavering faith in the rehabilitative power of Americanism exported abroad. A survey of Stratemeyer's competitors reveals a collective investment, after 1900 or so, in normalizing America's growing imperial influence overseas. If anything, early twentieth-century series books expanded the scope of young readers' sense of where US interests lay. Authors soon moved on to Latin America and the circum-Caribbean. The indirect imperialism of budding American investment beyond its borders became a particularly prominent fixation of later books (see chapter 5). But in the immediate aftermath of the War of 1898, boys' series fiction authors still concentrated on Cuba, the Philippines, and the nation's growing strategic commitment to East Asia.[33]

Several writers seized upon the cry of "Cuba libre," though none more quickly than the Starry Flag Series. In it, Hal Maynard, an American boy, partnered with Juan Ramirez, rebel soldier, to effect an end to Spanish tyranny in the Western Hemisphere. Much of the material would have looked familiar to any reader conversant with the era's popular fiction. The Cubans came across as "so grateful to this country for its friendly support," and spoke only to say "'Long live the United States!'" Meanwhile the Yankee, full of "grit—clear grit!" and with "tears glisten[ing] in his eyes," saluted the flag, which "floats a supreme warning that treachery and tyranny can never flourish in the New World!" Writers likewise wondered "how any American can live without finding life one long thrill of pride that he is part and parcel of the Stars and Stripes?" More important, Hal Maynard, the youthful protagonist, was described as "a bright, typical dashing American boy." He was not superhuman, writers stressed. He was "you," because "every American boy has implanted in him the seeds of heroism, awaiting only the sunshine of opportunity for development." "Thus," they concluded, "Hal Maynard will be representative of all American boys, and our readers, in following his adventures, will see done exactly what they would do themselves were they in the hero's place."[34]

The importance of such rhetoric to young readers should not be overlooked. Unlike older varieties of didactic youth literature, in which authors assumed a paternalistic or custodial role vis-à-vis their audience, series fiction seemed content to place boys on their own and watch them

Figure 2.3. "Don't Touch My Flag!" Prints depicting the pugnacious patriotism of American boys circulated during the War of 1898. Such images echoed themes omnipresent within the era's juvenile literature. Library of Congress Prints and Photographs Division.

flourish outside the home, beyond adult supervision. We never once see or hear of 15-year-old Hal Maynard's parents, and yet, rather than misbehave, he became a major player in US foreign relations. "All American boys," these authors insisted, could be trusted to help project American power abroad. Investment in empire was a wholesome outlet for a child's healthful desire for independence and influence.[35]

Inserting boy-heroes into the day's current events was a popular narrative strategy both for Stratemeyer and his fellow series fiction writers. The Army Boy series, written by Captain C. E. Kilbourne, followed the adventures of Donald Page and Harry Kearny, a pair of boys no less audacious than the Russell brothers. So that the audience might identify with the protagonists, Kilbourne frequently described them as "very young for the position they filled." But their faces exuded a self-confidence beyond their years, while their bodies were "beautifully set up, and moved with the grace of perfectly balanced muscles." Having earned the trust of adults, the two managed to find themselves at the front lines of nearly every conflict that developed during the era. The Boxer Rebellion was their first foray into combat, and the boys distinguished themselves with brave deeds best described as racially motivated acts of vengeance. Chinese aims in the uprising are anybody's guess; the closest thing to an explanation of the conflict comes when Don and Harry note that "isolated whites were holding back hordes of yellow fanatics, thirsting for their blood and for that of their wives and children." An anonymous "Yellow Peril" actuated by nothing other than cruelty threatened white civilization's outposts in China. Women and children, in particular, had been placed in mortal danger.[36]

The boys cannot accept such a state of affairs. Series characters, narrators noted, "believed too implicitly in the civilization of the white man and the supremacy of the Anglo-Saxon to admit [defeat]." If "no chink has any use for a foreigner," the protagonists therefore reasoned, restraining rules of engagement could be relaxed. Witness to a slaughter of Christian missionaries, Page and Kearny swear vengeance, vowing to fix "those slant-eyed heathen!" Justice, in these books, was a proposition best measured by the enemy's body count. By the end of the story, the boys boast of their many kills. For young people who encountered the Boxer Rebellion through Kilbourne's book, this intricate, if indeed violent, nationalist-religious struggle was reduced to a conflict between a barbarous and backward China and the ever-righteous forces of white and Christian civilization. American intervention was rationalized as something thrust upon the nation by a foe unwilling to respect both international law and the codes governing decent conduct. That particularly pertained to the treatment of "ladies." In one book, a character managed to pick a fight because "'I don't believe that any yellow man has a right to glare like that at an American girl.'" Luckily, "the superior athletic physique of the Anglo-Saxon bore up before the rushes of the Chinamen," so that maidens considered themselves "'thankful that we have American men instead of men of any other nation to defend us.'" Different boys in a different series came to essentially the same conclusions: "'You Chinese are a weak race, and haven't the back-bone to stand up for your rights.'"[37]

Another story inserted two young soldiers of fortune into the Philippine territory that Stratemeyer previously covered. Attached to the constabulary force then mopping up remnants of the insurgency, Don and Harry spend their days training a native police force and patrolling the jungle for disloyal Filipinos. But as the author makes clear, the Americans had little to work with in their attempts to instill civilized traits in a decidedly uncivilized people. Upon surveying their recruits, the boys reported "a wild looking crew [in whom] savagery and animal ferocity were the dominating features." The "only sign that a mind governed the short, heavy bodies" was the "alertness of eye common to all beings, both human and animal."[38]

The contrast between Filipino and American was bluntly drawn: "In the one was an almost animal lust for combat, in the other equal courage perfectly controlled." The American boys accepted their role as both military and racial superiors, remarking that the Natives "needed taming badly." The book did not invite readers to question why a pair of youngsters with almost no experience, no seniority, and no knowledge of the local terrain were given command positions. Instead, by summoning an endless reserve of "Anglo-Saxon grit," the boy-soldiers consistently impressed their mostly nameless and faceless Filipino underlings, to the point that "one impulsive native seized Don's hand and carried it to his lips," telling him that "it is fitting that you should command such men as I." The series' broader thesis dealt with the efficacy of force across America's new empire. "From outlawry, murder, and rapine a few years have brought us to peace and good feeling. From poverty, pestilence, and famine they have brought us to comparative affluence and comfort." This was all due to a race of men "whose executive genius and unselfish devotion to duty have made so great a success."[39]

The justice of the American cause and the righteousness of its boys eventually reformed the hardened criminal and rebel leader, Don Sanchez. In the last throes of life following a battle with the boys and their newly trained crack troops, this former foe validated the United States' imperial vision by admitting that "you have beaten me throughout young man, and now that all is over I am glad. I see a better, greater future for my country than such as I could have given her." The fantasies depicted in such conversations were those of white hero-worship on the part of a racial underclass admiring of and deferential to American youth.[40]

The Moro War on the Philippine archipelago's southern islands also attracted the attention of a few authors. *Uncle Sam's Boys in the Philippines*, seemingly written to refute reports of American military atrocities at Bud Dajo during the suppression of Muslim rebels, kept insisting that "Uncle Sam's troops have no quarrel with men and women following peaceful occupations. If these brown natives understood our people better they would not scurry to cover when khaki-clad men are passing on fighting bent." Kids were assured that whatever rumors they might hear to the contrary, "massacres" perpetrated by US soldiers in fact represented the just application of punitive power. The Moros "spat on the Flag," and unless they were "punished for it, the native respect for American authority in these islands will soon be less than nothing."[41]

Other stories also stayed in the Philippines to monitor the progress of the imperial project. In one, a "Young Scout" infiltrated an insurgent camp, captured its leader, and ensured that "the frightened natives ... made every effort to gain the good will of the Americans." Another had a Philippine rebel refuse to surrender, leading one "Gatling Gun Bill" to sputter, "Such insolence! I'll show him whether they have accepted American sovereignty or not." Soon enough, several "half-breed chinks" and "niggers" lay dead and a "boy with grit ... got [his] shoulder straps." The rivalry between a teacher and an officer in the colonial constabulary, both sent from the United States to pacify the Philippines, appeared in a different tale. Allan, the teacher, believes that soldiers are brutes, while Burt, the military man, mocks his civilian counterpart as "one of those he-schoolmarms" here "to teach the Filipina girls to wear panties under their skirts and the boys to wear collars and shoes." Trouble with the Natives, however, soon demonstrated the importance of a united front among Americans overseas: "a white man was a white man," after all, and the "splay-footed little niggers" needed to "knuckle down" before their benevolent Uncle Sam.[42]

All of this fiction, when combined, encouraged boys to prepare themselves for the reality of colonial power: It would be a difficult and often thankless commitment that required perseverance. Young readers may have wondered why, if the United States had freed Cuba, there were still soldiers being sent on occasion to settle elections and quell unrest. Native characters who arose to complain that the War of 1898 had not brought freedom but meant only "changing masters" needed to be answered. And they were, usually in the shape of declamatory oratory. In one soliloquy, boy spy Tom Holton unmasks himself at a Havana protest against US rule to declare that "Cuba is certainly to be left to the Cubans, but first, order must be restored here and the wheels of government set going." "Heed the voice of common sense," he cried. "Your country must walk before it can run." Holton asked his juvenile audience to wonder, where was the gratitude America had earned? "Now will you not thank us for setting upon its feet this new-born child among the nations? Is not that what should happen?" In such ways, readers were told to reconcile themselves to an indefinitely long occupation of several spots around the world. Stories swept the troubled transition to American rule abroad under the rug, hoping instead to ensure that when youths looked upon their country, they "saw a people greater, freer, and more powerful than any nation had ever been," a "bright and shining light among the nations." And one fine day, these authors gloated, American boys would glory to see the "brown scoundrels" of the world "forced to pay the Flag humble reverence." Did you know "the Spaniards . . . once lorded it over everybody?" one chum asked another while stationed at a new imperial outpost. His young friend's reply did not miss a beat: "I guess we'll do that now." As they sang in unison while standing athwart the new empire: "Long live the United States!"[43]

## Fans Write Back

Assumptions regarding how young readers reacted to these books are difficult to substantiate. Response theory, which speculates about the reception of texts, is a thicket. It provides little solid guidance regarding the diverse and historically contingent ways in which literature is read and comprehended. With children's books in particular, this disjuncture between the historian's interpretation and that of individual readers would seem even more difficult to resolve. Adults might scrawl marginalia, correspond with contemporaries, or maintain a journal, any of which can eventually assist scholars in understanding how works are received. Young people, on the other hand, did these things in only the rarest of circumstances.[44]

One source concerning the effects that series fiction may have had on the worldview of children who read them is the reflection of adults. Though difficult to locate, some few memoirs contain reminiscences of childhoods spent gobbling the formulaic plots of mass-produced books. Literary critic Henry Canby, for example, wrote of the genre in his 1934 autobiography. "All those books," he thought, "were such real determinants of inner life for readers brought up in the eighties and nineties that no one will ever understand the America of that day without reading and pondering [them]." "I cannot separate in my own memory," he continued, "the bands and cheering of '98, Hobson, Dewey, and manifest destiny in an expectant world, from the extravagant romanticism of the shallow, unphilosophical, unpsychological novels we had all been reading. One carried over into the other, and the same color was infused through both." Within these few pages of a longer memoir, Canby eloquently drew an explicit link between the imagery of empire, its reflection in popular literature, and his resulting engrossment in a widely shared sense of triumphalism. The series books he read as a teenager, Canby admitted with some embarrassment, fostered a possessive sense of investment in American empire; "we, like our period, were hot for expansion." Theodore Dreiser also wrote about the cheap fiction he purchased, "as might a drug addict," during the 1890s. He claimed to understand how "impossible, from a practical point of view," their plots were, but he devoured them because they dramatized the "freedom of action" he craved. And it was empire, specifically, that satisfied his hunger for some semblance of agency. "How often at that time," Dreiser recalled, "I trotted over the plains of Africa or Australia or Asia with these famous boy heroes" while "destroy[ing] all manner of savages and wild animals, and so with impunity invaded the wildest, the most dangerous and therefore the most fascinating regions!" But insights gleaned from memoirs are imperfect resources in any attempt to reconstruct the influence and meaning of juvenile stories. Clouded as they are by hindsight, memories can be a poor substitute for one's reaction upon first encountering a book. Other evidentiary sources must be found to discover the immediate impact of series fiction on youthful readers.[45]

Fan mail provides one such avenue for exploration. In a testament to Stratemeyer's enormous popularity and to the emerging celebrity culture of the early twentieth century, young readers around the country bombarded his publishing firm with thousands upon thousands of adulatory letters. These missives can help to gauge how Stratemeyer's readers understood the ideas and material presented in his books. Rather than appealing to an ahistorical, vaguely defined, or theorized "reader," this fan mail allows us to assess the reactions of actual adolescents as they sent their opinions to the author. Today, there survives only a miniscule amount of what was, at one time, an archive of children's writing tens of thousands of letters strong. It breaks the historian's heart to see a 1906 newspaper story about Edward Stratemeyer and read that "he files many of the [kids'] letters away until the amount becomes so large that it is necessary to destroy them. Recently he burned several hundred." The little that was spared the furnace, however, still warrants some scrutiny.[46]

As these are fan letters, they are characterized by, even self-selected for, their laudatory tone and enthusiastic embrace of Stratemeyer titles. Harry Morris of Long Branch, New Jersey, who we met at the introduction to this chapter, wrote Arthur Winfield (one of Stratemeyer's many pseudonyms) to "congratulate you on your fine work in writing books." Harry gushed that Winfield "wrote the best books ever," claiming that the author knew "how to put that touch in them that gets boys." Concluding with a request for an autographed picture, Harry closed by stating, "You deserve a lot of credit for writing such fine books and I know every real boy will eat them up." And then, in a revealing final line, Harry stated, "I always try to imitate the Rovers as much as I can." The Rover Boys, one of many popular series books written by Stratemeyer and his employees, were a group of high school boys who traveled widely as ambassadors of American superiority. The Rovers, however, are less important than the claim, made with pride, that this young fan saw them as role models. To what extent Harry Morris found it practicable to emulate his literary heroes we do not know. What his letter does make clear, though, is that the young correspondent drew an explicit link between what he called "real boys" and the xenophobic nationalism and resolute jingoism of series book characters like the Rovers.[47]

Harry Morris's letter is one of a number that expressed an urge to imitate or otherwise learn from the characters and environments described by Stratemeyer. Another boy, S. G. Reid, wrote from Richmond, Virginia, asking for "the courtesy of knowing whether the island of Suna Bola (to which you refer in 'Don Sturdy Captured by Head Hunters') is an actual island or merely a fictitious name." He noted that he was "interested in any island which is in the Pacific . . . and should like to praise you more for your writing about the conditions in that section of the globe." The letter gives an impression of the ways in which some boys turned to the Stratemeyer adventure series for information about exotic locales and foreign cultures. The syndicate's consistent depiction of those places as patently inferior to the United States feels more consequential when one considers the accolades books received from fans regarding their educational value.[48]

As profuse as Reid's praise for Stratemeyer's authentic portrayal of the South Pacific appears, it is not difficult to imagine the sort of lessons about race taught by a book that prominently referenced "head hunters" in its title. Don Sturdy's adventures across the world, while published decades after the Russell brothers' exploits in the War of 1898, perpetuate similar perspectives regarding an altruistic American hegemony and the inevitability (and desirability) of white racial dominance. Bruce Rhodes, a boy of 13 living in Jacksonville, Florida, would have agreed with his fellow Don Sturdy fan from Richmond. Bruce sent a note to Stratemeyer to say that he "often dreamed [he] was a close companion of the boys and was sharing some of their adventures with them." They seemed, to him, to be "the kind of people that any real boy would be proud to call his friends." "Thanks very much," he finished, "for giving the youth of America such an absorbing set of books."[49]

Robert McIntyre of Mount Vernon, New York, wrote the syndicate to say that he had "just finished a series of books that you have written called Don Sturdy and enjoyed them very much." Robert proudly declared that "since I started to read these books, I have pulled my geography mark in school up from 70% to 95%." McIntyre, and presumably boys like him, relied upon the Stratemeyer fiction factory to supply them with their early conceptions of the globe, world affairs, and America's place in them. Lillie Nickerson, of Baltimore, echoed those sentiments on behalf of her grandson. She wrote in to note that the two "derived much pleasure and information from reading your 'Don Sturdy' books" together. "He has the complete set," she stated, "and we have read them the second time with as much interest as the first, hunt[ing] up the various places mentioned, and discussing each chapter as we progress." Stratemeyer himself announced to readers that he aimed to "acquaint our boys with . . . Uncle Sam's new possessions" around the world. Fans, in turn, regularly praised Stratemeyer's books as learning tools. In doing so, they defied legions of professional librarians and teachers who denounced series fiction as intellectually deadening "trash" literature. Then as now, the greater the taboo, the more young people thrilled at the thought of transgression.[50]

Girls writing to Stratemeyer seemed particularly concerned with the idea of infringement. The syndicate did publish a good deal of series fiction marketed to young women, but very little of it took up issues like international relations or empire. Publishers sought to police a fairly rigid divide separating the sexes. Girls' series were almost invariably set domestically. Plots were driven by romantic rather than battlefield conquests. Even the few adventure series geared toward young women featured far more passive female protagonists than their counterparts marketed to boys. As literary scholar Ilana Nash pithily puts it, "hiking, driving, and flying heroines covered many miles geographically," but "advanced only a few feet ideologically."[51]

And yet, as with settler colonial storytellers, series fiction publishers were often approached by female fans devoted to ostensibly "boys'" books and dissatisfied by their favorite authors' depictions of one-dimensional women. Sisters Mary and Barbara Charnley, for example, wrote Victor Appleton to demand that he "*please* emphatically do *not* make Mrs. Sturdy and Ruth," series regulars, "so weepy and weak." Your books, they told Appleton, were "the only books we have that have enough action in them." But, they complained, "their insatiable love of thrilling and exciting adventure" would be better satisfied once female characters ceased to cower in almost every scene. Their assessment, it should be noted, was not mistaken. The syndicate did try to essentialize gender distinctions. Series writers' rough drafts of women's fiction were often rejected and sent back with notes that said, "the story has a boyish ring throughout which we will temper to conform with more girlish ideals." Some subjects, like the rough business of empire, were not meant for a young lady's "delicate" constitution. Girls, however, wrote in to contradict corporate sentiment regarding what comprised suitable subjects for their sex. Tracy Serrano was one among many young women who noted that "in the back of your hard-covered books, it states that boys 10 years to 14 read" them. Stratemeyer himself said that "I speak to boys, because my books are chiefly for them." But Serrano, as did others like her, simply shrugged that "I am a girl, and I enjoy your books better." "I am 10, but a girl," she reiterated, "and I *love* your books." It was all that mattered. Imperially minded fiction became a means for growing girls to flout adult mores.[52]

Joseph Schroth, writing from Sharpsburg, Pennsylvania, sums up common sentiments found in the fan mail written to the Stratemeyer syndicate from youths around the country:

> I just want to tell you that I am very fond of your books. I am a boy of 12 years old and I read a good many books. But I find that I like your books best. I have read every one of [the] Don Sturdy books. I think they are real boys books. I lend them to every boy I think will like adventure books and they all like them very much. Sometimes I wish I was Don Sturdy. It seems so true. Please excuse the writing I never used to read much until I read one of the Don Sturdy books. I like that there is a lot of knowledge in your books about inventions and different lands. Excuse me for being so friendly but it seems as tho' I know you very well. I guess I have said enough for one letter.

When Joseph spoke of the way that he brought his friends together through a shared interest in Stratemeyer's adventure stories, he offered clues about why circulation estimates are misleading. Stratemeyer's publishing house earned a single sale when Joseph bought his book. But in what is known as the pass-along effect, the boy handed his book to various friends, who themselves may have done the same, thereby disseminating it beyond the ability of historians to track reading patterns with much accuracy.[53]

But it is not simply that Stratemeyer's books became a basis for companionship among many boys. Rather, as Joseph's letter makes clear, the knowledge contained within those books often inspired improvisational play and the imaginary worlds youths constructed, whether alone or in groups. Recent scholarship has explored ways in which the recreational and leisure activities of children helped reproduce imperial values. Joseph Schroth, who drew connections in his own correspondence between what he learned from Stratemeyer's work and his own play, illustrates the link between the presentation of an imperialistic worldview within juvenile literature and the reproduction of that mentality in daily life. He was not the only one. Ansel Duncan wrote his favorite publishers to proclaim that "the United States is great—she couldn't be otherwise." "Doubtless," he continued, his country "will fulfill her part in the destiny of the Anglo-Saxon race in its upward and onward course *unless*," the little nativist-in-training hesitated, "she allows the foreign element within her borders to dominate her homes." Other boys displayed their immersion in an imperial moment by composing poems that declared "Our Cuban brothers must be free/From misrule and tyranny," and "This great Nation has decreed/To substitute for words the deed, at last, at last!" Seven-year-old Dan Wallingford, meanwhile, emptied out his piggy bank after the USS *Maine* exploded, and sent all 48 cents to, as he put it, "help build a new ship." Clearly youths were swept up in the creation of overseas empire, just as publishers had hoped they might be. For, although parents ruled the roost, writers claimed for themselves "the responsibility of guiding their early footsteps," because "the boy of to-day is the man of to-morrow" and "upon him will depend the welfare of future generations."[54]

Series book and periodical publishers as a class, in other words, were clearly self-conscious about their role in cajoling young people into becoming imperial cheerleaders. They repeated Edward Stratemeyer's pleas regarding the importance of a child's education in empire. At a propitious moment like 1898, one editor warned, "the boy who does not keep himself in touch with the world's progress is bound to hold narrow views. It will affect his business intelligence and his mental capacity to a greater extent than you would imagine." Whereas the rhetoric of settler colonialism had been thought adequate to socialize one generation, now "our boys" should "wish to broaden their views" as a means of encompassing America's new global expanse. Something had definitively changed, these authors said, after Uncle Sam's navy sent two Spanish fleets to the bottom of the sea. "We rank among the first of the great powers of the world, as we shall doubtless be for ages to come." But only if "every American boy remembers that he has a definite share in the national celebration. Do not let anyone forget his part." With so many new national responsibilities around the world, "every boy in this great Republic has much to do." It was time for every boy to "'roll up his sleeves' and help *do* it, by using his best brains and looking sharp for all the opportunities."[55]

The vividly described environments and inhabitants of Cuba, the Philippines, and elsewhere that appeared in, among others, the Old Glory and Don Sturdy series provided the settings children used to rehearse these new colonial obligations via games and play. During the run-up to the War of 1898, several publishers even offered to send instruction booklets, insignia, and badges for patriotic clubs that boys could found. What was "cowboys and Indians" for one generation may have been "Don Sturdy and the head hunters" for another. At the very least, the testimony of fans makes it clear that many young boys and girls were entirely immersed in the world that series fiction made. The knowledge about "different lands" that they credited their favorite authors with providing derived from a genre that spoke openly of white America's responsibility to remake the world in its own image. Piles of dead Filipino characters, meanwhile, proved that resistance was not simply futile, it could be fatal. As the Russell brothers sang in unison: "Anglo-Saxon blood is bound to rule the world!" The missives from many juvenile enthusiasts did not often sound very different. If kids deviated from the script, after all, they were deemed defective. "It is a poor sort of boy," one editor announced, "whose young blood does not tingle at the sight of a martial parade or a man-of-war swinging along at sea."[56]

But publishers could not simply compel ideological compliance from young people. Instead, there was a good deal of interplay between authors and readers. Stratemeyer was quite candid about the way he used fan mail to guide his storytelling choices. In an interview, he claimed that his "correspondents are scattered all over the country, and they sometimes give [me] suggestions which [I] am able to use to advantage in writing stories." Correspondence between the publishing company and its veritable army of ghostwriters also gestures to the influence juvenile audiences exerted over presses. For example, it was the original instinct of boardrooms nominally in control of content to, in their own words, "leave war out of these stories" as much as possible. But young fans bombarded publishers seeking their favorite authors' views on the subject. They clamored for talk of conflict in the pages of series fiction. Firms soon obliged. New marching orders now began to appear: Pacifistic sentimentality or ambivalence about the efficacy of armed force would be shoved aside. "Nothing should be put into stories," a company-wide directive read, "which would upset an over-zealous, patriotic reader." Tiny jingoes, in other words, had to have their views respected. There were simply too many letters resembling the one Stratemeyer received in 1906: "I like to read about war and I want to be a soldier some day but my mother does not want me to be one." Story outlines assigned to piecework writers for fleshing out also frequently contained phrases like "a number of fans have been asking for . . ." and "going over fan mail, we have decided . . ." Another anonymous author was informed that "you might want to watch items which would meet with the objections of readers in certain locales." Buried beneath the surface of seemingly banal business records is evidence of a publishing outfit attuned to the demands placed upon them by young readers. If turn-of-the-century series fiction firms propagated an imperial vision of America's growing global influence, they did so, in part, because that is what children themselves requested.[57]

By Stratemeyer's own admission, fans played some part in shaping the content of series books. Memoranda internal to the syndicate also hint at the ways in which juvenile feedback helped corporate officers discover what young people wanted to see in their fiction. We should be careful, therefore, in presuming that the relationships publishers cultivated with readers was one of absolute power over a captive audience. Rather, children themselves helped shape what was easily, in the early twentieth century, the most broadly popular component of youth culture. Juvenile demand fueled America's expanding culture of expansionism. Anti-imperialists meanwhile—those publicly opposed to a "large" policy after the War of 1898—tended to be older. Stratemeyer, his syndicate, and their competitors surely played some part in what was an age-graded imperialism. But even they were often responding only to the kind of globe-girdling country that junior citizens themselves wished to inherit.[58]

If juvenile publishing is better seen as a joint enterprise connecting youths and adult authors in the mutual affirmation of empire, however, there were other forms of media managed entirely by young people. Some of Stratemeyer's fan mail actually hinted at this pint-sized public sphere. Bruce Rhodes, for example, explained that "the reason I get such a 'kick' out of reading is that I have always wished to be an author of some kind." So fond of writing was he, in fact, that the boy began "editing a small one-sheet paper which I distribute to my friends around the neighborhood." It contained gossip, local news, book reviews, and editorials. And he was not alone in circulating such a periodical. Many boys and girls did so. This was the realm colloquially known as Amateurdom. Children and adolescents took a postbellum Christmas-present craze— the toy or "novelty" printing press—and used it to churn out piles of their own political commentary. Altogether, these amateur newspapers represent some of the most thoroughgoing youth engagement with imperial rhetoric on record.[59]

3

Empire's Amateurs

In May 1873, a Baltimore newspaper ran an editorial entitled "The Indians." It was a rather gory piece of prose. The writer decried the "treacheries, outrages, [and] murders" recently perpetrated by Modoc warriors. He then asked his readers to imagine women and children "lying lifeless and scalpless" and their settlements "burnt to the ground." Such scenery, it was said, "makes our blood boil, and our hearts cry for revenge." And so, the essay next asked, "are we, here in the East, to sit in our comfortable parlors and let our soldiers be slaughtered by savages?" "No!" went the defiant reply, which quickly took peace off the table. "The government has already spent millions of dollars in, we need not say, vain attempts to accomplish that object." The author instead suggested something far bloodier. "The only peace that can be made with Indians," his matter-of-fact proposal went, "is to exterminate the whole race." Then, and only then, would "our frontier settlers . . . have peace of mind in working their lands." The country could no longer allow its citizens "to be butchered in this way." Instead, as the entirely capitalized final sentence shouted, US authorities had to "EXTERMINATE THE INDIANS."[1]

Such sentiments were, of course, common enough to the periodicals that circulated postbellum America. Far more curious, however, is the identity of the writer: The person demanding this act of ferocious retribution was a teenaged boy. He, and thousands more adolescents like him, were the editors of, contributors to, and audience for a sizeable national network of so-called amateur newspapers. Printed with miniaturized toy (or hobby) presses on palm-sized pieces of paper, hundreds of thousands of these broadsheets circulated city blocks, suburban neighborhoods, and rural townships throughout the Gilded Age United States. For historians, they collectively represent one of the few great and virtually untapped public spheres left to excavate. But even more tantalizingly, young people, typically ranging from 10 to 20 years of age, controlled their content. Here lay the littlest republic of letters—a place its practitioners called "Amateurdom." Previous chapters have dealt with what adults wrote for juvenile audiences. This section examines what adolescents wanted to say to one another. In an arena affectionately nicknamed "the Dom," toy press tinkerers created one of the nation's first peer-oriented and broadly participatory youth cultures.[2]

For it turns out that though young people read story papers and other periodicals quite avidly, many of them also became producers within an active amateur newspaper scene that flourished from the late nineteenth to the early twentieth century. Most were small, cheaply assembled, and short in duration as their creators lost interest. But they were ubiquitous. As one early chronicler put it, the 1867 invention of the tabletop press meant that "a few dollars now enabled every boy and girl who wished it to rush into print." A variety of manufacturers, pushing slogans like "Every Boy a Ben Franklin," quickly multiplied the number of miniature presses available. Soon enough, "little, hand-printed papers in pretty bad typography broke out all over the country." Eventually, these individual endeavors, which the New York Times described as a "new epidemic among the boys," became at least loosely organized under the umbrella of the National Amateur Press Association (NAPA) and a variety of regional Amateur Press Associations (APAs). Much of the purpose of those organizations was to help facilitate communication between authors. "Amateur journals are printed for the benefit of receiving exchanges," one novice publisher claimed, and Amateurdom itself formed "a vast literary society whose members express their opinions, state their arguments upon topics under discussion, expound their theories, and thus improve their literary composition, through the columns of their papers." Participants considered it a kind of collective enterprise, and as such, a means to foster a sense of national adolescent community through debate and dialogue.[3]

The content of the papers varied wildly. Some amateurs simply told jokes, printed limericks, and repeated local gossip. Others acted as mock literary magazines, complete with fiction and poetry drafted by siblings and friends. But many more expressed a juvenile perspective on what were considered to be the pressing political issues of the day. What scholars are often conditioned to think of as implicitly "adult" affairs—such as military policy, electoral politics, or tariff schedules—in fact found vibrant expression within the pages of media produced by and for young people. And there was perhaps no single topic that seemed to generate more sustained interest among junior editorialists than American foreign relations, broadly construed. From Indian matters in the trans-Mississippi West to immigration and the War of 1898, youths around the country attempted to articulate their thinking on the United States and its relationship to the wider world. That vengeful young man from Baltimore by no means stood alone. He and many others like him repurposed racism, nativism, and imperialism in order to claim both cultural relevance and political legitimacy for themselves.

The sum total of so much juvenile discoursing, however, is difficult to characterize in any coherent way. Even a sympathetic 1882 observer, when asked to summarize "the Dom," became flustered enough to declare that "the style of these papers is so varied, and the papers themselves so numerous, that one is at a loss where to begin." Historians too have struggled to characterize the genre and its contributors. There are several reasons for this. One problem pertains to representativeness. Amateurs often claimed to speak for the youth of America, but the racial, gender, and class composition of the field belied such assertions. The overwhelming majority of participants, though regionally diverse, were middle-class youths from families of some means. The fact that they had the leisure time required to assemble their papers at a moment when so many other children were condemned to rot inside factories indicates their privilege.[4]

Moreover, Amateurdom was mostly a homogenously male and white affair; amateur presses themselves tended to be advertised with a promise to make "EVERY BOY HIS OWN PRINTER." But the proscriptive language did not deter every parent. A handful of "lady" editors and writers were active enough to inspire Louisa May Alcott's *Little Women*—the March sisters—to produce a weekly newspaper, the "Pickwick Portfolio." Some Black and Indian participants likewise clung to the margins of the endeavor. Their capacities, however, often came under attack in teenaged editorials denouncing civil rights "agitators" within their ranks.[5]

Another problem confronting historians attempting to discern perceptible patterns within the worldview of these children has to do with amateurdom's fractiousness. For instance, youths frequently fought off attacks by printing businesses, some of which resented the pretentions of their junior competitors. Prior to the existence of schools of journalism or any other process for the professional certification of journalists, adult newspapermen and -women also became somewhat prickly about the idea of mere children claiming status for themselves as editors. Moreover, the young people who published papers often vehemently disagreed with one another's assessments of North American and global affairs. Amateurs remained in constant contact with their peers and assiduously criticized fellow producers. The result was endemic ideological conflict. Contentiousness helped to continuously revitalize the field, generate new content, and draw additional participants into the fray. But it also places limits on what we can safely label as "orthodox opinion" among young people.[6]

The sheer volume of amateur imprints and their thematic capaciousness, however, speaks to the genre's broader importance. Whatever their limitations as a source, it is difficult to think of any other single record of youth opinion quite so large. It would be more surprising if such an abundant archive did not chronicle persistent disagreement within its ranks. But over and above the particularities that divided them, amateur newspapers confirm broad-based consensus among American adolescents on at least one subject: the value of their own particular perspective on important diplomatic issues. This is the assertion often hiding between the lines of editorial opinion regarding westward expansion, war, and exclusionary immigration policy. Youths used tabletop presses to dress-rehearse their still-crystallizing perspectives on American foreign relations. Amateur papers allowed adolescents to demonstrate the very maturity and intellectual seriousness—what one reporter called the "broadening of their outlook"—that developing discourses of childhood innocence and juvenile delinquency implicitly denied to the young.[7]

Boys seized upon Amateurdom to disprove, in effect, nineteenth-century newspaperman Horace Greeley's 1859 assertion that "the Indians are children." It was his sense that "any band of schoolboys from ten to fifteen years of age are quite as capable of ruling their appetites, devising and upholding a public policy, constituting and conducting a state or community as an average Indian tribe." Which was to say, neither were able to do so. For Greeley, the comparison highlighted indigenous incapacity and demonstrated that Natives "must die out." Turn-of-the-

Figure 3.1. Small tabletop presses like the one pictured here were popular among children during the 1870s and 1880s. They used them to produce amateur newspapers around the country. Courtesy of the National Museum of American History, Smithsonian Institution.

century arch-imperialists like Albert Beveridge only extended the analogy by justifying overseas expansion as the enactment of parental duties. The United States, he proposed, would govern its new "territories without their consent" just as "we govern our children without their consent." Young people, however, resented any analogy that likened them to "untutored savages." Within the pages of their own papers, therefore, adolescents demonstrated their mental acuity. In fact, they often did so by weighing in on the very "public policy" debates surrounding the Indian question or empire that Greeley, Beveridge, and others gestured to in their remarks. By distancing themselves from "childlike races," young people insisted upon their own political value to the United States. The same would hold true as other "barbaric" peoples around the world fell under the aegis of American authority.[8]

When a Baltimore teen demanded the extermination of an entire people, he unwittingly demonstrated the ways in which imperialistic ideas about the West (and beyond) were perpetuated across time. Studying how and why such sentiments became popular among the later nineteenth century's adolescents can help us better understand the pervasiveness, power, and longevity of both America's settler colonial practices and its increasingly international outlook. Both were frames of reference or perspectives on the world that required "buy-in" on the part of youths in order to entrench what historians have called America's Gilded Age "global dawn." In order to thrive, after all, empires must possess cross-generational appeal. Amateur newspapers provide important insight into how and why a sizeable slice of juvenile America welcomed this increasingly muscular role for the United States along its expanding frontiers. One way to understand the country's embrace of international interventionism must attend to the attractiveness that such ideas had for those too young to enact policy but old enough to participate in a cultural process of consensus-building. Young people's agency was often expressed not necessarily by challenging their parents' pro-expansionary politics, but rather, in the reaffirmation (and thus propagation) of imperial power structures.[9]

Frontier Fixations

As we have seen, conscious appeals to young people within juvenile publications helped armchair ideologues articulate the meaning, purpose, and stakes of American territorial expansion. In this way, empire's children became a crucial audience for adults' expansionist vision of North America. Amateurdom, in contrast, was a print universe created and policed by young people. It served as a space wherein adolescents worked through and articulated *for themselves* many of the perils, problems, and promises of the American West. One of the key avenues by which "the virgin vote" voiced a sense of national belonging, it turns out, was to express their commitment to (or engage in critiques of) the republic's settler colonial past, present, and future. Children ended up connecting themselves to each other but also the state (and the nation as "imagined community") through their investment in imperial politics.[10]

One could, of course, find a fair amount of breathless, blood-soaked coverage of settler colonial subjects within the pages of amateur papers. Such stories were not confined to any particular region or locale. Teen-aged journalists in San Francisco who carped about "the utter stupidity of our dealings with the Indians" and demanded "a war of extermination" did not sound terribly different from their counterparts in Ohio, who decreed that the country should be "wiping out every red-skin possible." An Ithaca paper published a bit of settlerist propaganda in the poem titled "A Pioneer's Home," while another editor in Beloit, Wisconsin, accepted for publication short stories written by neighbors and featuring white boys of "bone and muscle" who "conquered the Indian" by "gigantic blows" and rifle shots "between the eyes." The *Forest City Spark* denounced the "outrageous slaughter of whites in the far west" at the hands of "the red man," and "look[ed] forward to the time, not far distant, when the race shall be extinct." Even what passed for humor in these publications possessed an imperial inflection. One jokingly printed Indian proverbs such as "take care of the poor Indian and he will take hair of the white man." Another noted of recent Mesoamerican archaeological discoveries: "haven't we Indians enough now without bringing out any more?"[11]

Young writers often recycled elements of the settler colonial serials which dominated the Gilded Age's youth literary market. They marveled at the "overpowering hand of civilization" and remarked upon the "numerous evidences of cultivation, where a few centuries ago, the untutored savage held the ruling power." They celebrated the lives of those who "subdued the savage border to civilization" and proclaimed themselves "ready to reap the reward." There was boosterism that boasted about the "thundering tread of the advancing hosts of civilization" and the concomitant retreat of "wild beasts and wilder men." Others still heralded the "*genius of the age*" and the "onward march of progress" which transformed "a wilderness covered with wild grass" into "fruitful valleys surrendered to the peaceful conquest of the plowshare and sickle." It was common for amateurs to do as their elders did, abstracting a violent process of dispossession by deploying bloodless language to describe it. "Civilization," they said, "is the making of a land, the foundation of human happiness, and the means of turning forest lands into farms." Passive constructions did useful work by perpetuating a myth of national blamelessness. "Bands of wild savages," almost of their own volition, were said to have "marched off the field, one by one, to make room for civilization's progress."[12]

"But what progress!" another imprint exclaimed, reducing centuries of history to a simple formula: "as our pioneers advanced, the Indians retreated." And, like the larger literary milieu, youth publications denounced the "treachery and cunning" of the "half-clad savages" among whom "civilization could gain no foothold." If anything, one boy announced, "the subtle Red Men greatly retarded the advance of civilization" until swept aside so that "gloomy wastes" could be "converted into fertile fields." Another sheet mimicked the mockery of pacifist caricatures in juvenile fiction by jeering that, given the Native American's tendency to "dash down on the defenceless homes of our western pioneers," those who would "rise in a body and take pity on the 'poor, misguided and ill-used Indian'" ought to be forced to live amongst bands of "howling red-skins." It was with a shrug, therefore, that boys announced of "red men" and the "onward march of civilization": "they are doomed, a perishing race. It is so written in the Book of Fate." Amateurs may have been particularly nonchalant about the question of Indian extinction precisely because of their youth. Editorials at times mocked older people for their tendency to "worry and fret about the mistakes they have made." For the young, "all is glory." They indulged in "thoughts of the future and a considerate ignorance of the past." "Always looking back," meanwhile, was what gave a nation its "gray hairs." Adolescents arriving at what they called "the spring-time of life" naturally evinced more interest in stories showcasing progress. With storypaper Indians so regularly depicted as "losers" in the struggle for existence, young people seemed disinclined to mourn their apparent disappearance.[13]

The stock figure of the pioneers, on the other hand, regularly appeared as "winners" in the pages of amateur papers. These were persons whose lives were thought to embody the same purposeful and positive spirit teenagers claimed to crave themselves. Emulating settlers—in their supposed grit and perseverance—was considered a potential conduit to success. Some editors even sought out and then published commemorative interviews with exemplary local senior citizens who claimed to have had run-ins with Native Americans at an earlier point in time. Another asked its readers to wonder "what would a nation be without its pioneers." Animated by "the spirit of colonization," these were "men who brave every hardship, endure every privation, that their chosen land may, at some future time, teem with the comforts of the civilized world." Finishing with a dramatic flourish, the editorial spoke of an eternal drive to "move onward, to build new cities and win new states from the grasp of the Barbarian, to the wholesome protection of the Union." Leaving the country in the hands of "savagery" constituted a form of criminal negligence: Indians and Mexicans "had made scarcely any advance for a hundred years, and if left to themselves never would have made any."[14]

Hagiographic prose praised the "genuine men and women" who "launch out from home ... to face all the hardships and privations of a frontier life." To its pioneers "our country owes a vast debt of gratitude, for its developments, its wealth, and its high position among the civilized nations of the world." The degree to which any of this language—grandiose descriptions of settler-stimulated progress, environmental transformation, and the march of civilization—could just as easily be found between the covers of children's literature authored by adults is remarkable. It reflects the extent to which young minds proved receptive to the expansionist ethos that juvenile mass-culture endorsed. Such broad-based acquiescence among amateur writers in turn helped shape their political prescriptions for the era in which they lived.[15]

Papers became particularly preoccupied with the "problem" of indigenous resistance. Winona, Minnesota's *The Idler* expressed exasperation with "the Indian department," which had "effected no permanent cure" for the "atrocious outrages and barbarities" heaped upon "poor and defenseless settlers" by "depredating Indians." The editor hectored those who defended the "'noble red man'": if "the Indian ever possessed noble traits," he "has irrevocably lost them." It was obvious that "civilization is alien to his composition, the march of progress is not to his taste, and he can never feel anything but eternal enmity towards the caucasian race." A "mild and amicable course" could never be successful. "There [was] but one recourse," the article insisted, "and while it is severe, it must be used as a matter of self-protection": The United States had to pursue a "*war of extermination.*" A St. Louis boy, meanwhile, averred that "the development of the country is a duty." As such, anyone who "denounces our settlers, who are hastening this work, as persecutors of the Indian, is as idiotic as [they are] ignorant." The writer then went on to express his disbelief that "there are those who, through a sickly sentimentality or a love of notoriety, prate about the wrongs" done to "the noble savage, who is, generally speaking, a filthy and degraded brute." To those misguided philanthropists, he had a simple message: "this country is too valuable to humanity to be given up to grasshopper-hunting." The country's enemies were identified as "certain would-be orators, who utter much meaningless stuff about the condition of the Indian." Or, as another youth plainly put it: "We do not grieve the fate of the Indian."[16]

Commentaries such as these are curious in part because calls for wholesale eradication became framed as the reluctant duty of intellectually brave boys uncorrupted by the humanitarian cant of their elders. Some adults, these authors implied, were too fearful of the ethical consequences or political fallout accompanying any call for the harsh measures required to deal with what amateur papers construed as the cyclical (and thus intractable) problem of Native American violence. Older generations had become squeamish. They were paralyzed by their attempts to nuance an issue that younger minds did not have the patience to debate any longer. Decisiveness and certitude were luxuries hard-charging boys enjoyed, and some clearly relished the platform their papers provided to voice what they believed to be the simple and necessary (if brutal) solution to a long-running national debate over Indians in the West. Fed a steady diet of cheap fiction which itself depicted the West in Manichean tropes, some young readers seemed content to discuss the world around them in similarly truncated terms.

Some, but not all. As the century progressed, support for the federal government's civilizational initiatives began to materialize more often within the pages of the amateur press. A few young men seemed confident enough in their own assessments of the "Indian problem" to begin dispensing with a reflexively violent response to discontented indigenous people. Prior to the turn of the twentieth century, a handful of children's literature authors pushed for Peace Policy initiatives like allotment or boarding school–based generational uplift. Junior editorialists, on the other hand, began to express discomfort over the seeming wastefulness—in lives and treasure—of more aggressive approaches to national expansion. Virginia's *Crab*, for example, thought that "the only just and honest way to rid ourselves of the indian troubles" would be to "educate the numerous tribes that roam our Western Territories." As evidence, they pointed to the "marked difference" that distinguished "men of the forest . . . looking almost too hideous to be recognized as human" from the "polite and genteel" Natives who emerged from "a term of enlightenment" in the East. "Would not the government be only doing its duty in supporting an increased number of these Indian pupils for erudition," the editor asked? Another paper answered that question in the affirmative, insisting that "the Indian must be given citizenship [and] must be made a man, a part of the government, and not as now a 'government ward.'"[17]

Some of the impetus behind these calls for the erudite Indian seem to have emerged out of the same Native American academies founded by reformers like Richard Henry Pratt. Students at his longtime pet project, the Carlisle School, maintained an active correspondence with several white teenaged editors around the country. Samuel Townsend, a Pawnee student there, wrote to Holliston, Massachusetts' *Amateur Journal* (which then printed the letter) to declare that "those who thought at first that the Indians could not be taught to learn" have now "been convinced that they can." He further argued that reservations served no practical benefit except to retard the development of a people who might otherwise prove themselves quick studies. Material inequality, not racial degeneracy, explained the Native American's plight. As Townsend's conclusion stated, "I am sure white children would be as slow to learn under the same circumstances." He pleaded for young America's moral and financial support.[18]

Some fellow amateurs seemed to signal their encouragement by reprinting these appeals, complete with appended commentary which mirrored one youth's optimistic assertion that by "educating his children and his children's children, we may have civilized the Indians in time." Others spoke of amateurs printed by people otherwise "so far away from civilization" as "a worthy effort." When Indians "almost beyond the limits of civilization sent forth a bright amateur journal," it signaled positive change. Anglo-American teenaged journalists thereby construed their activities as more than a hobby. Junior presses could be, in and of themselves, instrumental to both the pacification of the West and the elevation of its "savage" denizens.[19]

It was moments like these that revealed Amateurdom's split personality. Many papers blithely replicated settlerist screeds devoted to the total annihilation of Native Americans. But in other, harder-to-find but still striking episodes, the toy press facilitated a climate of cross-racial contact among young people willing to abandon particularism in favor of a shared identity as fellow hobbyists. Novice printers could usually be counted on to reinvigorate existing power structures. Consensus, however, remained elusive. Some few seemed to relish the opportunity that this corner of the public sphere offered for independent expression. Dime novel discourse and series fiction dialogue also inspired, as we have seen, small pockets of resistance comprised of children who objected to the genre's mindless violence and masculine preening. Myriad youths embraced juvenile jingoism, but others dissented to denounce their books' shortcomings. Native peoples themselves, it seems, were sometimes a part of that latter crowd.[20]

The student bodies at various boarding schools, after all, often set up their own amateur press operations. Within the pages of these publications, they playfully utilized terms and concepts such as "savage" and "uncivilized" in ways different than most of their white contemporaries, including those who produced the bulk of Amateurdom's content. Such forums also resisted cultural eradication by allowing for the printed preservation of previously oral narrative traditions. The experience and terminology of colonization could thus be redeployed into something less potentially threatening. As one Crow youth, Harry Hand, insightfully observed, "we have read of many adventures of white people among Indians, but we never read of adventures told by Indians among white people. Why? Because the Indians have no newspaper through which to let the reading public know their side of many stories." In so saying, he cut to the core of Amateurdom's appeal to some indigenous people: It provided an accessible forum within which Anglo-centric storytelling paradigms could be challenged. The bulk of adolescent publications still remained wedded to the triumphalism of years past. What Hand bemoaned as the literary marketplace's oversaturation with "many adventures of white people among Indians" continued to characterize the juvenile press through its gradual decline as a popular medium of expression for adolescent America. But young white writers now had to grapple with at least a modicum of dissent within their ranks.[21]

It can be easy, of course, to overstate the liberatory potential of such rhetorical tinkering on the part of Indian students. Superintendents and other school administrators often encouraged (and exercised editorial control over) amateur literary endeavor among their charges. Challenges to these institutions' assimilationist bent were always more covert than clear. Yet despite such limitations, it is almost certain that at least a part of the road to an early twentieth-century efflorescence of Native American letters ran through Amateurdom. It partially integrated indigenous voices into a mainstream adolescent project, helped culturally disparate Indians bridge tribal divides, and provided a public arena where young Native people could begin to articulate their own visions of a future (and a country) that welcomed their input. For while, as one amateur Sioux writer assessed, "ever since the white man came to America, the Indian has been his dupe, because he has been too ignorant to look out for his own interests," it might still be possible for him "to hold his own" and "fight the white man with his own weapons." Literacy was the key. "They have a sharp weapon, called knowledge. They are fighting the Indians with this weapon. If we get this weapon of knowledge we shall get along with the white people." The Dom, therefore, was a linguistic whetstone. By providing practice in the art of self-expression, it helped hone the edges of words needed for a larger struggle. In the same way that American youths utilized these newspapers to promote their own political agenda and communicate across local and regional boundaries, so too did Native American students attempt something similar.[22]

## From the West to the World

The West was the clear focus of amateur authors who wished to weigh in on the exercise of American power. This is hardly surprising given that, as discussed in an earlier chapter, territorial expansion and settler colonial policymaking similarly transfixed the authors of literature read by young people. But, as surveys of dime novels and juvenile periodicals reveal, the frontier, as a story setting, gradually faded from view during the later nineteenth century. Of course, it by no means disappeared entirely. In some instances, the West even regained popularity, particularly during the early Cold War's Disney-inspired "cowboy" and "Davy Crockett" crazes. But, during the later 1880s and early 1890s—with the collapse of Indian military resistance and the Census Bureau's "closure" of the frontier—the region simply lost some of its attractiveness to authors and audiences alike. For those books seeking to shape children's engagement with the wider world, new sources of inspiration needed to be found. North America's pacification proved no less a dilemma for the teenaged editors of amateur papers. Young writers now seized upon issues like immigration and foreign interventionism as fit subjects for discussion.[23]

Much of their thinking about the efficacy of belligerence in the West seems to have found applicability as the adolescent gaze grew to encompass more of the world. Amateurdom's embrace of an activist state along the trans-Mississippi frontier cleared the rhetorical path for a similar flexing of national muscle in new contexts. On immigration, for example, most papers toed a hard line. "America for Americans" cried one boy, who complained that "our country is made the abode of foreign criminals, the lowest and vilest people that debase this fair world." His counterpart in Connecticut believed that "if all emigration to the United States was stopped the nation would be benefited greatly," while another called immigrants "creatures" who threatened "the utter destruction of law and order." Not even voters themselves, boys still worried that most "immigrants have acquired their citizenship by fraud" and vowed that "they *shall not* use our ballot box to subvert the time-honored institutions of our fathers." Youths predicted that "a nation practically in the control of a lot of ignorant foreigners—as America really is—need never expect to live long." And they then agitated to help shape the country they would soon inherit.[24]

As was true of the country's white population writ large, however, teenagers targeted the Chinese for particularly fierce condemnation. The "Mongolian horde," as one boy called transpacific immigration, necessitated a harsh response. They framed the issue, as did later Supreme Court cases upholding Chinese exclusion, as a question of national defense in the face of "invasion." The "only way to rid this country of this pest," declared one junior Know Nothing, was "to send *every one* back to China and not allow them to return under *any pretence whatever!*" Heated opposition to Asian immigration even had amateurs second-guess the very Founders they ordinarily revered. "There is one place in my opinion where our forefathers committed an error, and that was in making America a universal country." The revolutionary generation "doubtless had many reasons for doing this," but the Chinese, this lad from Worcester, Massachusetts indicated, made a mockery of the Declaration's appeal to equality. They were, after all, "a low, filthy, vicious people" guilty of "by far the worst type of barbarism ever exhibited on our shores." Tellingly, with the decline of the frontier as a setting for the short stories submitted to amateur editors, there appeared a noticeable uptick in the number of novice authors using "John Chinaman" as a stock figure meant to stand in for stupidity. Such sendups, complete with affected dialogue, also populated the era's children's literature. Many young people seemed content to figuratively ally with the Western mobs then brutalizing Chinese communities. They happily united with some of the era's leading children's periodicals like *The Golden Argosy*, which in 1891 lectured youths about "the keeping out of foreigners," denounced those countries "endeavoring to unload [their] indigent and criminal classes," and lamented that America had been transformed into a "dumping ground" for paupers.[25]

Anyone looking to children more generally for challenges to the Gilded Age's prevailing prejudices would be disappointed when perusing these papers. If the truism about the late nineteenth century has some basis in fact—that it represents a nadir in the nation's race relations—then Amateurdom reveals just how far down the age scale such intolerance traveled. So powerful and encompassing were ideas about white supremacy, they managed to twist the thinking of even the youngest citizens. Juvenile journalists seemed particularly eager to seize upon their nascent grasp of race science to police their own ranks. When a Philadelphia boy succinctly summarized his feelings on the issue, he spoke for many of his demographic bracket: "There is a real and apparent difference between a white and a black, other than color—a difference in mind, in morals and in body. He has never aided the progress of the world."[26]

And, of course, this rampant racism then affected their outlook on the wider world and its inhabitants of color. If "the global negro" was only ever "engaged in the delectable occupation of killing and eating each other," one boy reasoned, then the "intellect [of] the white" should be "engaged in moulding the destinies of empires [and] enlightening the world by new discoveries." The planet needed white Americans to spread "civilization and civilized pursuits." If African Americans at home exhibited a "paramount shiftlessness and worthlessness" and education only "serves to make a fool of him," what were boys led to expect from similarly situated people overseas? Another amateur answered that question with an appeal to the managerial responsibilities of what he called "the fittest race of natural selection." The "intelligent white cannot be ruled and follow the dictations of a black man." There were "natural inequalities existing between the white and black races," and the sooner this truth was acknowledged, the sooner advanced nations could begin "driving the colored race from the earth." Their "end must be death and inevitable extinction."[27]

The same casual calls to genocidal policy characterizing editorial comment on the West during the 1870s and 1880s now found a new home overseas. Or, as a New Hampshire novice reflected, "the mission of our race is evident—to civilize, Christianize, and give a universal language to the world." The American Anglo-Saxon had "taken Texas and California from the Mexicans." He had "been the power behind the ax that has swept away the inhospitable forest and behind the plow that has cultivated the hitherto unproductive soil of the meadows." And now it was time for "the present generation" to act. They "should become instruments in redeeming the world," from the "'dark continent'" to "the heathen lands of Asia." The most basic elements of the racialism and settler colonialism inherent to the era had shaped some children's conceptions of history, and those tropes were then repackaged as a motivational tactic meant to instill a sense of purpose in the up-and-coming generation.[28]

"Soon westward progress will end," one paper declared. It was a frightening prospect precisely because so much of the literature they read had depicted territorial expansionism as one of the boy's few plausible pathways to manly self-actualization and national notoriety. But, amateurs reassured one another, those who aspired to attain the same imperially inflected renown as their ancestors could rest easy with the knowledge that, as this article asserted, "new fields will be sought." If we choose to take youth politics seriously, then these pledges to pursue the exercise of power in distant places help provide at least a part of the explanation for the US public's increasing appetite for adventurism abroad. Among solidly bourgeois amateurs at least, growing up meant satisfying a growing hunger for additional outlets suited to national enterprise. The "exploring" or "pioneering" spirit frequently praised in the pages of media manufactured by kids themselves "must advance... into unknown lands." An erstwhile president of NAPA even speculated that Amateurdom itself would be instrumental to US-led global regeneration. Though "distinctly an American Institution, the time will probably come when, as enlightenment and liberty advance, Amateur Journalism will encircle the world."[29]

It is therefore unsurprising to find among amateurs a broad-based embrace of America's deepening global footprint. Editorials demanded that Congress fund the construction of an isthmian canal. Others cheered the US-backed overthrow of the Hawaiian monarchy. The "ever advancing forerunners of American civilization" would soon declare that "*southward* the star of empire takes its way." As if on cue, articles appeared avowing that as American capitalists had made themselves "the predominating element" below the border, "the acquisition of Mexico is both certain and desirable." Developmentalist discourse about the Western Hemisphere more generally was a fairly hot topic among adolescent amateurs considering future career prospects. They seemed to salivate over the "great mineral and agricultural wealth" that "will be thrown open to our enterprising fellow citizens." Given their prognostications pertaining to US power, it is hardly surprising to find that the novice press also supported increased defense spending. They eagerly anticipated the day when the nation's comparatively miniscule military establishment would "cease to be a butt for the ridicule of other nations in general."[30]

Cuba and the Philippines presented particularly fit opportunities to demonstrate newfound national power. Before the War of 1898 began, a number of papers called for intervention as an act of charity. As had been their wont in the West, kids usually demanded to know why the government dragged its feet in chastising malefactors. "What is this 'glorious land of the free' coming to," asked an 1896 editorial, "when it will not recognize those who are oppressed [and] tyrannized by a monarchical government?" But after the destruction of the navy ship, the USS *Maine*, in February 1898, and the commencement of hostilities two months later, junior jingoes lined up behind the effort. "*War!!* Barbarous Spain! Inhuman Brutes! United States Will Wipe Them Off the Earth!" one representative headline read. With most too young to serve in the armed forces, adolescents instead chose to print pieces of serial fiction set in Caribbean battlefields. Short stories with titles like "Darkest Cuba" and "How Walter Saved the Lone Star" allowed young people to enjoy vicarious triumphs in a war they claimed credit for having helped win. Indeed, the latter story ends with a supplicant rebel leader gratefully gripping the hand of the teenaged "Walter Clyde" to declare that "we owe our victories to that brave American lad."[31]

Unfortunately for the historian, however, it is harder to find much in the way of authentic amateur journalism as the 1890s ended. If the phenomenon can be described as a fad, by then the tabletop printing press craze had begun to die out. The archives of Amateurdom extend well into the twentieth century, but its contents represent the output of a deeply diminished number of participants. Hobbyists themselves now tended to be adults. They had picked up the habit as children but did not age out as most did. The material remains fascinating, but the perspective such publications represent seems less identifiably "youthful" in its orientation. While amateur newspapers did thrive as a young person's preoccupation, however, it acted as one of our clearest windows into the adolescent angle on multiple subjects. Not the least of these consisted of the relationship between the United States and the world.[32]

## Rehearsals for Adulthood

The expansionist ethos—both on the North American continent and beyond—proved enormously popular among most juvenile editors. Their thinking on foreign policy generally supported the exercise of American power, starting first in the West and then later around the world. These young men (and again, men comprised the overwhelming majority of writers) were clearly enamored by the idea of America as an important force in global affairs. They rarely missed an opportunity to demand the deployment of US military might as punishment for some perceived slight against national honor. And, they remained suspicious of forces—such as the "menace" of Chinese immigration—supposedly threatening the health of the republic. The body politic, in Amateurdom's discourse, appeared broadly analogous to their own changing bodies. Teenaged boys putting on weight, growing stronger, and eagerly anticipating the turn toward adulthood became attracted to similarly muscular rhetoric about their own country. Their pomposity echoed contemporaneous thinkers like Josiah Strong, whose broadly influential *Our Country* (1885) urged Americans to embrace their once-young country's rise to preeminence.[33]

Bombast, in other words, was common enough to Gilded Age reflections regarding the United States and the world. Young people indulged in it no less than their parents. But this is not to say that young and old came to such ideological convergence for the same reasons. The swaggering nationalism of junior journalists traced its origins, in part, to the particular problems of adolescence. By the later nineteenth century, the industrialized world was becoming a thoroughly age-graded hierarchy. Even a few years earlier, however, the Civil War generation had broadly recognized the legitimacy of youth activism. Indeed, the Wide Awakes, a junior auxiliary among early Republicans, was essential to the party's popularization (though not to be outdone, young Democratic "Chloroformers" soon mustered to "put the Wide Awakes to sleep"). But now postbellum pundits tried to play down juvenile political zealotry as potentially pernicious. Ideas stressing the inherently innocent (and thus apolitical) nature of childhood only gained broader social acceptance as educational institutions expanded in scope and further delayed teenage maturation. For middle-class offspring, childhood dependency became a prolonged affair as apprenticeships and other forms of employment were closed off to them. Young people led increasingly regulated lives once the chronological span of childhood slowly but surely extended. This proved vexing for more than a few such kids, and Amateurdom became an outlet by which they might vent their frustration. The numerous amateur editorials decrying compulsory education statutes as a species of slavery are revealing.[34]

Junior citizens felt they had been confined—legally and institutionally—to a state of irrelevancy. Hence one adolescent's assertion that "boys and young men [are] systematically suppressed" and another's gripe that "the women and the darkies" were not "half so badly used as the boys." Or, as an Illinois paper lamented, "to be a boy is to be somebody without a right in the world." Amateurdom therefore possessed obvious appeal to self-pitying adolescents. It encouraged free expression among people deeply resentful of society's failure to treat them with the seriousness they thought appropriate. Indeed, one particularly poetic youth forged an explicit link between an earlier abolitionist movement and the hobby press. In his mind, it represented "the emancipation of boyhood from the fetters of sixty centuries." The connection between complaints about youth disempowerment and America's need for an aggressive global posture hardly seems coincidental. Fantasies of personal and national power intertwined for many young people. At a moment in time when both the law and culture increasingly prescribed that teenagers be muzzled, adolescents sought to speak up.[35]

Amateur papers therefore often took the form of testimonials. Youthful writers insisted upon their instrumentality to both the country and its political life. "Upon the young men of to-day," went a characteristic refrain, "rests the hope of the future." Another crowed that "in less than one hundred years," the United States "has been placed among the first nations of the earth." And "what is the reason of this?" he asked. "Why simply because [of] the American boy" and his irrepressible "intention to excel." Contributing to Amateurdom's national conversation, editors thought, likewise provided an opportunity to exercise the press freedoms—that "glorious gift of birth-right under the American flag"—believed essential to self-government. They often hoped aloud that adults might see their efforts and recognize "with what an earnestness of zeal the youth of this land have [labored] to promote its further good." Articles performed a particularly melodramatic type of patriotism meant to conclusively prove that young people were ready for the duties and obligations of citizenship *now*. America, they insisted, had "the devotion of the youths who are soon to be the men and women of the world ready to give their lives for the old 'stars and stripes.'" "Be considerate, old fogies, of the boys" stated the warning of a Washington lad, "for the boys are the very life of the land."[36]

Some responded to the problems of adolescent depoliticization and disenfranchisement by directly proposing a lowering of the voting age. "What makes the man?," one such activist inquired. "Is it not a thorough knowledge of the government, the parties, the politics of his country?"

Amateurs regularly demonstrated such talents, and yet, "they *cannot vote!*" As such, to be a teen was only to be, as the editorial groused, "the *pretended* man." This crime could not be rectified until boys "had the rights and privileges of their elders." It was in the nation's best interest. For, as another amateur diagnosed, when adults tacitly encouraged political apathy among their offspring, they helped breed a broader disengagement from the democratic process. Youths were too often "encouraged to think that men were made for such work, and to them belonged the duty of all political matters." This was wrong, and so the article made a counterproposal. "We lovers of our country," American boys, "feel it to be our duty to cultivate a liking for politics and to watch with interest every action [our] country takes."[37]

But for those making the case for the social acceptability of civically engaged children, there was still the problem of evidence. Young people needed to demonstrate their aptitude in "adult" affairs. Based on how common commentary about the country's foreign relations materialized within the pages of amateur papers, it appears that youths found diplomatic dealings to be an ideal proving ground. As one editor commented about the subject: "Since it is so important that our American youth be properly instructed in their duties, what more appropriate place can be found for discussing these matters than in their publications 'of boys, for boys, by boys.'" The irony is that, in a medium virtually unmediated by adult input, young people still expressed a desire to "sound" more grown up. This led them to recapitulate the imperial rhetoric considered a hallmark of sophistication. Here was yet another means by which a messianic mentality regarding America's role in world affairs managed to cross over from one generation to the next. And in a testament to the significance of young people's early embrace of US empire, it is important to note, as does a history of Amateurdom written by one of its members, that the hobby press spawned hundreds of enthusiasts who later became influential newspaper editors and politicians.[38]

What seems more meaningful about these articles drafted by adolescents, however, has little to do with their capacity to impact adult decision-making. Any correlation between the two, after all, is a very difficult proposition to prove. Rather, it is more important to recall that the audience for such editorializing remained almost exclusively other young people. These small sheets of paper passed through the neighborhoods where amateurs circulated, while other hobbyists used the postal service to share their handiwork with one another. In that world of aspirational adulthood and a longed-for veneer of professionalism, language about America's role in both the West and the wider world became a sort of currency, a way of demonstrating one's seriousness, one's credentials, one's ability to speak and act as a mature and deliberative person, as opposed to an infantile romantic. Such posturing signaled to other readers that one had transcended the childish, sophomoric, or jejune.

This is evident in one Massachusetts-based teenaged editor's solicitation of articles from local kids with the promise that "young writers will find *Youth*," his amateur paper, "a good medium through which to express their thoughts. Articles must be original and free from slang and vulgarity to insure insertion." And how entirely appropriate, then, that the very first article provided to fulfill that request was entitled "Frontier Perils," lamented "peskey red skins" who were "a terror and a scourge to innocent frontier settlers," and resolved that every one of those "merciless foes" be summarily "shot or hanged." If young writers saw the amateur press as a forum through which they might share their still-crystallizing politics and thus demonstrate their credentials as budding adults and mature writers, it seems significant that they chose to do so by engaging with sorts of settler colonial tropes and expansionist politics that saturated the reading material publishers marketed to them.[39]

Examples abound across Amateurdom's voluminous record: Advocacy for hardline imperial policy in the West and elsewhere served as a litmus test meant to solidify many young people's earliest claims upon not only membership in the "Republic of Letters" but also a sense of belonging in the United States. Seizing upon settler colonial imagery in their own writing became, in other words, a means to access the status associated with what one scholar has recently called "imaginary citizenship." Juvenile saber-rattling allowed those (children, in this case) with neither the franchise nor most civil rights to posture for adult adulation and secure membership within the body politic. The bitter irony here was, of course, that while, according to publications like *Youth*, "slang and vulgarity" disqualified an author's submission, calling for the wholesale slaughter of a people signaled intellectual seriousness and pretensions to maturity.[40]

In the broadest sense, the dependence of young writers on settlerist messaging is indicative of intersections between youth culture and state-making during the Gilded Age and Progressive Era. If, as many scholars have suggested, territorial expansion, conquest, and colonization in the West, as historical processes, were crucial to the development of an American administrative apparatus, it was no less important in the growth of a self-conscious, national community of adolescents and their relationship to that polity. These young people explicitly adopted the language of settler colonialism at home and empire abroad, affirmed their support for state-sanctioned policies that forced Indians onto reservations and exterminated those who resisted, and proclaimed their loyalty to the American government responsible for carrying out such a program. In the newspaper articles they themselves wrote, the white settler was a heroic figure depicted as worthy of emulation—"there never was a hardier, braver, more self-sacrificing set of men on the face of the earth than [those who] penetrated the dark woods clothing the fertile lands," as the *Youth's Ledger* insisted. These laudatory literary productions served as a means to demonstrate young America's devotion to those same people (not to mention the policies their lives embodied) and thus, by extension, their own fitness, as emerging adults, for full membership within the society that empire had built.[41]

A young man in Yonkers announced as much, noting that "older and more practised" parents had no right to monopolize either public opinion or civic affairs. "People who learn to look ... for what the boys have to say would in many instances be surprised at the able manner in which they would handle the questions of the day." The act of discoursing within the public sphere, in other words, entitled the country's youths to a measure of respect. Or, as a Chico, California, amateur paper—named, fittingly if unimaginatively enough, the *Amateur*—mused, "time, in its steady march, will take from us those who now conduct the affairs of the State and these burdens must fall on younger shoulders." "As one by one those now in charge are called from earth," let us hope that "a young and vigorous mind may fill his place, and perpetuate the glory of our land." But how, we might ask, would America's young people do so? In the words of this juvenile journalist, what would the "mighty work before them" consist of, exactly?[42]

Perhaps an answer was to be found in the very next story, which ran directly beneath that youthful call to arms. Entitled "The Apache," the article noticed a recent attack on an Arizona community, and blamed Indians alone for "atrocious depredations," "murdering settlers," and "ravaging the country." The solution offered to such complex borderlands skirmishing, however, was simple enough: "The new Administration" should "act wisely and promptly, and cause this to be the last [uprising] by killing every bloody Indian in the tribe." This, an inducement to genocide, from the same novelty printing press that had, mere moments earlier, spoken so eloquently in urging "young men," other boys in the small town of Chico, to "see that our country's honour and glory is perpetuated." But that was the point. What might at first glance feel like a disjuncture or tonal shift was, in fact, not. The felt weight of future responsibilities to the state and notions of the child's role in what they themselves called a "model republic" could not be disentangled from the casual violence and exterminationist logic that filtered through an imperially infused mass media. It was not simply that "savages" in the far West and overseas should be colonized to curtail their "child-like" behavior. Rather, children themselves saw one another as essential to the continuation and culmination of expansionist policy and, by extension, national glory.[43]

This idea was perhaps most directly expressed by a boy from Kansas. In an 1884 essay entitled "Our Pioneers," he made a direct connection between the past work of settlers and the current struggles of schoolchildren like himself. First admiring earlier generations who cleared the land of people he called "barbarians," the novice newspaperman quickly shifted gears. For "after him," after all, "comes another pioneer," what the editorialist called "the pioneer of education." This was his term for those who toiled in the state's common schools, diligent boys "filled perhaps with an even nobler resolve." Adults, it was argued, forgot to grant these young trailblazers their due credit. The amateur press, therefore, became the outlet through which the hardships of the educational system could be appreciated for what at least some young people believed they were: another link in the chain of civilization. The country's "sons and daughters" passed through the school's doors, and "become purer, better, wiser than before." As such, "they too lend a helping hand" in securing national greatness. Their battles did not pit them against Indians, but nevertheless, their educational attainments "shall float the gallant ship of State." This young man's assessment may have been more elaborate and eloquent than most, but he broadly represented a strain of youth thinking attracted to imperial analogies for their explanatory power. It provides a curious complement to the way in which G. Stanley Hall and other early theorists of childhood development rooted their concepts in colonial frames of reference. Social scientists may have "created" adolescence as a category of analysis after 1900, but before that, young people themselves had articulated, more organically, a "teenaged" perspective. When junior citizens got together to praise the virtues of empire, they affirmed the age-based peer bonds coming to dominate how Americans related to one another.[44]

Juvenile reading material provided a vocabulary to young people seeking either to articulate their own place in the world or to position themselves as fit successors to what the popular literature they read dramatized as the conquest of North America. Amateur newspapers, meanwhile, afforded an arena within which adolescents from around the country could transcend local particularities to develop and rehearse an outlook on the world specific to their own age cohort. Recycling settlerist language, in other words, was more than children's rote recitation of what they had read someplace else. It was, instead, a political claim unto itself. Young people approached imperial discourse as a tool, one they might use to access the same power, privilege, and prestige that expansionist heroics seemed to confer upon their elders. When Frederick Jackson Turner famously called the frontier "a magic fountain of youth in which America continually bathed and was rejuvenated," he was not referring to actual youths (or their reading habits). But these were prescient words all the same. For as it turned out, the country's younger generations continued to breathe new life into the West (and the "greater West" of global empire) once they found rich significance for themselves in its rhetoric and representations.[45]

## Cosmopolitan Undercurrents

It is hard to see the mainstream of Amateurdom as anything other than committedly racist and implicitly expansionist. Nor is it surprising that most boys and girls failed to break free from the ideological constraints of their age. They penned prejudicial and ethnocentric editorials. They called for the indiscriminate murder of so-called savages in the West. They urged the expulsion of nonwhite "alien" peoples like the Chinese. And they evidenced a casual disregard for most claims to sovereignty made by "subalterns" within America's overseas empire at the turn of the twentieth century. The majority of amateur writers had their conception of the country's proper relationship to the wider world colored by chauvinism. American Anglo-Saxons had risen to become North America's rightful rulers. It stood to reason that this would be no less true as the United States more thoroughly embedded itself in global affairs after the Civil War.

Some of Amateurdom's adult observers commended junior journalists precisely because they appeared to embrace the status quo. In an 1871 write-up on the subject, for example, the *New York Times* praised "Young America" and its "amateur journalism," which had "grown from small beginnings up to really important and respectable proportions." For the nation's largest newspaper, the spectacle seemed far more wholesome than the "broken bones, dissipation, [and] great waste of time" that ordinarily characterized adolescent leisure. "The Dom" and its rapid rise fit squarely into broader self-congratulatory narratives of the republic's postbellum progress. But the *Times* was also quick to pat amateurs on the back for their apparent devotion to policing the present state of affairs. "We see no signs of revolutionary tendencies in the direction of women's rights or transcendental- and other -isms. Nor has radicalism so run riot in any of them as to make us tremble for the country." Breathing a sigh of relief, this columnist reassured parents that "the boys" were committed to the principle of hierarchy in both race and gender relations. The implicit promise here was that, with these boys in charge, nothing much would change.[46]

An 1878 episode among amateurs known as the "Civil Rights War" showcased their "healthful" impulse toward intolerance. The incident involved a 16-year-old Black youth named Herbert Clarke. He ran a Midwestern amateur newspaper, and, at a sparsely attended NAPA convention, emerged as the victor in a race for one of the umbrella organization's several vice presidencies. In response, nearly all Southern papers cried foul, and they were joined by a substantial number of northerners. In epithet-laden editorials that spanned the next few years, Clarke's detractors rehearsed the same white supremacist arguments against integration that their parents utilized to roll back Reconstruction and justify Jim Crow. One boy, who was a better bigot than he was a speller, declared himself "unalterbly opposed to the admittance of negroes because they are not the social, intellectual, or moral equals of the Caucasson race." Some proposed the creation of a separate, segregated "Colored Amateur Press Association." Another bombastic set of editors denounced NAPA's admittance of "niggers" and seceded to form an "Amateur Anti-negro Admission Association." Ironically, boys who bemoaned their own political powerlessness worked fairly hard to deny others a voice in adolescent affairs. Clarke, for his part, orchestrated a lengthy defense of his prerogative. "In the Republic of Letters," he pleaded, "there has never been any distinction save that of merit." Clarke therefore asked to be judged by the quality of his writing rather than the color of his skin. But it was not a successful appeal. NAPA eventually rewrote its constitution so as to prohibit nonwhites from joining the organization, while an unchastened Clarke later went on to found a Black newspaper.[47]

Yet, if the entire episode is emblematic of the broader antipathies that animated Amateurdom, it also sheds light on a smaller subculture of cosmopolitanism sitting at the community's edges. The *New York Times* might have spoken too soon when it pronounced Amateurdom devoid of countercultural creeds. Some papers, after all, rose to Clarke's defense. They rooted their willingness to embrace his candidacy as part of a broader push for toleration, which they argued ought to govern human affairs during a modernizing age. As the twentieth century approached, new transportation, industrial, and communications technologies (including the tabletop printing press) seemed to signal for the world's people a turn toward broader integration. In response, some boys more willingly embraced a self-consciously internationalist outlook. A small but vocal cohort penned editorials denouncing violence in the West, urging reconciliation between warring races, and counseling an assimilationist attitude toward immigrants. They also sought to sever the rhetorical linkages that had tied Amateurdom to dime novels and other forms of mass-produced sensational literature. This group of amateurs were always outnumbered by their more prejudiced brethren. But broadminded sentiments were common enough to become noticeable by the end of the nineteenth century.[48]

A Chicago imprint, for example, came out swinging when it declared that "our government's course with the Indians has been characterized from beginning to end with injustice and deceit." This had "done more to bring [the country] into disrepute probably than any other thing." As a result, "we cannot help blushing for shame, when we see how the Indians have been oppressed." Another observed that "the Indian race is the most abused race of the human family" and mocked the "white man [who] believes he is obliged to kill a human being because civilization demands it." One boy sarcastically wished that Native Americans "had killed the first settlers," for "they would now be a happy and prosperous race instead of an oppressed and hunted tribe." Some amateurs even composed overwrought odes to harried indigenes forced to flee their homelands. The *Young Aspirant*, meanwhile, denounced Denis Kearney's nativist Workingmen's Party and declared Chinese exclusion "dishonorable and unworthy of a christian people." Still another teenaged editor proclaimed, outright, that "the worst form of bigotry is prejudice on account of nationality, and a man who will despise a fellow creature because he was born on the other side of the Atlantic, is not worthy of the name 'American.'" To "point the finger of scorn at foreigners," he concluded, "shows a despicable spirit of intolerance, and an utter lack of patriotism."[49]

Some others reserved their condemnation for the piles of cheap fiction that helped shape the pro-expansion politics embraced by so many other young people. Junior iconoclasts instead demanded a more complex kind of juvenile literature. They chastised dime publications for their murderous main characters and hackneyed plots. An Iowa boy, for example, wrote an editorial in his amateur paper to complain that "the average school boy of today" was "devoted to the perusal of some most exciting adventure of a frontier or border ruffian who thinks it grand and smart to kill human beings." It was, he announced, "high time that this was stopped." Another paper similarly bemoaned "sensational stories, stories of the 'blood and thunder' kind," which "excited the [boy's] baser passions." More sensitive amateurs worried that glorifying the misdeeds of Indian killers helped perpetuate the mistreatment of Natives in desperate need of guidance. "Are we not our brothers' keepers," one such rebuke asked. Nonconformists did not, then, seem to reject the necessity of conquest. But much like adult Peace Policy advocates, they preferred to see the subjugation of Indians enacted through legal and cultural structures that would limit bloodshed and hasten the assimilation of Native Americans.⁵⁰

It is difficult to know what to make of these dissenting voices. In some ways, the rarity of empathetic editorials does little more than affirm the immense importance of the flash fiction they claimed to despise. Nearly all the amateurs who seemed skeptical of the dime novel's genocidal and nativist messaging also openly admitted to the genre's wild popularity. They urged teenaged contemporaries not to insert copycat cruelty into their own papers mostly because so many of them did. Even in 1882, *St. Nicholas*, a self-consciously "respectable" children's magazine, sifted through stacks of amateur newspapers only to announce that "we can not find a single story which can properly be reproduced here." So "many of them are poor imitations of the dime novel" that the magazine's editors had trouble distinguishing between the two. When the amateur publisher of a scathing critique of US Indian policy complained in the next issue that his article "brought to us considerable criticism regarding its being incorrect," he hinted at the relative unpopularity of what numerous detractors, following the lead of chest-thumping jingoes like Teddy Roosevelt, dismissed as "sickly sentimentalism." Boys whose editorial slant emanated a whiff of the "womanish" hazarded censure from their peers. Relatively few, therefore, seemed willing to run the risk. The reflexively misogynistic pose struck by many amateurs only seemed to reinforce that sort of thinking.⁵¹

Yet to ignore earnest and sustained disagreement with the thematic thrust of a generation's youth literature seems shortsighted. A variety of factors—including religious belief, individual conscience, and personal politics—seem to have motivated various youths to condemn international aggression and imperialist violence. Some must have relished the role of the bomb-throwing provocateur. For other young people, romanticizing the Indian's "freedom" proved attractive amidst the chafing constraints imposed upon them by both parents and teachers. And in still other ways, the denunciations of dime novels read like the class resentment of middling adolescents directed against forms of literature stereotypically considered the common man's fare. But even if their self-consciously enlightened perspectives did not approach mainstream status during the Gilded Age, it nevertheless foreshadowed a creeping cosmopolitanism within the content of children's literature.⁵²

What makes this language more remarkable, however, is the fact that such tolerant sentiment predated the widespread appearance of similar ideas in adult-authored literature for youths by at least a decade. Progressive political activism, later punctuated by a pacifistic backlash against the seemingly senseless slaughter of World War I, helped fuel the creativity of a new generation of children's writers. This cohort of authors stressed the importance of inclusivity and empathy in the education of America's youth. They hoped to establish a different world, one free from conflict and devoid of prejudice. It was their conviction that by reimagining children's literature, they could change the outlook of the country's youth and avoid perpetuating the nationalistic rivalries that had sent soldiers into an abattoir along the Western Front.[53]

Mass fiction bred insensitivity to suffering, fostered a fear of foreigners, and created a cohort of "infant Indian exterminators." Reading material informed by internationalism, on the other hand, might help raise a generation of Americans more willing to cooperate with the world's diverse inhabitants. Yet as the complaisant undercurrent within amateur papers suggests, children themselves actually anticipated this broader transformation by several years. Adult authors had to catch up with the younger members of an audience sometimes more open to liberal sentiments than imagined. The amateur press, at least as an avocation specific to young people, ceased to function by the early twentieth century. "The craze subsided," lamented one devotee "the Dom," "and most of the papers and magazines soon disappeared." Some of its more heterodox ideas, however, shortly gained broader acceptance among the makers of books for children.[54]

# 4

## Internationalist Impulses

Franklin K. Mathiews, chief librarian for the Boy Scouts of America, issued his cri de coeur in November 1914. The target? Edward Stratemeyer's literary syndicate, not to mention every other purveyor of what he called "mile-a-minute fiction." Such books, Mathiews complained, were neither written nor read. Instead, publishers merely manufactured them and young readers, to their detriment, only consumed them. Edification was absent from the equation. Series novels were too easily acquired and too quickly digested to be healthy. They served "no moral purpose" and possessed "no real intelligence." Cheap fiction sinned because it told "inflammable tale[s] of improbable adventure." "Indeed," the bibliophile jeered, "no popular character of history or legend or mythological story was ever more wise, more brave, more resourceful, than some of these up-to-the-minute boy heroes are made to appear." Worse than their implausibility, however, were the mental risks such fast-paced plots posed. "The fact is," Mathiews warned, "that the harm done is simply incalculable. I wish I could label each of these books: 'Explosives! Guaranteed to Blow Your Boy's Brains Out.'"[1]

The adverse effects for juvenile readers were numerous. For one, while "story books of the right sort stimulate and conserve" what Mathiews called the "noble faculty" of imagination, "those of the viler and cheaper sort, by overstimulation, debauch and vitiate, as brain and body are destroyed by strong drink." Moreover, the "modern 'thriller'" made "no effort to confine or direct or control" the "highly explosive elements" that often impelled children's behavior. Young minds fueled by the series book's ceaseless titillation would be less governable at best and given over to rank disobedience at worst. Sensational books helped spawn sensational crimes. The linkage between the two had already been firmly established in the minds of those who campaigned against dime novels in the 1870s and 1880s. Mathiews was an heir to their concerns, even as he targeted the newer, and as he believed, more pernicious force that was children's mass fiction.[2]

While this diatribe echoed earlier complaints, it also pointed toward something new. For, though Mathiews may have been one of the louder voices in the room, he by no means stood alone. The chorus to which he belonged collectively identified as Progressives. They comprised significant wings of the two major parties, often mounted independent political challenges, and set their sights on a slew of societal reforms. Everything from electoral procedure and the environment to urban development and food safety felt the force of Progressive pressure for change. Children, moreover, were a particular focus of their campaigns. Activists declared war against infant mortality, child labor, child abuse, and child poverty as perhaps the most pressing problems bred by industrial society. They oversaw the creation of a federal Children's Bureau designed to disseminate childrearing information and helped finance a nationwide child study movement that investigated juvenile development. And Progressives took these steps because they contended that transformational social change could best be achieved through aggressive youth outreach and training. Better books would make better citizens. Therefore, in ways that older figures like Anthony Comstock might only have dreamed, they brought an organizational acumen and scientifically minded reformism to the campaign for clean-minded children's literature. All told, the Progressives' actions helped remake the literary landscape for kids.[3]

Part of this transformation involved the genre's institutionalization. The same investment in expertise and professional guidance that steered Progressive thinking on other issues likewise structured their approach to the problem posed by mass-market children's literature. Franklin Mathiews was, in that sense, emblematic. His official title, that of "children's librarian," signaled a broader shift toward specialized training in the best practices required to meet the literary needs of young citizens. Progressives at the local, state, and national levels founded children's libraries throughout the United States. Segregated from adult reading rooms, these new spaces catered to the specific developmental needs of youths. They were, in turn, presided over by taxpayer-funded individuals clothed with the authority to steer young people toward "proper" prose. University programs meant to credential this new cohort of custodians in the "science" of managing a child's cultural diet also arose. Here lay one important instance of the Progressive movement's tendency to imagine the state as a species of parent. Actual parents in fact sometimes clashed with these officious librarians and their presumptuous efforts to police the reading habits of youths.[4]

Beyond the question of institutionalization, however, lay the problem of literary content. Children's librarians worked hard to shape the substance of books marketed to young readers. Much like Mathiews, they went to war against series fiction. Labeling it "trash," most of the new youth libraries absolutely refused to shelve it. Despite the ceaseless and always aggravating complaints of their patrons, some children's librarians even publicly burned cheap imprints. Furthermore, they used the professional periodicals and academic journals that grew up around (and served to legitimate) library schools to pen social scientific attacks against the baneful impact of popular fiction on young minds. Progressive reformers distributed what amounted to blacklists. Officially sanctioned circulars such as the highly influential *Winnetka Graded Book List* assisted staff members in separating worthy novels from the unworthy.[5]

Altogether, newly appointed gatekeepers sought to influence what publishers printed by bringing their moral authority (not to mention their libraries' considerable purchasing power) to bear against an industry thought dangerous to the nation's rising generation. They used the boycott as a tool to force reform. Their sworn enemies were the authors and publishers who, in Mathiews's words, "give no concern as to what they write or publish so long as it returns constantly the expected financial gain." Industrial capitalism's laissez-faire logic had not simply polluted rivers, poisoned provender, and perverted the political process. It was also busily transforming the minds of America's youth into sewers of iniquity. Policing such books, then, could improve both the republic's mental health and its domestic politics. But interestingly, so too did many Progressives come to believe that the fight for quality children's literature would help reshape America's international relations.[6]

Stratemeyer, for his part, had always believed as much. He explicitly argued that series fiction socialized America's youth into their imperial duties. Some Progressive thinkers, on the other hand, pointed to the naked nativism, racism, and militarism espoused by such books as a grievous wrong. Not only did those ideologies fuel bigotry in the United States, but, even worse, they became the basis for a brutal and murderous foreign policy. By desensitizing young people to the horrors of war and evils of ethnocentrism, cosmopolitans complained, mass fiction simply sustained a corrupt status quo. World War I provided all the evidence Progressive thinkers needed regarding the perverse impact of junior jingoism. The Stratemeyer Syndicate and other purveyors of "cultural trash" therefore had to be eradicated in favor of more broad-minded books. Soon enough, forward-looking writers began to publish children's literature meant to promote mutual understanding among the world's youth. The hope was to raise a generation allergic to aggression and committed to global harmony. Youth fiction thus comprised a critical but understudied component of a broader early twentieth-century movement called "cultural internationalism." This was, in short, the belief that a "peaceful world order could develop not just through the drafting of legal documents but through the efforts of individuals across national boundaries to promote . . . a more humane world." While ordinarily understood as an adult aspiration, kids were in fact key players. A good deal of the era's diplomacy was conducted by the mostly female writers and educators who spoke to them.[7]

The internationalist impulse among children's literature authors was not, of course, universally shared. The Stratemeyer Syndicate did not cease publishing during the 1910s and 1920s. Other writers profited from juvenile books that celebrated "ludic imperialism," portraying the wider world as a playground for the enactment of American authority. Plenty of Progressives, meanwhile, scorned pacifism, embraced racism and nativism as rooted in immutable scientific truth, and remained stalwart expansionists. This was the era, after all, during which was drawn a global color line. Yet for a small but deeply committed cohort of activist authors, children's literature became an outlet by which the virtues of open-mindedness might be propagated. They aimed for nothing less than the total reconstruction of relations between states around the world. By breeding into the next generation of America's young a revulsion for the petty particularisms of nation and color, authors expected to combat the spread of prejudice and end war. The "highway to peace," as *Scribner's* remarked about this ideological engineering project, would be built with "the soul of youth rather than of age." Using literature to remake the outlooks of children might initiate a "disarmament of the mind" and usher in a new era of global goodwill.[8]

It was a heady and ultimately unattainable dream. Warren Harding's winning political message in the election of 1920 counseled "not submergence in internationality, but sustainment in triumphant nationality." The United States rebuffed the League of Nations and retreated from transnationalism by passing restrictive immigration laws. Europe and East Asia descended into totalitarianism, rearmament, conflict, and genocide. Yet the short-term failure of Progressive authors to stave off global catastrophe does not signify the fruitlessness of their endeavor. When read across a longer timeline, interwar dreamers helped alter some of the core ideological tenets of mainstream American children's literature. By endorsing diversity, anti-racism, and pacifism, they helped sow the ideological seeds for much of today's youth publishing. At the very least, cooperationist voices serve as a reminder that empire's nursery raised its share of discontents. Something akin to imperial skepticism occasionally appeared in juvenile publications and needs to be understood in dynamic or symbiotic relation with the dominant discourse. The cosmopolitans who comprised a small but significant corner of the children's literary market professed a deep commitment to counter-expansionist foreign policy goals, even as they paradoxically championed America's destiny to become the first among equals overseas.[9]

Ecumenist Energies

Internationalist children's literature may have gained greater notoriety during the Progressive era, but it did not appear out of thin air. We have already seen some of its predecessors in imprints that fretted over the dime novel's exterminationist rhetoric. Other antecedents are to be found in the Millenialist doctrine and evangelical reading material circulated by Protestant missionary organizations during the nineteenth century. Indeed, virtually from the moment Puritans set foot upon the shores of North America, Christian printing presses concerned themselves with the moral welfare of young people. Stories espousing a "softer" settler colonialism, meant to convert rather than annihilate "heathen" Indians, frequently appeared in New England's juvenile tracts. Abolitionism was also a focus of early Christian children's literature.

Works such as *The Child's Anti-Slavery Book* sought to inculcate among Northern youth a hatred of bondage rooted in appeals to the spiritual equality of all souls. And once nineteenth-century sects began to found societies committed to evangelism overseas, Protestants soon saw more of the world portrayed in the pages of periodicals printed exclusively for these various churches' children. Young people, operating under the auspices of the Student Volunteer Movement, were often at the leading edge of an invigorated Gilded Age foreign mission movement. But they were also an important audience for the articulation of new norms meant to govern US global conduct. As a result, titles like *Children's Work for Children*, the *Heathen Children's Friend*, and the *Children's Missionary Friend* saturated the Christian children's literature market.[10]

Anti-imperialism is likely too strong a term to describe the politics of such publications. After all, American missionaries depended upon the military and economic infrastructure of various European empires in order to proselytize abroad, their aim to convert the world possessed expansionist overtones, and evangelists stationed abroad often became critical intermediaries who facilitated subsequent commercial and military penetration. Yet some of those same actors did, in their writing for young people, advocate a more restrained approach to intercultural affairs than much of the hard-charging frontier-themed children's literature that otherwise dominated the market. This nonaggressive sensibility was in part pragmatic. Successful missionaries could rarely afford to affect the same haughty airs prevalent in mainstream settler colonial youth fiction. But an ideological gap also separated the evangelical approach to juvenile foreign relations from its more secular counterpart. The young readers of missionary-themed children's literature heard a good deal more about brotherhood and toleration than those of their peers who exclusively perused cheap fiction. Whereas the merciful Christian was often depicted as foolish in the mainstream pro-expansionist children's press, that same figure proved heroic among readers of Protestant subgenres. Publications even encouraged American youths to play that part themselves by "adopting" a foreign child and raising money to pay for his or her education, room, and board at a missionary school.[11]

*Everyland*, a product of the Young People's Missionary Movement (an organization itself associated with the Student Volunteer Movement), was one of the most popular examples of a broader evangelical embrace of cosmopolitan sensibilities. Its preeminent purpose, like every other such magazine, was two-pronged: converting heathens abroad while Christianizing children at home. But it is crucial to note that by the fin-de-siècle, devout youngsters were being asked to embrace multiculturalism. The journal's subtitle, "A World Friendship Magazine for Boys and Girls," nicely encapsulates its editorial slant. "The chief object of *Everyland*," an introductory essay claimed, "is to help us get acquainted with our world neighbors, with the hope that we may all be friends." Articles furthered that goal by explicitly promising to connect "our readers" with "boys and girls in the far-away countries of the world." Each issue contained rich illustrations of life overseas, short stories, suggestions for activities and craftwork at home, and correspondence from children around the globe.[12]

It was the last function—letter writing and gift exchange between US children and foreigners at missionary stations abroad—that comprised much of *Everyland*'s content. Columns routinely invited youths to trade epistles with kids overseas. The idea was to create tangible connections between America's youth and their counterparts elsewhere. These magazines strived to transcend cultural barriers by demonstrating the real possibilities that existed for international harmony. The foreign was still exoticized while ethnic dissimilarities became fodder for comedy, but the basic lesson embedded in each article remained the same: The quest for universal salvation would require good Christians to transcend prejudice. In Westerns and colonial adventure fiction circulating among young people, racialism justified the violent dispossession of those deemed unassimilable. Kids' missionary material, on the other hand, placed a higher premium upon at least the cautious acceptance of divinely ordained diversity. Christian internationalism implicitly rejected nationalism as a kind of blasphemy, a rival faith that prevented people from fully embracing the peaceful (and transnational) teachings of Jesus.[13]

*Everyland* stressed the interconnectedness of all humanity by providing capsule biographies of various young people around the world. Adult evangelists wrote them intending to introduce American children to their charges overseas. For example, A. Hyatt Verrill, stationed in the West Indies, had readers say hello to "Beche, the Carib Boy." Helen Murphy wrote about "Natchez, the Brown Boy of Guam." Elizabeth Gurnee Anderson, meanwhile, explained that "you ought to know Ana Julia, a little eight-year-old girl, living in a village called Colon, far up in the mountains of Venezuela in South America." The stories' frequent asides chiding readers for laughing at some facet of a culture that "may sound funny to you" promoted more relativistic mind-sets. As the story of a Hawaiian lad's life concluded, the proverbial book could not be judged by its cover. "He might be any boy for boys are exactly alike except for their clothes. Our clothes are just as queer to other people as theirs are to us." And while kids abroad "may need our help," they "will help us, too, with the useful things [they] can make." Popular fiction's rendering of empire as a relationship of command was here replaced with descriptions of mutual dependence.[14]

Immigration also received different treatment within the pages of children's religious literature. In juvenile series fiction, a nativist logic prevailed. The criminal element was often coded as foreign-born, and immigrants, when they appeared, exhibited little intelligence. The readers of missionary magazines, by contrast, used the turn-of-the-century's influx of foreigners as evidence of America's superior national virtue. "Miss Gulliver's Travels," a regular column, best expressed that particular idea. "What a wonderfully varied family we Americans are! All the characteristics of mankind are ours, and in consequence the United States should be the richest of nations in mind, spirit, and good will." That multinational mosaic must then, her logic extended, become the basis for a new form of foreign relations. "Because I am an American," the argument went, "I am bound in sympathy to all the peoples of the earth from whom my fellow Americans are descended." And "when we consider that our American family is related to practically all the peoples in the world, then each one of us as an individual girl or boy is related to all peoples." So, her conclusion sang, "when we think of this relationship, the whole great earth seems like one home," and "when we go a-travelling, you and I" it helped "us to see and learn and also love, and thereby come to understand ourselves as Americans better than if we had remained at home digging in the back yard." America's heterogenous population, authors argued, would make the nation a natural leader in the internationalist movement. Such publications, in other words, did not challenge the exceptionalist creed propagated by Edward Stratemeyer. They instead insisted that it become the basis for a new, more restrained style of US-led global regeneration.[15]

The context, however—widespread xenophobic agitation for more restrictive immigration laws, a resurgent Ku Klux Klan (complete with Kiddie Klavern youth outreach groups) during the 1910s and 1920s, and a larger literary market that embraced aggressive US expansion—made such sentiments quite radical. But even when swimming against the ideological current, calls for global camaraderie did find at least some support. As one of the architects of the early twentieth-century Sunday School movement asserted, Christian juvenile publications aided the "increase of human fellowship the world over. The gradual broadening of the sympathies of children through acquaintance with real children of other lands and other conditions is itself a magnificent missionary enterprise." So too did young readers themselves write in with similar praise. An eighth grader named Tessie Gross echoed the encomiums of others when she enthused over the opportunity to become "very well acquainted with my brothers and sisters in foreign lands," the "children of different races and nationalities." Other youths described how the periodical structured their play. A Brooklyn boy claimed to be "making an Eskimo village" and teaching "people who come about our village," while a St. Paul child described a hide and seek game where "different parts of a room were fixed up to look like various lands." Kids "dressed up like the people of those lands . . . and we learned lots about which countries the missionaries belonged to." Of course, claims about the beneficent influence of Christian moralizing were always self-serving and rarely represented the lived experience of those at the receiving end of ministerial effort. Individuals overseas often perceived missionaries as invasive. At the rhetorical level, however, it is important to note how planetary proselytizing helped generate new ways of seeing the world—ways far more tolerant of human difference—for young readers at home in the United States.[16]

The influence of these magazines, of course, can be overstated. For one, they hardly spoke for all self-identified Christians. Catholics were a growing subset of the population virtually unrepresented in such publications. Other denominations, meanwhile, made their peace with the spread-eagle posturing meant to promote US imperial interests. More concretely, evangelical imprints lacked the capitalization and comprehensive distribution networks that allowed mass-market youth fiction to penetrate every corner of the country. But despite their minimal circulation, they did eventually inspire sweeping transformations to come. Reformers seized upon the multicultural messaging these periodicals espoused, secularized the content, and sought to expand beyond the realm of churchgoing children. Interwar internationalists, raised on a literary diet that differed from the rabidly expansionist dime novels and series fiction, vowed to try something new. Revulsion in the face of World War I's carnage offered those aspiring to fundamentally change the face of youth literature an opportunity to do so.[17]

## Teachers in the Trenches

The Great War was a series fiction fixation. Even before the conflict began, juvenile literature worked to inculcate the nationalism and venerate the militarism that proved so instrumental in mobilizing young men for combat duty. As was the case with the War of 1898, stories revolved around precocious youths placed in precarious situations. Some series fixated on the war's new technology, such as submarines and airplanes. Others took the form of spy thrillers, with young boys rooting out German saboteurs at home. Many more fixated on Uncle Sam's need for "preparedness." And with formal US entry into the conflict a reality by 1917, books quickly whisked readers onto the western front. Characters never questioned the struggle's absolute necessity, and plots uniformly depicted "the Hun" as a bloodthirsty foe bent on world domination. As such, the novels collectively acted as an informal youth auxiliary of the Committee on Public Information (CPI), the federal government's prowar propaganda arm.[18]

Both the breadth and depth of youth politicization was unlike anything the nation had ever attempted before. It shocked the consciences of skeptics. Progressive-era compulsory education laws, however, had made the process simpler. Young people now spent far more of their early lives housed in state-supported schools, where, as propagandists discovered, they were easily found. Hence the CPI's significant juvenile outreach efforts beginning in 1917, which involved school visits made by public speakers. Similarly patriotic marketing targeted children's movies and other forms of popular entertainment. Any number of adult-run juvenile organizations sought to prepare young citizens for the war. The Junior Red Cross recruited millions of kids to gather needed medical supplies. The Boy Scouts of America offered their services for civil defense. The Girl Scouts of America tended Victory Gardens at the behest of the United States Food Administration. The Young Men's and Young Women's Christian Associations likewise devoted their efforts to eventual American victory. And in classrooms, children threw themselves into letter-writing and craft-making campaigns meant to boost the morale of both the troops "over there" and the hundreds of thousands of young war orphans crowding Europe's refugee camps. All told, young people's efforts were Herculean.[19]

Some, starting with President Woodrow Wilson, heralded children's contributions to the American war effort as essential. Many more saw in youth indoctrination a harmless diversion, perhaps even a necessary one given the tendency of wartime social dislocation to breed juvenile delinquency. A much smaller but vocal cohort of critics, however, bemoaned the baneful influence of a country given over to militarism. Battlefields, they argued, should not be sanctified. If innocence was an essential condition of childhood, then surrounding young people with martial rhetoric could be construed as a form of abuse. Propaganda poisoned their otherwise pure minds, taught them to perceive the world prejudicially, and ultimately produced armed conflict. Even before the conflict began, pacifists had sought to use the classroom as a weapon *against* war. Organizations like the American School Peace League (itself only one part of a larger global peace movement), bankrolled by the Carnegie Endowment for International Peace, led by Progressive reformer Fannie Fern Andrews and populated by thousands of mostly female teachers, circulated dovish literature in schools throughout the country. Once the trenches were dug across the Atlantic, they encouraged students to "look upon this spectacle of human suffering and devastation with horror" and "take an interest in the movement which shall bring about the reign of law in place of the reign of the sword." Activists utilized the rhetoric of military mobilization but aimed to push young minds toward the pursuit of goodwill. New ways of thinking about and seeing the world would be required, and kids were considered most receptive to them. "One generation of teaching the principles of justice, peace, and international unity," Andrews insisted with characteristic certitude, "would revolutionize the world."[20]

Such political persuasions often came at great personal cost. Pacifists and conscientious objectors faced charges of disloyalty, heightened scrutiny from law enforcement, dismissal from their workplaces, and in some cases mob violence. Yet many persisted even in the face of opposition, and the targets of their campaigning were manifold. The draft, the munitions industry, and war profiteers all came under scrutiny. Other organizers, however, focused on young people. They sought to stamp out war by eliminating the means by which children initially learned to behave aggressively. School curriculums—particularly in physical education—which stressed soldierly drill and regimentation sparked outrage. Idealists drafted new textbooks that placed a premium on the theme of "world citizenship." Institutions like the Boy Scouts were denounced for their paramilitary trappings. Potentially corrupt playthings like toy troops, air rifles, and the Liberty Toy Company's "Modern Trench Warfare Kit" were condemned (and publicly burned) for fear that "when the boy gets used to pulling the trigger of a toy gun, it's not a long step toward pulling the trigger of a real one." Even the era's "trial of the century"—that of teenagers Nathan Leopold and Richard Loeb for the murder of young Bobby Franks—seemed to hinge on the capacity of war to make killers out of innocent kids; defense attorney Clarence Darrow's widely read summation argued that "young boys" like the infamous Leopold and Loeb, with "tales of death in their homes, their playgrounds, [and] their schools" during the Great War, had become thoroughly desensitized. Therefore, no small portion of some reformers' ire was directed at those who published children's literature glorifying combat. In so doing, one Progressive lamented, publishers accomplished little else than to "make possible the quick focusing of suppressed aggression on a scapegoat." As long as writers were paid to exalt conflict, "the cultural stone axe of war" would be "cherished as a major institution." Such monsters had already seduced youthful millions into a meat grinder. It could not be allowed to happen again.[21]

## Writing Racism and Militarism Out of the Script

The most industrious of these critics sought to rewrite the script then dominating juvenile fiction. As the pacifists' cry rang, "if we would have our boys hate war, we must not familiarize them with the arts of war." Part of that familiarity had been bred by sensationalistic series books. Authors therefore hoped to suffuse the children's literature market with contrary impulses toward multilateralism, cosmopolitanism, and pacifism, particularly during the interwar years. A growing class of Progressive-era child studies experts had convinced many that the prejudices which produced war and racism were largely a product of youthful habits. Activists who found those arguments compelling expected to inculcate very different values in juvenile audiences by emphasizing the "gifts" given to American society by its diverse constituent communities. That quest for harmonious heterogeneity, meanwhile, would extend outward beyond the nation's borders. Childhood, as a concept, and children, as a cohort, were thereby placed at the center of conversations meant to remake relations between states and reconceptualize the international order. *Parents* magazine, one of the era's most widely circulated periodicals, and a proponent of education in the interest of international goodwill, characteristically claimed that "getting acquainted with children of other lands through travel and books can help build attitudes that will abolish war." Only a "League of Nations built in the hearts of children," another educator insisted, could produce lasting world peace.[22]

Part of what allowed this literary output to break with past precedent was the fact that women stood at its center. They wrote most of it, staffed the children's libraries that stocked it, and taught the classes that assigned it. Female authors had, of course, produced young people's reading for generations, but, on the whole, it had been a trade dominated by men. By the early twentieth century, however, some women came to view this masculinist edge as one of the genre's major problems. Men were, for a variety of reasons, believed incapable of advocating for peace. At a biological level, they seemed hardwired for conflict and hopelessly addicted to military pageantry. As pacifist Katherine Devereux Blake diagnosed the problem, "men seldom *work* for peace. Women will."[23]

The composition of various antiwar organizations certainly suggested as much. Women prevailed among both the leadership and the rank and file. Much of this had to do with the institutional and ideological crossover that connected pacifism with the female-dominated temperance, women's suffrage, and feminist movements. Many members of one crusade would often transition to the others, though this should not imply that all shared the same politics. Far from it. Each organization had its more or less militant wings. Conflicts of personality and disagreements over goals and tactics fueled feuds. More important here, however, was the thoroughly politicized nature of the work many early twentieth-century female children's authors performed. They came to the task with the fierce conviction, forged in the era's struggles for women's rights, that the "gentler sex" was duty-bound to reimagine an international system ruined by masculine aggression. Iconoclasts like Jane Addams, Emily Balch, and their Women's International League for Peace and Freedom (WILPF) went to war against what they called America's "fetish of force." And they expected to enlist kids as troops for the battle ahead.[24]

Radical authors did not do so without resistance. They were fighting an uphill battle, with most of the era's textbooks deeply committed to US empire's propagation. The predominately male political and educational establishment attempted to undermine women's activism in several ways. Female teachers talking of peace, they complained, would feminize the nation's boys. Books that substituted "one-worldism" for patriotism were denounced as a danger to the nation's military preparedness. So-called realists disparaged cosmopolitanism as sentimental nonsense. If the country's defense establishment crumbled, the United States would lose its status as an emerging power and instead become an international laughingstock. Skeptics of the new children's literature likewise lambasted female authors as traitors who, in undermining the legitimacy of war as an instrument of policy, called the morality of America's past battlefield successes into question. As such, they threatened to unravel threads central to the tapestry that was the nation's heroic self-conception. These accusations were, of course, little more than mendacious misogyny. But collectively, they elicited one truth: In subverting the long-standing image of the masculine soldier as the foundation of national glory, these women challenged the prevailing social order. Their books posited that because the world had recently blundered into war, foreign policy would be far better served by new stewards. It was a task that would begin with children's reading material explicitly designed to prevent recurrent catastrophe.[25]

In believing as much, this new generation of authors represented the fullest expression of a broader Progressive commitment to implementing structural social change by transforming the individual's behavior. Walter Rauschenbusch, a minister of the Social Gospel and prominent philosopher of early Progressivism, argued that "the greatest contribution which any man can make to the social movement is the contribution of a regenerated personality." Washington Gladden, another Progressive pastor, likewise observed that the path to peace would require Americans to alter their "primary conceptions." "What we have got to have . . . is a different kind of men and women." Self-proclaimed Progressive president Theodore Roosevelt called this the "slow and patient inward transformation" that constituted the period's "great work of reconstruction." Teddy, famous for his "Big Stick" diplomacy, was certainly no pacifist. But the language each of these activists (among others) deployed is instructive. It reflected a broader consensus among the reform-minded that cultural change required personal renewal. What better place to begin the internationalist revolution, therefore, than to plant its seeds in the fertile soil of children's imaginations? "A far-sighted policy, such as the training of the young," said one crusader, "is preferable to the summary regulation of the adult." If, as *Parents* magazine insisted, "the natural mind, as seen in a child, [was] essentially honest, fair and tolerant," why not encourage young people to carry those basic values into adulthood?[26]

Two Progressive-era series stand out for their faith in such an enterprise: Lucy Fitch Perkins's "Twins" books and the L.C. Page Company's "Little Cousin" imprints. Each warrants sustained engagement, beginning with the former. Lucy Fitch Perkins was trained in drawing and painting, and she sat on the faculty at Brooklyn's prestigious Pratt Institute of Fine Arts. It was time spent illustrating textbooks during the early 1890s, however, that pulled her into the several aforementioned reform movements then orbiting American schools. Her mother-in-law, who helped run a settlement house, and her husband, a member of the municipal playground movement, also proved inspirational. Yet as Perkins herself explained, she had long felt called toward the internationalist movement. After relocating to the ethnic mélange that was postbellum Chicago, she had been "deeply impressed by a realization of the great task which rests primarily on the teachers of America in bringing a unified nation out of a heterogeneous mixture of races." And thus, she continued, "it occurred to me with an emphasis that has never left me, that anything which would promote mutual respect for the best which other nations bring to this shore would help to some degree in this process of Americanization," and, even more important, "world peace." When she began publishing in 1911, Perkins sensed that "the secluding barriers of nationalism were just ready to be pulled down by people in all countries who were willing to believe that children the world around are natural friends." By harnessing what she believed to be the child's inherent inclination toward tolerance, Perkins expected to promote improved understanding among the world's people. The fruits of her resolve to remake foreign relations by, as she put it, "increasing sympathy and understanding for the qualities of different races," were the Twins books. It was, Perkins admitted, "a really big theme," but one that could "be comprehended by children if . . . presented in a way that holds their interest."[27]

Each of the series's twenty-six volumes strived toward that lofty goal by following a simple rubric. In a savvy marketing move meant to enhance the series's appeal among readers of both sexes, youths were introduced to a set of foreign twins, one boy and one girl. Perkins, in other words, backed away from the explicitly masculine messaging of serialized imperialism; her internationalist inclinations helped to promote world harmony by, in part, embracing more egalitarian gender ideals. The books then proceeded to narrate a few days in the routine of these children overseas, depicting the food they ate, the clothes they wore, and the holidays they celebrated. Each set of Twins acted as "cultural goodwill ambassadors." Unlike Stratemeyer Syndicate imprints and children's missionary literature, ethnic differences were never used to legitimate American intrusion. Instead, the behaviors and habits of other people were described only as subjects of inquiry and interest. In that sense, the books became a juvenile companion to the adult-oriented and informationally minded travelogues, lectures, and slideshows comprising what has been called the era's "fictive travel movement." But in addition to a kind of vicarious globalization of the national mind, Perkins pursued a larger ideological project. She hoped such superficially neutral prose, the appendix of one Twins tale announced, would eventually ensure that "the citizens of America . . . never lose their sympathy with the things that are best in foreign lands." When combined, the "great national heroes" and "music, art, and literature" of other cultures were all supposed to "inspire our people" and "add richness to our American civilisation." By "the fusing of their highest ideals into our own," a new generation, an amalgam of all the globe's best traits, might help build a better world.[28]

INTERNATIONALIST IMPULSES | 135

Figure 4.1. Illustrations in internationalist children's literature often emphasized the importance of camaraderie among the world's youth. Of course, the terms of this global fellowship were to be set by the United States. Lucy Fitch Perkins, *The Mexican Twins* (Boston: Houghton Mifflin, 1915), frontispiece.

Part of Perkins's task, then, was to destigmatize foreign children in the eyes of her American audience. Rather than the "race-consciousness, xenophobia, and imperialism" propagated by the era's mass-market children's literature, Twins books encouraged readers to perceive the pleasures inherent to childhood anywhere. *The Japanese Twins*, for instance, subverted tropes comprising the so-called Yellow Peril, an ideology that had long legitimated restrictive immigration laws levied against Asians. Instead, Perkins asked her readers to imagine "anything nicer in this world than being Twins, and living with a Mother and Father and Grandmother and a Baby Brother, in a dear little house ... in the middle of the Happy Islands that lie in the Ocean of Peace." Meanwhile, *The Mexican Twins*, set on a "great hacienda ... in the wonderful country of Mexico," aimed "to establish a better understanding of a neighboring [nation]" and "foster a kindly feeling for its people." Most of the books simply showed mothers and fathers caring for their offspring as children set about the chores of the day. When Mrs. Chang rocked her son to sleep, "she patted him and sang to him, just like any mother in the world." When the Filipino Twins prepared rice, the Irish Twins porridge, and the Italian Twins macaroni, it was explained as nothing more than breakfast. Passages like these may read cloyingly today, but at the time, and for helping American kids imaginatively embrace distant lifeways, they represented an ideological about-face. The "odd" became normal. As one young enthusiast of the books reflected years later, "here was a whole book about twins, a boy and a girl who lived in Holland but who had experiences a girl in Portland, Oregon, could share."[29]

The otherwise positive portraits painted of other cultures were marred by occasional slippages into overt criticism. "Gypsies" assume the role of villain in several volumes, and were always portrayed as dirty and thieving. Germans, who tellingly failed to receive their own sympathetic Twins treatment, came across as aggressive and antagonistic in a few books. Nonwhite cultures were, in some instances, treated less seriously or respectfully than their European counterparts. *The Eskimo Twins* for example (setting aside the misnomer "Eskimo" itself), featured a tribal shaman whose obesity becomes the source of slapstick humor. The author also tended to sneak in asides about the silliness of pagan religious incantations. Most egregious may be the unfortunately titled *Pickaninny Twins*, with its affected dialogue and romanticized depictions of the Deep South's sunny simplicity. More broadly, Perkins never completed volumes dealing with any part of Africa, South America, or the Caribbean, with their large populations of Black people. With even "open-minded" authors engaging in racism of both commission and omission, it looked all the more imperative for writers of color to craft their own juvenile literature. Hence the emphasis of the Harlem Renaissance on what Langston Hughes called "the need for books that Negro parents and teachers can read to their children without hesitancy, books whose dark characters are not all clowns, and whose illustrations are not merely caricatures." Beneath the interwar era's white-dominated internationalism, therefore, lay more sweeping critiques of American iniquity. They gradually gathered steam before bursting to the surface by the mid-twentieth century (see the epilogue).[30]

Despite these shortcomings, however, many of Perkins's contemporaries judged her voice an influential one. The children's and school libraries that Progressives built disseminated her work at the expense of the Stratemeyer Syndicate, and strong sales tended to reflect their promotional efforts. A 1935 Chicago *Tribune* write-up about Lucy Fitch Perkins, on the occasion of her having sold her two millionth book, succinctly stated that "quietly, gently, but earnestly she has for twenty-five years been performing the humanizing task of making children conscious that other children, however far removed geographically, are their brothers." It was a longevity that spoke to her popularity. That same year, the League of Nations's library requested from Perkins's publisher a copy of each of her books to be shelved in Geneva as a tribute to "the assistance they rendered to international friendship." And beyond such institutional sanction, young people themselves seemed to receive Perkins's series with enthusiasm. The Twins books were translated into several languages, and the author's daughter remembered stacks of fan mail piling up in her mother's study. It was, she said, "a prodigious correspondence with children pretty well distributed over the planet." One affecting anecdote involved young people who wrote her in the 1930s, about to "burst into tears" for fear of armed conflict in East Asia. "'If there were a war with Japan,'" they cried, "'something might happen to the Japanese twins!'" Though this correspondence is lost to us today, Lucy Fitch Perkins, by the time of her death in 1937, remembered it "evidencing that [the] books had, in some measure, fulfilled [her] hope for them." After all, inspiring an overriding concern for distant people—not to mention an instinctual hatred of war—had been her purpose in writing children's books.[31]

The *Little Cousin* books preached much the same message. Their progenitor, an author by the name of Mary Hazelton Wade, even shared certain biographical details with Lucy Fitch Perkins. Wade, born to a prosperous middle-class New England family in 1860, was eventually appointed as a teacher in the town of Malden, Massachusetts. One of the era's self-styled New Women, Wade clearly prized her career. She climbed up through the school district's administrative apparatus, earned repeated election to the local board of education, and remained active in the causes of women's suffrage and Progressive reform more broadly. By 1901, her determination to effect change likewise led her to begin writing children's fiction. The *Little Cousin* books blended factual description of life overseas with cosmopolitan messaging, and they were explicitly designed as a counterweight to the violent sensationalism of the Stratemeyer Syndicate. Beginning with *Our Little Indian Cousin*, L.C. Page & Company ultimately released over thirty such titles. Most went through numerous printings, and the series proved profitable for the publisher. By the time the last book appeared in 1927, Wade herself had moved on to other pursuits. But various "guest" authors had by then been contracted to provide volumes covering most of the habitable world.[32]

The setup was simple. Each book detailed the life of one or two "little cousins" living in a particular country or region overseas. Typically, young readers experienced another child's routine for a few days. Occasionally, through some plot contrivance, an American youth would appear and befriend his or her "little cousin" in order to juxtapose the two cultures. More commonly, an omniscient narrator pointed out important contrasts. Several aspects of daily life were consistently called to the reader's attention. Foodstuffs, cooking, and table manners often appeared as important windows into other societies. Clothing and fashion also occupied a good deal of space in each book, as did games and play and relationships with parents and between siblings. The idea was, in the space of about one hundred pages, to provide a comprehensive and informative picture of life abroad in terms that an American child might find relatable.

It would be easy, of course, to locate the many ways in which Wade's books seem to celebrate US colonialism and reify racial hierarchy. She, along with most other authors who wrote for the *Little Cousin* series, could by today's standards hardly be accused of excessive enlightenment. Indigenous Hawaiians, for example, were called a "childlike people" who had, rather than fall victim to an 1893 American-led coup, simply seen "that they could not govern themselves" and politely "asked the United States to receive them into her family." According to Wade,

Cuba was also the beneficiary of Yankee noblesse oblige. When observing the "great hardship and suffering" inflicted upon the island by Spain, William McKinley's administration selflessly sprang into action because "such things must not be at our very doorway." Yet continued US involvement in Caribbean affairs—in this case Cuba's postwar status as an American protectorate—was clearly justified by the fact that islanders still "need[ed] the friendly help of their more fortunate neighbours."[33]

Rejecting America's philanthropic overtures, meanwhile, provided cause for condemnation. Rebellious Filipinos, then in the midst of a war for independence from the United States, were scolded as "wild and distrustful children" who "have no faith in us" and "do not wish to obey our laws." Some of Wade's co-authors (though never Wade herself) even continued to rely on pat formulations regarding the power of "Anglo-Saxon blood to counteract the inherent tendency of [other] races towards procrastination." And, like so many Progressives, she downplayed the brute force that built America's overseas empire. Instead, cultural change imposed from above was, if anything, an act of charity. Her background as a teacher situated her, in spirit, among the thousands of US educators who fanned out across the world after 1898 to tutor the country's newest pupils. Her books tended to marvel at young imperial subjects who "have never been in a public schoolroom in their lives" and crow that "these are only now becoming common since our people have taken [them] under their care." As did many of her fellow citizens, Wade presumed that the world's people inherently aspired to imitate American values and that a guileless Uncle Sam should help them do so. Internationalism and imperialism were not necessarily antithetical precepts. The United States was often portrayed as duty-bound to usher in a new era of global amity, while whites were usually spoken of as the only race sufficiently intelligent to lead the world toward the cooperationist age. A firm belief in American exceptionalism often awkwardly stood beside multilateral rhetoric. Sometimes the Stratemeyer Syndicate and its cosmopolite critics divided over means rather than ends. Both saw the good in US global stewardship, whether achieved through military or moral force. Each believed that their nation's values were universally aspired to by the world's population.[34]

Inconsistencies such as these, however, represent low-hanging fruit that, when plucked out of context, distort the more forward-thinking dimensions of Wade's work. She was hardly a rabid imperialist of the series fiction sort, and in fact just as often urged her young disciples to see cultural difference not in terms of racial deficiency but instead, overarching humanity. For, as Wade remarked in one of her earliest volumes, other children, though "quite different from ourselves in dress and appearance [and] language and habits," nevertheless must be seen as fundamentally equal to "their white cousins." "These differences are after all only *outside* ones," she stressed, and ultimately, "we are all bound closely together by one great divine nature." And so, "when you think of this, I hope you will be glad to turn your minds for a while to the home of your Brown Cousin," here, a Bornean boy, "and join him in his work and play." Moments like these, when compared to some of her apologies for American interventionism, make Wade's ideology difficult to pin down. Yet this assertion of the essentially familial relationship among the world's youth—we are all "little cousins" to one another, we "all belong to the same great family"—does regularly appear throughout her books. It manifested in a few different ways.[35]

For instance, Wade insisted that white American children (she never pretended to address any other audience) had no monopoly on the world's useful knowledge and no right to believe themselves implicitly superior. Yes, other young people "never saw an electric car or a steamboat" and "few of them dream of the stores of knowledge to be gained through the study of books." But supposedly "backward" people also "learned much of which their white cousins are ignorant." They thrived without items their "little white cousins would think they must have." Wade tried to defamiliarize the familiar for her audience and show them new ways of living and knowing that were perfectly adapted to other environments. "We hear of different fashions," characters abroad observe, "but ours are still the best for us." The accouterments of daily life in middle-class America were regularly called "queer things" from the perspective of others overseas, while outsiders' "exotic" innovations were "better than anything . . . that you could give [them]." Wade often remarked about some component of life elsewhere: "I wish I could have one like it myself." Reflexive assertions of absolute American superiority were much rarer. Youths overseas were often permitted to vocalize their own patriotism, as when Carl, a Swiss boy, proclaims that "'our country is the freest and best in all the world.'" His US interlocutor replied, "I love America the best," but, she continued, "father says we Americans can learn some good lessons from Switzerland." Both youngsters resolved to foster a relationship of mutual support and dialogue. As such, Wade jettisoned the rhetorical excesses of American jingoism.[36]

The young reader was asked to understand that though his or her counterpart abroad was "peculiar in his looks, his talk was in a strange tongue, his clothes were odd in colour and fit, his shoes were unlike ours, and everything about him would seem to you very unusual in appearance," that boy abroad "did not think he was a bit queer." What was more, "if he should see one of you in your home, or at school, or at play, he would . . . wonder at your peculiar ways and dress." Foreign peoples possessed no monopoly on oddity; American kids had their own idiosyncrasies put on parade as well. The question underlying all of these observations was: How different were these children to begin with? Kalitan, the indigenous Alaskan, revealed that despite his "swarthy" skin and "strange mixture" of facial features, "boys are boys all the world over," and a "fair-skinned" youth who met him would soon be "chattering away to his newly found friend as if he had known him all his life." Chie Lo, a Malaysian child featured in one volume, also helped provide an answer. When she "talked to her dolls and sang queer little songs to them" and when she "'made believe' they were eating," it was "just as other little girls play, far away across the great ocean." A Bedouin boy revealed something similar, given that "our little Arabian cousins have much in common with [us], in that they are taught to have a great respect for their elders, and particularly to be polite and thoughtful to strangers." Their society's tenets were therefore hardly alien but rather "all very delightful," and "if you ever wish to visit your little Arabian cousins, you will always be sure of a warm welcome."[37]

Even when correcting a people's supposed defects, Wade urged readers to rely upon the power of moral suasion rather than military force. As opposed to series books that depicted violence (or the threat thereof) as the only language "savages" actually spoke, the *Little Cousin* volumes urged patience with the foreigner's faults. Referring to a fondness for smoking among Southeast Asian children, Wade said only that "we must hope that the time will come when people will be wiser in some things." Rather than sending armies to compel change, the author argued that "we should send our love to the little boy." So too for the Turkish child taught to revere a "despotic" Sultan: "let us open the doors of our hearts to him, and let him feel our love and sympathy." While mainstream children's fiction frequently positioned racial difference and a hierarchy of civilizational achievement as adequate justification for American rule, Wade instead emphasized the importance of unity and shared governance rooted in certain basic similarities. Hence her introduction to *Our Little Porto Rican Cousin*, which called distinctions like the islanders' "dark skins" and "Spanish language" nothing more than "slight differences." More heavily stressed was their "belong[ing] to the same branch of the great human family as we do." Such language counteracted cultural forces equating dark skin with ugliness and malice. Your nonwhite cousins, she soothed, are "not only good-looking, but kind and lovable, we feel sure." Implicitly thumbing her nose at the era's resuscitated Klan and rabid nativists, Wade announced of "the great negro race" that "like all the peoples of all the races of men on this big earth, they belong to the human family."[38]

Ideas about the basic subjectivity that structured human understanding likewise abound in Wade's prose. Whatever young readers might otherwise imagine to be an expression of their Little Cousin's "backwardness" was usually attributed to the contingency of birth. A Caribbean boy, for example, loved the "cruel pleasure" of cockfighting, but the author urged readers to spare judgment because "Manuel has been brought up to think there is no pleasure like it." "We cannot blame them," she insisted, "for the customs of their country have made it seem quite right and proper." Likewise, the Armenian boy's "custom of living in a stable with the cattle seems strange, but so do all fashions which are unlike ours." And upon second glance, "it wasn't a bad way of building a home, was it?" Nor was the Siamese boy who wore earrings to be mocked, because "there was nothing strange about that" to him. Religious difference received similar treatment. Buddhism sounded foreign to the Christian child's ears, but Wade thought both sought roughly similar ends: "This is what we all do, is it not? For we long to do right and seek the light of love and wisdom." Similarly, an American in Alaska remarked that "it is a pity you [Thlinkits] could not send missionaries to the States," for "white people" might learn to be more honest. And considering the era's entrenched anti-Semitism, *Our Little Jewish Cousin* was impressive for its fundamentally humane portrayal of Judaism. Again and again, Wade and other popular Progressive children's authors exchanged the essentialism of more popular series for a gentler relativism.[39]

It was an imperfectly applied ideology to be sure. Authors like Wade still presumed a privilege to chide those who did not behave just as they wished. But it was certainly a different model for juvenile foreign relations, one that urged young Americans to approach the world's people not as antagonists but rather as playmates. This was a type of diplomacy that Wade envisioned taking place on street corners and in schoolrooms. "When you meet your little Italian cousins" around town, the author urged, try to "feel a little nearer and more friendly" toward them. People overseas were most often portrayed as potential partners from whom US youths could benefit: "Our little American cousins," went one such statement, "would perhaps be able to learn many valuable lessons from Our Little Hindu Cousins." The utility of cross-cultural comparisons was that it, in the words of one "cousin," allowed a person "to be broad-minded, and able to see your own shortcomings."[40]

Cultivating an introspective generation ensured "that all nations grow," for those "able to see their national deficiencies" would become "the reformers and the leaders" of the future. Such volumes were therefore explicitly designed to "awaken an interest in the minds of [their] young readers" and "inspire them with a desire for further knowledge of their cousins" elsewhere. On a long enough timeline, such admonitions would eventually pay diplomatic dividends. Children raised with a healthy respect and appreciation for their "cousins" elsewhere might prove more welcoming to immigrants and less likely to resolve their conflicts violently. Hence the rhetorical question Wade asked at the end of her book on Japan: "After all, isn't one reason why we live in this big world and are so different one from another, that we may learn from each other?" If we approached one another with healthy curiosity rather than hostility, Wade pleaded, the world would become a far more harmonious place.[41]

## Inescapable Imperialism

*Our Little Indian Cousin* perfectly encapsulated the basic philosophy of Wade's (and Perkins's) children's books. Speaking of the same people that an older generation of authors had gleefully mowed down in the service of America's territorial aggrandizement, these new Progressive voices now reproached young readers for the callousness dime literature popularized among them. "We call them savages," but why behave so heartlessly when "there are many things we could copy with profit from them. Don't you think so, children?" She instead dusted off ancient maxims to guide contemporary practice. "'Live and learn' is an old saying, and I think we would do well to remember it when we read about the lives of our cousins in many lands." It was a theory that echoed across many of the era's books beyond the prodigious output of Lucy Fitch Perkins and Mary Hazelton Wade.[42]

New authors followed in their footsteps, thematically speaking, and sought to capitalize on the success of those two innovators in the field of internationalist children's literature. The most famous of these might be the Doctor Doolittle books, written by Hugh Lofting, a traumatized World War I veteran whose fantastical plots, as he put it, taught kids to transcend the "tribal prejudices" that produced conflict and sought to inspire "a new Literature of World Friendship for Children." Other influential examples, however, included the Little People Everywhere series written by Etta Blaisdell McDonald and Julia Dalrymple, the Peeps at Many Lands series, and the Children of Other Lands books. Most read as derivative of one another. Virginia Olcott's World's Children series explicitly borrowed Wade's formulation by noting that her books catered to "boys and girls eager to see how their Dutch, French, Italian, Swiss, Norwegian and Swedish cousins live." She promised that "young readers" would ultimately "feel so happily at home" and "so intimately familiar with the customs and daily living" of those overseas that the world could not help but be drawn together in fellowship. Yet even copycat authors had to find an angle designed to distinguish their own output from the growing list of competitors. For Olcott, it was veracity. She claimed a diplomatic imprimatur for her work. The fact that "the consulates of various countries have given these books their enthusiastic approval" made her mission to promote new forms of foreign relations more official. The Children of Other Lands series, meanwhile, stood out for having been written by immigrants who reflected upon their childhoods in books such as *When I Was a Boy in Greece* or *When I Was a Boy in China*.[43]

The limitations of this Progressive-era children's literature were many. For one, the books were reductionist in their logic. They tended to condense complex cultural landscapes into a very few representative characteristics. The Netherlands became a showcase for tulips, dikes, windmills, and wooden shoes. Ireland, predictably, featured bogs, shamrocks, potatoes, St. Patrick, and leprechauns. China looked like a land of silks, Confucian scholarship, and bound feet. Though rarely described in anything other than neutral terms, these were still stereotypes. Arguably they promoted only a superficial understanding of foreign countries, while downplaying important differences *within* particular ethnic groups. This problem arose in part because most "internationalist" authors rarely journeyed beyond the borders of the United States. Instead they tended to consult travel narratives and tourist guidebooks. Writers therefore imagined internationalism as something that would unfold according to America's timetable. The apparent failings of the cultural gifts movement as a whole were shared by similarly themed children's literature: World friendship was far easier to cultivate in the abstract than in reality. It was too difficult to fully dissociate from a US-centric mind-set. Even Fannie Fern Andrews, the wellspring from whom so much of this advocacy flowed, insisted that "the United States [was] peculiarly fitted to take a leading part in world activity" and "world brotherhood [was] but the expansion of American faith." Uncle Sam, in other words, was supposed to set the terms for global fellowship.[44]

Lip service paid to the virtues of diversity in these books, meanwhile, was often belied by the persistent reality of racial and socioeconomic inequality. To some extent, the period's broader political climate was to blame for these oversights. Advocating for sweeping change during World War I and in the midst of the Russian Revolution, a time of "one hundred percent Americanism" and Red Scare paranoia, could be a dangerous proposition. The likelier culprit here, however, was a basic blindness to structural inequality on the part of authors whose privileges rarely exposed them to most of the prejudices they denounced. As a result, other road maps for reimagined foreign relations, such as the era's lively Pan-African and Marxist movements, never appeared in "respectable" internationalist children's literature. Perkins, Wade, and other white bourgeois liberals, undoubtedly threatened by such radicalism, deemed those ideas "disreputable" and thus unsuitable for the eyes and minds of young readers. Not until the Depression years and beyond did a thoroughly leftist politics begin to infiltrate reading material for mainstream youth audiences.[45]

Much harder to assess than these authors' arguments, however, is their impact on young readers. The fan mail sent to publishers does not appear to have been archived. Letters to the editor were not requested or printed. The widespread absence of youth input here may be related, in part, to the didactic nature of the ideological project. Progressive reformers more generally often relied on expertise (concentrated in the hands of a select few) and its mass application. As one assessment of the period's educational initiatives went, "teacher-activists saw themselves as working for children, not alongside them." Authors, many of them with previous classroom experience, tended to treat readers as passive pupils. Their young audience members were not approached as potential collaborators, but rather as individuals who needed to be guided toward a particular pedagogical outcome. In this case, it was the inculcation of an internationalist mind-set, which would then bring about a world community devoted to diplomacy rather than war.[46]

The more "hierarchical" manner in which these authors envisioned social change makes the fruits of their labor difficult to find. One register of its influence might be found in the frequency with which youths joined organizations promoting much the same message as Lucy Fitch Perkins, Mary Hazelton Wade, and their cohort of cosmopolitan children's authors. The period from roughly 1900 to the Depression years represented a high-water mark for juvenile institution-building more broadly. Partly, this was the Progressive instinct at play, with its implicit faith in the power of regulatory bodies to effect change. It was also related to the concurrent explosion of new school construction and more stringent compulsory education statutes. Young people were being pulled off the streets and pushed out of the workforce in larger numbers. Fears of juvenile delinquency necessitated their supervision for longer periods of time. Athletics, clubs, and other professionally managed organizations presented themselves as solutions to the problem posed by idle children. And, importantly, some of the largest of these groups were devoted to multicultural causes.[47]

During periods of international tumult and perceived national emergency, those associations could be harnessed to promote larger diplomatic imperatives. The Boy Scouts of America, the Girl Scouts of the United States of America, and other closely related entities tended to dominate the institutional arm of youth internationalism. Previously studied as indicative of domestic social currents, we now see the solidly transnational sensibilities that fueled the dramatic growth and burgeoning influence of scouting (beginning with the fact that it was imported to the United States from Britain). Not only do troops exist in hundreds of countries around the world, but, from very early on, the organizations erected platforms meant to promote cross-national fraternity. Jamborees and penpalships fostered ties between children of different cultural backgrounds. Branches were founded in the Philippines, Puerto Rico, and other overseas regions occupied by US military installations, as a means to acclimatize people to indirect American rule. Scouts of various sexes and ages regularly participated in a variety of pledge drives, relief measures, and morale-boosting enterprises meant to promote particular foreign policy outcomes. In pamphlets and assembled at parade grounds, they were appealed to directly as quasi-diplomats, promoters of a global fellowship of boyhood and girlhood that would, in the aftermath of the Great War, redeem a battle-weary world. The Girl Scouts expressed it best by emphasizing international friendship, meant to keep people "in close touch and sympathy with each other, although belonging to different countries." By doing so, "they will make a real bond not merely between the Governments, but between the Peoples themselves and they will see to it ... that we have no more of War." Of course, young people did not always toe the official line. At multinational conferences, they pursued their own forms of intercultural engagement rooted in transgressive behavior that scoutmasters found distasteful.[48]

Even as adults organized American children to serve as diplomatic auxiliaries, however, US policymakers increasingly set their sights on young people overseas as fit objects for rescue. Educational initiatives, as described above, were certainly a part of the equation. But youth-directed efforts proved far more diverse. There were several reasons why. First, the growing size and authority of the federal state meant that it began to assume a host of new responsibilities. As agents from the

Children's Bureau (founded in 1912), the National Youth administration (founded in 1935) and the White House Conference on Children and Youth (founded in 1909) intermingled with members of the state and war (later defense) departments, programs directed overseas began to take young people into account. Government agencies found that focusing on children provided both a more morally sound and politically useful justification for a number of policies. Complex initiatives were made palatable to the public if sold as "child-saving" endeavors. Children were increasingly seen as icons of purity and innocence; harnessing their rhetorical power became one way for state and nonstate actors to justify US ambitions overseas. Images of suffering children became a particularly potent means by which interwar Americans could be asked to care about human rights more broadly. Or, as historian Liisa Malkki has noted, children, as avatars for "basic human goodness (and symbols of world harmony); as sufferers; as seers of truth; as ambassadors of peace; and as embodiments of the future," do important political work.[49]

World War I acted as the departure point for this phenomenon. Herbert Hoover's massive postwar relief efforts and his contributions to multiple international accords outlining basic legal protections for the world's youth read like pages pulled from Perkins and Wade. He "insisted that the love of parents for their children was a universal sentiment, one on which international collaboration could be established." Hence his 1928 campaign's promise that he would be the "Children's President." One way to skirt George Washington's injunction against foreign entanglements, Hoover and others found, was to claim that a task so noble as feeding, clothing, and caring for helpless children was fundamentally apolitical. Red Cross bodies such as the Bureau of Needy Children and the European Relief Council established transatlantic toeholds for American political and commercial interests under the banner of child welfare. Children aided by the United States, moreover, would, they assumed, grow up to become citizens more positively disposed toward a beneficent Uncle Sam. The organization's youth auxiliary, the Junior Red Cross, also mobilized American schoolchildren during the 1910s and 1920s to raise money, collect food, and gather used clothing for their less fortunate peers overseas. As a result, US children were thinking more globally and asked to more regularly imagine their nation's role as both world policeman and planetary patron.[50]

Figure 4.2. Putting the principles of internationalist children's literature into practice under the auspices of the Junior Red Cross, millions of American kids shipped care packages and correspondence to disadvantaged children around the globe. Acquaintanceships with the world's people were meant to produce peace, but the program also helped reinforce an international hierarchy, which placed the United States atop other "child-like" supplicant nations. As this float proclaims, American youths pledged to protect childhoods "the world over." Library of Congress Prints and Photographs Division.

Other forms of fellowship advocated for by some of the era's children's authors also came into existence prior to World War II. Educational institutions celebrated International Good-Will Day. At the behest of organizations like the Woman's Peace Party and the League for a Durable Peace, school cafeterias held "Bazaars of Nations," where costumed children sold wares representing the artifacts of particular cultures. Children's International Summer Villages facilitated cross-cultural connectivity by allowing vacationing American students to host schoolchildren from around the world. Various youth groups and public schools organized correspondence campaigns and directed them toward the goal of building international understanding. To name only a few, the aforementioned Junior Red Cross, the American Field Service, the Boy Scouts, the Girl Scouts, the Camp Fire Girls, the National

Catholic Welfare Council, the National Council of Churches, and the American Friends Service Committee all instituted transnational youth penpal and student exchange programs. The Carnegie endowment was particularly active in funding International Alcoves at public libraries, along with Model Leagues of Nations and International Relations clubs at high schools around the country.[51]

Surveys of university students during the 1920s and 1930s also revealed, in the words of one social scientist at the time, "a decided trend toward 'international-mindedness.'" Each "chart and every table indicates this," he continued, and "it stands out in bold relief." When asked in straw polls and campus surveys, "the young usually came out on the side of enlightened internationalism." Nonbinding referendums showed consistent backing for the League of Nations, the World Court, and other institutions symbolizing a commitment to peace and diplomacy rather than war. In a similar vein, multiple campus communities successfully revolted against bylaws mandating ROTC military-style drills and training. Observers also thought that intercollegiate conferences like the National Student Committee for the Limitation of Armaments and the Intercollegiate Liberal League were well attended. Eventually these likeminded organizations merged, forming the National Student Forum. Its organ, a publication called *The New Student*, circulated numerous essays and petitions seeking to construct a transnational youth movement that would unite students from around the world in a campaign for cross-cultural friendship. So too did school newspapers from a number of universities regularly publish editorials expressing at least a vague desire for enhanced international cooperation.[52]

But it is exceedingly difficult to draw a straight line connecting the work of peace-minded Progressive-era children's authors and the multiple institutional expressions of liberal internationalist sentiment. The causal "smoking gun" can be an elusive instrument. And there were always countervailing impulses toward youth jingoism, not to mention apathy. In the case of college students, for example, campus newspapers reveal a far greater obsession with athletics and socializing than international subject matter. Ultimately, we can only point to a remarkable similarity in rhetoric that suffused such books and at least a portion of the period's rampant youth activism. Organizations that stressed the basic similarities that united the human family and expressed skepticism about the inherent legitimacy of US-led empire-building projects certainly sounded a great deal like Lucy Fitch Perkins, Mary Hazelton Wade, and other progenitors of the push to promote juvenile cosmopolitanism. And yet, for all of their material and emotional investment in the project, it is hard to find concrete evidence of lasting success. The League of Nations foundered. Nationalism and militarism soon plunged the world back into war on a scale never before seen. Many of the youth organizations so nobly committed to global camaraderie found themselves, in the 1940s and 1950s, repurposed to promote American patriotism. When viewed from this angle, Progressive-era visions of an international order remade by children raised to scorn prejudice only seem quixotic.

From another point of view, however, it is in fact a credit to these authors that the ideas they espoused—initially so controversial—look to us like something approaching common sense. What was at the time a radical break with the almost universally pro-expansion politics of mass-market children's media has now become the basis for what constitutes, among a sizeable swath of the nation's parents, an education in basic human decency. Try to live in peace with the world's people; be accepting of one another's differences; work to overcome prejudice: To the extent that children's literature today engages with the subject of foreign relations, these are its basic lessons. They are directly descended from evangelical and secular publications for young people disseminated around the turn of the twentieth century. If a "widening acceptance of foreigners within mainstream American life" has arisen in the last one hundred years or so, this juvenile literature must surely share some credit for the achievement.[53]

But it would require time for such ideas to take firmer root. The path to realizing what one reformer called "the international mind" was a tortuous one. Oppositional cultural pressures stigmatized cosmopolitanism as "sissyish." Series fiction authors often set up road blocks, creating characters who mocked the "long sentences and oily phrases" of "peacespouters" and urged kids to retain faith in the hard-nosed "diplomacy of a sixteen-inch gun and the statesmanship in a ton of steel." World War II also intervened, as most internationalists conceded that violence would be necessary to cut out the cancer of fascism. There was, therefore, hardly any slow but inexorable national journey toward greater global understanding and racial enlightenment. No genuine and deep-seated dedication to toleration could capture the imagination of the rising generation without direct investment on the part of youths themselves.[54]

More young people, that is, had to want to change the conversation surrounding America's role in the wider world. Junior citizens needed to feel—as they had during periods of settler colonial growth and overseas expansion—like a vital part of the diplomatic process. They yearned for more room on the political stage, more of a microphone to amplify their own voices. This was why one man reminisced that the "average youth" found the well-intentioned recommendations of his parents and teachers "dull": because in cheap fiction, "the boy . . . became, to himself, the centre of the universe—the world was his." It was what Edward Stratemeyer meant in declaring that "a wide-awake lad has no patience with that which he puts down as a 'study book' in disguise. He demands real flesh and blood heroes who do something."[55]

Such insights escaped the attention of Progressive children's authors. Rather than offering their youthful audience a platform for creative expression as had dime novels, series fiction, and amateur journals, world friendship publications instead presumed to lecture a largely inert clientele. The irony here, of course, is that some of the first systematically anti-imperialist children's texts were written by authors with a thoroughly micromanagerial or "colonial" approach to young readers—partly a side effect of the rigidly routinist behaviorism then coming into vogue among childcare experts. Therefore, even with powerful allies in the adult establishment, well-intentioned internationalists still found their ideas outpaced and their sales outstripped by media forms more popular with children themselves. The numbers are a staggering reminder of this fact. By 1930, an American Library Association study asking kids in thirty-four cities about their favorite books found that 98 percent religiously read "trash literature." Rather than their parents, teachers, and librarians telling them what they should consume, young people drifted to books more aggressive in stressing adolescent agency.[56]

The genre steadily becoming predominant among juvenile readers was derided by cultural gatekeepers as "pulp fiction." Incensed internationalists raged that it undercut their influence and made the United States "a jungle inhabited by the greatest aggregation of literate ignoramuses ever brought together under one flag." It was a debatable assessment, but the term "jungle" certainly rang true. The era's pulps invigorated youthful investment in American expansionism by transporting them to the tropical climates of Central America, South America, the Caribbean, and beyond. Kids themselves helped keep empire alive by scorning cosmopolitan literature and rallying around an imperially inflected popular culture. At virtually the same moment when reform-minded writers struggled to expunge the fetishization of violence from children's reading material, fiction firms continued to produce stories applauding aggression as necessary to the country's conduct of its foreign relations. The tensions between those two increasingly distinct strands within youth publishing would only escalate as the twentieth century progressed.[57]

5

## Dollar Diplomacy for the Price of a Few Nickels

Steve Yeager "had not quit his job, it had quit him." The young man, "still a boy" really, once rode herd along the Dry Sandy Valley for the Lone Star Cattle Company. But then settlers "homesteaded the water holes" and built "barb-wire fences across the range," driving away the livestock. That was bad enough. Uncle Sam, however, finished the job after he "sliced off most of the acreage still left and called it a forest reserve." Denied the land necessary for grazing, "the Lone Star Outfit had thrown up its hands, sold its holdings, and moved to Los Angeles to live." Did anyone, however, stop to consider the case of Steve Yeager? The poor lad, "who did not know Darwin from a carburetor, had by process of evolution been squeezed out of the occupation he had followed all of his" young life. Soon, "the joyous whoop of the puncher would not much longer be heard." Such were the boy's gloomy thoughts as he wandered the desert Southwest.[1]

Hark! In the distance! Was that the cry of someone in danger? Steve's morose musings were quickly interrupted by the scene he stumbled across. There, in the clearing just ahead, a "short, fat man with a cigar in his mouth" stood by while two ruffians struggled to subdue a beautiful woman. The young cowboy "did not stop to reason out the situation." Delay could mean the difference between life and death for the girl. Instead, he "shot forward," and "all the weight and muscle of one hundred and seventy pounds of live cowpuncher" connected with one scoundrel's head. "Villain No. 1 went to the ground as if a battering-ram had hit him between the eyes." Steve then turned to Villain No. 2. "'Lay hands on a lady, will you?'" he shouted. "'What's eatin' you? We ain't hurtin' her any, you mutt,'" retorted the rogue. But Steve was in no mood for conversation. Fists flew, and in short order, the man joined his fiendish friend in the deep sleep of unconsciousness. Our hero then turned to see if his damsel in distress was well.[2]

She began to laugh. The man chomping on a cigar, now furious, bellowed "Cut!" A nearby camera crew, concealed by some scrub, stopped rolling. Aides quickly raced to revive the men recently knocked out. And still the girl could not stop laughing. "'What d'you know about that, Billy?'" went her smiling remark. "'The rube swallowed it all. You gotta raise my salary.'" The movie set was now pandemonium. Cinematographers, costume designers, and extras surrounded Steve Yeager, "all expostulating at once." That's when he realized his mistake. The men nursing their concussions "were dressed wonderfully and amazingly as cowpunchers, but they were painted frauds in spite of the careful ostentation of their costumes." Actors, in other words. A stunt coordinator joked that this "real" fight scene looked better than anything the cast had ever put to film: "'Funny you lads can't ever pull off a fall like that!'" But the director was less amused. "'Say, you Rip Van Winkle,'" he remonstrated, "'think we came out here for the ozone? You spoiled the whole scene.'"³

With a sheepish grin, Steve fell to apologizing. "'It's on me, compadre. I'm a rube and anything else you like. And I sure am sorry for going off half-cocked.'" After the dust had dissipated, however, the "rescued" actress noticed her would-be champion. He "wore his splendid youth so jauntily and yet so casually that the gaze of a girl was likely to be drawn in his direction a second and a third time." "Fifteen years in the saddle had given him a toughness of fiber no city dweller could possibly equal." The boy had the right "look," there was no doubt about it. Therefore, he was offered a small role in the picture. "Sometimes Steve smiled" at the thought. "The director's ideas had largely been absorbed in New York from reading Western fiction." But, "so long as he drew down his two-fifty a day and had plenty of fun doing it," he "was no stickler for naked realism."⁴

Then things truly became interesting. While working on location in Arizona, Steve and his fellow actors were suddenly swept into the Mexican Revolution. Gonzales, an evil warlord, crossed the border, seized the film's cast, and held them hostage. This time, our cowboy hero rode to the rescue in earnest. Along with a detachment of US cavalry, Yeager freed the captives, deposed Gonzales, and installed the far friendlier General Culvera in his place. After those eventful few days, the young ranger came to some realizations about American power. A cruel quasi-dictatorial Mexican like Gonzales could never be anything but "'a savage, a child at statecraft.'" Steve, on the other hand, embodied a "great country," one that, "'if [it] should ever become aroused,'" could "'stamp men like him out as one does a spider.'" Therefore, at the point of a bayonet, the newly minted local chieftain promised that "'from to-day you shall see a new policy.'" As he solemnly swore, "'I mean to cultivate friendship with the United States, to see that the Mexico I rescue from tyrants is modeled upon that glorious republic.'" The Yankee boy was, in effect, credited with the redemption of a troubled neighboring nation.[5]

This wild tale of borderlands bravery was published by *The Argosy* in November 1915. One story among many printed by what had once been a didactic magazine known as *The Golden Argosy*, "Men in the Raw," as the title went, signaled several new directions in juvenile publishing. The audience for the reimagined *Argosy*—young people, namely—stayed the same. But its content changed. Most notable was the tongue-in-cheek transformation of the West into an open-air motion picture studio. Steve Yeager, the cowboy, complained about unemployment. No longer a civilizing agent locked in titanic struggle with Indian savagery, the best he could do was earn a few dollars a day playing the rough facsimile of a pioneer. Even that bit part, however, as Steve grumbled, had mostly been dreamed up by misguided studio executives. Where was the dime-novel frontier, which had been sold to earlier generations as a deeply consequential imperial arena?[6]

A year later, as if to drive the point home, *The Argosy* invited its readers to sound off on whether they wanted to read another settlerist tale ever again. "Have you soured on cowboys, the range, and Western stories?" the editors asked. Recently, they noted, "a big show called the 'Stampede' went broke at Coney Island . . . because not enough people were interested in rough riding, steer roping, and bronco busting to pay expenses." Perhaps boys had tired of "this so-called 'Western stuff.'" Fan mail touching upon the frontier seemed split. Some refused to quit the genre and wrote passionately in its defense. Others, however, like John S. from New Bedford, Massachusetts, expressed their exasperation with a dead letter. "It is simply punk," he declared, "and I regret to see my favorite magazine printing such buncombe."[7]

What, then, would young readers wish to see instead? Here too, Steve Yeager rode to the rescue. When the idle cowboy reinvented himself as a soldier of fortune, someone willing to invade a nearby nation and involve himself in its internal affairs, he revealed a thematic transformation in juvenile literature. From the early 1900s until the 1930s, authors increasingly asked their young audiences to become invested in a more interventionist American foreign policy. This was, after all, the moment when the United States became the world's leading exporter of goods and capital, an era characterized by dollar diplomacy and ultimatums issued from the decks of gunboats. The early twentieth century witnessed the confluence of multiple trends that necessitated a more active American state overseas. Corporations carved out fiefdoms abroad once consumer tastes evolved to include bananas, coffee, cacao, and other "fruits of empire." Thinkers theorized that endemic labor unrest and the perceived problem of industrial overproduction could be ameliorated by accessing foreign markets. The War of 1898 had planted the American flag in colonies and protectorates around the world. Plans for a US-built Panama Canal required new naval bases and a willingness to impinge upon the sovereignty of other nations. Theodore Roosevelt's corollary to the Monroe Doctrine maintained America's absolute right to police the Western Hemisphere. Protection for the country's rapidly expanding investments throughout the Caribbean and Latin America demanded the deployment of both marines and customs officers. And, as the story of Steve Yeager helped illustrate, revolution in Mexico and Central America spurred Uncle Sam to invade several times for the purpose of protecting the lives of his citizens and the security of their property.[8]

All of these events possess rich histories unto themselves. Authors of youth literature, however, acknowledged that a long-term national presence in Latin America (and beyond) was not sustainable unless the culture industry could persuade young people as to the logic of US leadership. A new crop of stories therefore appeared to help junior Americans navigate an increasingly puzzling tangle of banana wars and business ventures overseas. The "diplomacy of trade and investment" burst out of corporate boardrooms and into children's bedrooms. The "combination of bonds and battleships" characterizing the era were channeled into texts meant to inculcate among juvenile readers a sense of their future duties as hemispheric stewards.[9]

Some of these tales took the form of series fiction and replicated Edward Stratemeyer's influential work with the Spanish-American War. But just as much juvenile foreign relations circulated within the new and increasingly popular genre of the pulps. Pulp fiction, so-called for the rough wood-pulp paper upon which it was printed, directly descended from the late nineteenth century's dime novels. Dime publishers that had folded during the "Fiction Wars" of the 1890s often reconstituted themselves as producers of pulp. Cheap to manufacture and cheap to distribute, the pulps began to swamp newsstands with the appearance of their first iteration, *The Argosy*. By the 1920s, and with an estimated thirty million readers per month, they were—barring newspapers—the nation's most widely circulating publications. Distribution networks next went global, introducing cheap fiction to far-flung audiences and making them transnational texts. Some of the era's most famous characters—including Tarzan, Zorro, Conan the Barbarian, and The Shadow—jumped out of the pulps to become household names worldwide.[10]

More to the point here, however, was the fact that the pulps were wildly popular with American adolescents. Historians have not always appreciated this fact. They are often described as "adult" reading, the pastime of poorly educated factory workers and office girls. But that characterization largely derived from highbrow screeds attempting to demonize pulp fiction by associating it with female "frivolity" and "imbecile" immigrants. Harold Hersey, however, one of the most prolific editors in the business, claimed that "the largest portion of pulp magazine readers were children or adolescents." The magazines' short sentences, monosyllabic prose, and simple diction were meant, by design, to attract inexperienced young readers. Erle Stanley Gardner, author of countless pulp stories (and creator of the Perry Mason series) likewise posited that high school students were the biggest group of readers of the era's cheap fiction. Cultural critics similarly pointed to "substantial clans of American boys" as the pulps' principal fans. Even the Communist Party of the United States complained that their youth outreach efforts were frustrated by young people's hopeless addiction to sensationalistic fiction (though Soviet sympathizers did deem Tarzan acceptable because the character, while an orphaned aristocrat, had been raised by proletarian apes). Too many teenagers would not touch any other literature.[11]

To say such publications were easy to read is of course not to suggest, as their detractors did, that they were simplistic. In fact, the pulps became highly specialized publications that dealt with complex issues. They encompassed over two hundred titles marketed to niche fans of detective stories, romance, and science fiction. Among the most popular of these subgenres, however, was the adventure story. Between the pulps' brightly colored cover pages, meant to attract a buyer's eye, American protagonists departed their nation's shores in search of excitement abroad. There were mining engineers in Mexico. There were soldiers stationed in Haiti. There were mercenaries toppling dictators in Honduras. There were men "building radio stations in queer corners of the world." And there were cowboys imported to every part of the British Empire for the purpose of pacifying dark-skinned Natives. The occupation of each was prosaic enough, pointedly so, for, in the words of one such magazine, it was "the ordinary man who is the real knight errant of modern times, the man whose courage inspires him to sacrifice himself for others in the performance of his duty." But their "routine" work, when placed in transnational context, assumed added importance. They were collectively called "American empire builders," "he-men with iron in their blood and steel in their backbones," who struck out across the world in an effort to secure America's ascendancy. A diverse cast of characters, they nevertheless united around one common theme: the unquestionable right of the United States, now a global power, to involve itself in the affairs of distant people and places.[12]

Cheap fiction charged itself with translating, in terms that juvenile readers could appreciate, Secretary of State Richard Olney's bombastic 1895 claim that "today the United States is practically sovereign on this continent and its fiat is law upon the subjects to which it confines its interposition." Which was to say that the world ought to familiarize itself with America's willingness and capacity to assert its authority internationally. For the price of a few nickels, young people could be coached in the justifications underpinning the muscular foreign relations of global dollar diplomacy—policies of often racially motivated armed intrusion and paternalistically minded financial receivership. If, as has been said, this was the era in which the Monroe Doctrine became "virtually a canon of American political religion," then inquiry into the cultural processes that produced its apotheosis seems necessary. A wide variety of influences surely played their part. Underappreciated, however, has been the impact of children's media in fortifying the brawnier Monroe Doctrine that emerged around the turn of the twentieth century.[13]

Internationalists and pacifists may have simultaneously been working to cultivate among young America a more cosmopolitan outlook. But, for many children, the overwhelming popularity of pulp fiction meant their continuing immersion in a culture committed to the violent enactment of imperial agendas overseas. "Our stories will not be namby-pamby tales that leave a weak taste in the mouth," promised one such publication. A more assertive America required the "tales of adventure . . . in foreign climes" that befitted a perceived uptick in its global prominence. "Not that I want to preach or run a geography class," another editor joked, but, with the world's axis steadily tilting toward the United States, it was time for "stories which familiarize the reader with some section out of life, some spot on the globe, [or] some industry" vital to the country's deepening footprint abroad. Mass fiction thus became an important arena where hemispheric power relations played out.[14]

## Series Books, Pulp Fiction, and American Boys in "Greaser Land"

From the 1890s onward, juvenile periodicals brimmed with belligerent declarations of America's growing grandeur. "This great country of ours," crowed the *Army and Navy Weekly*, "has reached a point where interest cannot be confined to internal affairs. It is ready to branch out." In the United States, a "spirit of unrest" and the "desire to extend its empire to every part of the world" was "slowly but surely obtaining a foothold among our people." If this mission to make America "one of the grandest countries on the globe" were to succeed, however, "it is upon the boys of the present day that we must depend." Authors therefore imagined themselves as both cheerleaders and tour guides. They would see to it that young readers "acquire an early interest in our national defenses" and all else "necessary to carry our flag to other seas," while also providing any information required to manage new peoples and places entering the nation's sphere of influence. In his first address to Congress as president, Theodore Roosevelt posited that, "Whether we desire it or not, we must henceforth recognize that we have international duties no less than international rights." Popular kids' literature in the ensuing decades mostly worked to ensure that budding Americans *would* desire those duties.[15]

Series fiction of the sort pioneered by Edward Stratemeyer helped lead this charge. After the War of 1898 and US-Philippine War wound down, Stratemeyer simply turned his attention to new fields for American expansion. The most important of these were Latin America and the circum-Caribbean. After 1898, Stratemeyer argued, the Western Hemisphere seemed to have been thrown open to adventurous and ambitious Americans. In saying as much, he articulated for adolescents the messaging that other imperial evangelists had popularized among adult audiences. "The race that gained control of North America," John Fiske thundered, "must [now] become the dominant race of the world." Josiah Strong, in his 1885 best seller *Our Country*, sounded a similar note. He called the Americas a gift from God meant to train and strengthen the Anglo-Saxon race. The first step in the realization of Uncle Sam's global manifest destiny, Strong suggested, would be the conquest of Latin America. Combined armies of financial and fundamentalist missionaries might "move down upon Mexico, down upon Central and South America," and then further still until they had "people[d] the world with better and finer material." The "feebler and more abject races" already occupying the region would be swept aside. Likewise, naval strategists like Alfred Thayer Mahan insisted that national security and the "manifest destiny of the Republic *in the broadest sense*" would necessitate Latin American acquiescence. In arguing that the conquest of one continent had only prepared white Americans to subdue the next, theorists mirrored a shift in children's media from settler colonial dime novels to the early twentieth century's more globally inflected series books and pulp fiction. Now, however, authors helped US youths reimagine empire as less a question of taking territory (as had been true in the West, the Philippines, Guam, and Puerto Rico) and more a matter of indirect influence, investment, fiscal supervision, and narrowly targeted interventionism.[16]

Stratemeyer's contemporaneous "Pan-American Series" exemplified the new articles of faith articulated by prominent political economists. He emphasized the profit and prestige that awaited young people willing to seek their fortunes in foreign markets. The stories follow several boys on a school trip through Central and South America, but they read like prospectuses written by an investment firm. Stilted conversations drew attention to the munificence of financial schemers headquartered in the United States. "Peru to-day is on the border of a great awakening," the narrator claimed. "American capital is building railroads, developing mines, and discovering untold wealth in beds of coal, nitrates, oil, and other commodities." It was, in other words, "a country of great possibilities." By the end of the story, Stratemeyer's characters resolved to "some day come down here and go to work, [as] the resources of South America have struck them very forcibly ever since they had come on the journey." Early twentieth-century series books expanded the scope of young readers' sense of where US interests lay. The neocolonial nature of growing American speculation beyond its borders became a particularly prominent fixation of the era's juvenile literature. Plots helped concretize an abstraction like capitalism by purporting to show its transformative power.[17]

The books were just as quick to explain why no one need object that American corporations were looting the resources of other countries. Foreign wealth should remain open to US exploration and exploitation given the local population's idleness. Native guides leading boy-protagonists through their respective communities were heard to grumble that "the Yankees know not how to take it easy." Latin Americans whined that the *gringos* "want to walk, or run, or ride, or do something all the time." Locals usually spoke only to self-indict: "my countrymen," one admitted, "like only to rest, to sit and smoke, to sleep, or to talk." Reverting to the instructional tone of a guidebook, the narrator halted to assess the man's words. "These wild savages have always been what they are today—willing to work a little, hunt a little, sleep and dream a good deal, and never to be entirely trusted." In Mexico, "the great mass of the people are pretty primitive," and the country would never prosper until populated by "a race of steady, patient workers"; the "very atmosphere of the place suggested languor and inaction." South America was called "the land of 'Mañana (to-morrow),'" a place where "no one wishes to work too hard to-day." Admiring locals thus stared agape at the "feverish character" of the Yankee boys' activities and remarked that "you Americans will turn the world upside down some day!" There was supposed to be a "bracing effect" that "the presence of clean-cut Americans, who always went at a thing as if they meant it," had on perennially "vacillating, hesitating Latins."[18]

A tour of the West Indies confirmed those claims about a world largely populated by loafers. The key to promoting the steadying effect of American influence involved renditions of the region's ineptitude. Ideas about the United States as a civilized, stable, and cohesive country could blossom in the minds of youths when defined against its antithesis south of the border. This "must be a lazy-man's land," declared one boy upon his arrival in Puerto Rico. The authoritative voice of their teacher stepped in only to flesh out his pupil's prejudice. "To a certain extent it is," he lectured, "for many of the Porto Ricans have the habit of putting off till to-morrow what should be done to-day." His comments, however, had a happy ending. "San Juan used to be an awfully dirty town ... but as soon as our soldiers took hold they made the citizens clean up." Responding in a chorus of voices designed to draw in the audience as well, the boys could only marvel that "American energy must open their eyes!" Passages such as these characterized a generation of juvenile series fiction and reflect a broad-based effort on the part of adult authors to promote a sense of the rich rewards opened up to young people as a result of America's systematic expansion across the Western Hemisphere and beyond. What has been called an encompassing "culture of dollar diplomacy," which supposedly swapped bullets for bucks as an instrument of civilization, possessed its evangelists among adolescents. In matter-of-fact language, juvenile readers were told that "in any country to the south of the United States," we "must do police duty" to protect the "American capitalists who had invested large amounts of money in developing the great natural resources" of the region. Disaster might ensue should "foreign investors no longer feel that their capital was safe."[19]

Stories repeatedly returned to the redemptive power of American money (and money managers). The fictional country of Guanama—a stand-in for Central America more broadly—was certainly depicted as the beneficiary of both US capital and technocracy. We know this because the two Americans charged with administering the economy never seemed to talk about much else. "'We came to Guanama years ago—when she was a God-forsaken, half-governed little republic,'" and since then, "'we've saved her; we've built her up; we've prevented her from being gobbled by European powers; we've worked and we've slaved and we've done everything that mortals could do!'" Now, "masses of American money were coming into the country; new railroads were projected and even building. Towns were starting, factories were building up, and ice-plants and electric lines" too. With US assistance, "the

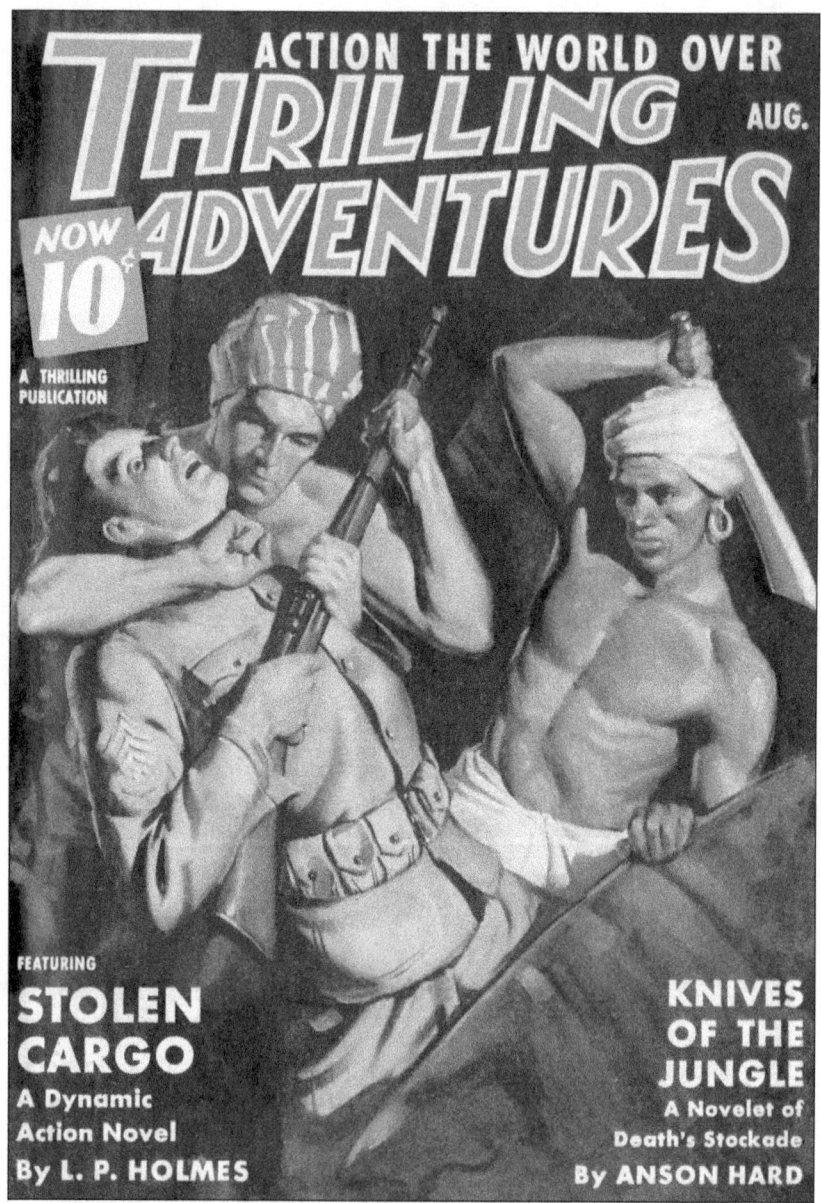

Figure 5.1. Pulp magazines increasingly placed Americans in exotic locations overseas in order to emphasize their country's growing global influence. *Thrilling Adventures* 30, no. 3 (August 1939).

little country was on the verge of unheard of prosperity and peace!" It was all possible, moreover, despite "'these condemned brown idiots,'" the country's bungling Native population. But with a splendid "American discipline" now "on its way to enforcement," the "beautiful inconsequentiality which characterizes the Guanaman people" could no longer impede progress.[20]

Nothing captured the sneering contempt that soaked the pages of pulps quite like the admission that the desires and demands of Latin Americans themselves were ultimately irrelevant. Yet for young readers, this was often little more than the dissemination of a dismissiveness already circulating among adult policymakers. Economic development among the "rotten little countries" comprising Latin America, scoffed one assistant secretary of state, could only succeed if "carried out without annoyance or molestation from the natives." Collectively, then, these stories became what are termed "conditioning structures," which help to embed a society's particular values or ethics by lending them an air of incontrovertibility. Pulps portrayed capitalist relations between peoples as a desirable universal standard, while depicting resistance to American entrepreneurship as both deviant and demanding redress.[21]

Countless tales cheered a new hierarchy taking shape within the nations of the Western Hemisphere. Latin American leaders—routinely demeaned as squabbling children—were being replaced by white experts trained in the United States and shipped abroad. The young men who performed heroic deeds were now often financial advisers managing capital, electricians constructing power grids, planters applying the principles of agricultural science, and railroad engineers building transit systems. Their training and proficiency gave them power over their dark-skinned charges, now mostly reimagined as prospective labor pools. American professionals, with their technical talent, were portrayed as the natural intellectual superiors to Latin Americans and showed no hesitation in ordering them around. All of these plot points exposed Progressivism as a double-edged sword. Some dreamers did campaign for a more enlightened children's literature, but many more perched in the pulps and preached a faith in credentials to legitimate the displacement of "ignorant" indigenous populations. Consent and democratic process could not be relied upon to promote development south of the United States. Instead, it was an undertaking, young readers were reminded, for the nations (and races) educated to the task and capable of the work. Put in the plain words of children's authors, "the greasers have got to take a back seat in this part of the world. We are a superior race, and they must bow to the inevitable." Books and periodicals repeatedly told youths that even an Open Door sometimes required a little kicking in.[22]

Yet, as this literature emphasized, those who rose to accomplish the tasks that Latin Americans could not or would not were little more than kids themselves. Barely pubescent foremen arrived from the United States and imposed order where chaos reigned. Ranches, mines, oil fields, banana plantations, and government offices would now turn a profit thanks to the executive acumen of white adolescents. Authors begged their readers to see these arrangements as entirely plausible. Of the "Go Ahead Boys" and their mastery of fully grown Mexican miners, writer Ross Kay simply said, "they are normal, healthy American boys fond of travel and adventure and naturally are meeting experiences such as come to men doing what they are doing." He had "no desire to make his young heroes either preternaturally brilliant or possessed of too precocious brains." It was simply that the "self-reliance, determination," and "ability to decide quickly and to act promptly" which American boys "acquired in the early years" naturally placed them in positions of authority over "lesser" peoples overseas. When, as at a Venezuelan oil platform, "the peons were childish," "ruminated young derrick man Tough Haggert," it took little to outwit them. Youths like him, "with blue eyes, frank and clear," which "stamped his race as did his Nordic features," spent the pages of short stories gleefully crushing incipient union organizing. What has been termed a discourse of "race management"— the "science" of enhancing efficiency by exploiting perceived biological distinctions between workers—found a happy home in the pages of juvenile fiction. The American expertise these books celebrated consisted of technical training but also an innate ability to "handle" heterogenous minions.[23]

Thus, troublesome employees like a "Pedro Gato" quickly learned the folly of crossing duos like the "Young Engineers." "The first thing you'll have to learn to do," insubordinate underlings learned, "will be to treat us with the proper courtesy." Blows rained, "sending Greaser bull[ies] to the earth" until they became compliant. Belligerent boys were the proud servants of capitalist transformation, for their "hands had slashed the scar of civilization" within wildernesses beyond America's borders. But they did not simply build things. Practicing the art of race-based management appeared here as its own contribution to progress. In fact, some publications acted as recruiters for the process. Pulp magazines like *Wide World Adventures* contained sections offering suggestions to young people curious about careers in South America and elsewhere. Youth fiction, meanwhile, transformed transnational business ventures into a reasonable expectation for growing Americans. Even Stratemeyer's personal correspondence with enthusiastic readers reiterated the essential role the United States must play in unlocking the world's untapped wealth. Replying to a boy who asked for information about a career as a mining engineer abroad, the author observed that "we are undoubtedly living in the greatest commercial age this old world of ours has ever witnessed." But, he emphasized, it required the ingenuity and pluck characteristic of Americans to succeed.[24]

It might also necessitate the persuasive power of military force. Boys' books frequently saw characters commit to deposing unfriendly regimes. Dollar diplomacy, which its practitioners often described as an enlightened alternative to war, had a sharp edge. Neighboring nations that abused Uncle Sam's "generosity" or seized the property of American corporations might find themselves attacked or occupied by US forces. Children's authors, however, were always careful to stress the necessity of these interventions. Series fiction and pulp stories encouraged young readers to think of American influence abroad as invited, advantageous, and, given the helplessness of foreign peoples, even moral. "In dealing with contumacious South American states," proclaimed one pulp story about a naval ensign operating another country's treasury, "their great sister republic occasionally finds it necessary to employ what might be described as strong-arm diplomacy." The right of the United States "to seize a custom house and pocket all the receipts until the amount of the claims has been collected" did not depend on whether or not some puny "mushroom republic desired it" but only that "a great sister republic concluded that such a course was necessary." Coyote Pete, a frontier stereotype and mercenary in Mexico, expressed a similar idea. Speaking of the interminable cycle of revolutions that seemed to plague Latin America, he could only conclude that "they sure do need our restrainin' hand." Or, as another writer announced, "it required a strong hand to rule such a people" as lived south of the border. The implications of this language were clear: American youths should become comfortable with their country's mastery of Latin America as a matter of course. If "Greaser Government" meant "anarchy, lawlessness," and a "disregard for either the lives or property of people," there was no other choice.²⁵

First, young readers had been asked to imagine themselves as instrumental to the conquest of a continent. Then, they joined the ranks of soldiers liberating Cuba and the Philippines. Now, authors coaxed kids to accept a dramatically expanded role for the republic in new corners of the globe. Because Mexico was "a hotbed of incurable anarchy," the "United States *must* put an end to the numberless outrages" endangering lives and livelihoods; if some South American "dagos" tried to gun down Americans, then "the United States government would blow the whole blamed country out of existence." Though an earlier generation of writers insisted that America's most important mission was the eradication of savagery at home, now "the United States [could] no longer be called a civilized and honorable nation if Army and Navy men" failed "to uphold our government and the rights of American citizens" wherever they went. And, while Indians had once prompted youths to threaten barbarous foes with summary extermination, boys now strutted through places like Honduras to menacingly declare: "'I hope you will do nothing that will bring down upon you the displeasure of the United States Government.'" Pulps announced the birth of a new diplomatic principle, one that superseded all international law: the "'perfect right of an American to protect the property and interests of others of his nationality.'" An invigorated Uncle Sam assured juvenile readers that he "'looks after his citizens, no matter how humble or in how remote a corner of the world they may be.'"²⁶

That newly announced creed first appeared close to home, even if it quickly radiated outward. The 1910 Mexican Revolution, encompassing a series of violent regional rebellions, coups, and counter-coups (in which the United States was deeply implicated), acted as a catalyst for discussion among young readers regarding the propriety of unilateral American intercession. With newspapers between 1914 and 1917 reporting on President Woodrow Wilson's various invasions at Veracruz and northern Mexico, authors translated events for junior citizens. One popular series, written under the name Lieutenant Howard Payson, chronicled the adventures of a group of Boy Scouts from Long Island. One of the boys' entrepreneurial uncles owned property south of the border and asked the group to guard his ranch from insurgents during the Revolution. While attending to that task, they became swept up in the struggle and ultimately assisted in the roundup of rabble-rousers. Witness to much belligerence among a dizzying array of political factions, the Eagle Patrol Scouts could only chuckle over the "foolish Mexicans fighting among themselves." Their main concern was the question of when the conflict would "go too far," whereupon "Uncle Sam, in his character of policeman for the Western Hemisphere, might have to try to restore peace to [a] harassed country."[27]

The contours of the Mexican conflict are described only vaguely in this literature, lending a sense of inconsequence to the whole affair. A multifaceted situation was reduced to little more than "gangs of Greasers" hoping to "leap across the Rio Grande, do a little gentlemanly looting," and "murder a few gringos if need be." Authors portrayed American intervention as the only alternative to anarchy, given depictions of Mexicans as incompetent and timid. Heroes with names like "Flume McCool" said that Latinos largely resembled "little children" with their "primitive ignorance" and an "ability to be diverted, fascinated, amused, and hoodwinked," while manly mining engineers like "Red Richards" declared that "most greasers are cowards." Battles between rival factions, meanwhile, were rendered as little more than comic spectacle. Witness to one such action, a troop of young scouts sarcastically exclaimed that "from the racket, you'd think they'd done something real wonderful." The boys agreed that all the sound and fury signified nothing save that "Spanish-American dispositions are ever excitable, and whatever they do is generally accomplished with much noise and confusion." Eventually entering the fray themselves in order to protect a few defenseless peasants, the teenaged combatants gun down countless Mexican partisans. "I guess we're showing the natives"—regularly referred to as "greasers"—"what Boy Scouts can do, eh?" Force, it seemed, was the only language that inferior races could be made to understand, and now, gloated these authors, "'the United States possesses force enough to bring all Mexicans to their senses.'" Payson's messaging portrayed violent conflict as an invigorating experience for young men and a redemptive one for racial inferiors abroad. American force of arms had once pacified a continent. Now, boys were told, that same influence would be brought to bear against the seemingly trivial squabbling of nearby nations. By the early twentieth century, a more muscular Monroe Doctrine found ready expression in much of the reading marketed to the nation's youth.[28]

Other authors consistently echoed these themes and images. Fremont B. Deering's Border Boys series and H. Irving Hancock's Uncle Sam's Boys series amounted to predictable extensions of this approach. The Border Boys, in one adventure, found themselves surrounded and ambushed by a crew of "swarthy Mexicans . . . dark-skinned and black-orbed . . . with villainous countenances." Yet despite being outnumbered and outgunned, the boys had little trouble outwitting and escaping their enemies. In the battle that ensued, "the Mexicans [found] out as their kind has done before, that a party of brave Americans is more than a match for twice their number in a fight." Or, as another set of boy heroes declared: "Twelve Americans are enough to lick fifty Mexicans!" For, unlike their foes whose "boiling Latin blood" was characterized by "meaningless frenzies of rage," the Americans calmly "marshaled their faculties and set themselves to [a] task." Irrational emotional display characterized inferior races. "Black Ramon," for example, one particularly "bad hombre," convulsed in "a fit of black Latin rage not so very different from the tantrums we occasionally find in our own nurseries." Yet in saying as much, children's authors simply channeled the same "wisdom" circulating among the nation's diplomatic elite. No less than Secretary of State James G. Blaine himself had dismissed Central America's population as "hot-blooded" and unreasonable, so much so that "when they are excited and get to fighting they do not know when to stop."[29]

Emphasizing both the dark skin and infantile qualities of the world's malefactors, Deering added his books to the chorus of voices blaming so-called primitive peoples for their own predicaments. The country could not tolerate neighboring nations who refused to respect American interests. Even as their activities in Mexico seemed to destabilize local communities and exacerbate the very disorder the Border Boys denounced, they solemnly swore that their mission was only to usher in that day when "Mexico should be known as a land of law and order like the United States." Until then, however, it was implied that young readers should not overly concern themselves with others' objections to America's activist foreign policy.[30]

More insidiously, writers sometimes attempted to legitimize US policy aims by forcing nonwhite characters to ventriloquize their support for them. In these stories, Americans never intruded but were instead invited to intervene. Boy-inventor Frank Reade, for example, successfully mediated Venezuela's 1890s border crisis with Britain as a local official "doffed his sombrero," "bowed low," and declared: "'America and Venezuela are one. We are brothers. Venezuela owes a debt to Uncle Sam.'" Afterward, "whenever the native Venezuelans were met, they treated the American travelers with marked distinction. 'The Americans are our friends,' they declared. 'We will never be untrue to them.'" Other episodes involved some wise member of the community who would beg pardon for his unenlightened countrymen and their misguided opposition to Uncle Sam's beneficence. Señor Bilbao, one such quisling, quacked that "the strained relations between our countries" largely derived from "ignorant and superstitious" peons "who misunderstand Americans." The old gentleman apologized for their ingratitude; "'my wretched country is given over to an unruly element who are in the majority.'" A Yankee airman assented. "'Bilbao is one of those Mexicans who has an excellent knowledge of the States, and realizes that we Americans want to be on friendly terms with our neighbors.'" In most cases, however, the opinions of foreign peoples about their own countries did not much matter. "'Greasers will never understand our motives'" in intervening, sighed another story's characters, "'for we think along entirely different lines.'" Even poor Señor Bilbao, showcased as a voice of reason, was dismissed by his American "allies": "'the old man seems friendly,'" they admitted, "'but he's a Mexican. I wouldn't trust one of them with a misfit key to a hall bedroom.'"[31]

Such literature did not, of course, live in a political vacuum. When the United States deployed troops across the region or bombarded a port city, it incensed foreign and domestic critics. Detractors denounced American aggression, while claiming that bankers and corrupt corporations used taxpayer-funded troops as their own private security forces. Anti-imperialists flooded Congress with petitions condemning the extraterritorial exploitation of capitalists. Influential platforms like *The Atlantic* published stories that painted the era's foreign relations as a "dark picture," a "rotten mess." But pulp fiction held firm in its commitment to the legitimacy of America's hemispheric mandate. Protagonists parroted objections to overseas occupation in order to demolish them. Though the early twentieth century was an era of surging anticolonial nationalism, young readers could be forgiven for their lack of awareness on the subject. And if, as Theodore Roosevelt complained, "nothing could be further from truth" than the proposition that "our assertion of the Monroe Doctrine implied or carried with it an assumption of superiority" over sister republics, children's authors certainly never received that memo. Their stories consistently made claims to the contrary. Dollar diplomacy's discontents, of which there were more than a few, rarely found much of a foothold in the mass fiction most kids read. That absence impoverished the ability (or desire) of many young people, at least early in life, to systematically challenge and dismantle imperial ideology.[32]

In "Deserter," for example, disgruntled Marine Ralph Quinlan, stationed in Nicaragua, launched a lengthy diatribe damning his officers and his Uncle Sam. "'What's it all for?'" he asked. "'What business have we got down here? So Washington can be the big boss of Central America! So Wall Street can make more money! Curse the country, the flag, and all the rest of that rot!'" By the end of the story, however, the mutineer had been set straight. As the foreman at an American-owned coffee plantation explained, "'if Nicaragua is unable to protect the lives and property of innocent people from outlaws, then some government that can, should.'" Quinlan instead redirected his rage to "'people, safe in the States, [who] say that Americans should stay home [and] believe we're exploiting the poor, downtrodden native.'"[33]

It was unclear who the country's greater enemy was: "brown rats" who took potshots at khaki-clad troops stationed abroad or the agitators at home questioning America's rightful responsibilities overseas. While a disillusioned Banana War veteran like Smedley Butler made headlines by complaining that his service overseas transformed him into "a gangster for capitalism," pulp fiction proactively defended the justice and indispensability of police actions. Meanwhile, when Native populations protested violations of their sovereignty, they were shown to be in error. "Our attitude toward the South American republics has been misunderstood," said one seventeen-year-old secret State Department agent. "We have endeavored to sustain the 'big-brother' feeling, and to try to show that we were not trying to take hold of any of the weaker nations." The "shocking reveal" of many pulp adventure stories involved the exposure of a vociferous critic of American foreign policy as either a fraud or a foreign power's puppet. Expressions of inchoate indigenous anti-imperialism were called counterfeit. Such sentiments perfectly parroted the pronouncements of officials like Secretary of State Philander Knox, who consistently called dollar diplomacy the "benevolent supervision" of struggling sister republics.[34]

The paradox unaddressed by such platitudes was the contradiction between a professed commitment to international political stability and the equally firmly held belief that nonwhite peoples were utterly incapable of self-rule. This was, in effect, a recipe for nearly nonstop interventionism. Cheap fiction only confirmed the necessity of white American stewardship over a large part of the world's surface and helped to popularize an evolving interpretation of the Monroe Doctrine emphasizing US regional supremacy rather than cooperative control. What choice was there, given the incorrigibly "hot-tempered, revolution-loving South Americans" who populated the pulps' pages? Was it the United States' own actions that destabilized the region? Nonsense, not when "'revolutions have become a habit down there.'" The "'natives couldn't do without them,'" characters joked, and "'you can't be a Central American till you have the habit.'" Latin Americans claiming they "do not like Yankees" for their "arrogant and overbearing" ways and their tendency to "interfere too much" were deemed misguided. The intelligent class below the equator were "all friendly to Americans," for "they realize the good they have done the country and the capital they have brought into it."[35]

But, just as important, the imperial culture industry dramatized for boys their own capabilities and instrumentality in meeting America's emerging international obligations. Hence the delight that authors seemed to take in having their adolescent protagonists lecture the "nasty little brown rats" who dared defy America's presumed right to control neighboring nations. To the revolutionaries shooting at marines and pillaging US property, the message was clear. "'You can't understand what the United States has done for this country. You don't know what gratitude is. You don't know what decency, even, means.'" To remedy such thanklessness, characters promised that "'the United States will send forces down here [and] *you'll get yours!*'" US capital and corporations were portrayed as so self-evidently advantageous that punitive expeditions seemed less like a conscious choice and more a common-sense solution.[36]

Indeed, the regularity with which nearby nations were literally threatened with a spanking is telling. After all, "'they were a lot of children, to be lured this way by a white stick of candy and back again by a striped one.'" That sure did sound a lot like the testimony of actual American troops, who, when asked to answer for alleged atrocities before Congress, insisted, "we were all embued with the fact that we were the trustees of a huge estate that belonged to minors." The appeal of the pulps' paternalistic rhetoric to young readers should be apparent. The imperial fantasy being sold was one in which barely pubescent protagonists could assume a parent's prerogative to punishment vis-à-vis grown men overseas. US hemispheric hegemony proved attractive for its inversion of age-based power relations. The deployment of troops to troubled zones, moreover, became much more intelligible for young readers if the occupied could be imagined as infantile and unruly, as perhaps they too had once been. Paternalistic prose naturalized America's claim to control the region by cloaking the exercise of power as a guardian's prerogative. The broader political culture powerfully reinforced the pretense. Newspaper editorials spoke of "baby republics" who "so richly merit a spanking." Responses to the Argentine foreign minister's proposed Drago Doctrine, which declared militarized debt collection illegal, were rooted in a claim that the United States could "not guarantee any state against punishment if it misconducts itself." After all, as Secretary of State William Jennings Bryan later observed of Latin Americans, they are "our political children." What mischievous adolescent, himself once taken to the woodshed, could not be made to understand that logic?[37]

As a result, the punitive duties of armed forces called upon to defend American interests overseas in the early twentieth century received particular attention in these books. Readers were exhorted to respect soldiers without qualification and associate a nation's prominence with its capacity to project force across the globe. One publication asked the American boy to become "an enthusiastic believer in the strength and glory of the republic of which he sought to be a worthy son" and contemplate "the future of his own homeland as a world power." Exuberant descriptions of military equipment achieved the same ends. Characters were portrayed as "feasting on the strong, proud lines" of battleships as "their staunch young hearts swelled with pride." The size of the armaments, meanwhile, stirred in their "breasts the emotions of love of coun-

Figure 5.2. Pulp magazines were part of a broader political culture that infantilized Latin Americans in order to justify frequent US military intervention. In this cartoon, "naughty" Nicaragua faces punishment for a refusal to sacrifice his sovereignty and accept the terms of the Monroe Doctrine. "There Is Nothing These People Respect and Follow Like Power," *Baltimore Sun* (1910).

try" and ultimately overawed them: "just then neither felt like speaking." Healthy boys ought to become ecstatic at the sight of heavy weaponry, and they could be coached to do so. G. Harvey Ralph, author of yet another popular set of books for boys, made this clear in his introductions. He expressed a "fond hope that herein [youths] will find pleasure, instruction and inspiration; that they may increase and grow in usefulness, self-reliance, patriotism and unselfishness, and ever become fonder and fonder of their country and its institutions."[38]

Yet their books, like so many others at the time, were set in some of the key strategic nodes of the nation's new empire. South America, Central America, and the Panama Canal became the backdrop against which tales of adventure and incident unfolded. Pulp fiction likewise dramatized the United States' occupation of various Caribbean countries. Barbarous "black devils" in the region arose to "slay the white dictators who have taken our liberty from us!" They promised to see "every white man, and every white woman, and every white child . . . thrown into the sea." It was all to be expected, readers were reminded, because "a nigger's a nigger, and a voodoo drum sets 'em all going," so that "gone was his 'education,' gone was the thin veneer of civilization." Brave Yankee troops stationed there became the bulwark separating order from chaos. But America's increasing commitments abroad would require a rising generation educated as to their obligations within those new arenas. Hence, when words such as "usefulness" and "patriotism" were utilized by series writers, they assumed an imperial guise. The "institutions" for which they sought to instill fondness were those charged with policing an increasingly hefty pool of colonies, protectorates, corporate fiefdoms, and subjects. The messaging was hardly ineffectual. Marines stationed in Haiti during the US occupation, for example, often partly attributed their enlistment to the influence of adventure-oriented fiction for boys.[39]

It is interesting, however, to note the sheer number of stories that justified jingoistic military intervention abroad meant purely to coerce a respect for the American flag. In other words, the nexus of ideals for which the flag supposedly stands rarely warranted discussion. Instead, any foreigner's refusal to venerate Old Glory immediately triggered a violent response. The Broncho Rider Boys saluted General Funston's plan to "'make [Mexicans] respect the American flag.'" A Battleship Boy was "'commended for having resented a gross insult to the Flag."' By beating a "whole crowd of howling greasers" who stomped on the star-spangled banner, his commander beamed, "'you showed yourself a true American, one worthy of the Flag you serve under.'" A Motorcycle Boy likewise thrashed a citizen of the fictional South American nation of "Chilovia" for daring to abuse Old Glory. "'I could not stand to see the flag of my country grossly insulted,' he explained, and "any American would have done the same thing, or have shown that he wasn't fit to be a citizen." There had been no choice in the matter. "It is not safe to insult their flag," the recently cowed "Chilovians" conceded, an issue, the narrator added, "in which they had just received a very striking object lesson." The question that lurked in the shadows of so many stories was why the United States even pretended to honor the autonomy of Latin America's "mongrel" republics. If, as Dave Darrin and his chum Dan Dalzell calculated, nearby nations would not defer to "the great United States" and its wishes, "'then these people are not fit to have a government of their own.' 'That's my opinion, too,' Dave rejoined with a shrug of his shoulders." Yet their sham sovereignty would have to continue because annexation was impossible. "'I should hate to think of having to welcome the Mexicans as fellow citizens of our great republic,' Dave exclaimed, with a gesture of disgust." The same could surely be said for most of the Western Hemisphere's denizens.[40]

Between the 1890s and the 1920s, wherever Latin Americans looked, they saw evidence of an increasingly heavy-handed US interventionism. Yankee warships patrolled their coasts and shelled their shores. American marines marched through their cities and countrysides. Wall Street bankers and extraterritorial investment firms exercised a controlling interest in their economies. The Washington, DC establishment meddled in their internal affairs and scrambled their relations with other supposedly sovereign Central and South American states. For many Spanish-speaking peoples, all of this seemed like evidence of their own degradation. As the United States attempted to transform the Western Hemisphere into its own *Zollverein*, that policy's supposed beneficiaries complained of catastrophe. "All protectorates are humiliating," one such diatribe read, "because they are the denial of the means to independence, from which is derived the right to be." *Hispanismo* critics of "*El Yanki's*" imperial pretensions increasingly portrayed the United States as

Latin America's principal enemy. They urged regional solidarity in the face of "the North American peril," and lamented that in Uncle Sam's professions of "friendship for them there will always be disdain; in their progress a conquest; in their policy, a desire for hegemony." Revolutionaries like Augusto Sandino armed themselves against "North American piratical assassins," "blond beasts," "oligarchs," and their indigenous collaborators who sought to "reduce the entire region to the status of an Anglo-Saxon colony."[41]

The juvenile literature dramatizing this chain of events, however, rarely paused to consider those objections. Dan Dalzell, boy hero serving in the very naval forces that were busily chipping away at Latin American sovereignty, spoke of his 1914 deployment to Veracruz as "a spanking expedition" designed to discipline unruly Mexican children. Summing up an excursion ashore that had resulted in the deaths of countless combatants, the character could only remark "with a broad grin": "We had an interesting time while it lasted.'" And neither he nor the United States were done. "'There is a world full of interesting times ahead of us,'" his conclusion sang, and "'we'll find them in every quarter of the globe.'" Violence, armed incursion, and power politics—all the rudiments of an expanding American empire—were reduced to childish pleasure and adolescent antics. Fun, in a word. But those good times had real-world ramifications. Policy choices of consequence, once portrayed as inconsequential entertainment, became that much more difficult to challenge for those raised in an imperial nursery. Within some of the country's literary corners, widespread, sustained, and systemic opposition to Uncle Sam's belligerence became harder to achieve in part due to the consensus kids' books tried to build around an "indispensable" America's stabilizing and civilizing role in the hemisphere. The "Dan Dalzells" of the world stood in stark relief to the "Mexican twins" and "South American cousins" concurrently trying to teach their readers about the joys of transnational fraternity.[42]

## All Around the World

By the 1920s and 1930s, and as talk above of planetary hijinks helps illustrate, pulp magazine adventure fiction began to focus less on the Western Hemisphere. Latin America looked as though it had been conquered by some combination of commerce and coercion. Now the wider world became a more explicit focus for authors selling cheap fiction to the nation's young people. This global turn among youth literature did not, of course, appear out of thin air. From the 1860s to the 1890s, authors such as William Taylor Adams (better known as "Oliver Optic") and Hezekiah Butterworth had written books comprising the *Young America Abroad* and *Zig-Zag Journeys* series. Those volumes, however, were long on information and short on plot. An adult, accompanying juvenile travelers, would typically rattle off a series of facts about a foreign city or landmark. The intended audience mostly encompassed the educated middle and upper classes. Optic, Butterworth, and others like them may have had their critics, but most agreed that they represented stepping-stones on the road to more reputable reading.[43]

The same was not said about the pulps. Bête noire of the respectability crowd, mass culture nevertheless gathered a wide following among adolescents attracted to stories eschewing a self-consciously educational tone. This is not to say, however, that there was no instructional dimension to pulp fiction. Early twentieth-century truths lurked between the lines of these stories. Boys and girls learned about the immutability of racial hierarchies. They heard about an increasing global demand for American expertise and manufactures. And, most important, readers were asked to imagine their country as irreversibly integrated into the international order. Pulps placed US citizens everywhere during the years prior to World War II. Collectively, bulk publications helped to familiarize young people with America's potential to restructure the planet along lines more amenable to its own interests and desires. Progress required a Yankee ingenuity "for getting work out of natives." It took American brawn "to hammer away on the engineering projects that bring civilization to the wilds."[44]

Tales told of economic opportunities for entrepreneurs, while sanitizing the violence of capitalist penetration by transforming it into an exciting escapade. Radio operators like the fan favorite "Peter the Brazen" struggled to "civilize" China. Mahogany cutters instructed Senegal's "somewhat stupid inhabitants" in gathering up a lucrative commodity. Engineers sent to construct infrastructure inspired a "devoted, almost doglike fidelity" among their nonwhite subordinates. Prospectors "chose to go wandering in the forbidding heart of Africa looking for mineral concessions." Copal traders with "a sharp eye for business" and the preternatural power to "smell a bargain ten miles off" scoured jungles in search of trade. The "Dark Continent" possessed its dangers, but "there [was] no stronger call to the vibrant heart of red-blooded young manhood" than its siren sound. One always risked "going native" or becoming "foul with the poison of Africa," something akin to Kurtz's fate in *Heart of Darkness*. But in these stories, the protagonists usually triumphed. The force of will required to overcome adversity was attributed to a boy's "pride of his race, of his nationality." Americans exuded a "promise of energy and white idealism" that propelled them forward, and they refused to allow themselves to "become a laughingstock—no; worse than that, an object of pity—for . . . grinning blacks and half-castes!" There was a sense that in newly arrived Americans, "man-eating, sinister continent[s]" had finally met their match. A trans-imperial motif emerged in the pulp fiction of the 1920s, one that narrated colonial crossings and insisted that the US nationals shown pushing against the boundaries of foreign realms should no longer consider themselves a peripheral people.[45]

So much so, in fact, that a sizeable number of stories began to imply that European empires might be more effectively run by boy heroes imported from the United States. A fair number of accounts, for example, featured American adolescents who joined the French Foreign Legion and fought to maintain civilizational footholds overseas. Even more common, however, were tales focused on the British Empire. Juvenile literature had always exhibited an ambivalence about British power. Long-standing cultural and economic ties, along with a perceived Anglo-Saxon racial kinship, seemed to necessitate feelings of transatlantic fellowship. Yet countervailing currents of Anglophobia also coursed through many stories. Britain was still, after all, a rival power competing with the United States for global supremacy. It is curious, then, to notice that, as the twentieth century progressed, American pulp fiction frequently featured characters from the United States (maybe more specifically from the West) who arrived at some remote corner of Britain's empire and volunteered to accomplish a feat that local administrators could not. The messaging was mixed. White conquerors joined hands to advance the interests of civilization. Yet that call to cooperative enterprise collided with contrary claims about the superior managerial capacities of Americans. The nation's supposed exceptionalism—rooted, ironically, in its anti-colonial struggle for independence from Britain—now came full circle in youth fiction positing protagonists who could better run their former mother country's empire.[46]

Tarzan, easily the most famous adventure pulp character, was only the tip of the iceberg. In South Africa, for example, "Dynamite" Drury, a "Yankee" who "used to be a cowman in one of them wild West states," was said to "know the niggers better than they know themselves." And more to the point, he was "a hard case" hardly "in the same class as the other men," someone "without a peer as a horseman." When a sticky situation confronted his commanding officers, they knew that "Dynamite" would succeed thanks to a "keen wit," "scoutcraft," and an "essential manliness" lacking among the British troopers. That was mostly because, as Drury believed, Britons "think more of the way yuh polish your buttons an' the way yuh manicure your nails than how a man sits a horse or handles his shootin' irons. Gawd! It's a wonder to me that they can get anythin' done, they're that damned clean." Moreover, "they don't understand niggers," while the American claimed to have "got a sort of a knack with them." Heir to a national struggle to destroy Indian "savagery," Dynamite's civilizing work in Africa, as he put it, "just comes natural like." Having once redeemed the West for civilization, adolescent adventurers now "freed [Africa] of the black yoke."[47]

Similar scenes played out elsewhere, as Americans lectured British officials on how to correctly colonize a people. An audacious frontiersman, for example, fought to rescue India from a second sepoy rebellion. When he vowed that the subcontinent "will be saved and not a white woman will even have to blush, much less turn pale," the ruling council's chambers, "for the first time in all the years of its existence, echoed with a cheer." Otherwise decorous aristocrats, at the sight of their Yankee savior, "became as enthusiastic as boys." Meanwhile, the Australian aboriginal's "sheer wanton impulse to murder" and "ratlike cunning" proved unequal to the intelligence of an American serving in Queensland's constabulary. In Burma, a sniveling and cowardly London administrator named Fortescue was put in his place by Haskin, his savvy subordinate from the United States. The latter was guilty of "a breach . . . of every regulation of official conduct," and was told that "in controlling these natives, rules are inviolable." Haskin replied that "rules are best kept in their place—in books on office shelves. It happens to be men who are required out here, not theories." Upon hearing such cheek from a son of Uncle Sam, the pompous aristocrat's "plump neck swelled bright turkey red." Naturally, the idealist, kidnapped by headhunters and tortured, was proven wrong. When the American effected a rescue, Fortescue abandoned his romanticism. Conversations like these contrasted a stagnant, hidebound Edwardian Empire with its more dynamic and energetic American counterpart. They also juxtaposed Yankee masculinity with British effeminacy. While Britons offered "improving lectures on the moral responsibility owed to backward peoples" and their "sympathies with native self-government," US citizens acted.[48]

Why? Larry Addison, an American stationed at a remote rubber plantation in British Guiana, called it "pride of blood." Witness to imperiled members of their own race, adventurers were stirred to combat. "I don't pose as any sniveling missionary or hypocritical evangelist," Addison confessed, "but it galls me like the devil to see a white man cringing in front of a lot of rats. There is such a thing as pride of blood, you know." Another story, featuring a construction foreman in Formosa, made a similar point about the need to "establish 'face,'" defined as "the confident strength and superiority which comes to a white man who has lived long among savage races." American traders at Borneo, meanwhile, were said to be "white folks . . . feverishly anxious to vindicate the honor of their race," while those in Mexico revolted against "conditions here . . . that no white man of any pride of race or history can tolerate." One man announced the moral to his story as plainly as possible: "'There's one rule I hold to—that white men have got to stick together.'" The terminology varied, but the implication was consistent: Any failure to uphold Anglo-Saxon honor in one setting might prove damaging elsewhere. In 1898, Britons had urged Americans to take up the white man's burden. By the 1920s, pulp magazines turned the tables by showing their adolescent audiences that white American men had a responsibility to stand guard at Britain's global outposts of civilization. No matter the reasons that brought them abroad, their countrymen were responsible for policing the racial hierarchy essential to order everywhere. "White men are what this country needs," these protagonists proclaimed, "white men with guts!" Such sentiments exemplify the bigotry that built the era's so-called Great White Walls. As Jim Crow segregation, apartheid, and comprehensive immigration restriction took shape around Angloworld during the early twentieth century, cheap fiction prepared those prejudices for children's consumption.[49]

In doing so, pulp authors echoed the race theorists then rising to prominence in the United States. Men like Lothrop Stoddard and Madison Grant urged measures meant to counteract a "rising tide of color" that would soon jeopardize white world supremacy. They fretted over miscegenation and amalgamation for the threat each posed to Anglo-Saxon racial integrity. The "supremacy of the Anglo-Saxon race" and "the subordination of the Latin" was for them an unshakeable conviction; among Americans, the "only question involved" was "the imperative necessity for opening up these countries to civilization." And, more to the point, such scientific segregationists were akin to household names. Newspapers reprinted their speeches, *Saturday Evening Post* editorials recommended their books, and President Warren Harding favorably referenced their research on the race issue. The adult authors of fiction read by adolescents must have been conversant in, at the very least, a vernacular version of such theorizing. Pulp magazines therefore often contained adventure stories that transformed the thick and impenetrable academic language used by eugenicists into engaging and action-packed narratives. They reheated the era's racial revanchism for juvenile consumers. Stories lionized Americans who went into the world, took the fight to "colored" challengers, and preserved a "pride of race" necessary to white survival. They featured heroes who set to "the saving of a nation, or rather, of all that remained of the whole Caucasian race, in the only way in which it could be saved—by awakening its deadened, dormant courage."[50]

For many eugenicists, however, the race question often intersected with a rabid anti-communism. In *The Revolt against Civilization*, Stoddard insisted that the Bolshevik Revolution in Russia had been planned and executed by Jews and other genetic defectives. The United States, after experiencing a post–World War I Red Scare, soon settled into a more general hostility toward revolutionary labor radicalism. All of this manifested itself in the pulps, which often shipped American mercenaries into the Soviet Union to battle collectivist thuggery. Communist soldiers were shrugged off as "a bunch of flat tires" and real "bozos." An American agriculturalist in the Ukraine denounced the "damned collectivized farm system," refused to "share equally with shiftless peasants without a ruble to their names," and organized a successful revolt against the local Red Army faction. US engineers battled the "Bolsheveki"— described as "scarcely human" with "eyes that had never warmed to pity or kindness"—in Siberia. And Lieutenant Dick Saunders outwitted the wicked Rimski's plot to destroy the Panama Canal. "The Industrial Revolution and the Brotherhood of Man are sweeping through the world," proclaimed the conspirator. "Nothing can stop them. Not even the great and powerful United States." Such Marxist machinations, however, were no match for the daring deeds of a determined American.[51]

## From "Greasers" to Good Neighbors

During the first third of the twentieth century, the children and adolescents targeted by pulp writers and series book authors were being coached to see more and more of the world as an American field of action. Fiction featured workers erecting the scaffolding of civilization in remote locations. Stories set adventurers to the task of managing Native employees and policing a white supremacist racial hierarchy. Tales told of military personnel punishing peoples who foolishly refused to accept Uncle Sam's benevolent embrace. Altogether, these sensationalistic accounts repeatedly insisted upon the indisputable right of the United States to exercise a controlling share of the world's commerce. And they positioned the nation's armed forces as a useful tool for pacifying much larger slices of the earth's surface. Therefore, to the cast of characters credited as the architects of early twentieth-century informal empire— investment bankers, corporate managers, and military advisers, among others—we must add the authors of youth fiction. Collectively, they labored to legitimate and normalize the actions of policymakers and acclimate their audiences to America's enhanced role overseas. They were not the only voices in the room, of course. Books like Charles Finger's *Tales from Silver Lands*—which respectfully retold the folktales of Central and South America—were heralded as exemplary children's books. Finger even won a Newbery Medal in 1925. But where his sales registered in the thousands, pulps circulated by the millions. Prizes could be awarded by distinguished panels of social scientists, but kids, who voted with their nickels and dimes, chose other champions.[52]

One wonders where this literature might have taken young readers had events not intervened. After all, the increasingly aggressive foreign relations embraced by pulp writers had begun to imply that with the remnants of the Spanish Empire safely in American hands, French and British territory would be next. Before the full realization of that eventuality unfolded within the pages of cheap juvenile fiction, however, the global economy collapsed. And to the list of the Great Depression's wide-ranging impacts must be added a sea change within the literature marketed to young readers. With capitalists now vilified, it no longer made sense to herald the emancipatory power of American money abroad. With corporations now persona non grata, pulps could no longer praise the transformative power of US-trained workforces overseas. And with the region's republics uttering what Secretary of State Henry Stimson called a constant "cry against domination and imperialism," it was difficult to sustain the fiction of American munificence. At least not with a straight face.[53]

Junior citizens had been asked to believe in a future where financial and military might had made their country a world power. But that illusion now clashed with the realities of widespread unemployment, parental poverty, and revolution abroad. Genre fantasies of a virile US imperial influence withered in the face of national economic emasculation and the refusal of many Latin Americans to be ruled. New crops of stories routinely crucified the enterprisers they had previously championed. A decidedly inward turn characterized most children's media during the Depression years—even a stalwart imperialist like Edward Stratemeyer redirected his Syndicate's gaze toward the Hardy Boys' and Nancy Drew's thoroughly domestic mysteries.[54]

Shifts in federal foreign policy likewise took their toll. President Franklin Delano Roosevelt, seeking to continue a retooling of Inter-American relations begun during the administration of Herbert Hoover, committed to a new set of principles collectively called the Good Neighbor policy. At the 1933 Pan-American Conference in Montevideo, Secretary of State Cordell Hull formally announced that "no state has the right to intervene in the internal or external affairs of another." It was a pledge ratified by the US Senate soon thereafter. Almost immediately, Roosevelt's new approach bore fruit. The marines occupying Nicaragua and Haiti were called home. The Platt Amendment granting Uncle Sam a unilateral right to intervene in Cuban affairs was abrogated. New regulatory agencies and reciprocal trade agreements were designed to curtail the worst abuses of dollar diplomacy. None of these measures, of course, wholly decoupled Latin America from the United States. Rhetoric encouraging international partnership often masked a persistent American desire to maintain its hemispheric hegemony. The means by which Washington, DC and Wall Street could do so, however, became subtler. Theodore Roosevelt's Big Stick had been expensive to swing and often provoked resentment among those nations that the United States most aggressively policed. Insofar as these "South American things" went, FDR privately remarked, "give them a share. They think they are just as good as we are and many of them are." Soft power could achieve the same ends at a lower cost and with fewer indignities heaped upon nearby populations.[55]

Promoting amicable relations between the Western Hemisphere's nations seemed a particularly prudent policy as totalitarian regimes rose to power in Italy, Germany, Japan, and elsewhere. Friendship with Latin America might be necessary to counterbalance the fascist menace in both East Asia and Europe. Young people thus began to receive new messages. Walt Disney cartoons like *Saludos Amigos* and *The Three Caballeros* showcased for children the promise of positive hemispheric relations. Radio shows tempered their tone in an effort to foster more constructive connections throughout America's sphere of influence. School districts attempted to cultivate goodwill by celebrating Pan-American Day. Civic organizations facilitated hemispheric correspondence clubs. Walking back the more abject racism and imperialism espoused by the pulps, various outlets now downplayed negative stereotypes regarding the region and its peoples. Themes emphasizing not coercion but cooperation with Latin America proliferated within youth culture. Much of this rhetoric, of course, ignored the fact that multiple neighboring nations had by then devolved into brutal dictatorships. Witness to one strongman after another using US-trained constabularies to crush democracy, an embittered Peruvian observed that FDR made himself "the Good Neighbor of tyrants." Children's reading, however, had already shifted its gaze homeward, leaving the wreckage of several decades of American meddling unexamined.[56]

More important, the arena where young people were most likely to encounter juvenile foreign relations discourse shifted. Pulp and series fiction, while not disappearing, saw their sales to the youth market decline across the 1930s. In their stead rose the next and most dominant children's media platform the United States had yet seen: comic books. This was not a question of one cultural format simply replacing another. It was instead an evolutionary process known as "remediation," whereby several interwar pulp publishers slowly transformed to become the country's largest comic book clearinghouses. Their gradual conversion makes a great deal of sense. Each relied upon similar storytelling devices, and both utilized industrial production methods. Together, they spilled enormous quantities of ink instructing young Americans about their global responsibilities. Ultimately, comic books fought World War II, became important explainers of US objectives during the Cold War, and channeled children's patriotism into the country's drive for international supremacy. Superheroes, superhuman soldiers, and secret agents piled up on the bedroom floors of young people across the nation, hoping to ensure their commitment to the American Century's actualization.[57]

# 6

## Comic Book Cold War

"The next half of the American Century," exclaimed Harry Truman, "is yours!" But this observation, from July 1950, was not made in the Oval Office. The President instead spoke to the nation's boys and girls as a comic book character. Fawcett Publishers' *Captain Marvel Adventures* invited an illustrated version of the Chief Executive to appear alongside their titular superhero, and he did so in an adventure titled "Captain Marvel and the American Century." The story itself involved one of the series' regular villains, Dr. Sivana, conspiring to replace the "American Century" with the "Sivana Century." Predictably, the plot failed, and in the last panels, Truman appeared to address his youthful audience. We have "led all civilization in enormous strides forward." Now, "in your hands," he warned, "rests the fate of America, of democracy, and of freedom! It is a sacred trust!" Here lay Henry Luce's concept of the American Century repackaged for children's consumption. The United States' status as a global power was no longer—as in earlier generations of juvenile literature—something to which young people should aspire. It was now a precondition requiring their effort to preserve.[1]

Comic books provide one of the more fascinating glimpses into how foreign policy programs were made palatable for young readers. Their wild popularity makes the genre essential to any understanding of children's engagement with international affairs. Growing out of turn-of-the-century newspaper cartoons and pulp fiction, comic books, which first appeared during the Depression years, had attained complete dominance of the youth literary market by the end of World War II. Wary parents and academic scolds spoke of the comic craze as an "intellectual narcotic," a "hypodermic injection" of sensationalism that made "the child impatient with better though quieter stories." Surveys conducted at the time both by the federal government and the industry itself certainly revealed something akin to addiction: An astonishing 95 percent of boys and 91 percent of girls aged 6–11 claimed to read comics regularly, and those figures dropped only slightly for those aged 12–18. *Publisher's Weekly* reported that by 1953, Americans spent over $1 billion on comic books. And the rising action of those diverse publications—from superhero epics to high school romance—was rarely divorced from broader conversations about American engagement with the wider world. Such plot points represented a response to demand. Big firms like Marvel, DC, as well as specialty outfits like EC and Quality, collected reams of market research as a means to understand their audience. At least through the Vietnam War, kids claimed to find fun in the country's growing global footprint.[2]

Given their omnipresence in the lives of wartime and postwar American youths, comic books should be considered the twentieth century's most significant species of children's literature. The sheer numbers in play, however—tens of millions of issues circulating and hundreds of titles to choose from—make an exhaustive survey of the genre beyond the reach of this chapter. Only a fraction of the industry's total output appears here. Yet we must appreciate that comic books were everywhere, and as such, played a vital role in the Cold War era's politicization of the country's youngest citizens. The idea was to assure juvenile readers that they too were key players in the broader struggle against the forces of oppression, that children were soldiers in, as another publication put it, a "secret battle taking place . . . between communism and democracy for the youth of America." Exhortations such as these were in turn paired with portraits of Soviet villainy and Marxist machinations.[3]

Comic books often explicitly made the case for foreign interventionism, and, as such, helped manage the country's transition to a new imperial style. Gone were the aspirations to territorial aggrandizement, direct colonial rule, and fiscal management. Instead, America's young people learned about a United States whose outposts girdled the globe largely by invitation. "Little Cold Warriors," as historian Victoria Grieve aptly calls the era's children, consumed popular culture which "socialized them into the new global balance of power" and "explained the role of the United States on new frontiers in Third World Nations." An inquiry into various comic books published from the late 1940s to the early 1960s reveals that the genre was among the most important tools used to both mobilize the country's youth in the struggle against communism and ensure the safeguarding of an American Century. It was the era's key contact point between kids and international affairs. For, as one contemporary study said of comic books: "through them boys, and girls too, may participate vicariously in [the] most important 'business' of today's adult world." The language and imagery used by comic books implied that this business mostly meant safeguarding democracy rather than subjugating Natives. A mixture of developmentalist dreaming and hard-nosed military deployment suffused their colorful pages.[4]

Confident predictions regarding the comic book juggernaut's staying power, however, proved illusory. Several factors jointly worked to weaken the industry by the time America's involvement in the Vietnam War escalated. For one, as had happened with dime novels, comic books became the victims of their own success once publishers oversaturated the market to chase diminishing returns. Fallout from several high-profile congressional investigations into the genre's "subversive" messaging, meanwhile, also slashed profit margins. Yet the real culprit responsible for curtailing the comic industry was technological change. As television entered the American home, other sources of entertainment rapidly retreated. For younger baby boomers and Generation X, "the tube" became their entry point into America's relationship with the wider world. The comic book companies that survived this period of contraction tended to consolidate. In a bid to avoid further alienating an already diminished audience, they stripped from their catalogs the close coverage of foreign affairs that had characterized earlier editions. The turbulent Sixties shattered what had once approximated an industry-wide consensus regarding the inherent benevolence of US world leadership. For the most part, mainstream comics now refused to tackle a subject the country itself had divided over.

## Comics and Containment

The postwar period, of course, did not suddenly inject international relations into what had been an apolitical genre. Far from it. World War II acted as an important catalyst. By March 1941, months before the United States' official entry into the fray, Captain America had already declared war on the Axis powers by knocking out Hitler. Following the attack on Pearl Harbor, superheroes derided America First, the German-American Bund, and other organizations for their

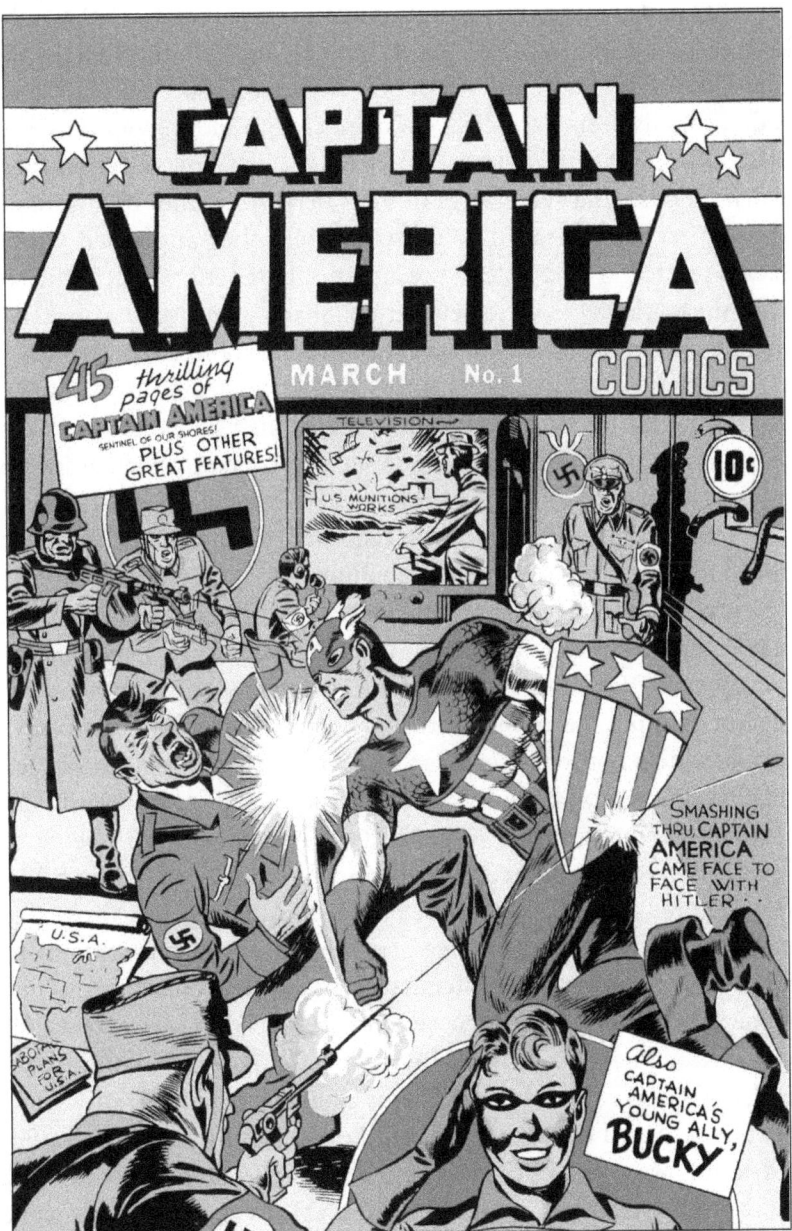

Figure 6.1. By March 1941, months before the United States officially entered World War II, Captain America had already given the Axis powers a *casus belli* by knocking out Hitler. After 1945, comic books were no less aggressive in prosecuting the Cold War against communist foes. *Captain America Comics* no. 1 (March 1941).

cowardly and treasonable actions. Superman requested that youths donate to the American Red Cross. Batman and Robin called for the collection of scrap metal and paper. Aquaman asserted that "you, reader, can also serve the cause of democracy and freedom! *Buy war bonds and stamps!*" Other characters taught kids how to ration their favorite foods. The secretaries of State, Treasury, and War were all afforded regular editorial columns wherein they addressed young readers regarding their role in the larger military effort. The Office of War Information worked closely with publishing houses to ensure that comic book storylines reaffirmed the country's objectives. In piles of fan mail sent to publishers, children spoke about their own spontaneous organization of clubs meant to police their neighborhoods and raise money earmarked for soldiers serving overseas. Such activities augmented larger campaigns—at the federal, state, and local levels—designed to foster juvenile patriotism and direct youthful energy toward the needs of the wartime economy.[5]

New realities in the lived experience of childhood, meanwhile, made it easier than ever before to reach and rapidly mobilize large numbers of young people. The continued tightening of compulsory public education laws, for example, meant that by the 1940s, nearly all of the nation's children were now housed together in large institutions for much of their daily lives. This proved convenient for those attempting to disseminate information among them. So too had the number of youth-centered organizations mushroomed. The Boy Scouts, Girl Scouts, Camp Fire Girls, Future Farmers of America, 4-H, YMCA, Junior Red Cross, and similar groups devoted themselves, fully or in large part, to structuring children's lives. Adult leaders tended to herald such collectives as disciplinary, bodies which by their very nature helped to curb supposedly skyrocketing rates of juvenile delinquency. Young people, on the other hand, embraced voluntary associations as an opportunity to strengthen peer bonds. And it was within the confines of growing schools and affiliated youth organizations that comic books circulated in large numbers. A low price of ten cents made them affordable to many children, while their fungible format enabled easy exchange. This meant that comics enjoyed an exceptionally high pass-along circulation. Young people, now institutionally aggregated, traded and loaned them like a sort of currency. Their ubiquity thus made comic books a potent messenger.[6]

While it would be a stretch to describe the wartime comics business as an appendage of the national government's propaganda machine, there can be no denying a close relationship between the two. A federal agency, known as the Writers' War Board, sought to steer storylines and coordinate relations between private publishers and Uncle Sam. As a result, each found profit and purpose in the other. More important here, however, was the American state's acknowledgment of young people as a crucial constituency in the explication and conduct of foreign affairs. That idea was an old one that extended back to the Civil War. But in terms of scale, and the close attention paid to messaging by government agencies, comic books represented something new. Private citizens had long promoted certain foreign policy programs among the young, particularly during periods of conflict. But they had done so largely of their own free will. Now, more conscious and systematic efforts were made to conjoin children's literature with national diplomatic imperatives and federally articulated foreign policy. Youth culture thus became even more thoroughly politicized during the wartime and postwar periods as part of an effort to purchase kids' loyalty and assent.[7]

Comic book companies, for their part, reassured young readers regarding their indispensable contributions to the country's success. One publisher, for example, addressed fans in late 1945 with "a salute to you and all the rest of you in appreciation of the fine job you did to help win this epic victory. Maybe you think that buying War Stamps and War Bonds, saving scrap metal and waste paper were of minor importance," the letter concluded, "but all those little things put together by a lot of people like you working in cooperation add up to a tremendous contribution." The rapid deterioration of US-Soviet relations characterizing the onset of the Cold War only augmented that impulse to invest children in international affairs. Hence Harry Truman's cameo in *Captain Marvel Adventures*.[8]

With so many publishers entering the comic book industry at the end of the war, however, it is difficult to pinpoint any single message broadcast to the country's youth. World War II comics benefited from a clarity of purpose: identifiable enemies in the Axis and an obvious objective in Allied victory. After 1945 the picture became muddled. Wartime rationing and production controls ceased, meaning that more businesses began to print comics with the hope of profiting from the youth market's seemingly unquenchable thirst for illustrated adventure. This, in turn, meant a flurry of new titles and a host of fresh storylines. Older plot devices receded as firms struggled to find formulas that could distinguish them from their numerous competitors. Superheroes who had led the fight against fascism during World War II were some of the first casualties of the new Cold War. Superman, Batman, Captain America, Green Lantern, and the Flash all saw their sales figures sag after V-E and V-J days. The new battle against communism was instead waged by spies and soldiers, and told within the pages of war, espionage, and adventure comic books. This would be, by and large, a human rather than superhuman struggle.[9]

The next generation of postwar comics assumed for itself a raft of new responsibilities. One of those was the induction of young readers into what publishers repeatedly referred to as an "atomic age." The phrase possessed expansive connotations. It referred to the grim prospect of nuclear annihilation, but also heralded exciting technological advances. "*This* is the Atom Age!" one such comic announced. "The *unbelievable* has already begun to come true!" Children were asked to cultivate a healthy respect for radioactivity's destructive power, while at the same time anticipating its potential to improve human civilization. Various comics proudly showcased scientific breakthroughs in defense technology. In doing so, they expressed a hope that children might sleep soundly knowing that America possessed the means to keep its people safe. Attack submarines, assault helicopters, jet packs, the Convair F-102 ("America's Atom-Age Airplane!"), and satellites were among the many machines described in obsessive detail. One story was even told from the perspective of a new military computer, "the supreme achievement of mankind's genius in the field of aerial defense" and a representation of "man's desire to live in peace [and] prevent war's crackling fires from searing his land!" Comic books placed these marvels of mechanical engineering upon pedestals and, in effect, asked young people to worship at their altars. Not for the first (or last) time in American history, junior citizens were told to view their country's global influence as the natural expression of its superior capacity for inventiveness.[10]

In the very earliest years of the Cold War, an inchoate Soviet adversary had not yet thoroughly crystallized. US monopolization of atomic weaponry, at least until its proliferation in 1949, initially allowed for magnanimity to influence comic book depictions of a newly nuclear world. Instead of focusing on Marxist villainy, writers tended to emphasize the need for peaceful coexistence and international cooperation in the management of such devastating devices. Richly illustrated panels portrayed the blasted ruins of American cities flattened by fission. The enemy, however, was never named. Human beings more generally—irresponsible and emotional—were portrayed as the authors of their own destruction. "We, the editors," announced one such comic, "feel we are performing a significant service by presenting dramatic stories of LIMITED thermonuclear battle!" In part, they promised, the "stories will be reassuring insofar as they will demonstrate how amazingly powerful and fantastically ingenious our country's atomic defenses are!" Moreover, "by giving an insight into these weapons' terrifying potential, the stories will reinforce your fervent desire to help prevent an all-out war in the Atom Age!" A Fawcett Comics tale stressed something similar. After a character awakens from the bad dream of a nuclear attack, he admits that "The atomic war itself would be MUCH WORSE!" So, a final cautionary note sounds, "I guess we'd all better learn to live and get along together—one nation with all other nations and one person with all other persons—so that the terrible atomic war will never occur!" "It is the common duty of all of us," another comic claimed, "to work incessantly to prevent the suicidal thermonuclear holocaust of total war in the Atom Age!"[11]

This state of relative neutrality quickly changed. With news of Iron Curtains, the "Fall of China," Berlin Blockades, and atomic espionage all accumulating by 1950, comic books less often hesitated to call out the country's enemies by name. Stories about atomic power no longer pushed international cooperation. Now it was "in spite of *our* efforts for peace" that "the ambitions of communist dictators make the danger of an atomic attack a grave possibility." "Commies," "Reds," "Red rats," "Red Hordes" and other such appellations crowded the pages of comic book children's literature. Instead of generalized anxieties about nuclear apocalypse, stories sought to reaffirm the undeniable superiority of the American way of life. Portrayals of military technology were increasingly politicized: The weaponry would "blast a path to freedom" and "pound a lesson into the Russians . . . that we mean business!" Writers used a variety of tactics to dramatize for young readers the distinctions between their own prospects for prosperity and those behind the Iron Curtain. Figures like Captain America were dusted off and rebranded as "Commie Smashers," while kids were told that even "with the coming of peace" in 1945, "there was still no rest for them. Communism was spreading its ugly tentacles all over the world!" Youths needed to enlist in the struggle. Containment would be the child's duty too.[12]

"Enemies," however, were now more often construed as ideological. Earlier children's texts had painted Indians, Filipinos, and others fundamentally antagonistic by right of their race or blood. But with eugenic thinking discredited by its links to Nazi and Japanese crimes against humanity, authors sought new methods to demonize America's adversaries. Here lay an indication of the creeping influence exercised by an earlier generation of internationalist children's literature. Deep down, all the world's people, irrespective of race, were the same; what united them was an aspiration to lead fundamentally "American" lives. Comics often stressed as much. One common approach was to feign testimony regarding the twin horrors of tyranny and deprivation characterizing communist-controlled countries. An ordinary Romanian truck driver told covert agent Pete Trask that "everything is worse under the Reds! Not only did they seize our liberties—but the food from our mouths as well! When will we be free of this curse?" A Korean laborer whispered of "communists telling us they're friends of the poor workman and poor farmer" even as "they kick us and steal our food." Chinese peasants testified that Chairman Mao and his ilk were "a selfish, ruthless, power-mad tyranny out to enslave the world!" One especially odd twist appeared in a science fiction story where "neutral" aliens arrive to observe the Cold War, but ultimately decide to aid Americans because they were the "only group" that seemed "decent and courageous," not "brutalized or cruel as are the others."[13]

Protagonists, however, were also eager to point out that leftist governments rarely spoke for their citizens. The "people wait for liberation," one character explained, while another offered his assurances that those who chanted "Down with US imperialism" or "Kill the capitalist" were simply "puppets" pulled by "the fine hand of the Kremlin." The vast majority of the Eastern bloc was depicted as sympathetic to American ideals and prepared for "the future victory of freedom over evil!" So too did leaders *behind the bamboo curtain* of communist China have "great cause to be desperate, suspicious, worried and troubled" thanks to the eventual "revolt they knew would erupt!" This was made easy for young readers to believe because communist villains often openly confessed that "we only deceive the poor with talk of leisure and plenty for the workers! It is all *lies*! Power is what we want!" Marvel Boy's exploits in "Upper Stalinia" hammered home for kids the Comintern's insincerity. Why, after all, were "commies, champions of the *common* people, heroes of the *downtrodden masses*" always "wearing the finest clothing, riding in the sleekest limousines, eating the grandest food, living in the most expensive hotels, and amassing great sums of United States currency by fair means or foul! What *hypocrisy!*"[14]

But it was also clear that the emancipation of foreign people from totalitarian slavery would depend upon Uncle Sam's initiative. Local populations, particularly when "nonwhite," were routinely depicted as helpless and incompetent. Echoing many American leaders at the time, comic book protagonists denounced decolonization or anti-imperialism as Trojan horses designed to enable Soviet infiltration of the developing world. Young readers were reassured that public opinion within war-torn Europe and the Global South thoroughly backed American-led interventionism. Any character questioning the unilateral right of US personnel to deploy abroad was either quickly revealed as a double agent or experienced a change of heart regarding the virtues of democracy and capitalism. Most stories ended with overseas populations expressing gratitude to their American benefactors. "God bless the Americans!" went the more broadly representative cry of blighted Berliners amidst the US-led 1949 airlift. "You Americans have *proved* that you *are* concerned about the German people, and that you want to help us in our *fight for freedom!*" Comic plotlines leaped around the world, often providing remarkably detailed (if stilted) information about various countries and regions. They read like the stripped-down explainers of international relations adults encountered in *Foreign Affairs* or the *Atlantic*.[15]

In Nicaragua, "Carmela," once the lover of an avowed Marxist, is quickly shown the folly of her ways by a US agent. "Communists?" she eventually spits, "I *hate* them!" The "reds," after all, "would make slaves of us and destroy our freedoms." At story's end, readers were assured that Carmela's conversion could be repeated throughout the region: "Central America," the comic crowed, "is safely on our side!" In South

Korea, grateful officials declared that only "with the assistance of Americans like yourself, we can smash *any* Communist plot!" A *John Wayne Adventure Comics* episode sent the film star, now an anti-communist agent, to an unnamed Arab state for the purpose of crushing a strike that had crippled oil production. Naturally, the labor agitators are revealed as Russians in makeup and costumes, counterfeit "Moslems" who "answer to Ivan and pray to Moscow!" Oil, "the life blood of nations, bought with the blood of men, that freedom may live," resumes its flow as a Middle Eastern crowd cheers: "Great work, John!" Egypt, meanwhile, was depicted as "restless, violent, [and] stirred by the maelstrom of modern global politics." What American operatives condescended to call "misguided Egyptians" were supposedly rallying to the "Anubis Party." This organization instructed their countrymen to "eject the Americans from our land!" and represented a direct threat to US security interests. Like clockwork, the group is revealed as a "Communist Party 'front'" while Egyptian nationalists protesting neocolonial meddling could be dismissed as "crazy fanatics" who "belong in an asylum!" Anti-American sentiment, in other words, was not only illegitimate but in some literal sense insane.[16]

That no one of sound mind could find communism attractive was a point driven home by another comic titled "The Deserters to Red Doom." In it, American soldiers stationed in Berlin suddenly began to defect, "writing letters to their grieving parents, letters spouting commie party-line lies." Panels portraying distraught mothers were meant to demonstrate for children reading at home the agonies their own parents might experience should they perpetrate similar disloyalty. "I don't understand," one woman sobbed. "Our son accuses America of war-mongering and other things! How could our boy say such terrible things about his own country?" Breaking ties with one's nation, junior citizens were warned, would break the hearts of beloved parents. And yet, once again, diligent detective work exposed the entire scenario as a Soviet plot. The G.I.s had not elected to desert. No real American would. Instead, they had been the victims of an experiment in mind control. "I had a feeling it was all a commie trick! I believe in our army!" went the comic's concluding paragraph. "The commies keep trying to hypnotize the free world with propaganda . . . but *we're wise to them!*" Many other stories similarly sought to impress upon young readers the perils of perfidy and the unnatural origins of Soviet sympathies. The overall message, however, was one of hope. Characters stoically broke through the fourth wall to announce that "if there's a war, we'll be ready!" or "freedom will live!" The United States, swore superspy Doug Grant, consistently "outfought and outwitted the Reds, and we can do it *every time!*" A generation regularly reminded of their own potential for nuclear annihilation thus overwhelmingly gravitated toward reading material that depicted American leadership as competent and promised them a happy ending. Part of the purpose of Cold War comic books was to promote a politics of reassurance. Assuaging the atomic anxieties of young people worked to embed a sense of American invincibility in a rising generation who would one day be responsible for carrying on the struggle against communist tyranny.[17]

Reassurance, however, was usually paired with discussions of deterrence—a term that, when used at the time, referred to a suite of US policies meant to derail Soviet aggression. Comics distilled these diplomatic initiatives and foreign policy plans so that children could easily comprehend their significance. Writers lifted the terminology from newspapers and other media made for adults and repackaged that reading material for their younger audience. Secret agents trumpeted the Voice of America—what one villain denounced as "lies beamed to our happy workers and allies"—and its important commission countering communist propaganda. High-ranking officials depicted the dangers of deviating from a containment strategy. Rationalizations for bloated defense budgets surfaced with warnings that "only a strong America can prevent *Atomic War!*" or "to permit our atomic muscles to grow flabby ... would merely invite *atomic attack* by an enemy, stronger and less responsible than ourselves!" Comics also disclosed Marshall Plan details and praised administrators for "bring[ing] light to all parts of the world" and to whom "we owe the continuance of our cherished heritage of freedom." The settings for these comic book Cold War adventures, meanwhile, included almost every corner of the world. The plots thus familiarized children with America's mushrooming global security concerns. But in an effort to promote among youthful readers the sense that they were privy to top secret information, characters would at times utter phrases like "censorship stops me from telling you where my new assignment was" or "Editor's Note: For security reasons, actual plans have been censored." Audience investment increased when comics claimed to traffic in vital details related to the consequential struggle against totalitarian oppression.[18]

What were intractable issues in real life, comic books guaranteed their readers, possessed potentially simple solutions. In "A Blow for Freedom," a young East Berlin girl "trying to cross those few feet that separated the worlds of slavery and freedom" was detained by a sadistic Soviet colonel. A chivalrous soldier in the American army decided to intervene by striking the woman's captors. When a minister lodged the predictable complaints in Washington, DC, US officials told the Russian premier "to go soak his head! There will be no apology!" The PFC's punch was instead heralded as "another blow struck for freedom" wherein "the Reds suffered a big defeat in the eyes of mankind!" Another story, "The Commissar's Girl," chronicled the competition between an American and a communist for an East German girl's affection. After the GI hits several of his "Red" romantic rivals, the woman becomes smitten, and the two are soon married. Given the elusiveness of Cold War victory, reductionist fairy tales flourished between the covers of comic books. The accounts served twin purposes. It was wish fulfillment for adult writers and, for juveniles, an encapsulation of a much larger conflict's confusing contours. Boy-meets-girl escapades helpfully condensed geopolitical entanglements.[19]

Romantic interludes more generally became a common metaphor for Cold War rivalries. Sexually maturing adolescents may have found such predicaments particularly potent stand-ins for broader foreign policy problems. Typically, some femme fatale seduced her prey and started to "sway him toward the communists" until he was urged "to be a man again" and reassert himself. Wavering women, meanwhile, often discovered the joys of freedom in the arms of an American paramour. "It was *love* that made me see the light," cried one such character, "that forced me to realize that all the Reds of this world were the implacable enemies of decent people everywhere who were merely seeking a little happiness for themselves! I made my choice, sweetheart. I'm on *your* side now!" Other stories were stranger. In one, titled "Mademoiselle Mig," a male American pilot and Soviet female ace become stranded together on a small island. They begin to debate ideology, an argument that ends with him asking, "What do you know of freedom? You've never tasted it! I re-

Figure 6.2. As the American Century enhanced the nation's strategic commitments overseas, children avidly read millions of comic books a year that dramatized those diplomatic maneuvers. Library of Congress Prints and Photographs Division.

ally feel sorry for you! You'll go through the rest of your life with never an idea of love, or beauty or freedom . . . or even truth!" The point is then punctuated with a kiss forced upon the communist's lips. She, of course, is instantly infatuated, and soon sacrifices herself so her new lover might live. With her dying breath, the reformed Russki declares: "Do not bother with me, American. I shall die happy, knowing I have spent a moment as a . . . woman!" Such martyrs, however, merely "died for the right to love and live—for the same values we're trying to protect! And we'll protect those and all democratic rights—*just as long as American countrymen are on the job!*" Freedom's forces would triumph even on the battlefield of love, thanks to the overawing virility of men from the United States. Marxism, on the other hand, seemed to unsex its female devotees. One spy, after shooting a Red temptress, pointedly pronounced that "she is no woman," but instead "a dangerous, venomous rattlesnake" which, "like all dangerous beasts and enemies of peace and society, must be destroyed."[20]

Comics more generally tended to treat women as ill-suited to the rigors of Cold War conflict. When the genre wrestled with the issue of foreign relations, it almost always did so in volumes marketed to boys. The messaging insisted that wives and mothers play more passive roles. Their duty lay in cheering and comforting men wearied by the many burdens that warding off the Red menace entailed. The occasional issue that featured a female lead came to telling conclusions. An *Atom-Age Combat* titled "My Rival," for example, found the wife of an American pilot bemoaning the long hours her husband spent up in the air. She construed the man's jet a romantic rival, but those petty jealousies were eventually allayed. "This is a strange age we live in," the woman's concluding confession cried out, "with forces at our disposal that nobody ever dreamed were possible!" As a result, "wives have to learn to live with this age, not to be jealous of how it drains their husband's strength and minds, but to be patient and understanding!" Such explicit epiphanies regarding the wisdom of sex segregation were more often left implicit. Yet they aligned entirely with the baby boom's "best" medical science, adamant as it was that "being a woman means acceptance of her primary role, that of conceiving and bearing a child."[21]

Women who did become more directly involved in Cold War politics soon found themselves in over their heads. An issue of *Daring Confessions* titled "Backyard Battleground" made this clear. It told the story of Ann Booth, an average American teenager smitten with Bart Edwards, captain of the high school baseball team. But Bart had a dirty secret: He was a communist. "I was a chump," Ann later admitted. "I took the bait—hook, line, and sinker." Bart had made "communism sound so right," and soon enough, the hapless girl was an accessory to several crimes committed by her fanatical new friends. When Bill, a kindly neighbor, tries to extricate her from the club, he ends up dead. A final twist finds Ann's confession being recorded from inside a jail cell. "For all of my tomorrows," she weeps, "I'll hear Bill's last scream. I'll always remember that my vile indoctrination into communism murdered him as surely as if my own hand had pulled the trigger of the gun that killed him!" Romance comics like *Daring Confessions*, targeting adolescent girls, proved enormously popular upon their introduction in the late 1940s. References to broader political crises and the topic of foreign relations, however, remained rare. Still, the occasional story such as "Behind the Romantic Curtain" did broach the subject. When characters cried out, "I'm not going to let myself fall in love with a rotten Communist! I'm not! I swear it!," they gave teenaged expression to corresponding diplomatic denunciations of communism made within national security circles. NSC-68, the 1950 document enabling America's "forever war" against the Soviet Union, could not have said it any better or more succinctly than the protagonists of adventures like "Communist Kisses!"[22]

When international issues did arise, romantic plots resolved such that they reinscribed midcentury motifs regarding the "irrational" woman's greater susceptibility to propaganda. Cold War girls, as recent studies of *Seventeen* magazine (among others) have revealed, still perused a good deal of globally minded and overtly political literary output. Seeking out such content in comics, however, generally required that they read material marketed to their brothers and boyfriends. The "world," as depicted by amorous volumes, rarely extended beyond the borders of the school grounds, soda shop, or drive-in theater. The rivalries that structured female lives, comics could lead one to believe, had almost nothing to do with those that divided democracies and dictatorships. Romance serials generally sought to fortify the pronatalist position regarding a woman's "natural" inclinations toward heterosexual marriage and childrearing. Plots tended to resolve along such lines, as did an array of "Love IQ" and "Romantic Aptitude" tests ubiquitous within such comics. Girls who received low scores on those quizzes were subtly shamed into behavioral reforms that promised to make them more attractive to potential mates. The era more broadly obsessed over sexual deviance as a threat to national security, and comics proved no less committed to such idealizations. Managing a stable nuclear family (and ensuring the proper political loyalties of her children) would be the average American woman's primary contribution to foreign relations in the atomic age. As the think tank Parenthood in a Free Nation insisted, maternalism took on "new and strategic significance" during a Cold War where "democracy is facing acid tests for survival." Even the era's most popular "how to" dating guide proclaimed that because "the very existence of our democratic form of government depends upon happy family life . . . you might even say that the future of our whole country rests right in the hands of us teen-age girls." Why threaten those already burdened hands, the presumption went, with deeply unfeminine reading material?[23]

Correspondence with publishers, however, reveals that such sentiments did not always describe reality for comic book audiences. After all, "masculine" war periodicals often received letters from female fans who claimed that while "most of the mail you receive is from boys, my girl friends and I have been enjoying every single magazine you've turned out." "You may think your magazine appeals only to men," another reader noted, but "I want you to know that I enjoy it as much as any man!" Some, like a Marcia Moore from San Diego, construed their reading choices as a subtle critique of military culture. "I may be only a girl," she wrote, "but nothing can keep me away from your combat comics! After all, they never did let girls on the 'front lines'—so I guess the only alternative is to join you and Easy Co. where the action is!" More forceful missives noted that "the ladies did contribute to the war effort," so, "when are you going to give us gals a break, and dream up a female counterpart" to "your great DC battle stars?" In numbers we might only speculate about, girls (and presumably boys) defied publishers' attempts at gender segmentation. Much of that phenomenon pointed to the apparent appeal of war among juvenile consumers.[24]

## Comic Book Combatants

Few subjects at the time consumed more colored ink than US justifications for the use of force. The Korean War, which began during the summer of 1950, proved to be of particular interest. Comic book companies discovered in the conflict a perfect opportunity to juxtapose American heroism and communist barbarity. Part of this project involved framing events on the Korean peninsula in a manner considered intelligible to young audiences. Comics provided an easy-to-understand primer for complex events. In a few pictures and words, the origins of an entire war were brought to life. Manichaean motifs clarified the stakes: "[T]he world is taking sides in one of the greatest struggles of mankind! Democracy versus tyranny! The U.S. versus the Iron Curtain! This is the time of decision!" "This Is Korea" put it most plainly in describing the arena as "a war of the freedom-loving people of the world against a menace that plotted to engulf them all!"[25]

Though too young to fight, children were nevertheless approached as a constituency whose consent lent additional legitimacy to the conflict. That is, they were explicitly asked to decide where their allegiances lay. But because events in Korea (and beyond) appeared much hazier in both their origins and objectives than the war that had ended in 1945, comic book publishers explored new approaches to explication less dependent upon superheroes. Much of the comic book's Korea coverage featured ordinary American troops coming to some important realization about the absolute necessity of their country's power as a counterweight to communist oppression. The man who "wondered what I was fighting for ... what it was all about" could later exclaim: "Now I know! Freedom, all colors, all creeds, any place in the world, freedom!" Another story entitled "Why We Fight" put it just as simply. "What's happening here *must* be checked before it spreads across the waters to our own country, our own people! *That's* what we're fighting for, what every American must fight for, in any land, at any time!" Korea was "a proving ground between two forces, the cause of democracy and the grim force of world-wide communism." One particularly shocking attempt to elicit young people's emotional investment in the conflict was the *Battlefield* comic's regular "Atrocity Story" segment. Histrionic panels illustrated "the entire civilian population of the state of Nevada" lined up and machine-gunned, or "every human being in Inglewood, California being tied and gagged and then buried alive." "*Brutal? Barbaric? Appalling? Yes!*" And "but for the grace of God it could have happened here in America." The "civilized world," of which American kids were instructed to consider themselves, had to stand up against "the Reds' savage brutality." Children's media made the case not only for one specific war, but a permanent war footing between contrary ideologies. Comics cloaked American interests as human interests.[26]

*American Air Forces*, for example, hoped juvenile audiences might better appreciate the necessity for US deployment overseas (as part of a larger UN mission) if it depicted the struggle as one meant to preserve the lives of young people like themselves. A story titled "Secret of the Tunnel," for example, surveyed the shattered life of a Korean girl named Tu Shan. Ripped from her parents' hands by cruel communist soldiers, she was then sent to a reeducation camp "to be indoctrinated into the Red way of life." At first, the comic cried out, "there seemed no hope for her." But soon enough, they observed, "in other corners of the world, people were rising to fight against the onslaught of Red terror!" An American soldier vowed that once "our forces go forward . . . the Reds are licked, but good!" A different tale begins with a young GI who witnessed the slaughter of women and children at the hands of communist forces. "Those could've been my folks, this could be our farm! If it happens here," his epiphany urged, "it could happen anywheres, I reckon!" If Marxism menaced someone somewhere, comics claimed, it was a threat to free peoples everywhere. As a narrator stepped in to tell us, the soldier "suddenly knew what a farm boy from Ohio was doing there in Korea, with a gun in his hands instead of a plow!" The basic setup became common enough to be considered a trope: defenseless children frogmarched off to some fetid prison camp as the only motive Americans needed to intercede. Such imagery played off of the basic fears of abandonment and alienation that comic writers knew their young audience would understand. It also helped to perpetuate what became, as the twentieth century progressed, a broader political language that utilized the threat of child endangerment as a means to "sell" US military interventionism as selfless sacrifice. The iconography of international emergencies increasingly depended upon imperiled youth as a justification for violent reprisals.[27]

Of course, if that failed to work, writers might always place older themes in service of newer Cold War ends. As one American soldier noted while standing over the corpses of recently routed Chinese troops, "like our forefathers said of the Injuns—a good Red is a *dead Red*! Now they're *all* good and dead!" Koreans, meanwhile, tend to come across as bit players in their own history. Tens of thousands of them fought alongside UN forces, and yet, overviews of the conflict instead noted that Korea was "an ancient land" where "American blood is spilled daily." The "Iowa farm boys" who fought "side by side with boys from the sidewalks of Brooklyn" have "come across the world to give [Korea] liberty." "Hopefully," the passage concluded, "all Koreans look to the future, when that liberty will, with the help of the US and the United Nations, become a fact!" Locals often appear in stories only to rehearse justifications for outside intervention. Many an apathetic villager was eventually persuaded to exclaim that "Now I see the truth! Reds bring violence and servitude [and] Americans bring honor and peace!" Comics portrayed an inveterate "Oriental" passivity as a problem more generally. As a rule, civilians were expected to have "the patience to wait" for "the men who will save their country, their way of life." One American character spoke for much of the genre when he shrugged and said of his "inscrutable" Korean allies, "I guess we'll never really get to understand these people!" Even when a South Korean boy was gunned down by Chinese troops for screaming "Give-um me liberty or give-um me death!" the most an American soldier could muster in reply was to say "You were okay!" Nevertheless, to whatever extent publishers felt Asians *could* be understood, comic books exerted authority as interpreters helping young people to formulate their first impressions of the world's regions.[28]

If allies could be derided or dismissed, enemies were often dehumanized. "Is the enemy human?" one comic asked. Two soldiers in a 1952 *War Comics* number debate the point, but when the more empathetic of them is captured and tortured, he learns the awful truth. "They ain't people! They're animals that walk on two legs! That's why we're fightin' this war! To show them animals they can't turn the world into a jungle! The commies resigned from the human race!" As his dying realization went, "Never trust the enemy . . . never trust the enemy." Medics were also often depicted saving the lives of North Korean prisoners, only to see their patients turn around and attempt to commit murder. The doctor who defended the decision to operate on a wounded communist by arguing that "he's a human being, isn't he?" had his question answered in the negative. Youths were told that neither the normal rules of engagement nor standards governing POW treatment could be honored on Cold War battlefields. "Wise up!" characters insisted. Because "them crumbs live for only one reason, to spread the commie malarkey all over the world, there ain't no place for sympathy!" As illustrated Americans breathed their last, they beamed hard-won knowledge to young readers. "I wish I could live to tell . . . all the free people in the world," one such man gasped, "the lesson I've learned . . . they *are* different from us . . . dirty, treacherous!" Yet no matter how nefarious their nemeses, youthful readers were always promised victory. Enemy troops were continuously forced to admit their own inferiority. "We bow before you," they groveled. "You have more brains in little finger than *all* communists put together have in stupid heads!"[29]

## Comic Books as a Cooperative Venture

Combat adventures emphasized the relentless single-mindedness of Marxist militaries. The persistence and deviousness of communist scheming also occupied a good deal of the comic book writer's time. Talk of hypnosis and sudden defection lent the impression that nearly anyone could be susceptible to transformation. Kent Blake, yet another American spy on the Cold War's front lines, wondered aloud, after catching a Soviet saboteur, "how a man . . . can turn communist?" "Who knows," replied a partner, "but there are many like him . . . men we'd never suspect!" Staring out at the audience in a knowing manner, the story asserted that "It's up to you . . . to save America from these scum!" In the face of communist attempts at bribery, readers were instructed to reply: "I am a rich man. I'm a free American, that's the kind of riches you rats don't know about!" As a response to the enemy's persuasive powers, kids were told to show strength: "I'm going to teach you how a product of the soft, decadent Western democracies can fight!" Pride in their country, in other words, was supposed to make youths vigilant. No one was above suspicion, but patriotic self-care could ward off the worst of communism's attempts to "turn all of mankind into Red slaves!" Commit to "win the war in Korea," readers were told, and "rout out the Red rats on the home front! Do everything you can to help us stop the Communist ravage that is at your very front gates!" In the communists' "ruthless battle against the forces of freedom and liberty, their cause cannot, *must not* succeed, if we are to continue our American way of life!"[30]

Invocations of "we" or the second person were clearly meant to mobilize young people—both ideologically and materially—in the global struggle against communism. But we might wonder about the efficacy of such appeals. As was the case with juvenile series fiction, one of the few ways to access children's reactions to popular media was found in fan mail. At least a few comic books regularly printed reader responses, and while these missives are by no means comprehensive, they represent one of the few surviving glimpses at how young people confronted the American Century's challenges. Opinions ran the gamut from complacency to condemnation of comic book content, but at the very least, junior citizens, as they had in the past, seemed prepared to insist upon the validity of their own perspectives. Publishers, meanwhile, always admitted that fans played an important role in determining the focus of particular comic series. One firm prefaced their war narrative with a reference to piles of letters demanding such stories: "Your wishes have been our command, boys!" Another company memorandum extended thanks to "all of you who have already written in. Each and every letter has been carefully read, digested, and acted upon!" And, because "the majority of your letters favored the war stories, insisting on more of this type," the publication "now consists almost entirely of stories dealing with war." As with so many other forms of children's media, comic book subject matter testified to a dynamic rather than dictatorial relationship between authors and readers. "Won't you write and let us know what you think?" implored many publishers.[31]

Particularly popular comics therefore inspired kids to send letters expressing a nascent outlook upon the world. The young man who wrote to Iron Man to rebuke him, stating that his disregard for international law might provoke World War III, represents one of many informative sources. Other youths felt compelled to weigh in on the pressing problem of Cold War civil rights, suggesting how widely dispersed across the age scale such issues had become by the 1950s. Responses in support of and opposed to a comic depicting the heroics of a mixed-race American military unit in Korea were particularly fierce. "This story stinks," announced one irate reader, for "I would not care to have a nigger eat at the same table with me, or anybody else with self-respect that I know." Another complained that the "story is strictly for the burds! What are you going to do? Dedicate your magazine to niggers? Those stories are going to lose a lot of costomers for you, I'll bet." As a parting rhetorical shot exploded, "the writer ought to spend a vacation in the Congo!!!"[32]

More enthusiastic, however, was an Arkansas boy who applauded efforts to transcend trivial bigotries. Referring to his own generation, he claimed that "we are ready to join hands and present a truly united front to the world." The youth also showed a conversational familiarity with international politics. For example, he namedropped the Soviet premier, claiming that cosmopolitan comics helped present "a picture to make Malenkov bolt his door and hide under the bed, for he is smart enough to know that when we destroy unfounded prejudice in our culture, we are destroying the only real chance the foreign aggressor ever had to enslave the American people." Though an unusually expressive letter, it still points to the ways in which comic books did help to structure the outlooks of young readers. The conviction that communistic plots sought to enthrall unsuspecting American children suffused the genre and subsequently leaked into their perception of events. Yet here was one enthusiast insisting that his age cohort could help combat a societal evil. Some even developed a sense that the young would accomplish what eluded adults. After all, noted one boy's assessment, comics were "doing a wonderful job breaking down race-prejudice, even better than a whole town of politicians."[33]

Other readers sought to shape comic book content. Some had frivolous objections, like the San Diego boy who wrote EC comics to say that "sometimes you got too much love and girls in the stories." More supportive missives encouraged publishers to churn out tales of a political tenor, such as the boy from El Paso who requested that a company "keep publishing stories like that," for "they will do a lot of good for a lot of people." Cold War themes, another enthusiast echoed, "are doing a wonderful service to the country . . . because if nothing else is accomplished, you've made people think." Young people could likewise lash out against what they perceived to be anti-American attitudes espoused by some writers: "If I could have my way, that [author] would be sent to the USSR, a country where sentiments like those are appreciated." Disagreement certainly flourished among fans. What united them, however, was the conviction that comic books played an important role in shaping national discourse. Hence the investment of readers attempting to take hold of the tiller and steer these companies, thematically speaking, in particular rhetorical directions. Control over the editorial voice of their cherished titles offered junior citizens an opportunity to shape what they rightly saw as a national conversation among their peers. Some wished to see potentially divisive subjects expunged, because "we're supposed to be a loving country." Others affected conscientiousness, complaining that comics might lend the impression that "the only war being fought is in Korea" when children's media might be doing more by "helping to wage war on the shocking injustices in our own home towns." All seemed to concur that comic books provided a portal for the young, one that allowed them to connect with pressing political questions.[34]

And children could then, in turn, act. They had been asked to do so. *Battle* regularly ran a "Fight for Freedom!" insert urging American children to join the "individuals, groups, and armies all over the world" that "have risked and still risk their lives to split the shackles of communist slavery!" Charlton Comics included a section called "Your Role in the Cold War" in each of its titles, which lauded (and urged youths to defend) an "American way of life that is without parallel in the civilized world!" Youths, often encouraged by publishers, sometimes took positive steps to enact concrete change at home and abroad. As the *New York Times* reported in 1956, "social-minded" comics asked youngsters to donate shoelaces for war orphans, and soon enough, they "poured in" by the hundreds of thousands, "accompanied by enthusiastic if ungrammatical letters." One boy argued that the genre "awakened me from a lethargic slumber" and instilled a desire to combat "prejudice and hate," while another "experienced a desire to do something about the conditions that exist today." Furthermore, fans responded to publishers' appeals for alertness and patriotic sacrifice in curious but not unpredictable ways. When comics insisted that "we *all* [do] our part in fighting those Reds as every American must do" and noted that the Cold War placed "*every* American, from the biggest to the smallest, in the service of his country," well-meaning endeavors ensued. Interviews conducted with retired comic publishers reveal details about readers' earnest and at times overzealous responses. They wrote to their favorite characters, announcing the formation of neighborhood patrols meant to observe friends and neighbors for evidence of seditious activity. They created clubs with names like "The Sentinels of Liberty" and informed local police departments about strange comings and goings. Some, understandably confused, sought to report suspect behavior to their cherished heroes. One writer even remembered receiving a letter from a boy who testified to hearing "strange noises" emanating from his parents' bedroom at night. This climate of paranoia, however, which some comic books helped to foster, soon turned against the genre's principal publishers. The Red Scare of the 1950s possessed important ramifications for the industry.[35]

Government Issued

The relationship between publishers and foreign policymakers was usually amicable. At particular flashpoints, however, such as the aforementioned Red Scare, it could sour. Tennessee senator Estes Kefauver, for example, seized upon the social scientific research of noted comic book skeptic Fredric Wertham to pin blame on the business for a perceived uptick in juvenile delinquency. The House Un-American Activities Committee (HUAC) claimed to find communist infiltration of the industry, all part of a Russian conspiracy to poison the minds of America's youth. Moreover, political leaders feared that excessively violent comics, which circulated throughout many countries, painted a negative portrait of American society among foreign youths. An anti-comic campaign soon took shape, and it quickly became transatlantic in nature. Canada, Britain, France, and other nations passed legislation meant to police the content of illustrated publications and push back against the seeming malevolence of America's creeping cultural hegemony.[36]

In the United States, representatives from comic companies were hauled before congressional panels and asked to publicly profess their loyalty. The resulting media frenzy was circus-like. Politicians jockeyed for the spotlight by accusing publishers of child endangerment, while industry insiders alternately parried their critics with contrition and derision. Meanwhile, a grassroots campaign led by parents and educators began to take shape. Municipalities passed laws banning the sale of "obscene literature," while vigilante groups collected and burned comic books. Here was the hatred once levied against dime novels and series books, resuscitated and reinvigorated. Interestingly, anti-comic sentiment had some adults reevaluating ancient animosities. They now considered "the old dime novels in which an occasional redskin bit the dust classic literature [when] compared to the sadistic drivel pouring from the presses today."[37]

The detective and horror subgenres were targets of special condemnation. Their depraved depictions of grisly murder scenes were said to have inspired copycat crimes among adolescents. Entertaining Comics (EC) in particular aroused the ire of activists seeking to cleanse comic books. Unlike so many other publishers, the company's owner, William Gaines, along with its editor, Harvey Kurtzman, neither kowtowed before Congress nor shied away from unpopular ideas. EC titles such as *Shock SuspenStories*, *Tales from the Crypt*, and *Tales of Suspense* provide a fascinating contrast with approaches to the Cold War that were more common among their competitors. While most comics refused to question the pieties of the American Century, some very few sought to expose its hypocrisies. In one bleak satire of the Red Scare ironically titled "The Patriots," a mob kills a suspected "commie" for failing to salute the flag only to discover he was a blameless blind man. Another tale told of a Korean War veteran who came home to castigate his fellow citizens for refusing to honor the sacrifices of Black troops. Science fiction–infused narratives likewise denounced the lunacy of an incessant arms race and preached "peace and friendship" between superpowers so that humanity might "go forth to meet our destiny." Idealistically illustrated panels portrayed American and Soviet soldiers reaching across the Iron Curtain, shaking hands, exclaiming "it is good that we are friends at last," and urging everyone to "forget our differences and work together." EC's United States was infested with racism, greed, groupthink, and hubris, and young readers were asked to self-scrutinize before casting stones at external enemies. It was an uncommon editorial slant, but a useful reminder that not all comic book publishers promoted the same perspective on the Cold War.[38]

Self-appointed crusaders for children's morals, however, misconstrued these exceptional cases as evidence of the industry's broader threat to juvenile citizens. Civic associations thus experimented with buyback programs, blacklists, boycotts, and other tools meant to curtail the comic book's pernicious influence. The FBI, for its part, opened countersubversive investigations targeting EC and likeminded publishers. But the solution most parties eventually settled upon was the so-called Comics Code of 1954. It represented a set of rules governing comic book content, imposed by the industry upon itself in order to forestall harsher forms of censorship. Consulting with educators, social scientists, and religious leaders, publishers crafted a set of standards regarding decent language and acceptable images. The genre, after all, had been deemed disproportionately responsible for adolescent misbehavior. To scrub the content of comics, therefore, was to create cleaner-minded youths in the United States. As the code itself read, "the comic book medium, having come of age on the American cultural scene, must measure up to its responsibilities" and "make a positive contribution to contemporary life." Comics, recently suffering reputational damage, sought to burnish their patriotic credentials. Never mind the fact that American communists *themselves* denounced comic books—with their worshipful attitude toward superhero strongmen—as fundamentally fascist. Attempting to assuage critics who saw Marxist bogeymen infiltrating an industry wildly popular with children, publishers amplified their already ebullient Americanism.[39]

Whatever doubt there could have been about the comics' allegiance had to disappear. The so-called General Standards policed by publishers therefore explicitly stated that "government officials and respected institutions shall never be presented in such a way as to create disrespect for established authority" and "in every instance good shall triumph over evil." Now, as a matter of policy, communists were portrayed as wicked, while the wisdom and justice of American foreign policy could not be questioned. Publishers repudiated the small gestures that had been previously made toward shared governance between rival superpowers. Comics whose content indicated a refusal to honor this new code were not granted the "Seal of Approval" prominently displayed on the covers of compliant publications. When retailers declined to stock merchandise that had not been certified by industry censors, they brought nonconformists to heel. EC ended up as one of the Comics Code's first casualties. By 1956, only one of the company's imprints survived, and then only because it rebranded as a magazine instead of a comic book: the irreverent periodical *MAD*.[40]

Uncle Sam was among the parties more interested in the industry's realignment during the 1950s. The comic book's influence was by then an undeniable phenomenon. Indeed, with publications for sale on several continents, the comic had gone global. But, in the eyes of many, the genre had been irrevocably tainted. The question became, how could a world power effectively wield such publications as a force for good? One answer was for the federal government to circulate its own comic books as part of a larger campaign to "sell the American way." Many were relatively innocuous treatises covering topics like civil defense, federal farm programs, and public health initiatives such as polio vaccination. Once weaponized by the CIA, the United States Information Agency (USIA), the Department of Defense, and other bureaucratic entities, diplomatic comic books disseminated throughout much of the Global South as a means to win young hearts and minds to the nation's specific developmental aims. A 1962 *Newsday* article on the subject called it a "comic warfare technique" meant to mold "impressionable minds from the mud huts of Peru to the mud huts of Tanganyika." The programs were cer-

Figure 6.3. Beginning in the 1950s and continuing to the present day, the State Department, Central Intelligence Agency, Department of Defense, and other federal agencies began to print and circulate comic books overseas in an effort to win young hearts and minds. In this particular comic, the title of which translates as "The Plunderers," Fidel Castro's communist government in Cuba is depicted as corrupt and tyrannical. Courtesy of the Stephen O. Murray and Keelung Hong Special Collections, Michigan State University Libraries, East Lansing, MI.

tainly ambitious, appearing in at least 45 languages and distributed free of charge to 60 or more countries. Edward R. Murrow, the USIA's most famous director, explicitly argued that the "purpose of the comic book is to get the American message across to many who would comprehend it only in this form."[41]

*Los Secuestradores* and *Escuela de Traidores*, for example, were Spanish-language comics smuggled into Cuba as a way to undermine the Castro regime. *Los Expoliadores* circulated in Latin America as a means to bolster support for the Alliance for Progress. *Los Apuros de Nerón* used a cartoonish family to herald the virtues of free and fair elections in Mexico. For those living behind the Iron Curtain, *On to the Goal!* outlined the virtues of defection. Chinese-language comics were smuggled out of Hong Kong and onto the mainland with messages that asked people to "be not deceived by communist promises," for "they end in slavery." South Vietnamese children, meanwhile, were given comics that demonized both the Viet Cong and North Vietnamese. Smaller conflicts received similar treatment. Even the people of Grenada, as late as 1983, saw a series of comic books that explained their own plight and concluded with a recently liberated community cheering "'Hooray! We are free! God bless daddy Reagan! God bless America!'" So too, for that matter, has the contemporary War on Terror been fought on illustrated battlefields. In 2005, US Special Operations Command began to solicit contractors capable of publishing comic books for Iraqi kids. "In order to achieve long-term peace and stability in the Middle East," the advertisement read, "the youth need to be reached. One effective means of influencing [them] is through the use of comic books." Since the Civil War at least, then, children in the United States have been approached as constituents in the construction of US imperial fantasies. But with World War II and the imperatives of the American Century, something new emerged: a wish to win the allegiance of young people overseas as well. The American state itself had now entered the children's literature industry. Publications printed for juvenile audiences abroad were deemed essential not only to securing a postwar peace but also perpetuating it across time. Comics remained (and continue to remain) central to that struggle.[42]

Other interest groups also jumped on the comic book bandwagon. Conservative organizations, convinced of mainstream comics' irrevocably leftist leanings, sought to circulate their own vision of the international order. The American Legion, Fraternal Order of Police, Catholic councils, John Birch Society, Young Americans for Freedom and allied associations printed their own comic books for dissemination among the nation's youth. They designed this educational programming to prevent children from becoming "red diaper babies," for, as their argument went, "the corruption of youth is always tied in with the fostering of hatred of America!" "Patriotic" imprints produced comics where protagonists such as J. Edgar Hoover and Allen Dulles warned young Americans about communism, "the major menace of our time," one that "threatens the existence of our civilization!" The Catechetical Guild released *Is This Tomorrow?* "for one purpose—*to make you think*! To make you more alert to the menace of communism!" Right-wing groups enlisted high-ranking military personnel to defend nuclear deterrence programs, denounce demands for disarmament, and condemn the supposed sickness that was UN "one-worldism." The American Legion, warning members that "The Commies Go After the Kids," commissioned its own comics to counteract what it considered a concerted effort to "undermine the loyalty of American children to their traditions, their way of life, and their form of government." An advocacy group known as the Liberty Lobby urged "young people to distribute throughout neighborhoods" picture stories that urged their generation to "*wake up*" regarding "international communism's goal of world domination."[43]

Conservative comics never circulated to the same extent as their mainstream counterparts. Not even remotely. The former were printed by the thousands, the latter by the millions. Moreover, corporate publications could rely on transcontinental distribution networks that placed them inside drugstores and outside newsstands across the nation. Anticommunist propaganda, by comparison, tended to rely on less comprehensive delivery methods. Parents were urged to take them for their kids' sake. Churches were asked to pass them out at Sunday school. Yet for all the right-wing handwringing about American comics as a Soviet subterfuge, it's hard to distinguish between the messaging of comics and their counterparts printed by the government and conservative associations. Both appeared overwhelmingly committed to the idea of the American Century. Each remained wedded to the same basic proposition: The United States had a moral imperative to combat the global communist menace. It was a conviction that led comics to initially embrace intervention in Vietnam. And, ironically, the resulting slow-motion catastrophe in Southeast Asia proved terminal for the genre's willingness to foster among young readers a belief in America's unquestioned right to global preeminence.

Collapse

From a steadily increasing stream of military advisers under John F. Kennedy to Lyndon Johnson's post-Tonkin deployment of ground troops, Vietnam is often discussed as an arena where America's Cold War turned hot. Yet the same cannot be said for the country's comic book Cold War. Southeast Asia, with only limited exception, proved as much a quagmire for the comics industry as it did for US military strategists. Illustrators initially dove in enthusiastically, much as they had during the conflict in Korea. They expected to provide primers for the war in Vietnam, while also using the region's jungles as a setting for heroic narratives celebrating America's armed commitment to democratic self-determination. With their credibility damaged during the Red Scare's multiple investigatory hearings, publishers saw the war as an opportunity to reestablish the comic industry's patriotic bona fides. By the end of the 1960s, however, those sanguine expectations had been proven premature.

References to Vietnam prior to the Kennedy administration were few and far between. The rare story that broached the subject did so to applaud Foreign Legionnaires for beating back nationalist fanatics. "The Dirty War" in 1953, for example, explicitly sought to "salute the French and Loyalists in Indo-China, whose gallant stand against overwhelming odds is winning the admiration of free peoples throughout the world." France's disaster at Dien Bien Phu the next year, followed by the partition of Vietnam at the Seventeenth Parallel, seemed to temporarily settle the issue in the eyes of comic authors. More pressing events attracted their attention, even as the Asian nation became more restive once UN-mandated elections failed to materialize.[44]

As the number of US military personnel sent to aid South Vietnam increased under JFK, comic book interest in the area revived. Their coverage repeated a few particular talking points. One was the absolute necessity of American involvement. Comics depicted the Viet Cong as ruthless butchers, painted South Vietnamese regular troops (the ARVN) as cowards, and showed the country's peasantry as unable to help themselves. "Where are our defenders," cried a fictional village recently put to the torch, "WHERE ARE THEY?!" If, as one American soldier supposed, "these people got no belly for fighting the guerrillas," then it became Uncle Sam's clear obligation to once again step in and beat back communist brutality. An adventure titled "A Walk in the Sun" made the case for intervention most pointedly. In it, avowedly neutral Vietnamese elders are given a tour of the carnage caused by the Viet Cong. We see looted hamlets, executed civilians, and maltreated orphans, but, just as important, the charitable contributions of American agencies. "We were fools," civilians sheepishly confessed. "You showed us that as you fed our hungry, buried our dead and saved our children, Yankee. We will do our part to fight the Red dogs!" One is left with the impression, though, that the wavering peasantry who rallied to the American-led military effort were meant as stand-ins for uncertain readers at home in the United States. Youths previously unable to identify Vietnam on a map were now presented with a pressing case for their country's involvement.[45]

Indeed, if information about Southeast Asia was in short supply, comics tried to fill that void with useful knowledge meant to generate among child readers their tacit consent for further escalation of the conflict there. Features like "Customs of Vietnam" and "The Enemy in Viet Nam" explored the region's supposed exoticism, while describing the typical Viet Cong guerrilla as "a scrawny, unkept 100-pounder who barely comes up to the average GI's shoulders." Yet boys were warned not to dismiss them due to their diminutive size. The Red enemy in Vietnam was the "scorpion in a haystack": "cruel, cunning, and tough" but "elusive as a smoke wisp." Laos was likewise the subject of an instructional insert, though the essay assumed a dismissive tone by referring to the country as "landlocked," "lackadaisical," and "truly underdeveloped." Of course, the story still ended with a member of the Royal Laotian Army offering his "eternal thanks" to an American soldier embedded in his unit. "Yanks," he turned directly to the reader to announce, "I salute you!" This was all by way of praising what comics portrayed as America's humanitarian "helping hand." Even Marvel's Iron Man initially announced his support for military deployment. The beloved superhero made his debut in March 1963 when defense contractor Anthony Stark devoted his weapons research to "solving [America's] problem in Vietnam." Captured by Wong-Chu, a communist guerrilla warlord, Stark built himself an indestructible suit and pledged to "defeat this grinning, smirking, red terrorist!" "Scientist Anthony Stark," readers were assured, would never "neglect America's Cold War struggle against the Communist menace!"[46]

But this promise could not ultimately be kept. Comic book portrayals of Vietnam refused to move off the shelves. Dell and Charlton Comics, widely acknowledged as the industry's more conservative wing, had bet heavily on the war and lost. So too did other firms see their coverage of the conflict circulate with little popular interest. By 1966, even *Newsweek* noticed slack sales among comics committed to championing America's military efforts in Southeast Asia. Children's literature, went their diagnosis, was "having much the same kind of trouble holding reader support for their war that the Administration is having rallying support for the real war." A host of factors, both internal and external to the comics industry, helped drive the diminishing popularity not only of the Vietnam War but also of foreign relations topics more broadly.[47]

Price hikes, for one, had only recently pushed the average cost of a comic book above ten cents, a move some blamed for shrinking revenues. So too had the Comics Code driven away customers by oversanitizing the genre. Far more significant, however, was the countercultural politicization of large numbers of young people during the 1960s. Civil rights activism, revolts on college campuses, and even increased agitation at the high school level were all powered by what historians have come to call the era's "Youthquake." The sorts of platitudes about the "American way of life" and its implicit virtue that comic books had long peddled began to lose traction. Adolescents in particular became far more comfortable challenging the fictions that had sustained comic renditions of the American Century. Perhaps they could not cast ballots, but they still managed to vote with their nickels and dimes. They simply were not "buying into" imperial adventurism overseas. Publishers responded by redirecting their efforts away from the globally inflected narratives of the 1940s and '50s.[48]

None of this is to suggest that comics ceased to engage with the issue of international relations. The subject still came up occasionally, but it was more often background noise. When political consensus gave way to an age of fractiousness, comics responded by excising potentially divisive material. Graphic novels and more specialized publications meant for niche audiences soon arose to more directly confront thornier issues. Mainstream comics, meanwhile, played it safe. They calculated that politics no longer stopped at the water's edge. Foreign affairs now *had* a politics to it, which is to say, it was something that engendered widespread disagreement. Fan mail bore this out. The back pages of comic books became battlegrounds. Some conservative adolescents found the genre's messaging useful. They wrote to say "thanks for the inspiration," and praised editors for their eagerness to show "that teenagers are willing to fight for their freedom and independence—even to the death." Others saw coverage of the conflict as inherently demoralizing. "Do you seriously expect to make money with a war magazine that publishes nothing but anti-war stories?" quipped one California boy. More responses contradicted the complainers and expressed their appreciation for comics that "show what war really is, and what terrifying outcomes it can produce." The conflict's apparent intractability seemed to raise the stakes that much higher. "As a youngster reading the newspapers every morning," admitted one boy, "the war in Vietnam means something to me—but if it keeps up, I'm eventually going to wind up there myself."[49]

It was most common for readers to request "a new angle on war stories," one that did not simplistically depict Americans as "super-human." "I am sick, sick, sick of these exaggerated war stories," groaned one boy, while another faulted a publisher for his "terribly nationalistic" artwork: "Why not tell of the enemy's emotions and feeling toward *his* enemy?" The promises that Cold War comics had been making about the free world's invincibility ran headlong into a Southeast Asian stalemate. It looked to some youths as though America's empire no longer had any clothes, and they wanted their popular culture to reflect new realities. The harsh words of two Illinois boys help exemplify much of that displeasure. They were "thoroughly disgusted with your G.I. Combat comic books," which "make it look like war is just a big game." "We have news for you! Men are getting killed in Vietnam this very day!" Young people, the critics claimed, would no longer subscribe to "ridiculous theories such as Americans Always Win, Americans Never Get Killed, [and] Any American Can Beat Up Any Enemy With One Hand Tied Behind His Back."[50]

Dispiriting nightly news reports from contemporary battlefronts clashed with the sunnier imagery of children's literature, creating more cognitive dissonance than some comic book fans could bear. The result was disillusionment. And disillusionment inspired letters like that from little Randy Moore, who wrote to show his scorn for battle comics. "War is nothing but a disease," he observed, "a disease passed on from generation to generation." "It is," moreover, "a silly game that grown-ups play." Here, comic book correspondence enabled the expression of pubescent politics and provided a place to safely critique adult power structures. "The thing that puzzles me is that a little kid like me knows that war is wrong, but how come the grown-ups don't know it yet?" Claims of youthful moral superiority soon suffused a genre originally devoted to ensuring children's compliance with the American Century's dictates. Now they were writing Iron Man to call him a "profiteering, capitalist, war-mongering pig."[51]

Damage control became necessary. An industry already hemorrhaging readers could hardly afford to alienate more young people by wading into such treacherous waters. The later 1950s and 1960s were a period of recession for comic book publishers. Readership declined. Distribution networks crumbled. Many firms folded while others consolidated. In that unfriendly business environment, direct and immediately recognizable depictions of world affairs were often shelved by cautious companies. War comics, meanwhile, abandoned the contentiousness of jungle conflict and retreated into rose-colored remembrances of World War II. In effect admitting American defeat before the official ceasefire was signed in 1973, fans frequently wrote in to request the return of older heroes from periods of greater confidence regarding US relations with the wider world. One exasperated DC editor gave vent to industry-wide sentiment when he asserted that "the war in Vietnam was a big glorified guerrilla scrap," "unglamorous," and thus an expository dead end.[52]

It was, in that climate, the superhero who ultimately emerged victorious. Seeking to exploit audience nostalgia and resuscitate formerly lucrative storylines, the so-called Silver Age of comics saw old crusaders dusted off to do battle within fictional and fantastical worlds mostly divorced from the messiness of Cold War realities. New characters, on the other hand, were often depicted as visibly diverse "mutants" or "outcasts" who appealed to countercultural sensibilities. Antiracism and anticolonialism defined comic book content by the late 1960s, while the number of antiheroes deformed by laboratory experiments and military testing raised questions about the costs associated with America's single-minded pursuit of victory over the Soviet Union.[53]

The country where over 90% of its youth could report reading roughly the same comics, however, was dead and gone. Only the smallest fraction of that crowd remained devoted to the genre; today it is estimated at less than one-half of 1% of the US population. Comic books transitioned from the mass market to what is known as a "direct" market. The common sight of them for sale at grocery stores, pharmacies, and other neighborhood emporiums vanished. Now they were mostly being retailed at specialty shops catering to a smaller cohort of collectors who themselves skewed older. When asked to account for this seismic shift in the nation's cultural appetite, publishers, writers, illustrators, distributors, politicians, educators, and many other interest groups all pointed to their own pet scapegoats. Each could list many reasons why the single most dominant phenomenon in the history of American children's literature had been so dramatically diminished. But the largest letters of the proverbial writing on the wall spelled one word: television.[54]

# Epilogue

*The Empire Writes Back*

"Y-o-o-o-o Joe!" went the G.I. Joes' signature battle cry. Beginning in 1983, millions of young viewers tuned in to see their favorite animated action heroes do battle with devious foes. *G.I. Joe*, a cartoon television series, chronicled "America's daring, highly trained Special Mission Force," an organization whose purpose was "to defend human freedom against Cobra, a ruthless terrorist organization determined to rule the world." Like clockwork, each episode featured some new diabolical plot cooked up by archvillains Destro and Cobra Commander. They attempted to ransom futuristic military hardware. They constructed portals to different dimensions. They sought to melt the polar ice caps. They even tried to steal the state of Alaska. But, just as reliably, Cobra's dependence upon comically inept henchmen and the Joes' undaunted courage spelled disaster for such wicked designs. G.I. Joe, "he never gives up, he's always there," the theme song promised, "fighting for freedom over land and air."[1]

At a superficial level, *G.I. Joe* looked like a continuation of the serialized adventure fiction that had captivated kids' imaginations since the Civil War; the cartoon's producers had even recruited animators from the ranks of Cold War comic book writers and illustrators. The medium changed, of course, once television replaced print as the more influential means of children's acculturation. But how different were the stories themselves? After all, soldiers, described as "real American heroes," traveled the world as a sort of police force meant to defend political ideals closely associated with those of the United States. Likewise, some episodes mimicked the foreign policy concerns of the day. In one incident, the G.I. Joes appeared to reenact the "liberation" of Grenada. Another installment found the Joes committed to guaranteeing a steady flow of oil out of the Middle East. The futuristic weaponry channeled contemporary chatter surrounding the Strategic Defensive Initiative and a 1980s US military buildup more broadly. Indeed, if one squints hard enough, he or she might be able to detect a Reaganesque, "Morning in America" sheen to the show. As confident men and women of action, G.I. Joes took the fight to the enemy, never backed down, and were not paralyzed by malaise.[2]

Yet that interpretation of the series does not withstand much scrutiny. *G.I. Joe*'s politics are far more nebulous. Most episodes seem to consciously eschew any embeddedness in the era's international affairs. The theme song's talk of "real American heroes" was to a great extent belied by the show's visuals and dialogue. Characters are only "American" in the vaguest sense. The flag rarely flies. Neither the Soviet Union nor communism appear. There is minimal discussion about ideology of any kind. Instead, children watched only a more generalized struggle between good and evil. The apolitical content of *G.I. Joe* mostly stemmed from its commercial purposes. The series was designed, first and foremost, to sell toys. The Joes had been action figures before they became animated heroes, and Hasbro, their manufacturer, bankrolled the show as a prolonged piece of product placement. Plots and settings revolved around the introduction of new characters and equipment about to appear on store shelves. Market forces seemed to necessitate a certain detachment from contentious current events. A parent's electoral preferences could not be allowed to constrain consumer choice.[3]

The popular entertainment purchased by previous generations of children had not shied away from direct engagement with American foreign relations. Stories set in the West, the Philippines, Cuba, and elsewhere had openly avowed a commitment to US aggrandizement and addressed the country's kids as imperial inheritors. Now, from the 1960s onward, overt assertions of America's right to rule a hemisphere and manage the world's modernization became much harder to find in children's media. As *G.I. Joe* suggests, it was true of television, but it was also true of books and periodicals. Empire's nursery slowly became a dilapidated and disused structure as the second half of the twentieth century progressed. The sources of this thematic transformation seem worthy of comment.

Part of youth literature's disengagement from a directly imperial ideology can be traced to the process known as "generational disaffiliation." In effect, the monumental scale of America's debacle in Vietnam had,

EPILOGUE | 227

Figure E.1. Across the second half of the twentieth century, television became the dominant form of children's media. But as parents remained immersed in the world's current events, America's young people heard less and less about the subject of foreign relations. Library of Congress Prints and Photographs Division.

for many, exposed a hollowness at the heart of their country's pretensions to principled global leadership. Convinced that the failures of their elders had led to stalemate and stagnation in Southeast Asia, some Americans proceeded to reject exceptionalism and expansionism as the bankrupt values of a blundering establishment. Anti-war and civil rights protestors, typically young themselves, questioned what they saw as the reflexive and simple-minded patriotism of their forbears. Critics were exhausted by children's literature that stressed a need for the spread of American values abroad when it was clear that those same values had failed to take root at home. All of this occurred amidst a postmodern transformation within children's reading material more generally, where "the didactic edge of earlier books"—their "confident dissemination of clear values"—simply disappeared.[4]

Individuals involved in the 1960s and 1970s several rights revolutions—America's "Third Founding"—soon infiltrated the ranks of youth publishing. Plugging into the longer-standing pluralistic currents of Christian ecumenists and interwar internationalists, these new writers and publishers more fully abandoned the unrestrained racism and nativism that had previously populated the pages of mainstream children's reading material. Instead, they taught the virtues of tolerance, acceptance, and open-mindedness. Cultural differences once presented to American kids as a justification for subjugation were now depicted as desirable. Nonwhite peoples formerly stigmatized as racial "others" were now more often approached with care and conciliation. Parents and their children were encouraged to perceive borders as productive sites of conversation and mutual exploration rather than the staging grounds for armed incursion.[5]

It is important to note that a large part of the pressure for this turnaround bubbled up from within the empire itself. Postwar decolonization and "Third Worldism" delegitimated openly imperialist literature. Peoples with direct experience as colonial or quasi-colonial subjects increasingly wrote back to their oppressors, penning juvenile fiction that attested to their own humanity. Native American authors documented the difficulties of reservation life, endemic poverty, and cultural dislocation. Black writers spoke of the lingering effects of slavery and the impact of entrenched racism, but also celebrated African American contributions to the country's history. Hispanic immigrants, often in proudly bilingual books, recounted the challenges of assimilation and the importance of maintaining a sense of connectedness with their heritage. Puerto Rican literary lights sought to instill confidence in children (and diasporic youth) regarding their island and its past. Filipino nationalists triumphantly sang of their independence from an imperious Uncle Sam. Chamorro chroniclers preserved the indigenous language and customs that Guam's US-operated educational system had sought to eradicate. Vietnamese Americans narrated the horrors of prolonged military conflict and the tribulations endured by "boat people." The list of contributors is almost endless, and the influence of their pushback against US empire is undeniable. White supremacist power dynamics championed for a century came under heightened scrutiny. Implicit in all of this output was a reimagining of whose stories mattered to the history of the United States in the world.[6]

This is not to say, of course, that the more troubling aspects of older youth literature have entirely disappeared. Definite strides toward inclusivity and multivocality have been made, but there is still room for improvement. Problems of representation and representativeness continue to plague the industry. As one recent survey observed, since the year 2000 only 10% of children's books are about people of color, while less than 5% have been written by nonwhite authors. Given the growing heterogeneity of America's population, this is a glaring disparity. There remains broad consensus among sociologists and media scholars that when young people cannot see or hear themselves within popular culture, feelings of inadequacy can fester. It is also the case that white children profit from their familiarization with difference. As Nancy Larrick argued in a famous 1965 article often said to have spurred the recent quest for literary diversification, "nonwhite children are learning to read and to understand the American way of life in books which either omit them entirely or scarcely mention them." Even more telling was her appeal to the discourse of juvenile foreign relations. Multicultural youth media, she concluded, was "urgently needed for world cooperation."[7]

A worrying trend, however, has been the recent resurgence of imperially minded series fiction among homeschooling families who self identify as conservative. The books of Edward Stratemeyer, G. A. Henty, and other turn-of-the-century authors have been dusted off, reprinted, and marketed to parents as an alternative to the liberal dogma now being peddled to kids by teachers and librarians. Older children's authors, on the other hand, teach what are considered by some to be desirable lessons in patriotism, manliness, and respect for authority. "America is not only suffering from a shortage of heroes in its public life," observes one account of the genre's revival, but also "from a shortage of heroes in its children's literature, too." "Most of today's children's books," reactionaries moan, "are populated by prissy paragons of indeterminate sex who spend their lives working in shelters for the homeless, lamenting the fate of native Americans, and questioning gender stereotypes." And so, "a growing number of Americans are turning in frustration" to writers of "a decidedly different kidney": those "celebrating the twin virtues of . . . imperialism and Victorian manliness." Publishing company spokespeople have been quoted as being captivated by the "mixture of historical accuracy and political incorrectness" espoused by more ancient authors. In bygone characters, they see "the rugged independence of Errol Flynn and John Wayne." In books that "preach the virtues of family loyalty, female modesty, and patriotism," they perceive a remedy for "politically correct yuckiness." Other activists have recently suggested that communities "pool their resources and open children's librar[ies] where parents [don't] have to worry about their children being propagandized by Wokeness." These beliefs are hardly insignificant, given the approximately two million students homeschooled each year in the United States. It is a number projected only to increase.[8]

Children themselves, as always, remain resilient literary producers. The Internet is alive with evidence of their creative endeavors. Various social media platforms are filled with varieties of kids' storytelling. They post pictures that narrate their perspective on life. They record and upload videos in response to a wide array of more or less political issues. And, in response to their own favorite books, television shows, and films, they also compose their own fan fiction. The latter represents a particularly elaborate public sphere that derives from worlds originally created by adult authors but that adolescents seize to suit their own purposes. In all of this online juvenile discourse, there is a considerable similarity to the novice novellas and amateur newspapers circulated by earlier generations. One can see it in the communal and collaborative nature of chat rooms and message boards, as well as the less encouraging ways in which anonymity allows for a sometimes shocking degree of insensitivity.[9]

As prodigious as this outpouring of creative writing has been, however, it does not regularly broach the subject of foreign relations. With limited exceptions (like immigration and climate change), young people seem less directly engaged with diplomatic questions than they did at earlier junctures in American history. The most popular children's books tend to be set in fantasy realms where allusions to foreign affairs are oblique at best. In the same way that the disastrous Vietnam War caused comic books to jettison any clear concern with international relations, so too have many other forms of youth literature beat a hasty retreat from the fiascos in Afghanistan and Iraq. One could, of course, argue that the politics of empire have simply migrated to newer forms of children's media. The "forever war" against terrorism, a global scramble for diminishing supplies of natural resources, and other transnational subjects do at times appear in today's blockbuster entertainment. Popular platforms like the Marvel "cinematic universe," as well as various video games, have openly collaborated with the American military to propagandize youths and boost recruitment. Their messaging, however, is far more muddled than the juvenile foreign relations of former years. Understandably, contemporary diplomacy seems not to have captured the imaginations of US youth in quite the same way that previous generations eagerly embraced a burgeoning American Century. This may be another manifestation of what has been called an end to the country's victory culture.[10]

No one should shed a tear over the widespread discrediting—at least among youth publishers—of sensationalized settler colonialism and serialized imperialism. Only a depraved mind could harbor nostalgia for children's books championing the right of "Anglo-Saxon blood" to rule the world. Perhaps, however, we should be careful not to throw out the baby with the bath water. Valorizing empire is not a healthy instinct, but the genre's disengagement from foreign relations might do rising generations of American citizens a disservice. For, though many families have abandoned the imperial nursery, the United States has hardly divested itself of empire. Indeed, a "politics of childhood"—whereby postwar American interventionism is rationalized as the selfless act of "child-saving"—has only fueled its growth. With real annual military expenditures exceeding $1 trillion, bases scattered around the globe, fleets deployed in every ocean, and drones circling the skies above several continents, the federal government is an indisputable hegemon. Everywhere around the planet, young people (including those growing up in the country's several overseas territories) are forced to reckon with Uncle's Sam's imperial influence. Why should American children be any different?[11]

Teaching youths to turn a blind eye toward empire carries with it an inherent danger. By ignoring imperialism, kids' literature both wildly misrepresents the relationship of the United States to the world and implicitly transforms America's activities abroad into inconsequential background noise. Authors who avoid the issue help to cultivate an air of mystery around international relations while simultaneously provincializing their readers. Silence within popular media reinforces a belief that the diplomatic arena should remain a province of the privileged. Only those educated at elite institutions, it is implied, possess the qualifications to form an opinion on the subject. Once upon a time, young people were asked to think through complex questions about American foreign relations. They were often taught reprehensible ideas, but they clearly embraced the topic with a good deal of enthusiasm. It might be worthwhile to (re)consider the value of more direct and thoroughgoing appeals to junior citizens regarding the subject of international affairs. At the very least, this would demystify diplomacy and shore up the notion that in a democracy, ordinary people can and should exercise plenary power over policymaking. An unaccountable national security state thrives in part by convincing citizens that military and diplomatic decisions are best left in the hands of pedigreed experts. This is an easier idea to sell when the young are not raised to wrestle with such issues. The youthful zeal of earlier generations, if directed toward nobler ends, could recast America's role in the world.[12]

In the United States, an imperial mission materialized at the same time that ideas about childhood as a distinct phase in life took firmer cultural root. Empire became a national project of supposedly great moral purpose, but so too did childrearing. The two processes almost inevitably intertwined. Young people were approached as junior partners in the country's imperial enterprise, even as their enthusiastic embrace of expansion assured empire's endurance. It is disturbing to watch adults teach white children about their role as the rightful rulers of supposedly inferior peoples. More alarming still was the eagerness with which those same youths often rushed to accept their colonial responsibilities. But these facts need not trigger despair. It is true that many kids were once proud partners in the making of US empire. Could they not now, however, become allies in its unmaking as well? America's relationship to the wider world, after all, still has a good deal of growing up left to do.

ACKNOWLEDGMENTS

This book is indebted to so many wonderful people. It began its life in a graduate seminar taught by Kathy Peiss at the University of Pennsylvania. With Kathy's encouragement, what started as a short research paper gradually expanded in scope and scale. Her insight and editorial work were instrumental in getting this project off the ground. Dan Richter and Michael Zuckerman, my other mentors and friends at Penn, likewise read early drafts and offered encouragement. I owe so much to the stellar graduate program there.

At NYU Press, let me thank Clara Platter, who worked as a tireless advocate for this endeavor. She and her fantastic team put in so much of the hard but often unseen editorial and manual labor required to transform words on the screen into a book. I am also thankful to the fantastic readers who helped shape the manuscript in its early stages. Jennifer Helgren, Daniel Immerwahr, James Marten, and another anonymous reviewer helped to refine and polish so many rough edges. If there's anything good here, it's largely due to their input. So too have many friends and colleagues at SHAFR, SHEAR, the OAH, and the AHA patiently read or listened to portions of this project and given me invaluable guidance. Small portions of this book previously appeared in the *Journal of the Gilded Age and Progressive Era*, the *Western Historical Quarterly*, and *Modern American History*, and I would also like to thank those editors for their permission to republish.

I am likewise grateful for the army of archivists and librarians around the country who helped me track down almost two centuries worth of children's literature. I wish to thank the curators and staff at the American Antiquarian Society, the Baldwin Library of Historical Children's Literature at the University of Florida, the Comic Art Collection at Michigan State University, the Cotsen Children's Library at Princeton University, the Cushing Library at Texas A&M University, the Library of Congress, the National Archives at College Park, the New York Public Library, the Northern Illinois University Library, the Smithsonian, the University of Minnesota Library, the University of Oregon Library, and the University of Wisconsin Library. And a special thank you to the American Antiquarian Society, the Baldwin Library, and the Cotsen Library for the fellowships that made much of this research possible.

It has also been my good fortune to find a happy home in the History Department at Texas A&M University. The university itself deserves special thanks for making an Arts and Humanities Fellowship available, which financed several summers worth of travel and accommodation. So too did the generous fellowship endowed by Ray A. Rothrock help make this book a reality. The College of Liberal Arts' Faculty Development Leave program, meanwhile, provided me with a release from teaching. The Melbern G. Glasscock Center for Humanities Research at Texas A&M University provided a generous publication assistance grant. And last but by no means least, a very hearty thank you to all of my friends and colleagues in the History Department. In seminar rooms, hallways, dinner tables, and local bars, we've shared the ideas (and laughs) that make for better scholarship.

The same goes for all my friends and family. Josh and his fantastic family, the UCSD gang, the old crew from Penn: You know who you are, and you're the best. To my sisters Lauren and Allison, my "brothers" Brock and Adam, my nephew Hollis, the extended family down in Florida, and of course Carol and Jerry, I love you all. Excuse me, I mean, I love y'all. And, of course, here's to the memory of my mother and father, who sacrificed so much to give their kids happy childhoods and great educations.

The book is dedicated to Katherine and our good boy Hudson. They make life wonderful.

# NOTES

## INTRODUCTION

1 Henry R. Luce, "The American Century," *Life* (February 17, 1941), 61–65. A. G. Hopkins discusses Luce and the larger subject of US imperialism in *American Empire: A Global History* (Princeton, NJ: Princeton University Press, 2018), 443–450.
2 Ellen Key, *The Century of the Child* (New York: Putnam's, 1900).
3 The connection between "The American Century" and "The Century of the Child" is helpfully suggested in Susan Eckelmann Berghel, Sara Fieldston, and Paul Renfro, "Introduction," Eckelmann Berghel, Fieldston, and Renfro, eds., *Growing Up America: Youth and Politics Since 1945* (Athens: University of Georgia Press, 2019), 8. Children and the adult quest for young people's "consent" in Courtney Weikle-Mills, *Imaginary Citizens: Child Readers and the Limits of American Independence, 1640–1868* (Baltimore, MD: Johns Hopkins University Press, 2013). Little scholarship exists on the linkages between children's literature and US foreign relations, but a nice overview can be found in Karen Sands-O'Connor and Marietta Frank, eds., *Internationalism in Children's Series* (New York: Palgrave Macmillan, 2014). On the development of "childhood" as a social and legal category in the United States, see Stephen Mintz, *Huck's Raft: A History of American Childhood* (Cambridge, MA: Harvard University Press, 2004).
4 Thomas Borstelmann, *Just Like Us: The American Struggle to Understand Foreigners* (New York: Columbia University Press, 2020) provides an important statement on why we should consider popular culture and the evolution of mainstream American attitudes toward foreign peoples to be components of the history of the United States in the world. Patrick Brantlinger, *Rule of Darkness: Imperialism and British Literature, 1830–1914* (Ithaca, NY: Cornell University Press, 1988), 190, notes that "much imperialist discourse was . . . directed at a specifically adolescent audience, the future rulers of the world." "Hegemonic habits of thought" was inspired by Walter Nugent's *Habits of Empire: A History of American Expansion* (New York: Knopf, 2008). An important early investigation into the shaping power of children's literature is R. Gordon Kelly, "Literature and the Historian," *American Quarterly* 26, no. 2 (May 1974): 141–159. On empire, see Paul A. Kramer, "Power and Connection: Imperial Histories of the United States in the World," *American Historical Review* 116, no. 5 (December 2011): 1348–1391. As Kramer recommends, this book will not engage in hairsplitting over what, precisely,

empire "is." *Empire's Nursery* will instead use the term "imperial" as a category of analysis—signifying asymmetries of political, economic, and cultural power between the United States and the world—meant to tie together a wide array of children's literature that, though thematically and chronologically diverse, shared an interest in legitimating the exercise of American authority over "inferior" peoples.

5  On the "constructedness" of empire and the necessity of stories to sustain it, see Edward W. Said, *Culture and Imperialism* (New York: Knopf, 1993). Mary Renda, *Taking Haiti: Military Occupation and the Culture of U.S. Imperialism* (Chapel Hill: UNC Press, 2001), 6, notes that writers often help introduce the idea of empire while erasing the violent processes by which empires are built. The role of "representational machines" and the legitimization of empire is described in Ricardo D. Salvatore, "The Enterprise of Knowledge: Representational Machines of Informal Empire," in Gilbert M. Joseph, Catherine C. Legrand, and Ricardo D. Salvatore, eds., *Close Encounters of Empire: Writing the Cultural History of Latin American Relations* (Durham, NC: Duke University Press, 1998), 69–104, and Stephen Greenblatt, *Marvelous Possessions: The Wonder of the New World* (Chicago: University of Chicago Press, 1991).

6  On the broader theme of the American empire's concealment, see Daniel Immerwahr, *How to Hide an Empire: A History of the Greater United States* (New York: Farrar, Straus, and Giroux, 2019). A connection between childhood and imperial innocence has been suggested by Ariel Dorfman, *The Empire's Old Clothes: What the Lone Ranger, Babar, and Other Innocent Heroes Do to Our Minds* (New York: Pantheon Books, 1983), 199–210. These ideas about images of childhood innocence helping to "soften" the application of American power owe something to Mischa Honeck, *Our Frontier Is the World: The Boy Scouts in the Age of American Ascendancy* (Ithaca, NY: Cornell University Press, 2018), 13, who argues that youth culture "sanitize[d] the bloody work empire and allay[ed] anxieties about the future in a century marred by ideological conflict, war, depression, and nuclear war." More generally, Robin Bernstein chronicles "the use of childhood to make political projects appear innocuous, natural, and therefore justified" in *Racial Innocence: Performing American Childhood from Slavery to Civil Rights* (New York: NYU Press, 2011), 33.

7  Literature covering the history of the United States and the world is voluminous and still growing exponentially. A solid overview of the subject is Ian Tyrrell's *Transnational Nation: United States History in Global Perspective Since 1789*, 2nd ed. (New York: Palgrave Macmillan, 2015). On diplomatic history's expanding cast of characters, see Thomas Zeiler, "The Diplomatic History Bandwagon: A State of the Field," *Journal of American History* 95, no. 4 (March 2009): 1053–1073.

8  On these ideas more broadly, see Corinne T. Field and Nicholas L. Syrett, "Chronological Age: A Useful Category of Analysis," *American Historical Review* 125, no. 2 (April 2020): 371–459, and James Marten, "Childhood Studies and History: Catching a Culture in High Relief," in Anna Mae Duane, ed., *The Children's*

*Table: Childhood Studies and the Humanities* (Athens: University of Georgia Press, 2013), 49–60. A pioneering cohort of scholars is currently working to connect the histories of childhood and foreign relations in the United States. An important statement on this subfield can be found in the multiple pathbreaking essays that comprise the "Transnational Generations" forum. See *Diplomatic History* 38, no. 2 (April 2014): 233–298. Among the historians most influential upon my thinking here have been Jennifer Helgren, *American Girls and Global Responsibility: A New Relation to the World During the Early Cold War* (New Brunswick, NJ: Rutgers University Press, 2017); Victoria M. Grieve, *Little Cold Warriors: American Childhood in the 1950s* (New York: Oxford University Press, 2018); Sara Fieldston, *Raising the World: Child Welfare in the American Century* (Cambridge, MA: Harvard University Press, 2015); Margaret Peacock, *Innocent Weapons: The Soviet and American Politics of Childhood in the Cold War* (Chapel Hill: UNC Press, 2014); Anita Casavantes Bradford, *The Revolution Is for the Children: The Politics of Childhood in Havana and Miami, 1959–1962* (Chapel Hill: UNC Press, 2014); Ann Marie Kordas, *The Politics of Childhood in Cold War America* (London: Pickering and Chatto, 2013). Collectively, these (and other) historians, along with this book, wish to respond to the call for studies of the United States in the world that place greater emphasis on childhood and youth made by Akira Iriye in *Global and Transnational History: The Past, Present, and Future* (New York: Palgrave Macmillan, 2013), 70–71.

9  Roscoe Kiper, "American Boys and the Future," *The American Boy* (June 1903): 246. Demographic statistics located in Priscilla Ferguson Clement, *Growing Pains: Children in the Industrial Age, 1850–1890* (New York: Twayne, 1997), 1. This book follows in the footsteps of most scholars of American childhood in seeing 20 years of age as, very roughly, a cutoff point for historical inquiry. With some exceptions, 21 has usually signaled the formal entry into adulthood for many people. The book also elects not to finely parse the term "child" in an effort to display various scholars' diverse usage and deployment of the term. There are, of course, gradations within that span (infancy, adolescence, etc.) and experiential differences dependent upon factors such as race and gender, but time and space constraints necessitate that these be downplayed in favor of a broader overview. On terminology and the age of majority, see Howard Chudacoff, *How Old Are You?: Age Consciousness in American Culture* (Princeton, NJ: Princeton University Press, 1989).

10 The literature on masculinity and American empire is now voluminous. Important to my thinking here has been Kristin L. Hoganson, *Fighting for American Manhood: How Gender Politics Provoked the Spanish-American and Philippine-American Wars* (New Haven, CT: Yale University Press, 1998); Gail Bederman, *Manliness & Civilization: A Cultural History of Gender and Race in the United States, 1880–1917* (Chicago: University of Chicago Press, 1995); and Amy S. Greenberg, *Manifest Manhood and the Antebellum American Empire* (Cambridge: Cambridge University Press, 2005).

11 "Jim Crow Colonialism" in Peter Schmidt, *Sitting in Darkness: New South Fiction, Education, and the Rise of Jim Crow Colonialism, 1865–1920* (Jackson: University of Mississippi Press, 2008). On race and US foreign policy more broadly, see Robert Vitalis, *White World Order, Black Power Politics: The Birth of American International Relations* (Ithaca, NY: Cornell University Press, 2015); Matthew Frye Jacobson, *Barbarian Virtues: The United States Encounters Foreign Peoples at Home and Abroad, 1876–1917* (New York: Hill and Wang, 2000) and Michael L. Krenn, *The Color of Empire: Race and American Foreign Relations* (Washington, DC: Potomac Books, 2006). On how children "learn" race, see Jennifer Ritterhouse, *Growing Up Jim Crow: How Black and White Children Learned Race* (Chapel Hill: UNC Press, 2006). Childhood and the reification of racial categories in Caroline F. Levander, *Cradle of Liberty: Race, the Child, and National Belonging from Thomas Jefferson to W.E.B. DuBois* (Durham, NC: Duke University Press, 2006).

12 On the rise of a more "global outlook" among Americans, see Frank Ninkovich, *Global Dawn: The Cultural Foundation of American Internationalism, 1865–1890* (Cambridge, MA: Harvard University Press, 2009). Imperialism's cultural component is theorized in Said, *Culture and Imperialism*. Specific attention to the literary culture of US empire is discussed in Andy Doolen, *Territories of Empire: U.S. Writing from the Louisiana Purchase to Mexican Independence* (New York: Oxford University Press, 2014); Meg Wesling, *Empire's Proxy: American Literature and U.S. Imperialism in the Philippines* (New York: NYU Press, 2011); John Carlos Rowe, *Literary Culture and U.S. Imperialism: From the Revolution to World War II* (New York: Oxford University Press, 2000) and Richard Slotkin's "trilogy" on frontier violence: *Regeneration Through Violence: The Mythology of the American Frontier, 1600–1860* (Middletown, CT: Wesleyan University Press, 1973); *The Fatal Environment: The Myth of the Frontier in the Age of Industrialization, 1800–1890* (New York: Atheneum, 1985); and *Gunfighter Nation: The Myth of the Frontier in Twentieth-Century America* (New York: Atheneum, 1992). The historiography of the British Empire has been far more active in incorporating children's literature. See, for example, Michelle J. Smith, *From Colonial to Modern: Transnational Girlhood in Canadian, Australian, and New Zealand Children's Literature, 1840–1940* (Toronto: University of Toronto Press, 2018); Kristine Alexander, *Guiding Modern Girls: Girlhood, Empire, and Internationalism in the 1920s and 1930s* (Vancouver: UBC Press, 2017); Joseph Bristow, *Empire Boys: Adventures in a Man's World* (London: Routledge, 2016); Bradley Deane, *Masculinity and the New Imperialism: Rewriting Manhood in British Popular Literature, 1870–1914* (Cambridge: Cambridge University Press, 2014); Michelle J. Smith, *Empire in British Girls' Literature and Culture: Imperial Girls, 1880–1915* (New York: Palgrave Macmillan, 2011); Kirsten Drotner, *English Children and Their Magazines, 1751–1945* (New Haven, CT: Yale University Press, 1988); Megan Norcia, *Gaming Empire in Children's British Board Games, 1836–1860* (New York: Routledge, 2019); Fiona Paisley, "Childhood and Race: Growing Up in the Empire," in Philippa Levine, ed., *Gender and Empire* (New York: Oxford University Press, 2004), 240–259; Jeffrey Richards, ed.,

*Imperialism and Juvenile Literature* (Manchester: Manchester University Press, 1989); and Cecil D. Eby, *The Road to Armageddon: The Marital Spirit in English Popular Literature, 1870–1914* (Durham, NC: Duke University Press, 1987).

13  On children as the colonized "other," see Perry Nodelman, "The Other: Orientalism, Colonialism, and Children's Literature," *Children's Literature Association Quarterly* 17, no. 1 (1992): 32, and M. Daphne Kutzer, *Empire's Children: Empire and Imperialism in Classic British Children's Books* (New York: Garland, 2000), xvi, who works from an "underlying assumption . . . that children are colonized by the books they read." Regarding the nebulous manner in which youths read texts, see Daniel T. Rodgers, *The Work Ethic in Industrial America* (Chicago: University of Chicago Press, 1974), 127–128. Marah Gubar discusses the need for scholars of children's literature to address the writing of young people themselves in "On Not Defining Children's Literature," *PMLA* 126, no. 1 (2011): 209–216. On the ways in which audiences "did not submissively receive hegemonic cultural messages" but "actively negotiated the meanings of fiction" and "used texts in their own ways," see Charles Johanningsmeier, "Understanding Readers of Fiction in American Periodicals, 1880–1914," in Christine Bold, ed., *The Oxford History of Popular Print Culture, Volume Six, U.S. Popular Print Culture, 1860–1920* (New York: Oxford University Press, 2011), 591–610, quoted on p. 592. The polyvocality of texts is described in Amy Beth Aronson, *Taking Liberties: Early American Women's Magazines and Their Readers* (Westport, CT: Praeger, 2002).

14  As Mischa Honeck argues, "children sustain the edifice of empire." See "Friends of the Free World: The Boy Scouts and the Juvenilization of America's Cold War Empire," in Eckelmann Berghel, Fieldston, and Renfro eds., *Growing Up America*, 36–37. Youth influence over the media they consume is covered in Margaret Cassidy, *Children, Media, and American History: Printed Poison, Pernicious Stuff, and Other Terrible Temptations* (New York: Routledge, 2018) and Christine Alexander and Juliet McMaster, eds., *The Child Writer from Austen to Woolf* (Cambridge: Cambridge University Press, 2005), 1–7, but see also Alicia Brazeau, "'I Must Have My Gossip with the Young Folks': Letter Writing and Literacy in The Boys' and Girls' Magazine and Fireside Companion," *Children's Literature Association Quarterly* 38, no. 2 (2013): 159–176, and Paul B. Ringel's idea of child readers as "participatory consumers" of their books and magazines in *Commercializing Childhood: Children's Magazines, Urban Gentility, and the Ideal of the Child Consumer in the United States, 1823–1918* (Amherst: University of Massachusetts Press, 2015), 113. In "Print Networks and Youth Information Culture: Young People, Amateur Publishing, and Children's Periodicals, 1867–1890" (PhD diss., University of Illinois at Urbana-Champaign, 2017), 97–98, Dawn Michelle Smith also posits a collaborative relationship between adult authors and young readers. The "power relationships were asymmetrical," she argues, but the "influences were bidirectional." For a more skeptical take on children's agency, however, see Sarah Maza, "The Kids Aren't All Right: Historians and the Problem of Childhood," *American Historical Review* 125, no. 4 (October 2020): 1261–1285.

15 Children and the replication of power structures in James E. Block, *Crucible of Consent: American Child Rearing and the Forging of Liberal Society* (Cambridge, MA: Harvard University Press, 2012), and Karen Sánchez-Eppler, *Dependent States: The Child's Part in Nineteenth-Century American Culture* (Chicago: University of Chicago Press, 2005), xv–xvii, who urges us not to see young people merely as "passive receptors of culture." Compliance in Jessica Isaac, "Compliant Circulation: Children's Writing, American Periodicals, and Public Culture, 1839–1882," (PhD diss., University of Pittsburgh, 2015). See also Susan A. Miller, "Assent as Agency in the Early Years of the Children of the American Revolution," *Journal of the History of Childhood and Youth* 9, no. 1 (Winter 2016): 48–65; Mona Gleason, "Avoiding the Agency Trap: Caveats for Historians of Children, Youth, and Education," *History of Education* 45, no. 4 (2016): 446–459; or Marah Gubar, "The Hermeneutics of Recuperation: What a Kinship-Model Approach to Children's Agency Could Do for Children's Literature and Childhood Studies," *Jeunesse: Young People, Texts, Cultures* 8, no. 1 (Summer 2016): 291–310. These thoughts also owe something to the questions raised by Elliott West and Paula Petrik in "Introduction," *Small Worlds: Children and Adolescents in America, 1850–1950* (Lawrence: University Press of Kansas, 1992), 1–8.

16 "New sensibilities" in Steven Mintz, "Why the History of Childhood Matters," *Journal of the History of Childhood and Youth* 5, no. 1 (Winter 2012): 22.

17 For empire as a "way of life," see T. J. Jackson Lears, *Rebirth of a Nation: The Making of Modern America, 1877–1920* (New York: Harper Collins, 2009), chap. 7, and William Appleman Williams, *Empire as a Way of Life: An Essay on the Causes and Character of America's Present Predicament, Along with a Few Thoughts about an Alternative* (New York: Oxford University Press, 1980).

18 The "age-segmentation" of books is discussed in Sarah Wadsworth, *In the Company of Books: Literature and Its "Classes" in Nineteenth-Century America* (Amherst: University of Massachusetts Press, 2006). On the importance of children's literature to the articulation of ideas about childhood, see Patricia Crain, *Reading Children: Literacy, Property, and the Dilemmas of Childhood in Nineteenth-Century America* (Philadelphia: University of Pennsylvania Press, 2016). The most comprehensive account of the nineteenth century's creation of a "priceless child" is Viviana A. Zelizer, *Pricing the Priceless Child: The Changing Social Value of Children* (New York: Basic Books, 1985).

19 On colonization and the "child-like" savage, see Jacobson, *Barbarian Virtues*, 142. The rhetorical use of children as a justification for foreign policy programs is discussed in Karen Dubinsky, "Children, Ideology, and Iconography: How Babies Rule the World," *Journal of the History of Childhood and Youth* 5, no. 1 (Winter 2012): 5–13.

20 On this earlier era of largely didactic children's literature, see Anne Scott MacLeod, *American Childhood: Essays on Children's Literature of the Nineteenth and Twentieth Centuries* (Athens: University of Georgia Press, 1994), 87–98 and Gil-

lian Brown, *The Consent of the Governed: The Lockean Legacy in Early American Culture* (Cambridge, MA: Harvard University Press, 2001).

21  On the disparate and "regional" nature of antebellum and wartime children's literature, see James Marten, *The Children's Civil War* (Chapel Hill: UNC Press, 1998), 31–67. On empire as an integrative force among young people (albeit in the British context), see Troy Boone, *Youth of Darkest England: Working-Class Children at the Heart of Victorian Empire* (New York: Routledge, 2005).

22  "Anthony Comstock Lecture," *New York Tribune*, March 5, 1884 and quoted in Gail Schmunk Murray, *American Children's Literature and the Construction of Childhood* (New York: Twayne, 1998), 80; Charles M. Harvey, "The Dime Novel in American Life," *The Atlantic* 100 (July 1907): 44–45. The transition from children's work to children's education is most succinctly outlined in Peter Stearns, *Childhood in World History* (New York: Routledge, 2006), 55, which argues that the "modern model" of childhood involved the shift "from work to schooling." This "meant . . . that children turned from being . . . economic assets to becoming absolute economic liabilities." On literature, empire, and the thirst for adventure, see Jimmy L. Bryan, *The American Elsewhere: Adventure and Manliness in the Age of Expansion* (Lawrence: University Press of Kansas, 2017).

23  Textbooks and US empire in Clif Stratton, *Education for Empire: American Schools, Race, and the Paths of Good Citizenship* (Berkeley: University of California Press, 2016).

24  An excellent overview of the history of the "popular press," loosely defined by its affordability and accessibility, can be found in Christine Bold's introduction to Bold, ed., *The Oxford History of Popular Print Culture*, 1–22. The capsule history of American children's literature presented here is drawn from Gillian Avery, *Behold the Child: American Children and Their Books, 1621–1922* (Baltimore, MD: Johns Hopkins University Press, 1994). Civil War juvenile fiction is described in Alice Fahs, *The Imagined Civil War: Popular Literature of the North and South, 1861–1865* (Chapel Hill: UNC Press, 2001), 256–286, and Sam Pickering, "A Boy's Own War," *New England Quarterly* 48, no. 3 (September 1975): 362–377. On the nineteenth-century rise of children's cheap fiction and the adult-led backlash, see Margaret Cassidy, "'Concerning Printed Poison': Nineteenth-Century American Adults' Ambivalence about Children's Interactions with Cheap Fiction," *Journal of the History of Childhood and Youth* 8, no. 2 (Spring 2015): 211–228, and Vicki Anderson, *The Dime Novel in Children's Literature* (Jefferson, NC: McFarland, 2004). Shelley Streeby's work on the popular press and antebellum imperialism has been formative to my thinking about mass children's media. See *American Sensations: Class, Empire, and the Production of Popular Culture* (Berkeley: University of California Press, 2002). On the long nineteenth century's popular fiction (but with little attention paid to young people), see Nancy Bentley, *Frantic Panoramas: American Literature and Mass Culture, 1870–1920* (Philadelphia: University of Pennsylvania Press, 2009), and Hugh McIntosh, *Guilty Pleasures: Popular Novels and American Audiences in the Long Nineteenth Century* (Charlottesville:

University of Virginia Press, 2018). Youth periodicals and the thematic shift away from genteel liberal Protestant values are discussed in Ringel, *Commercializing Childhood*.

25  Working-class youth culture in David Nasaw, *Children of the City: At Work and At Play* (Garden City, NY: Anchor Press/Doubleday, 1985), and Clement, *Growing Pains*.

26  On the fundamental connection between whiteness and the early romanticizing of childhood, see Bernstein, *Racial Innocence*. Representations of nonwhite children in juvenile literature are discussed in Donnarae MacCann, *White Supremacy in Children's Literature: Characterizations of African Americans from 1830–1900* (New York: Routledge, 1998). On the childhoods of colonized children, see A. J. Angulo, *Empire and Education: A History of Greed and Goodwill from the War of 1898 to the War on Terror* (New York: Palgrave Macmillan, 2012); Jonathan Zimmerman, *Innocents Abroad: American Teachers in the American Century* (Cambridge, MA: Harvard University Press, 2006); Solsiree Del Moral, *Negotiating Empire: The Cultural Politics of Schools in Puerto Rico, 1898–1952* (Madison: University of Wisconsin Press, 2013); and Sarah Steinbock-Pratt, *Educating the Empire: American Teachers and Contested Colonization in the Philippines* (Cambridge: Cambridge University Press, 2019). The limitations of a study confined to "popular" fiction is somewhat offset by the fact that the genre's popularity forced more "respectable" books and publications to adopt the trappings of mass literature. Paul Ringel calls this hybrid form "genteel sensationalism." See Ringel, *Commercializing Childhood*, 11 and 73–89. This is not to suggest that nonwhite children's literature was nonexistent, but rather to argue that its content less often directly addressed questions of foreign relations. For examples of Black children's literature, see Katharine Capshaw and Anna Mae Duane, *Who Writes for Black Children? African-American Children's Literature Before 1900* (Minneapolis: University of Minnesota Press, 2017), and Nazera Sadiq Wright, *Black Girlhood in the Nineteenth Century* (Urbana: University of Illinois Press, 2016). And, of course, Black literature for adults often discussed the subjects of diplomacy and empire, as demonstrated in John Cullen Gruesser, *The Empire Abroad and the Empire at Home: African American Literature and the Era of Overseas Expansion* (Athens: University of Georgia Press, 2012), and Gretchen Murphy, *Shadowing the White Man's Burden: U.S. Imperialism and the Problem of the Color Line* (New York: NYU Press, 2010). Julia L. Mickenberg argues that the postwar children's literature industry became a haven for communists, leftists, and fellow travelers. See *Learning from the Left: Children's Literature, the Cold War, and Radical Politics in the United States* (New York: Oxford University Press, 2006).

27  Kutzer, *Empire's Children*, xiii.

28  As Melani McAlister, *Epic Encounters: Culture, Media, and U.S. Interests in the Middle East, 1945–2000* (Berkeley: University of California Press, 2001), 4, argues, culture is not a frivolous footnote to the superstructures that "matter" to foreign relations, but rather deserves "a central place in an analysis of the production

and reproduction of U.S. power." There are many excellent histories covering the popular culture of US empire. Crucial to my thinking here have been Kristin L. Hoganson, *Consumers' Imperium: The Global Production of American Domesticity, 1865–1920* (Chapel Hill: UNC Press, 2007); Amy S. Greenberg, *Manifest Manhood*; Amy Kaplan, *The Anarchy of Empire in the Making of U.S. Culture* (Cambridge, MA: Harvard University Press, 2002); Renda, *Taking Haiti*; Amy Kaplan and Donald E. Pease, eds., *Cultures of United States Imperialism* (Durham, NC: Duke University Press, 1993); Michael Hunt, *Ideology and U.S. Foreign Policy*, rev. ed. (New Haven, CT: Yale University Press, 2009); and Talya Zemach-Bersin, "Imperial Pedagogies: Education for American Globalism, 1898–1950" (PhD diss., Yale University, 2015).

29 Luce, "American Century," 61–65.

## 1. HOW THE WEST WAS FUN

1 Harry Harrison, "An Adventure with the Indians," *True Gazette* 2, no. 4 (April 1873) in the American Antiquarian Society Amateur Story Collection (hereafter AAS).

2 Following James Belich, settler colonialism refers to a nexus of practices and ideas that involved a demographically dominant population of white settlers displacing indigenous peoples, seizing and then reengineering their land to accommodate capitalist development, and legitimating those actions through an appeal to divine will, racial predilections, or some other interpretive fiction. See Belich, *Replenishing the Earth: The Settler Revolution and the Rise of Angloworld, 1783–1939* (New York: Oxford University Press, 2009). The literature on settler colonialism is voluminous, but, for the US case, see Walter L. Hixson, *American Settler Colonialism: A History* (New York: Palgrave Macmillan, 2013) and Adam Dahl, *Empire of the People: Settler Colonialism and the Foundations of Modern Democratic Thought* (Lawrence: University Press of Kansas, 2018). The Gilded Age commemoration of violence against Modoc Indians is covered in Boyd Cothran, *Remembering the Modoc War: Redemptive Violence and the Making of American Innocence* (Chapel Hill: UNC Press, 2014).

3 The mythologization of the frontier is discussed in Richard Slotkin, *Gunfighter Nation: The Myth of the Frontier in Twentieth Century America* (New York: Macmillan, 1992); Christine Bold, *The Frontier Club: Popular Westerns and Cultural Power, 1880–1924* (New York: Oxford University Press, 2013); Christine Bold, *Selling the Wild West: Popular Western Fiction, 1860–1960* (Bloomington: Indiana University Press, 1987); and Greg Grandin, *The End of the Myth: From the Frontier to the Border Wall in the Mind of America* (New York: Metropolitan Books, 2019).

4 Karen Sánchez-Eppler, *Dependent States: The Child's Part in Nineteenth-Century American Culture* (Chicago: University of Chicago Press, 2005), xv; Grandin, *The End of the Myth*, 5.

5 Scott E. Casper et al., eds., *A History of the Book in America: Volume Three, The Industrial Book, 1840–1880* (Chapel Hill: UNC Press, 2007), and J. Randolph

Cox, "Dime Novels," in Christine Bold, ed., *The Oxford History of Popular Print Culture, Volume Six, U.S. Popular Print Culture, 1860–1920* (New York: Oxford University Press, 2011), 63–80. Cox, "Dime Novels," 77, notes that "in time the general level of [dime novel] readership shifted to boys aged eight to sixteen years old." Dime novel dissemination during the Civil War and its transformation into "youth literature" is discussed in Alice Fahs, *The Imagined Civil War: Popular Literature of the North and South, 1861–1865* (Chapel Hill: UNC Press, 2001), 225–286. Older but still influential studies on the rise of the dime novel include Michael Denning, *Mechanic Accents: Dime Novels and Working-Class Culture in America* (New York: Verso, 1987), and Daryl Jones, *The Dime Novel Western* (Bowling Green, OH: Popular Press, 1978), though Denning rejects the thesis that dime novels were a young person's delight much before the 1890s.

6  W. H. Bishop, "Story-Paper Literature," *The Atlantic* 44 (September 1879): 384; "trysting places" quoted in Charles M. Harvey, "The Dime Novel in American Life," *The Atlantic* 100 (July 1907): 37. On dime novels as a "children's genre," see Martin Woodside, *Frontiers of Boyhood: Imagining America Past and Future* (Norman: University of Oklahoma Press, 2020), 45–78. Robert H. Vine, *The American West: An Interpretive History* (Boston: Little, Brown, 1973), 274, estimated that two-thirds of the dime literature produced between 1860 and 1898 was set in the trans-Mississippi West. Paul B. Ringel, *Commercializing Childhood: Children's Magazines, Urban Gentility, and the Ideal of the Child Consumer in the United States, 1823–1918* (Amherst: University of Massachusetts Press, 2015), 11 and 73–89, defines attempts to graft bourgeois didacticism atop popular fiction's sensibilities as "genteel sensationalism." More general coverage of the "cheap fiction" read by the era's young people and the changing form of children's media in Margaret M. Cassidy, *Children, Media, and American History: Printed Poison, Pernicious Stuff, and Other Terrible Temptations* (New York: Routledge, 2018); Ryan K. Anderson, *Frank Meriwell and the Fiction of All-American Boyhood: The Progressive-Era Creation of the Schoolboy Sports Story* (Fayetteville: University of Arkansas Press, 2015); Shelley Streeby, *American Sensations: Class, Empire, and the Production of Popular Culture* (Berkeley: University of California Press, 2002); Shelley Streeby, "Dime Novels and the Rise of Mass-Market Genres," in Leonard Cassuto et al., eds., *Cambridge History of the American Novel* (Cambridge: Cambridge University Press, 2011): 586–599; and Paul J. Erickson, "Judging Books By Their Covers: Format, the Implied Reader, and the 'Degeneration' of the Dime Novel," *Transcendental Quarterly* 12, no. 3 (December 1998): 247–263. Of course, school textbooks from the era often trafficked in similar themes, thus creating a kind of cultural feedback loop. See Laurence M. Hauptman, "Westward the Course of Empire: Geography Schoolbooks and Manifest Destiny, 1783–1893," *The Historian* 40, no. 3 (May 1978): 423–440.

7  "Grim Walker's Vengeance: The Story of an Indian Fighter," *Golden Argosy* 5, no. 15 (March 12, 1887): 238–239; James McCabe, Jr., *Planting the Wilderness; or, The Pioneer Boys, a Story of Frontier Life* (Boston: Lee and Shepard, 1875), 1; Editor of

"The Youth's Casket," *The Burning Village and Other Indian Stories* (New York: Blakeman and Mason, 1862), 6–9; "To Young America" in Samuel Woodworth Cozzens, *Crossing the Quicksands; or, The Veritable Adventures of Hal and Ned Upon the Pacific Slope* (Boston: Lee and Shepard, 1877), 3. The youthfulness of the dime novel's audience discussed in Vicki Anderson, *The Dime Novel in Children's Literature* (Jefferson, NC: McFarland, 2005). Ringel, *Commercializing Childhood*, 113–114, notes the collapse of multiple "respectable" children's periodicals during the 1870s and suggests they failed because they offered "no perspective on young people's roles in modern society" and refused to accept children as "participatory consumers" in the making of American history.

8  Samuel Fletcher, *Red Men of the Woods; or, Long Bob the Sharp Shooting Hunter* (New York: George Munro, 1865) and reprinted as Beadle's Frontier Series No. 59 (Cleveland, OH: Arthur Westbrook, 1909), 9–10; George Robinson, *The Red Star of the Seminoles: A Tale of Wild Life on the Border* (New York: George Munro, 1868) and reprinted as Beadle's Frontier Series No. 54 (Cleveland, OH: Arthur Westbrook, 1909), 9; Dangerfield Burr, "Buffalo Bill's Four; or, Custer's Shadow," *New York Dime Library* 58, no. 750 (March 8, 1893), 11; John W. Mackey, *The Shawnee Witch: A Romance of the Western Border* (New York: George Munro, 1868) and reprinted as Beadle's Frontier Series No. 47 (Cleveland, OH: Arthur Westbrook, 1908), 9–11.

9  Samuel Fletcher, *Harry Hardskull* (New York: George Munro, 1868) and reprinted as Beadle's Frontier Series No. 50 (Cleveland, OH: Arthur Westbrook, 1909), 12; Col. Ralph Fenton, "Little Red Cloud, The Boy Indian Chief," *Young Men of America* 13, no. 627 (September 12, 1889): 2; Quelton, "The Massacre on the Sweetwater," *Golden Hours* 28, no. 715 (October 12, 1901), 16; "Chasing the Apaches," *Youth's Companion* 60, no. 1 (January 6, 1887): 4; Mackey, *The Shawnee Witch*. Similar examples include: John Willis Hays, "Attacked by Apaches: An Adventure at Zuni," *Youth's Companion* 59, no. 30 (August 5, 1886): 295; John Willis Hays, "Besieged," *Youth's Companion* 60, no. 6 (February 10, 1887): 51; Fred E. Fanning, "The Sergeant's Story," *Youth's Companion* 60, no. 20 (May 19, 1887): 226; Will C. Barnes, "Raided by Apaches: A True Story of Cowboy Life in Arizona," *Youth's Companion* 61, no. 3 (January 19, 1888): 27; or Lt. R. G. Carter, "The Cow-boys' Verdict," *Youth's Companion* 61, no. 8 (February 23, 1888): 94.

10  Fletcher, *Red Men of the Woods*, 18, 25–26; Joseph F. Henderson, *Roving Dick, Hunter* (New York: George Munro, 1867) and reprinted as Beadle's Frontier Series No. 68 (Cleveland, OH: Arthur Westbrook, 1909), 32; Burr, "Buffalo Bill's Four," 25; Gus Williams, "The Spectre of El Paso," *The Boys' Own* 3, no. 53 (October 10, 1874): 1–2; Elwin Gerry Davis, "Snatched from the Fire," *Golden Hours* 28, no. 718 (November 2, 1901): 7. On the era's politics of rape, see Crystal Feimster, *Southern Horrors: Women and the Politics of Rape and Lynching* (Cambridge, MA: Harvard University Press, 2009).

11  Lt. Howard Payson, *The Boy Scouts on the Range* (New York: A. L. Burt, 1911), 244–245, 252; C. H. Pearson, *The Cabin on the Prairie* (Boston: Lee and Shepard,

1870), 186, 180–181; William West Wilder, "Cowboy Chris, the Desert Centaur," *Western Weekly* 2, no. 68 (1897): 4.

12 William Barrows, *The General; or, Twelve Nights in the Hunter's Camp, a Narrative of Real Life* (Boston: Lee and Shepard, 1871), iii, 116–117, 159; J. Springer, *Big-Hearted Joe: An Indian Tale* (New York: George Munro, 1865) and reprinted as Beadle's Frontier Series No. 72 (Cleveland, OH: Arthur Westbrook, 1909), 9; "Sitting Bull and the Outbreak of 1876," *Golden Argosy* (May 23, 1885): 197; Edward A. Rand, "The Young Rifleman Going West; Or, the Cost of Settling the Republic," *Golden Argosy* 1, no. 15 (March 17, 1883): 115. Similar sentiments regarding the retreat of Mexican culture in California can be found in Samuel Woodworth Cozzens, *Crossing the Quicksands; or, The Veritable Adventures of Hal and Ned Upon the Pacific Slope* (Boston: Lee and Shepard, 1877), 304–305. "Imperialist Nostalgia" in Renato Rosaldo, *Culture and Truth* (Boston: Beacon Press, 1989).

13 Edward S. Ellis, "Blazing Arrow: A Tale of the Frontier," *The Argosy* (November 7, 1891): 141; Ralph Morgan, "Saving the Life of Boone: A True Incident in the Early Settlement of Kentucky," *Golden Argosy* (May 23, 1885): 198; Jacob Abbott, *Aboriginal America* (New York: Sheldon, 1860), 255–257, 277, 287–288. The broader connection between popular culture and racialized thinking is explored in Linda Frost, *Never One Nation: Freaks, Savages, and Whiteness* (Minneapolis: University of Minnesota Press, 2005).

14 "The Tariff Question," *Golden Argosy* 1, no. 12 (February 24, 1883): 92; James McCabe, Jr., *Planting the Wilderness; or, The Pioneer Boys, a Story of Frontier Life* (Boston: Lee and Shepard, 1875), 1; Elijah Kellogg, *Lion Ben of Elm Island* (Boston: Lee and Shepard, 1869), 5–6; Elijah Kellogg, *Brought to the Front; or, the Young Defenders* (Boston: Lee and Shepard, 1876), 5–6; Elijah Kellogg, *The Mission of the Black Rifle; or, On the Trail* (Boston: Lee and Shepard, 1876), 5–6. Ellen Boucher discusses "the transformative power of the settler colonies" that "permeated . . . children's books more generally" in *Empire's Children: Child Emigration, Welfare, and the Decline of the British World, 1869–1967* (New York: Cambridge University Press, 2014), 37–38.

15 See, for example, E. V. Smalley, "Home-Seeking in the West," *Youth's Companion* 59, no. 19 (May 13, 1886): 186–187; J. T. Trowbridge, "With the Colorado Cowboys," *Youth's Companion* 60, no. 10 (March 10, 1887): 99–100.

16 Advertisement in *Harper's Round Table* 2, no. 23 (September 1899): 502–503; Col. Prentiss Ingraham, *Buffalo Bill's Pledged Pard or, True to the End* (New York: Street and Smith, 1904), 2.

17 "Two Distinguished Friends of the *Army and Navy Weekly*," *Army and Navy Weekly: A Weekly Publication for Our Boys* 1, no. 3 (July 3, 1897). Interplay between audience and authors in Bold, *Selling the Wild West*, 31–35.

18 "Buffalo Bill's Trail of the Ghost Dancers; or, The Sioux Chief's Secret," *Buffalo Bill Stories* 46 (March 29, 1902): 28; "Buffalo Bill's Phantom Hunt; or, The Gold Guide of Colorado Canyon," *Buffalo Bill Stories* 49 (April 19, 1902), 68.

19   New York Public Library, Stratemeyer Syndicate Records, Box 56, Folder 1, S. G. Reid to Publishers, June 10, 1933; New York Public Library, Stratemeyer Syndicate Records, Box 56, Folder 1, Robert McIntyre to Publishers, October 1, 1930; Letter to Old Pard, *Boys of America* 1 (October 4, 1902): 15; Emily L.C. to editor, *Demorest's Young America* 4, no. 45 (July 1870): 352; Anna Alice to editor, *Demorest's Young America* 3 (May 1869): 273–274. Though much of the *extant* fan mail was written in the 1910–1930s, it was composed in response to work that had often been in print (and reissued) for many years prior, or, work that recycled the same settlerist themes present in material written during the 1870s and 1880s. The writing of actual children is enormously difficult to find in the archives because so much of it was treated as ephemeral; as a result, that which does survive warrants investigation, so long as the conclusions drawn are treated as tentative. It might also be noted that British imperial children's fiction also solicited a good deal of reader feedback in the form of letters to the editor. See Janis Dawson, "Our Girls in the Family of Nations: Girls' Culture and Empire in Victorian Girls' Magazines," in Karen Sands-O'Connor and Marietta A. Frank, eds., *Internationalism in Children's Series* (New York: Palgrave Macmillan, 2014): 38–55.
20   "Buffalo Bill's Victories," *Buffalo Bill Stories* 31 (December 14, 1901): 28; Thurston and McShane in "Buffalo Bill's Victories," *Buffalo Bill Stories* 35 (January 11, 1902): 27–28; William D. Howells, "My Year in a Log-Cabin: A Bit of Autobiography," *Youth's Companion* 60, no. 19 (May 12, 1887): 214. For similarly themed fan mail see also "Buffalo Bill's Run-Down; or The Red Hand Renegade's Death," *Buffalo Bill Stories* 65 (August 9, 1902): 29–30. On settler colonial toys and imperial play more generally, see Howard Chudacoff, *Children at Play: An American History* (New York: NYU Press, 2007), 79 and 129, and Gary Cross, *Kids' Stuff: Toys and the Changing World of American Childhood* (Cambridge, MA: Harvard University Press, 1997), 87 and 156.
21   "Buffalo Bill in the Bad Lands; or, Trailing the Veiled Squaw," *Buffalo Bill Stories* 45 (March 22, 1902): 29; McCabe, *Planting the Wilderness*, 110–111.
22   Jane Harris to editors, *Complete Story Magazine* 4, no. 5 (July 1925): 143; New York Public Library, Stratemeyer Syndicate Records, Box 56, Folder 1, Fan Mail, Mary Wolstencroft to Grosset and Dunlap, November 16, 1931; "more excitement" quoted in Jane H. Hunter, *How Young Ladies Became Girls: The Victorian Origins of American Girlhood (New Haven, CT: Yale University Press, 2002)*, 80; "Trading Post," *Frontier Stories* 13, no. 8 (Spring 1937): 127; Mary Domalski to "Old Pard," *Boys of America* 2, no. 72 (February 14, 1903): 15. "Cowards and weaklings" in "The Trading Post," *Frontier Stories* 13, no. 8 (1937): 127.
23   Anna Newman to editors, *Wide World Adventures* 18, no. 2 (June 1930): 294; Louise to BBW, in "Around the Camp Fire with Our Boys," *Boys' Best Weekly* 2, no. 57 (1910): 26. Popular literature for girls in Carolyn Carpan, *Sisters, Schoolgirls, and Sleuths: Girls' Series Books in America* (Lanham, MD: Scarecrow Press, 2008).
24   Mazie R. to BBW, in "Around the Camp Fire with Our Boys," *Boys Best Weekly* 2, no. 58 (1910): 26. On the ordinarily "masculine" thrust of Western popular culture,

see Jimmy L. Bryan, *The American Elsewhere: Adventure and Manliness in the Age of Expansion* (Lawrence: University Press of Kansas, 2017), and Daniel Worden, *Masculine Style: The American West and Literary Modernism* (New York: Palgrave Macmillan, 2011).

25 J. L. Harbour, "Among the Pueblos," *Golden Argosy* 1, no. 20 (April 21, 1883): 158. Adolescence in Joseph Kett, *Rites of Passage: Adolescence in America, 1790 to the Present* (New York: Basic Books, 1977). The rise of age-graded institutions discussed in Chudacoff, *How Old Are You?* and Reed Ueda, *Avenues to Adulthood: The Origins of the High School and Social Mobility in an American Suburb* (New York: Cambridge University Press, 1987). On the shift away from age-mixing and juvenile politicization, see Jon Grinspan, *The Virgin Vote: How Young Americans Made Democracy Social, Politics Personal, and Voting Popular in the Nineteenth Century* (Chapel Hill: UNC Press, 2016). By contrast, Hunter, *How Young Ladies Became Girls*, discusses the ways in which late nineteenth-century American girls could sometimes experience school (and its raucous peer culture) as something that freed them from the imprisoning demands of domestic propriety.

26 Louisa May Alcott, "Eight Cousins," *St. Nicholas* 2 (August 1875): 616–618; J. L. Harbour, "A Sermon for Boys," *The Argosy* 13, no. 468 (November 21, 1891): 301; Jack Crawford, "Boys and 'Blood and Thunder' Reading," *American Boy* 2, no. 7 (May 1901): 208; and for similar "sermons," see also Quelton, "Adventures on the Border: Stories of a Scout and Hunter Told at the Evening Camp Fire," *Golden Hours: A Weekly Journal of Good Literature for Young Folks* 28, no. 712 (September 21, 1901): 16, or Anonymous, "False Notions About the Cow-boy's Life," *Youth's Companion* 60, no. 39 (September 29, 1887): 407–408. Alcott's admonitions ring somewhat false, given her early career as an author of sensational fiction. See Madeleine Stern, *Louisa May Alcott: From Blood & Thunder to Hearth & Home* (Boston: Northeastern University Press, 1998). Of course, even as these authors warned against juvenile travel to the West, charitable organizations chartered orphan trains to ship thousands of indigent children to "wholesome" frontier families. See Linda Gordon, *The Great Arizona Orphan Abduction* (Cambridge, MA: Harvard University Press, 1999).

27 Edmund Lester Pearson, *Dime Novels; or, Following an Old Trail in Popular Literature* (Boston: Little, Brown, 1929), 222–255 and quoted at 238, 244, 250, 254; Anonymous, "Young Dick Turpin," *Golden Argosy* 3, no. 15 (March 14, 1885): 116.

28 Unknown author, "A True Tale of Western Warfare," *Youth: A Journal of the Youth, By the Youth, and for the Youth* 1, no. 6 (June 1885): 1 in AAS; Unknown author, "A Stage Ride to California," *The Meteor* 2, no. 4 (June 1884): 1 in AAS; Winslow, "Pete Lewis' Story," *The Eagle* 2, no. 1 (March 1877) in Edwin Hadley Smith Collection of Amateur Papers at the University of Wisconsin (hereafter EHS) vol. 32; Unknown author, "A Romance of Red Canyon," *Youth* 2, no. 5 (May 1886): 2 in AAS; Thomas H. Kerr, "The White Chief," 1, no. 2 (August 1875) in EHS vol. 21. Similarly violent amateur stories include Edgar P. Slade, "A Trapper's Tale," *Novelty*

*Advertiser* 1, no. 9 (September 1876): 1–2 in EHS vol. 27, and Charles E. Hellings, "A Border Tale," *Weekly Gazette* 2, no. 35 (October 1876): 1 in EHS vol. 29.

29  Charles E. Hellings, "The Scout," *Weekly Gazette* 2, no. 33 (September 1876): 1–2 in EHS vol. 29; Kerr, "The White Chief"; Unknown author, "A Tale of the Frontier," *Youth's Ledger* 2, no. 15 (February 1887) in AAS; Yankey Sam, *Jack Johnson, or, The Wild Man of the Prairie* (Vienna, NJ: Zander Snyder, 1876), 2 in AAS; Unknown author, "The Lost Mine," *Typographic Budget* 2, no. 4 (December 1875): 2–3 in EHS vol. 21. Beadle quoted in Edmund Lester Pearson, *Dime Novels; or, Following an Old Trail in Popular Literature* (Boston: Little, Brown, 1929), 99.

30  Edgar P. Slade, *Dashing Dick! Or the Terror of the Camanches* (Jasper, IN: Benjamin Doane, 1876), 2; Incognito, "Adventure of a Boy Ranger," *The Stranger* 1, no. 4 (April 1876): 3 in EHS vol. 28.

31  Geoffrey Randolph, "Old Tim's Leap," *Amateur Gazette* 1, no. 4 (August 1877): 1 in AAS.

32  Wash., "Buffalo Ned, The Boy Trapper," *Young Advertiser* 1, no. 3 (September 1872): 1 in AAS; Unknown author, "Squint-Eye, the Squatter," *The Meteor* 1, no. 7 (July 1874) in AAS; Author Unknown, "A Luckey Escape," *The Argus* 2, no. 1 (December 1884): 5–6 in AAS; Cornelius Shea, *Frank and Hal; or, The Magicians of the Plains* (Tottenville, NY: C. Shea, 1879) in AAS. Similarly structured amateur stories include "A Story of Adventure," *Chester Hill Times* 1, no. 9 (May 1878): 1–2 in AAS, or Edgar P. Slade, "On the Trail; also the Border Giant: A Tale of Indian Peril," *Luck and Pluck* 2, no. 4 (February 1877) in EHS vol. 33.

33  Judson Monclair, "Wantega, War God of the Choctaws," *Amateur Times* 2, no. 3 (October 1872) in AAS. Similar amateur stories include A. H. Scott, "Sandy Mike," *Boys' Messenger* 1, no. 1 (August 1873) in AAS, and An Amateur, "The Trapper's Escape," *Shooting-Stick* 1, no. 4 (June 1875) in EHS vol. 21. The longevity of the frontier mythos described by Grandin, *End of the Myth*.

34  Thomas Elliott, "The Hero of the West," *Boys' and Girls' Journal* 4, no. 2 (January 18, 1851): 25–27; Carlos Vane, "My First Adventure," *Boys' Own* 1, no. 22 (March 7, 1874): 349; Francis Mackey, "The Boy Scout," *Boys' Own* 2, no. 30 (May 2, 1874): 470; Edgar P. Slade, *A Close Call: A Story of the Plains* (Washington, DC, 1876), 3, 11 in AAS. Kit Carson was a figure popular with amateur authors. See also "The Prairie Duel, A Tale Founded Upon Facts," *Young America* 1, no. 5 (n.d.) in AAS, and "Kit Carson," *Keystone Banner* 1, no. 3 (November 1885) in AAS. On youth periodicals as a platform for children's storytelling, see Anna M. Redcay, "'Live to Learn and Learn to Live': The St. Nicholas League and the Vocation of Childhood," *Children's Literature* 39 (2011): 58–84.

35  Walter Mott to "Old Pard," *Boys of America* 2 no. 2 (October 11, 1902): 15; James Benson to "Old Pard," *Boys of America* 2 no. 89 (June 13, 1903): 15; "Crescent Reading Club," Racine, Wis. to "Old Pard," *Boys of America* 1 (October 4, 1902): 15; Frank Freeman to Old Pard, *Boys of America* 2, no. 73 (February 21, 1903): 15; James Benson to Old Pard, *Boys of America* 2, no. 89 (June 13, 1903): 15. For similar language, themes, and exchange among authors, see also "An Expert Marksman,"

*Scalping Sam, the Silent Slayer* (Brooklyn, NY, 1876); Frank D. Creekbaum, *Charlie Clipper* (Ripley, OH, 1878) in AAS; Thomas H. Kerr, *Border Jack, Perils of the Frontier* (Rockland, ME, 1872) in AAS.

36  Michael Warner, "Publics and Counterpublics," *Public Culture* 14, no. 1 (Winter 2002): 49–90.

37  Mona Gleason, "Avoiding the Agency Trap: Caveats for Historians of Children, Youth, and Education," *History of Education* 45, no. 4 (2016): 446–459. Juvenile expressions of empathy for Indians were considerably rarer but not unheard of. See, for example, "The Red Men of America," *Boys' and Girls' Journal* 4, no. 19 (September 13, 1851): 310.

38  By no means was all of the amateur fiction penned by girls set in the West. The girls often drafted poetry and fiction more "domestic" in its orientation. The subject matter often revolved around romantic suitors. See, for example, Bessie Murray, "Millie Lee, or, Three Christmas Eves," *Youth's Journal* 3, no. 1 (January 1875) in EHS vol. 21. On popular fiction as an important feminist outlet, see Nan Enstad, *Ladies of Labor, Girls of Adventure: Working Women, Popular Culture, and Labor Politics at the Turn of the Twentieth Century* (New York: Columbia University Press, 1999). On the appearance of dime romance fiction meant for girls (and simultaneous "masculinization" of the frontier), see Streeby, "Dime Novels and the Rise of Mass-Market Genres," 586–587 and 594–595.

39  "Fred's Adventure," *Badger News Boy* 1, no. 2 (October 1875), in AAS; T. E. LeGraph, "Mad Betsy, the Scourge of the Apaches," *Western Shore* 2, no. 1 (August 1875): 8 in EHS vol. 21; Thomas Kerr, "The White Chief," *Western Shore* vol. 2, no. 1 (August 1875): 9–10 in EHS vol. 21.

40  Alice Lane, "The Old Cabin," *Semi-Monthly* 2, no. 21 (July 1883) in AAS.

41  "Patty the Girl Rifle Shot," *Buffalo Bill's Rifle Rangers* no. 4 (June 8, 1901). Girls' amateur writing may have been connected in part to the later nineteenth-century enshrinement of certain exceptionally violent frontier females such as Hannah Duston or Calamity Jane. See Barbara Cutter, "The Female Indian Killer Memorialized: Hannah Duston and the Nineteenth-Century Feminization of Violence," *Journal of Women's History* 20, no. 2 (2008): 10–33. It is also important to note that at least some frontier fiction featured female protagonists. Janet Dean observes that while the genre was eventually written by and for men, "the first dime novel Western was written by a woman and about a woman." See Dean, "Calamities of Convention in a Dime Novel Western," in Lydia Cushman Schurman and Deidre Johnson, eds., *Scorned Literature: Essays on the History and Criticism of Popular Mass-Produced Fiction* (Westport, CT: Greenwood Press, 2002), 36–50, quoted at p. 37. "Manifest Domesticity" in Amy Kaplan, *The Anarchy of Empire in the Making of U.S. Culture* (Cambridge, MA: Harvard University Press, 2002), 23–50.

42  Bishop, "Story-Paper Literature," 385. "New girls" and their refusal to act as Victorian-era "parlor ornaments" discussed in Hunter, *How Young Ladies Became Girls*, 4–6, and, on girls' reading and writing more broadly, 38–90. Female characters and frontier-themed pulps are discussed in Renée M. Sentilles, *American*

*Tomboys, 1850–1915* (Amherst, MA: University of Massachusetts Press, 2018), 73–94. By the turn of the twentieth century, some girls' organizations focused on outdoor activity were more willing to embrace the role female pioneers had played in American history. See Susan A. Miller, *Growing Girls: The Natural Origins of Girls' Organizations in America* (New Brunswick, NJ: Rutgers University Press, 2007).

43 Thomas Wentworth Higginson, as quoted in Richard Darling, *The Rise of Children's Book Reviewing in America, 1865–1881* (New York: Bowker, 1968), 57.

44 A shift toward broader themes of tolerance and acceptance in Progressive-era children's literature described in Diana Selig, *Americans All: The Cultural Gifts Movement* (Cambridge, MA: Harvard University Press, 2008). This transformation was broadly paralleled by a similar one among adult reading material. See Sherry L. Smith, *Reimagining Indians: Native Americans through Anglo Eyes, 1880–1940* (New York: Oxford University Press, 2000). The politics of Indian assimilation discussed in C. Joseph Genetin-Pilawa, *Crooked Paths to Allotment: The Fight Over Federal Indian Policy after the Civil War* (Chapel Hill: UNC Press, 2012).

45 Francis Rolt-Wheeler, *The Boy with the U.S. Indians* (Boston: Lothrop, Lee and Shepard, 1913), vii–viii.

46 Rolt-Wheeler, *The Boy with the U.S. Indians*, vii–viii. For similar children's literature, see Ernest Thompson Seton, *Two Little Savages* (New York: Grosset & Dunlap, 1911); Mary Hazelton Wade, *Our Little Indian Cousin* (Boston: L.C. Page, 1901); or Emma M. Maguire, *Two Little Indians* (Chicago: A. Flanagan, 1919).

47 A shift away from a militarized Indian policy covered in Cathleen Cahill, *Federal Fathers and Mothers: A Social History of the United States Indian Service, 1869–1933* (Chapel Hill: UNC Press, 2011). The struggle to supplant celebratory accounts of settler colonialism was also reflected in the institutional histories of early twentieth-century organizations such as the Boy Scouts, the Woodcraft Indians, and the Boy Pioneers. See Mischa Honeck, *Our Frontier Is the World: The Boy Scouts in the Age of American Ascendancy* (Ithaca, NY: Cornell University Press, 2018).

48 "Every third boy" in Bishop, "Story-Paper Literature," 385; "entering wedge" quoted in Jani L. Baker, "'A really big theme': Americanization and World-Peace Internationalism and/as Nationalism in Lucy Fitch Perkins' Twins Series," in Karen Sands-O'Connor and Marietta A. Frank, eds., *Internationalism in Children's Series* (New York: Palgrave Macmillan, 2014), 92.

49 *Indian Stories Retold from St. Nicholas* (New York: Century, 1905), 22, 28, 44, 87. Books of Indian legends packaged for children became very popular in the early twentieth century. See, for example, Ethel C. Brill, *The Boy Who Went to the East* (New York: E. P. Dutton, 1917); Margaret Bemister, *Thirty Indian Legends* (New York: Macmillan, 1912); Julia Darrow Cowles, *Indian Nature Myths* (Chicago: A. Flanagan, 1921); and Elaine Eastman, *Indian Legends Retold* (Boston: Little, Brown, 1919). Imperialist nostalgia in Brian W. Dippie, *The Vanishing American: White Attitudes and U.S. Indian Policy* (Middletown, CT: Wesleyan University Press, 1982).

50 Quelton, "The Massacre on the Sweetwater," *Golden Hours: A Weekly Journal of Good Literature for Young Folks* 28, no. 715 (October 12, 1901): 16; Alfred Damon Runyon, "The Dying Race," *Complete Story Magazine* 1, no. 5 (October 25, 1924): 140. And, of course, the Depression Era also witnessed the immense popularity of Laura Ingalls Wilder's Little House on the Prairie series. See Caroline Fraser, *Prairie Fires: The American Dreams of Laura Ingalls Wilder* (New York: Metropolitan Books, 2017).

51 On the shifting depiction of Indians more broadly, see Philip J. Deloria, *Playing Indian* (New Haven, CT: Yale University Press, 1998). Sherman Alexie and Louise Erdrich may be among the best known of these Native American authors, but it is also interesting to note that latter-day Newbery-winning children's books such as *The Courage of Sarah Noble* began to feature settler heroes who befriend rather than butcher nearby Indians. See Alice Dalgliesh, *The Courage of Sarah Noble* (New York: Simon & Schuster, 1986). The complex history of this literature lies beyond the scope of this chapter, but see Frederick E. Hoxie, *Talking Back to Civilization: Indian Voices from the Progressive Era* (New York: Bedford/St. Martin's, 2001), and Amelia V. Katanski, *Learning to Write "Indian": The Boarding School Experience and American Indian Literature* (Norman: University of Oklahoma Press, 2007). There is also some evidence to suggest that Native Americans read dime novels against the grain in order to reclaim them as "indigenous texts." See Christine Bold, "Did Indians Read Dime Novels?: Re-Indigenising the Western at the Turn of the Twentieth Century," in Ken Gelder, ed., *New Directions in Popular Fiction: Genre, Distribution, and Reproduction* (New York: Palgrave Macmillan, 2016): 135–156.

52 Nicola K. Beisel, *Imperiled Innocents: Anthony Comstock and Family Reproduction in Victorian America* (Princeton, NJ: Princeton University Press, 1997). Dawn Keetley draws direct connections between Pomeroy and frontier fiction in "The Injuries of Reading: Jesse Pomeroy and the Dire Effects of Dime Novels," *Journal of American Studies* 47, no. 3 (August 2013): 673–697. The antisocial impact of cheap children's fiction was an obsession of the era. See, for example, Thomas Travis, *The Young Malefactor: A Study in Juvenile Delinquency, Its Causes and Treatment* (New York: Crowell, 1908), 160–161, which found "counterfeiting and even murder springing from bad reading."

53 Unknown author, "Plots," *Boys of Gotham* 1, no. 4 (September 1878) in AAS.

54 Will W. Bartlett, "Are Blood and Thunder Stories Injurious?" *All Sorts* 2, no. 6 (April 1877) in EHS vol. 30.

## 2. SERIALIZED IMPERIALISM

1 Harry Morris to Arthur Winfield, May 30, 1933, Box 56, Folder 1, and Stratemeyer quoted in "Newark Author, Great Favorite with Young Folks, Talks of Stories for Boys," Box 319, Folder Clippings Re: E. Stratemeyer, 1906–1927, both of which are located in the New York Public Library's Stratemeyer Syndicate Records (hereafter NYPL SSR).

2   For a general history of series fiction, including but not limited to the Stratemeyer Syndicate, see Faye Riter Kensinger, *Children of the Series and How They Grew, Or a Century of Heroines and Heroes, Romantic, Comic, Moral* (Bowling Green, OH: Bowling Green State University Press, 1987). The postbellum antecedents to Stratemeyer's fiction factory are discussed in Michael Denning, *Mechanic Accents: Dime Novels and Working-Class Culture in America* (New York: Verso, 1987), 17–26.

3   Edward Stratemeyer, *American Boys' Life of Theodore Roosevelt* (Boston: Lee and Shepard, 1904), 296. "Greater United States" and the transition from continental settler colonialism to overseas imperialism described in Daniel Immerwahr, *How to Hide an Empire: A History of the Greater United States* (New York: Farrar, Straus and Giroux, 2019). "Cultural globalism" in Sam Lebovic, "From War Junk to Educational Exchange: The World War II Origins of the Fulbright Program and the Foundations of American Cultural Globalism, 1945–1950," *Diplomatic History* 37, no. 2 (2013): 280–312. Stratemeyer did not entirely turn away from the West, as his multistory "Pioneer Series" would suggest. But it was downplayed in favor of a more international emphasis. On series fiction and the persistence of the West as a setting and symbol for children, see Kathleen Chamberlain, "The Bobbsey Twins Hit the Trail: Or, Out West with Children's Series Fiction," *Children's Literature Association Quarterly* 17, no. 1 (Spring 1992): 9–15.

4   Stratemeyer quoted in "Newark Author, Great Favorite with Young Folks, Talks of Stories for Boys," Box 319, Folder Clippings Re: E. Stratemeyer, 1906–1927, in NYPL SSR; George T. Dunlap, *The Fleeting Years* (New York: Privately Printed, 1937), 74. Of course, classrooms and textbooks also played a crucial role in legitimating "American economic power through empire-building projects both at home and abroad." See Clif Stratton, *Education for Empire: American Schools, Race, and the Paths of Good Citizenship* (Oakland: University of California Press, 2016), 2. It was Stratemeyer's sense, however, that when this information was presented to children as "schoolwork," it became less palatable. On Stratemeyer and US imperialism more broadly, see Peter J. Hugill, "Building Aerial Empires: Technology and Geopolitics in American Juvenalia Through the 1930s," *Journal of Transatlantic Studies* 16, no. 4 (2018): 323–355. Imperial themes in the era's youth literature are also described in Sharon Delmendo, *The Star-Entangled Banner: One Hundred Years of America in the Philippines* (New Brunswick, NJ: Rutgers University Press, 2004), 47–85, and MicKenzie Fasteland, "Empire and Adolescence: Whiteness and Gendered Citizenship in American Young Adult Literature, 1904–1951" (PhD diss., University of Michigan, 2016).

5   Stratemeyer quoted in Deidre Johnson, *Edward Stratemeyer and the Stratemeyer Syndicate* (New York: Twayne, 1993), 78. The frequently foreign settings of his books' plots, moreover, aimed explicitly to teach the values of American citizenship by contrasting them with its inferior counterparts abroad. On the later nineteenth-century rise of a more thoroughly "globalized" United States, see Frank Ninkovich, *Global Dawn: The Cultural Foundations of American Interna-*

*tionalism, 1865–1890* (Cambridge, MA: Harvard University Press, 2009); Robert Kagan, *Dangerous Nation: America's Place in the World from Its Earliest Days to the Dawn of the Twentieth Century* (New York: Vintage, 2007); Jay Sexton, *A Nation Forged by Crisis: A New American History* (New York: Basic Books, 2018).

6  Quoted in Peter A. Soderbergh, "The Great Book War: Edward Stratemeyer and the Boy Scouts of America," *New Jersey History* 9, no. 4 (Winter 1973): 246.

7  William C. Sprague, *American Boy Magazine* (January 1899), ix.

8  Beveridge quoted in Kristin Hoganson, *Fighting for American Manhood: How Gender Politics Provoked the Spanish-American and Philippine-American Wars* (New Haven, CT: Yale University Press, 1998), 158–162; Frank Norris, "The Frontier Gone at Last," 1902, repr. in *Frank Norris: Novels and Essays* (New York: Library of America, 1986), 1184; Jack London quoted in George C. Herring, *From Colony to Superpower: U.S. Foreign Relations Since 1776* (New York: Oxford University Press, 2008), 338; Roosevelt's "boyish" nature in David Healy, *U.S. Expansionism: The Imperialist Urge in the 1890s* (Madison: University of Wisconsin Press, 1970), 110.

9  The editor of *Journeys Through Bookland*, 1909, as quoted in Peter A. Soderbergh, "The Stratemeyer Strain: Educators and the Juvenile Series Book, 1900–1973," *Journal of Popular Culture* 7 (Spring 1974): 864; Peter Hulme, *Rescuing Cuba: Adventure and Masculinity in the 1890s* (College Park, MD: Latin American Studies Center, 1996), 1–33, and Louis A. Pérez, Jr., "Incurring a Debt of Gratitude: 1898 and the Moral Sources of United States Hegemony in Cuba," *American Historical Review* 104, no. 2 (April 1999): 356–398.

10  This is an admittedly simplified version of a much more complex story. See Ryan K. Anderson, *Frank Merriwell and the Fiction of All-American Boyhood: The Progressive Era Creation of the Schoolboy Sports Story* (Fayetteville: University of Arkansas Press, 2015), 41–47.

11  On the arrest and prosecution of dime publishers for printing "indecent" material, see Martin Woodside, *Frontiers of Boyhood: Imagining America, Past and Future* (Norman: University of Oklahoma Press, 2020), 57–58. Prolific as he was, very little scholarly literature about Edward Stratemeyer exists. See Deidre Johnson, *Edward Stratemeyer and the Stratemeyer Syndicate* (New York: Twayne, 1993), and Trudi Abel, "'A Man of Letters, A Man of Business': Edward Stratemeyer and the Adolescent Reader, 1890–1930" (PhD diss., Rutgers University, 1993). Stratemeyer actually corresponded with Alger, at times soliciting advice. See NYPL SSR, Box 1, Folders 1–2. On the campaign against cheap literature, see Margaret Cassidy, "Concerning Printed Poison: Nineteenth-Century American Adults' Ambivalence about Children's Interactions with Cheap Fiction," *Journal of the History of Childhood and Youth* 8, no. 2 (Spring 2015): 211–228.

12  On Adams, Alger, and series fiction devoted to the inculcation of a work ethic, see Daniel T. Rodgers, *The Work Ethic in Industrial America, 1850–1920* (Chicago: University of Chicago Press, 1974), 125–152, though Michael Zuckerman, *Almost Chosen People: Oblique Biographies in the American Grain* (Berkeley: University

of California Press, 1993), 219–238, cautions us that Alger's supposed "self-made men" were, in reality, hardly representative of truly capitalistic values. On Henty and other British juvenile series fiction writers, see Peter J. Hugill, "Imperialism and Manliness in Edwardian Boys' Novels," *Ecumene* 6, no. 3 (1999): 318–340; M. Daphne Kutzer, *Empire's Children: Empire and Imperialism in Classic British Children's Books* (New York: Garland, 2000), and Joseph Bristow, *Empire Boys: Adventures in a Man's World* (New York: Routledge, 2017). A very few of Henty's books portrayed colonial life in the American West. See, for example, Henty, *Redskin and Cowboy: A Tale of the Western Plains* (London: Blackie, 1892). One American enthusiast remembered that Henty gave American boys more of "a due appreciation of the British Empire than all of Cecil Rhodes' scholarships" combined. See James Lea Cate, "With Henty in Texas: A Tale of a Boy's Historian," *Southwestern Historical Quarterly* 68, no. 2 (October 1964): 153.

13  Lydia Cushman Schurman and Deidre Johnson, eds., *Scorned Literature: Essays on the History and Criticism of Popular Mass-Produced Fiction in America* (Westport, CT: Greenwood Press, 2002).

14  *Under Dewey at Manila or, The War Fortunes of a Castaway* (Boston: Lee and Shepard, 1898), the first of Stratemeyer's six-book "Old Glory Series," sold 6,000 copies when it was released in November 1898 for the Christmas season. The book's sequel, *Fighting in Cuban Waters*, registered advance sales of more than 2,000 copies, and from its release in August 1899 through Christmas of that year, it sold more than 16,000 copies. Based on these sales figures, Lee and Shepard Publishing was able to negotiate for shelf space at several different department stores throughout the country, further expanding Stratemeyer's hold over the marketplace. Complete sales data for the entire series have not yet been discovered; what exists has been extracted from the surviving correspondence between Stratemeyer and his publisher. See Abel, "A Man of Letters, A Man of Business," 110, 139, 217–218. These books had wide circulation beyond what sketchy sales data reveal. Libraries and public schools reported heavy borrowing of Stratemeyer's work, and anecdotal evidence suggests an informal but widespread "book trade" among boys who bought these novels and shared them. On the popularity of Stratemeyer among schoolchildren and at libraries, see Soderbergh, "The Stratemeyer Strain," 864–872. An early twentieth-century survey of public school children, known as the *Winnetka Graded Book List*, found that 98% of pupils surveyed were familiar with at least some of Stratemeyer's works. See Carleton Washburne and Mabel Vogel, "Supplement to the Winnetka Graded Book List," *Elementary English Review* 4 (February 1927): 47–52 and (March 1927): 66–73. It should be noted, however, that prior to 1898, youth periodicals had attempted to drum up kids' support for *Cuba libre*. See, for example, Juan Romero, "My Escape from Morro Castle," *Youth's Companion* 59, no. 11 (March 18, 1886): 99.

15  Stratemeyer quoted in Johnson, *Edward Stratemeyer and the Stratemeyer Syndicate*, 5; Franklin M. Reck, *The American Boy Anthology* (New York: Crowell, 1951), viii; Lorinda B. Cohoon, *Serialized Citizenships: Periodicals, Books, and American*

*Boys, 1840–1911* (Lanham, MD: Scarecrow Press, 2006), quoted on p. 152. In Stratemeyer, *American Boys' Life of Theodore Roosevelt*, 1–2, he reprinted much of TR's "Strenuous Life" speech and remarked that "from it American boys of to-day, and in generations to come, may gain lessons that will do them much good." Juvenile degeneration discussed in T. J. Jackson Lears, *No Place of Grace: Antimodernism and the Transformation of American Culture, 1800–1920* (Chicago: University of Chicago Press, 1981), quoted ("menstruate") at 104, and Gail Bederman, *Manliness and Civilization: A Cultural History of Gender and Race in the United States, 1880–1917* (Chicago: University of Chicago Press, 1995).

16 Boyology, "Boy Problem," and adolescent emasculation discussed in Julia Grant, *The Boy Problem: Educating Boys in Urban America, 1870–1970* (Baltimore: Johns Hopkins University Press, 2014); E. Anthony Rotundo, *American Manhood: Transformations in Masculinity from the Revolution to the Modern Era* (New York: Basic Books, 1993), 222–246; and Bederman, *Manliness and Civilization*, 77–120 and quoted at p. 98. This last sentence is a reference to Frances Hodgson Burnett's *Little Lord Fauntleroy* (New York: Scribner's, 1886), a blockbuster children's book that theorists like G. Stanley Hall believed gave birth to the pathology of the "mama's boy."

17 Edward Stratemeyer, *Under MacArthur in Luzon or, Last Battles in the Philippines* (Boston: Lee and Shepard, 1901), v; Capt. Ralph Bonehill [Edward Stratemeyer], *A Sailor Boy with Dewey or, Afloat in the Philippines* (New York: Mershon, 1899), 164.

18 On the increasingly age-segmented nature of reading habits, see Anne Scott MacLeod, *American Childhood: Essays on Children's Literature of the Nineteenth and Twentieth Centuries* (Athens: University of Georgia Press, 1994), 114–126. MacLeod argues that generational distinctions in reading material are a relatively recent phenomenon, replacing an older model of more group- or family-oriented reading habits.

19 On the comforts of genre fiction, see John G. Cawelti, *Adventure, Mystery, and Romance: Formula Stories as Art and Popular Culture* (Chicago: University of Chicago Press, 1976), 1–35; Johnson, *Edward Stratemeyer and the Stratemeyer Syndicate*, ix–xi; and Meghan O'Rourke, "Nancy Drew's Father," *New Yorker* (November 1, 2004), 120–129. Edward Stratemeyer, *Under Otis in the Philippines or, A Young Officer in the Tropics* (Boston: Lee and Shepard, 1899), 329. Malolos was the seat of Emilio Aguinaldo's "rebel" government. Its capture did not so much end the war as disperse it across the Philippines's various islands.

20 Clifford Putney, *Muscular Christianity: Manhood and Sports in Protestant America, 1880–1920* (Cambridge, MA: Harvard University Press, 2001); Rotundo, *American Manhood*, 222–284.

21 Edward Stratemeyer, *A Young Volunteer in Cuba or, Fighting for the Single Star* (Boston: Lee and Shepard, 1898), 143; Edward Stratemeyer, *Under Dewey at Manila or, The War Fortunes of a Castaway* (Boston: Lee and Shepard, 1898), 17–18.

22 Stratemeyer, *A Young Volunteer in Cuba*, 80; Stratemeyer, *Under Otis*, 1–2, 331. "Prosaic duties" quoted in Cassidy, "Concerning Printed Poison," 219.

23  Stratemeyer, *Under Otis*, 12; Stratemeyer, *Under Dewey at Manila*, 216.
24  Hulme, *Rescuing Cuba*; Hoganson, *Fighting for American Manhood*.
25  Roosevelt quoted in Archibald Roosevelt, ed., *Theodore Roosevelt on Race, Riots, Reds, and Crime* (West Sayville, NY: Probe Press, 1968), 87. Overviews of the shift in war aims and the racialization of occupied zones in Paul A. Kramer, *The Blood of Government: Race, Empire, the United States, and the Philippines* (Chapel Hill: UNC Press, 2006), and Louis A. Pérez, Jr., *The War of 1898: The United States and Cuba in History and Historiography* (Chapel Hill: UNC Press, 1998).
26  Stratemeyer, *Under Otis in the Philippines*, 205. On the subject of nativism in series fiction more broadly, see J. Frederick MacDonald, "'The Foreigner' in Juvenile Series Fiction, 1900–1945," *Journal of Popular Culture* 8 (January 1974): 534–548.
27  Stratemeyer, *Under Otis in the Philippines*, 205; Edward Stratemeyer, *The Campaign of the Jungle or, Under Lawton through Luzon* (Boston: Lee and Shepard, 1900), 125.
28  Stratemeyer, *A Young Volunteer in Cuba*, 191–92; Stratemeyer, *A Sailor Boy with Dewey*, 163; Senator Albert Beveridge, *Congressional Record*, 56th Congress, 1st Session, 708; Stratemeyer, *American Boys' Life of Theodore Roosevelt*, 200.
29  Stratemeyer, *Under Dewey at Manila*, 40; Stratemeyer, *The Campaign of the Jungle*, 125; Stratemeyer, *Fighting in Cuban Waters or, Under Schley on the Brooklyn* (Boston: Lee and Shepard, 1899), 191–213; Stratemeyer, *A Young Volunteer in Cuba*, 170, 240, 194; Capt. Ralph Bonehill [Edward Stratemeyer], *When Santiago Fell or, The War Adventures of Two Chums* (Chicago: Geo. M. Hill Co., 1899), iii–iv; Stratemeyer, *A Sailor Boy with Dewey*, iii.
30  Bonehill, *When Santiago Fell*, 32; Stratemeyer, *Under Dewey at Manila*, 143–144; Edward Stratemeyer, *When Santiago Fell or, The War Adventures of Two Chums* (Boston: Lee and Shepard, 1899), 166.
31  Stratemeyer, *Campaign of the Jungle*, 166–175. This was, of course, wishful thinking on Stratemeyer's part. Sexual liaisons between American soldiers and Filipino or Cuban women were quite common. See Paul A. Kramer, "Colonial Crossings: Prostitution, Disease, and the Boundaries of Empire during the Philippine-American War," in Emily Rosenberg and Shanon Fitzpatrick, eds., *Body and Nation: The Global Realm of U.S. Body Politics in the Twentieth Century* (Durham, NC: Duke University Press, 2014), 17–41.
32  Stratemeyer, *Under Otis in the Philippines*, 247, 37; Stratemeyer, *Campaign of the Jungle*, 11; Stratemeyer, *A Sailor Boy with Dewey*, 77.
33  So too has the informal imperialism enabled by American investment capital interested American historians. Some of the more important studies of this phenomenon include Emily Rosenberg, *Spreading the American Dream: American Economic and Cultural Expansion, 1890–1945* (New York: Hill and Wang, 1982); Walter LaFeber, *The New Empire: An Interpretation of American Expansion, 1860–1898* (Ithaca, NY: Cornell University Press, 1998); Mona Domosh, *American Commodities in an Age of Empire* (New York: Routledge, 2006); Megan Black, *The Global Interior: Mineral Frontiers and American Power* (Cambridge, MA: Harvard

University Press, 2018). It might also be noted that series fiction alone was not the only venue where young people could read about American exploits during the War of 1898. Juvenile magazines were brimming with references to the conflict's major engagements. See, for example, *Harper's Round Table* 2, no. 13 (November 1898).

34  Douglas Wells, "The First Gun; or, Hal Maynard's Strong Command," *Starry Flag Weekly* 3 (May 21, 1898): 5, 26; Douglas Wells, "Under Blanco's Eye; or, Hal Maynard Among the Cuban Insurgents," *Starry Flag Weekly* 1 (May 7, 1898): 3, 14–15, and 32.

35  On an older "custodial" model of children's fiction and the transition to precocious protagonists, see Paul B. Ringel, *Commercializing Childhood: Children's Magazines, Urban Gentility, and the Ideal of the American Child, 1823–1918* (Amherst: University of Massachusetts Press, 2015).

36  Captain C. E. Kilbourne, *An Army Boy in Mexico* (Philadelphia: Penn, 1914), 22; Kilbourne, *An Army Boy in Pekin* (Philadelphia: Penn, 1912), 35. Charles Kilbourne was himself a decorated veteran of multiple conflicts. He transformed his first-hand knowledge of foreign battlefields into a lucrative part-time position as an author of boys' books. See also Elbridge S. Brooks, *Under the Allied Flags: A Boy's Adventures in the International War Against the Boxers and China* (Boston: Lothrop, 1901). On the era's obsession with the "Yellow Peril," see John Kuo Wei Tchen, "The Yellow Claw: The Optical Unconscious in Anglo-American Political Culture," in Christine Bold, ed., *The Oxford History of Popular Print Culture, Volume Six: U.S. Popular Print Culture, 1860–1920* (New York: Oxford University Press, 2011), 477–500.

37  Brooks, *Under the Allied Flags*, 141; Kilbourne, *An Army Boy in Pekin*, 15, 35, 323; H. Irving Hancock, *Dave Darrin on the Asiatic Station; or, Winning Lieutenant's Commissions on the Admiral's Flagship* (Philadelphia: Henry Altemus, 1919), 12, 114, 135–136; Yates Stirling, Jr., *A United States Midshipman in China* (Philadelphia: Penn, 1909), 175–176.

38  Captain C. E. Kilbourne, *An Army Boy in the Philippines* (Philadelphia: Penn, 1913), 17.

39  Ibid., 49–55, 309, 5.

40  Ibid., 345.

41  H. Irving Hancock, *Uncle Sam's Boys in the Philippines; or, Following the Flag Against the Moros* (Philadelphia: Henry Altemus, 1912), 112, 122, 190; On the Moro War and continuing unrest in the Philippines, see Oliver Charbonneau, *Civilizational Imperatives: Americans, Moros, and the Colonial World* (Ithaca, NY: Cornell University Press, 2020).

42  B. J. Bishop, "General Funston's Young Scout; or, Aguinaldo's Last Trail," *Golden Hours* 28, no. 708 (August 24, 1901): 7; Oscar Hatch Hawley, "Gatling Gun Bill," *Popular Magazine* 2, no. 5 (September 1904): 109–112; H. G. Fry, "The Devil of Maamet: A Novelette of the Philippines," *Wide World Adventures* 14, no. 3 (July 1929): 395–421.

43 Lawrence Perry, "Cleared for Action," *The Argosy* 70, no. 2 (September 1912): 339 and 357; H. Irving Hancock, *Uncle Sam's Boys in the Philippines*, 253; Cyrus Townsend Brady, "By Command of the Commodore," 4, no. 3 (July 1905): 5–6 and 14–15.
44 Karen Sánchez-Eppler, *Dependent States: The Child's Part in Nineteenth-Century American Culture (Chicago: University of Chicago Press, 2005)*, is an important exception for the way it analyzes some of the very few extant nineteenth-century children's diaries.
45 Henry Seidel Canby, *The Age of Confidence: Life in the Nineties* (New York: Farrar and Rinehart, 1934), 191, 195, 205; Theodore Dreiser, *Dawn* (New York: H. Liveright, 1931), 125–126.
46 "Sent Odd Letters to Story Writer," *Newark Sunday Call* (April 8, 1906) in NYPL SSR, Box 319, Clippings Re: E. Stratemeyer, 1906–1927. A small portion of what was originally a much larger collection of fan mail is currently housed at both the New York Public Library's Stratemeyer Syndicate Records (NYPL SSR) and the University of Oregon's Knight Library (UOL). Unfortunately, none of the surviving fan mail predates the late 1920s. Yet if used carefully and speculatively, it can still be a useful source when applied to earlier Stratemeyer series largely because his literary formulas changed so little from 1898 until his death in 1930. And, even after his passing, his daughters continued to run the syndicate much as their father had. New characters appeared, but their views on the world did not change much. As the largest literary syndicate, Stratemeyer received the bulk of children's fan mail. Sadly, fan mail written to the authors of competing series fiction firms does not, to my knowledge, exist any longer.
47 Harry Morris to Arthur Winfield, May 30, 1933, Box 56, Folder 1, NYPL SSR.
48 S. G. Reid to Victor Appleton, June 10, 1933, Box 56, Folder 1, NYPL SSR.
49 Bruce Rhodes to Edward Stratemeyer, January 9, 1933, Box 56, Folder 2, NYPL SSR.
50 Robert McIntyre to Victor Appleton, October 1, 1930, Box 56, Folder 1, NYPL SSR; Lillie M. Nickerson to Victor Appleton, May 15, 1933, Box 56, Folder 1, NYPL SSR; Stratemeyer, *A Sailor Boy with Dewey*, iii. The educators' backlash against series fiction discussed in Margaret Cassidy, *Children, Media, and American History: Printed Poison, Pernicious Stuff, and Other Terrible Temptations* (New York: Routledge, 2018).
51 Girls' series books discussed in Ilana Nash, *American Sweethearts: Teenage Girls in Twentieth-Century Popular Culture* (Bloomington: Indiana University Press, 2006), quoted on p. 32; Carolyn Carpan, *Sisters, Schoolgirls, and Sleuths: Girls' Series Books in America* (Lanham, MD: Scarecrow Press, 2009); and Emily Hamilton-Honey, *Turning the Pages of American Girlhood: The Evolution of Girls' Series Fiction, 1865–1930* (Jefferson, NC: McFarland, 2013).
52 Mary Vernon and Barbara Charnley to Victor Appleton, n.d., Box 56, Folder 1, NYPL SSR [emphasis in original]; Tracy Serrano to Syndicate, Box 56, Folder 7, NYPL SSR. Company correspondence with series ghost writers found in Box 31,

Microfilm Reel 6, NYPL SSR. Stratemeyer on "boys" in Box 319, Clippings Re: E. Stratemeyer, 1906–1927.

53  Joseph Schroth to Victor Appleton, January 1, 1932, Box 56, Folder 2, NYPL SSR. Johnson, *Edward Stratemeyer and the Stratemeyer Syndicate*, 110, notes that girls' series always remained secondary. Stratemeyer created more than twice as many boys' series before his death in 1930.

54  Ansel Duncan to *American Boy* 3, no. 11 (September 1902): 331; Author unknown, "Uncle Sam to Senor Don," *Half-Holiday* 10, no. 15 (May 14, 1898): 23; Dan Wallingford in "The Story of an Ill-Fated Battleship," *Half-Holiday* 10, no. 8 (March 26, 1898): 44.

55  "Current News of the World: Plainly Told for Youthful Readers," *Half-Holiday* 10, no. 13 (April 30, 1898): 41–44; Edward S. Ellis, "From Tent to White House," *Half-Holiday* 1, no. 18 (June 4, 1898): 23; "The Fourth of July," *American Boy* 1, no. 9 (July 1900): n.p.; "Our Navy and What It Can Be," *The Argosy* 13, no. 468 (November 21, 1891): 210.

56  Stratemeyer, *Under Otis in the Philippines*, 82; Enrique H. Lewis, "American Naval Apprentice Life," *Half-Holiday* 10, no. 12 (April 23, 1898): 19. "1898 Clubs" in C. L. Robertson, "Uniformed Cadet Corps," *Half-Holiday* 1, no. 16 (May 21, 1898): 17–19 and *Starry Flag Weekly* 10 (July 9, 1898): 32. Megan A. Norcia, *Gaming Empire in Children's British Board Games, 1836–1860* (New York: Routledge, 2019). For a look at inter-imperial racial Anglo-Saxonism in juvenile literature, see Paul A. Kramer, "Empires, Exceptions, and Anglo-Saxons: Race and Rule between the British and United States Empires, 1880–1910," *Journal of American History* 88, no. 4 (March 2002): 1342–1344, and more generally in Stuart Anderson, *Race and Rapprochement: Anglo-Saxonism and Anglo-American Relations, 1895–1904* (Rutherford, NJ: Fairleigh Dickinson University Press, 1981). Youth periodicals were also invested in such sentiments. See "The Future of the English-Speaking Races," *Youth's Companion* 61, no. 44 (November 1, 1888): 557–558, or John A. Logan, "England and America," in Samuel Fallows, ed., *The Young American Annual* (New York: Juvenile Publishing, 1890), 448.

57  "Newark Author, Great Favorite with Young Folks, Talks of Stories for Boys," NYPL SSR, Box 319, Clippings Re: E. Stratemeyer, 1906–1927. The "soldier" boy is also discussed in that interview. Stratemeyer Syndicate business records and internal memoranda (disjointedly) gathered in NYPL, SSR, Box 31, Microfilm Reel 6. Sarah Lindey, "Boys Write Back: Self-Education and Periodical Authorship in Late-Nineteenth-Century Story Papers," *American Periodicals* 21, no. 1 (2011): 72–73 notes authors "allow[ed] youth to help direct and produce the print entertainment they consumed." For a similar point, see Anderson, *Frank Merriwell and the Fiction of All-American Boyhood*, xix, who notes that series fiction "reader letters influenced, but did not dictate the story's direction."

58  On age as the critical factor dividing pro- from anti-imperialists, see Robert L. Beisner, *Twelve Against Empire: The Anti-Imperialists, 1898–1900* (New York: McGraw-Hill, 1971), 228. The most vocal anti-imperialists averaged almost 70

years old, which meant they would mostly have read didactic antebellum children's literature.
59 Bruce Rhodes to Franklin W. Dixon, January 9, 1933, Box 56, Folder 1, NYPL SSR.

## 3. EMPIRE'S AMATEURS

1 "The Indians," *Young Idea* 2, no. 4 (May 1873) in American Antiquarian Society's Amateur Newspaper Collection. Importantly, this boy's rhetoric nearly repeated the very phrase, "utter extermination," which William Tecumseh Sherman, commander of all US forces, had used in an April 19, 1873 interview with the *Army and Navy Journal*. The Gilded Age commemoration of violence against Modoc Indians specifically is covered in Boyd Cothran, *Remembering the Modoc War: Redemptive Violence and the Making of American Innocence* (Chapel Hill: UNC Press, 2014).

2 The historical literature on amateur journalism is sparse, but see Paula Petrik, "The Youngest Fourth Estate: The Novelty Toy Printing Press and Adolescence, 1870–1886," in Elliott West and Paula Petrik, eds., *Small Worlds: Children and Adolescence, 1850–1950* (Lawrence: University Press of Kansas, 1992): 125–142 and note 4 for circulation figures; Lara Langer Cohen, "'The Emancipation of Boyhood': Postbellum Teenage Subculture and the Amateur Press," *Common-place* 14, no. 1 (Fall 2013); Ann Fabian, "Amateur Authors," in Scott E. Casper, Stephen W. Nissenbaum, and Michael Winship, eds., *A History of the Book in America: Volume Three The Industrial Book, 1840–1880* (Chapel Hill: UNC Press, 2007), 407–415; Jessica Isaac, "Compliant Circulation: Children's Writing, American Periodicals, and Public Culture, 1839–1882," (PhD diss., University of Pittsburgh, 2015); Jessica Isaac, "Youthful Enterprises: Amateur Newspapers and the Pre-History of Adolescence, 1867–1883," *American Periodicals* 22 no. 2 (2012): 158–177; and Dawn Michelle Smith, "Print Networks and Youth Information Culture: Young People, Amateur Publishing, and Children's Periodicals, 1867–1890" (PhD diss., University of Illinois at Urbana-Champaign, 2017). And, on the technology of the toy press itself, see Elizabeth M. Harris, *Personal Impressions: The Small Printing Press in Nineteenth-Century America* (Boston: David R. Godine, 2004). The major collections of amateur newspapers are held at the American Antiquarian Society (hereafter AAS) and the University of Wisconsin Library's Edwin Hadley Smith Collection of Amateur Newspapers (hereafter EHS). This chapter follows in the footsteps of many scholars of American childhood in seeing 20 as, very roughly, a cutoff point for historical inquiry. There are, of course, gradations within that span (infancy, adolescence, etc.) and exceptions to it, but, for much of the nation's history, age 21 has signaled one's formal entry into adulthood. See Howard Chudacoff, *How Old Are You?: Age Consciousness in American Culture* (Princeton, NJ: Princeton University Press, 1989).

3 "Amateur Journalism," *Illustrated American* 8 (September 26, 1891): 261; Thomas G. Harrison, *The Career and Reminiscences of an Amateur Journalist and a History of Amateur Journalism* (Indianapolis, IN: Self-published, 1883), 16; "Ben Franklin"

in Smith, "Print Networks and Youth Information Culture," 138; "The Amateur Casuals in Journalism," *New York Times*, October 9, 1871. Smith, in "Print Networks and Youth Information Culture," is particularly adept at demonstrating Amateurdom's deeply networked nature. While it is important to note that handwritten "amateur papers" in America date back to the eighteenth century and involved literary luminaries such as Nathaniel Hawthorne, the hobby did not reach its apogee until the invention of the miniature press after the Civil War. The overwhelming majority of amateur publishers were white, male, and middle class, though some few African Americans and women did participate. Some interesting work has also been done on a few surviving editions of amateur newspapers circulated by Indian students at Native American boarding schools. See Lisa K. Neuman, "Indian Play: Students, Wordplay, and the Ideologies of Indianness at a School for Native Americans," *American Indian Quarterly* 32, no. 2 (Spring 2008): 178–203; Jennifer Bess, "More than a Food Fight: Intellectual Traditions and Cultural Continuity in Chilocco's *Indian School Journal*, 1902–1918" *American Indian Quarterly* 37, nos. 1–2 (2013): 77–110.
4 Harlan H. Ballard, "Amateur Newspapers," *St. Nicholas* (July 1882): 723.
5 Ballard, "Amateur Newspapers," 718; Louisa May Alcott, *Little Women* (New York: Penguin, 1989), 99–104. The "Pickwick Portfolio" was itself modeled after a handwritten amateur newspaper that a younger Alcott and her sisters had issued. And there is at least some evidence that Alcott's book inspired other girls to produce their own amateur newspapers. See Daniel Shealy, "The Growth of Little Things: Louisa May Alcott and the Lukens Sisters' Family Newspaper," *Resources for American Literary Study* 30 (2005): 160–177.
6 The attacks of professional printers and journalists are described in Smith, "Print Networks and Youth Information Culture," 180–182.
7 H. Tecumseh Cook, "Amateur Journalism," *American Boy* 5, no. 9 (July 1904): 278. On the era's obsession with molding America's youth, see David I. Macleod, *Building Character in the American Boy: The Boy Scouts, YMCA, and their Forerunners, 1870–1920* (Madison: University of Wisconsin Press, 1983).
8 Horace Greeley, "Lo! The Poor Indian!" in *An Overland Journey, from New York to San Francisco, in the Summer of 1859* (New York: C.M. Saxton, Barker, 1860), 151; Albert J. Beveridge, "The March of the Flag," September 16, 1898, in James A. Henretta, ed., *Documents for America's History: Vol. 2 Since 1865* (New York: Bedford/St. Martin's, 2011), 164. Nineteenth-century adult authors often likened boys to "savages." On this phenomenon, see Kenneth B. Kidd, *Making American Boys: Boyology and the Feral Tale* (Minneapolis: University of Minnesota Press, 2004), 54–59.
9 Multiple studies of America's globalization attach a particular significance to the later nineteenth century. See Frank A. Ninkovich, *Global Dawn: The Cultural Foundation of American Internationalism, 1865–1890* (Cambridge, MA: Harvard University Press, 2009), and Emily Rosenberg, ed., *A World Connecting, 1870–1945* (Cambridge, MA: Harvard University Press, 2012).

10 On the broader subject of nineteenth-century youth political activism, see Grinspan, *The Virgin Vote*, and James Marten, *The Children's Civil War* (Chapel Hill: UNC Press, 1998).
11 San Francisco *Drops of Ink*, "The Apache Farce," 1, no. 3 (July 1886) and Fostoria, OH *Amateur Gazette*, "Old Tim's Leap," 1, no. 4 (Aug. 1877) both in AAS. "A Pioneer Home," *Our Happy Hours* 1, no. 5 (Winter 1885): 1–4, in EHS vol. 77; "The Red Man," *Forest City Spark* 1, no. 5 (October 1885): 3 in EHS vol. 76; *American Banner* 2, no. 13 (February 1877) in AAS; *Boys of Buffalo* 1, no. 1 (January 1877) in AAS.
12 "An Evening Scene," *The Criterion* 3, no. 1 (May 1883) in AAS; "Facing Indians," *Aurora Index* 1, no. 3 (May 1883) in AAS; "Wisconsin and Minnesota," *Home Diary* 3, no. 54 (August 1867) in AAS; "Genius of the Age," *The Microgram* 4, no. 4 (September 1883) in AAS; "Civilization," *The Patriot* 1, no. 2 (September 1886) in EHS vol. 82. As noted by Smith, "Print Networks and Youth Information Culture," 205, "young amateurs read and interact[ed] with story papers, but also . . . modeled their stories after the serialized fiction they read."
13 "Our Indians," *Enterprise* 1, no. 7 (January 1879) in AAS; "The Making of America," *New Century* 2, no. 5 (May 1885) in AAS; "Editorial," *Thunderbolt* 3, no. 8 (October 1886): 5 in EHS vol. 84; "The Doomed Race," *Little Rhody* 1, no. 6 (October 1878) in EHS vol. 42; "Youth and Old Age," *Patriot* 1, no. 1 (August 1886) in EHS vol. 83.
14 Examples of interviews include "Early Life on the Wabash," *Prairie City Gem* 1, no. 1 (March 1876), 6–7 in EHS vol. 28, and "An Indian Adventure," *New England Star* 2, no. 4 (April 1875), 6 in EHS vol. 20; "Our Pioneers," *Kansas Zephyr* 4, no. 1 (January 1884) in AAS.
15 "California's Growth," *Monthly Pomonaite* 1, no. 6 (January 1886) in AAS; "Going West," *Morrill's Monthly Prairie Leaflet* 3, no. 21 (November 1877) in EHS vol. 34.
16 "The Indian Problem," *The Idler* 1, no. 2 (August 1882) in AAS; "Lo! The Poor Indian," *Scratches and Sketches* 1, no. 1 (October 1873) in AAS; "The Making of America," *New Century* 2, no. 5 (May 1885) in AAS. One might note that the *Scratches and Sketches* editorial uses for its title the very phrase, "Lo! The Poor Indian," which Horace Greeley used to introduce his article, referenced in this chapter's introduction, comparing American children and "childlike" Native Americans. It is probably not a coincidence.
17 "Educating Indians," *The Crab* 1, no. 6 (June 1879) in AAS; "A Few Thoughts on the Indian Question," *The Dart* 7, no. 1 (October 1883) in AAS. David Wallace Adams, *Education for Extinction: American Indians and the Boarding School Experience, 1875–1928* (Lawrence: University Press of Kansas, 1995).
18 "Letter from Carlisle," *Amateur Journal* 3, no. 5 (May 1886) in AAS.
19 "Editorial Comment," *Youth* 2, no. 5 (May 1886) in AAS; "Editorial Comment," *Youth* 2, no. 2 (February 1886) in AAS; "Editorial Note," *New Century* 2, no. 2 (February 1885) in AAS. Some of the era's children's periodicals printed similarly encouraging reports. See "Indian Education," *Golden Argosy* 2, no. 29 (June 21,

1884): 226, which sought to "greatly stimulate public sentiment in behalf of the educational plan of settling the Indian problem."

20   Native American student engagement with the public sphere is discussed in Susan Scheckel, "'To make something of the Indian': Hampton Institute and the Uses of Popular Print Culture," in Christine Bold, ed., *The Oxford History of Popular Print Culture, Volume Six, U.S. Popular Print Culture, 1860–1920* (New York: Oxford University Press, 2011), 417–436.

21   Hand quoted in Jacqueline Emery, "Writing Against Erasure: Native American Students at Hampton Institute and the Periodical Press," *American Periodicals* 22, no. 2 (2012): 189.

22   Quoted in *Southern Workman and Hampton School Record* 22, no. 3 (March 1894): 44–45. Some interesting work has been done on a few surviving editions of amateur newspapers circulated by Indian students at Native American boarding schools. See Lisa K. Neuman, "Indian Play: Students, Wordplay, and the Ideologies of Indianness at a School for Native Americans," *American Indian Quarterly* 32, no. 2 (Spring 2008): 178–203; Amelia V. Katanski, *Learning to Write "Indian": The Boarding School Experience and American Indian Literature* (Norman: University of Oklahoma Press, 2007).

23   Disney's West discussed in Steven Watts, *The Magic Kingdom: Walt Disney and the American Way of Life* (Columbia: University of Missouri Press, 1997).

24   "America for Americans," *Monthly Pamonaite* 2, no. 1 (August 1886) in AAS; "Brass Filings," *Brass City Herald* 2, no. 5 (January 1887) in AAS; "The Commune," *Crescent* 1, no. 4 (August 1878) in AAS; "Editor's Sanctum," *Cornucopia* 2, no. 3 (April 1872) in AAS; "Land of the Free," *Editor's Eye* 1, no. 3 (January 1879) in EHS vol. 48. Immigration and the United States in the world discussed by Donna Gabaccia, *Foreign Relations: American Immigration in Global Perspective* (Princeton, NJ: Princeton University Press, 2012).

25   "The Heathen Chinee," *Monthly Pomonaite* 1, no. 6 (January 1886) in AAS; "The Chinese," *Amateur Tribune* 1, no. 6 (October 1878) in AAS. Examples of anti-Chinese "humor" in "A Vulgar Crank," *Stylus* 2, no. 2 (October 1885) in AAS, or "Ah Sin Was His Name," *Eagle* 1, no. 3 (December 1884) in AAS; "Increase and Decrease," *Golden Argosy* 13, no. 476 (January 1892): 288. J. Frederick MacDonald, "'The Foreigner' in Juvenile Series Fiction, 1900–1945," *Journal of Popular Culture* 8 (January 1974): 534–548. Anti-Chinese sentiment explored in Beth Lew-Williams, *The Chinese Must Go: Violence, Exclusion, and the Making of the Alien in America* (Cambridge, MA: Harvard University Press, 2018).

26   "The U.A.P.A. and the Negro," *Amateur Press* 1, no. 4 (May 1898) in AAS. Robin Bernstein has examined how nineteenth-century children communicated ideas about race to one another. See "Children's Books, Dolls, and the Performance of Race; or, The Possibility of Children's Literature," *PMLA* 126, no. 1 (January 2011): 166–167.

27   "The U.A.P.A. and the Negro," *Amateur Press* 1, no. 4 (May 1898) in AAS; "The Negro of the South," *Eastern Amateur* 1, no. 3 (April 1898) in AAS; "The Inevitable Extinction of the Colored Races," *Psyche* 1, no. 1 (April 1882) in AAS.

28 "Anglo Saxon Leadership," *Our Optic* 2, no. 5 (May 1886) in AAS.
29 "Editorial," *Monthly Pamonaite* 1, no. 10 (May 1886) in AAS; Harrison, *Career and Reminiscences of an Amateur Journalist*, 80.
30 "Panama Canal," *American Headlight* 4, no. 8 (January 1889) in AAS; "Hawaii," *Some Remarks* 1, no. 1 (January 1894) in AAS; "Southward the Star of Empire," *Monthly Pamonaite* 1, no. 10 (May 1886) in AAS; "Editorial," *Monthly Pamonaite* 2, no. 2 (September 1886) in AAS; "Forgotten Mexico," *Appeal* 4, no. 22 (May 1891) in AAS; "Our Navy," *Acorn* 1, no. 3 (October 1886) in AAS.
31 "War!!" *Semi-Occasional Cedar Pointer* 3, no. 1 (May 1898) in AAS; "Darkest Cuba," *Amateur* n.d., in AAS; "How Walter Saved the Lone Star," *Leaves from the Press* 1, no. 5 (October 1897) in AAS. For similar stories about Cuba, see "Fame and Fortune, or the Adventures of Rad Clennan," *Dauntless* 1, no. 4 (July 1877) in EHS vol. 32 or "The Traders of the Gulf," *Keystone Magazine* 2, no. 1 (November 1877) in EHS vol. 33; "The Fourth of July," *Amateur Record* 1, no. 6 (July 15, 1898) in AAS.
32 The decline of amateur journalism is described in Petrik, "Youngest Fourth Estate." Changes to the laws governing US mail also played a part. By 1880, it had become, for most boys, prohibitively expensive to maintain the postal exchanges that had originally allowed Amateurdom to flourish.
33 Gilded Age America's imperial bluster in Walter Nugent, *Habits of Empire: A History of American Expansion* (New York: Knopf, 2008).
34 "Compulsory Education," *Boys of Atlanta* 1, no. 5 (February 1875) in EHS vol. 19. The rise of "adolescence" as a social and analytical category has sparked much debate. Scholars disagree on its origins and periodization. Kent Baxter, *The Modern Age: Turn of the Century American Culture and the Invention of Adolescence* (Tuscaloosa: University of Alabama Press, 2008), and Joseph Kett, *Rites of Passage: Adolescence in America, 1790 to the Present* (New York: Basic Books, 1977) emphasize the turn of the century, the middle class, and high schools. Grace Palladino, *Teenagers: An American History* (New York: Basic Books, 1996) places greater emphasis on the Great Depression in fomenting adolescent culture. Sarah E. Chinn, *Inventing Modern Adolescence: The Children of Immigrants in Turn-of-the-Century America* (New Brunswick, NJ: Rutgers University Press, 2009) traces the origins of adolescence to the largely working-class culture of young immigrants. But rather than pinpoint the definitive origins of adolescence, it may be more useful to think of it as a polygenetic affect, something that coalesced out of disparate strands. Such is the implicit contention of Thomas Hine in *The Rise and Fall of the American Teenager: A New History of the American Adolescent Experience* (New York: Harper Perennial, 2000). Youth depoliticization discussed in Grinspan, *The Virgin Vote*, and on the Wide Awakes, see Jon Grinspan, "'Young Men for War': The Wide Awakes and Abraham Lincoln's 1860 Presidential Campaign," *Journal of American History* 96, no. 2 (September 2009): 357–378. As noted in chapter 1, and in contrast to the mostly male purveyors of amateur papers, girls often saw classrooms as liberatory spaces. See Jane H. Hunter, *How Young Ladies*

*Became Girls: The Victorian Origins of American Girlhood* (New Haven, CT: Yale University Press, 2002).
35 "Editorial," *Illinois Amateur* in AAS; "Editorial," in *Idyllic Hours* in AAS and see also Cohen, "Emancipation of Boyhood."
36 "Young Men in Politics," *Amateur Journal* 4, no. 22 (September 1882) in AAS; "Progress," *Boy's Companion* 1, no. 5 (February 1875) in EHS vol. 19; "Loyal Sons of America," *Amateur Advertiser* 1, no. 7 (March 1879) in AAS; "Our Country," *Golden Dawn* 2, no. 6 (June 1895) in AAS; "Fourth of July and the Boys," *Dawn* 1, no. 4 (July 1876) in EHS vol. 24.
37 "Boy Suffrage," *Young American's Monthly* 5, no. 3 (May 1873) in AAS; "Politics," *Scientific Amateur* 1, no. 3 (April 1872) in AAS.
38 "Politics," *Young Aspirant* 3, no. 7 (October 1878) in AAS. Some few amateurs, however, did question the propriety of political talk in adolescent newspapers. See, for example, "What Good Is Politics in Amateur Papers?" *Young American's Monthly* 4, no. 2 (July 1872) in AAS. The biographies of prominent amateurs discussed in Truman J. Spencer, *The History of Amateur Journalism* (New York: The Fossils, 1957).
39 "Frontier Perils," *Youth* 1, no. 8 (August 1885): 4 in AAS.
40 "Imaginary citizenship" in Courtney Weikle-Mills, *Imaginary Citizens: Child Readers and the Limits of American Independence, 1640–1868* (Baltimore, MD: Johns Hopkins University Press, 2013).
41 *Youth's Ledger*, "A Tale of the Frontier" 2, no. 15 (February 1887) in AAS.
42 A. W. Dingwall, "Amateur Papers: As They Are, and As They Should Be," *Press* 2, no. 16 (November 1877): 1 in AAS; "America's Young Men," *Chico Amateur* 1, no. 1 (June 1885): 1 in AAS.
43 "The Apache," *Chico Amateur* 1, no. 1 (June 1885) in AAS. There is a voluminous historiography on the West and the state. Particularly relevant here is Stephen J. Rockwell, *Indian Affairs and the Administrative State in the Nineteenth Century* (New York: Cambridge University Press, 2010), and Benjamin Madley, *An American Genocide: The United States and the California Indian Catastrophe, 1846–1873* (New Haven, CT: Yale University Press, 2016). On the "savage-as-child," see Matthew Frye Jacobson, *Barbarian Virtues: The United States Encounters Foreign Peoples at Home and Abroad* (New York: Hill and Wang, 2000).
44 "Our Pioneers," *Kansas Zephyr* 4, no. 1 (January 1884) in AAS. "Adolescence" as a "colonial" concept described in Gail Bederman, *Manliness and Civilization: A Cultural History of Gender and Race in the United States, 1880–1917* (Chicago: University of Chicago Press, 1995). On age-gradations and American society, see Chudacoff, *How Old Are You?*.
45 Frederick Jackson Turner, "Address at the Dedication of a New High School Building in Portage, Wisconsin," January 1, 1896. On Amateurdom and the articulation of a distinctly adolescent perspective, see Isaac, "Youthful Enterprises," 158–159. Of course, this is not to exclude other types of "play-acting" within Amateurdom. Karen Sánchez-Eppler, *Dependent States: The Child's Part in Nineteenth-*

*Century American Culture* (Chicago: University of Chicago Press, 2005), chap. 4, imagines amateur newspaper editors to be "playing at class" by mimicking middle-class adult work.
46 "The Amateur Casuals in Journalism," *New York Times*, October 9, 1871.
47 "Editorial," *Amateur Press* 1, no. 9 (November 1898) in AAS. The "Civil Rights War" covered in Harrison, *Career and Reminiscences of an Amateur Journalist*, 66, Petrik, "The Youngest Fourth Estate," 131–134, and Clarke quoted in Cohen, "Emancipation of Boyhood."
48 Smith, "Print Networks and Youth Information Culture," 13–14 posits a similar shift toward a softer, more literary aesthetic among amateurs by the early 1880s.
49 "Our Indian Wars," *Editor's Eye* 1, no. 1 (November 1878) in EHS vol. 41; "Editorial," *Aspirant* 1, no. 2 (February 1879) in AAS; "The Indian's Farewell," *Buffalo Amateur* 1, no. 3 (August 1878) in AAS; "The Chinese Question," *Young Aspirant* 3, no. 12 (March 1879) in AAS; "Editorial," *Our Own Journal* 5, no. 10 (June 1881) in AAS. A similar hope for national atonement expressed in "The Treatment of the North American Indian," *Souvenir* 1, nos. 4–5 (June and July 1886) in EHS vol. 84.
50 "Fiction," *Hawkeye Boy* 4, no. 19 (March 1879) in AAS; "The Three Stumbling Blocks to the Advancement of Amateurdom," *Young Americans' Comrade* 4, no. 5 (January 1873) in AAS; "Dime Novels," *Literary Companion* 1, no. 1 (March 1884) in AAS. By 1878, reformers amended the NAPA constitution in an attempt to exclude boys whose papers trafficked in "cheap" literature. The politics of Indian assimilation discussed in C. Joseph Genetin-Pilawa, *Crooked Paths to Allotment: The Fight Over Federal Indian Policy after the Civil War* (Chapel Hill: UNC Press, 2012).
51 Ballard, "Amateur Newspapers," 725–726. Some girls did publish amateur papers, and even editorialized in favor of women's rights. But they were mostly surrounded by boys who generally insisted on policing rigid distinctions between the sexes. See, for example, one boy's discussion of the "sentimental disease" that was women's suffrage: "Girls' Education," *Youth* 1, no. 10 (October 1885) in AAS. Petrik, "Youngest Fourth Estate," discusses a campaign within NAPA to demean the work of female editors and diminish the role of girls within the organization. On Roosevelt, bravado, and "womanish emotionalism," see Bederman, *Manliness and Civilization*.
52 "Captain Jack," *Editor's Eye* 1, no. 2 (December 1878) in EHS vol. 41. As an ex-president of NAPA himself noted, "sensational literature, of the 'blood and thunder' class had been predominant during Amateurdom's early years ... and remained in favor among a large class of journals for some time." See Harrison, *Career and Reminiscences of an Amateur Journalist*, 47.
53 The broad outlines of this shift described by Diana Selig, *Americans All: The Cultural Gifts Movement* (Cambridge, MA: Harvard University Press, 2008).
54 Frank H. Severance, "The Periodical Press of Buffalo, 1811–1915," *Publications of the Buffalo Historical Society* (Buffalo, NY: Buffalo Historical Society, 1915), 192. Smith, "Print Networks and Youth Information Culture," argues that "Ama-

teurdom" in its original form had mostly disappeared by 1890, a victim of both changing tastes and new postal regulations that denied amateurs discounted bulk rates. But it might also be noted that amateur presses were given something of a second life by the growing number of high schools in America. As those institutions proliferated after the turn of the twentieth century, high school newspapers sprang into existence. They depended upon the same technology as the amateur press and often engaged in similar sorts of networked exchange. On the early high school newspaper and its importance to a nascent teenaged peer culture, see Hunter, *How Young Ladies Became Girls*, 222–260, and Reed Ueda, *Avenues to Adulthood: The Origins of the High School and Social Mobility in an American Suburb* (New York: Cambridge University Press, 1987), 123–125.

## 4. INTERNATIONALIST IMPULSES

1. Franklin K. Mathiews, "Blowing Out the Boy's Brains," *Outlook* (November 18, 1914): 652–653.
2. Ibid. The era's librarians were almost universally opposed to the circulation of series fiction as "worthless drivel that would corrupt the minds of young people." See Emily Hamilton-Honey, "Guardians of Morality: Librarians and Girls' Series Fiction, 1890–1950," *Library Trends* 60, no. 4 (Spring 2012): 765–785, quoted on p. 770.
3. Histories of the Progressive movement writ large include Michael McGerr, *A Fierce Discontent: The Rise and Fall of the Progressive Movement in America, 1870–1920* (New York: Free Press, 2003); Alan Dawley, *Changing the World: American Progressives in War and Revolution* (Princeton, NJ: Princeton University Press, 2003); and T. J. Jackson Lears, *Rebirth of a Nation: The Making of Modern America, 1877–1920* (New York: Harper Perennial, 2009). On Progressivism, child study, and children more particularly, see Kriste Lindenmeyer, *A Right to Childhood: The U.S. Children's Bureau and Child Welfare, 1912–1946* (Urbana: University of Illinois Press, 1997), and Janet Golden, *Babies Made Us Modern: How Infants Brought America into the Twentieth Century* (New York: Cambridge University Press, 2018).
4. A short but excellent overview of the children's library movement can be found in Kathleen Chamberlain, "'Wise Censorship': Cultural Authority and the Scorning of Juvenile Series Books, 1890–1940," Lydia Cushman and Deidre Johnson, eds., *Scorned Literature: Essays on the History and Criticism of Popular Mass-Produced Fiction in America* (Westport, CT: Greenwood Press, 2002): 187–211. See also Jacalyn Eddy, *Bookwomen: Creating an Empire in Children's Book Publishing, 1919–1939* (Madison: University of Wisconsin Press, 2006), and Anne Lundin, *Constructing the Canon of Children's Literature: Beyond Library Walls and Ivory Towers* (New York: Routledge, 2004). On the Progressive state as "superparent," see Mary Ann Mason, *From Father's Property to Children's Rights: The History of Child Custody in the United States* (New York: Columbia University Press, 1994), 85–119.
5. These efforts at suppression have been dubbed the "Fairy Tale Wars." See MicKenzie Fasteland, "Empire and Adolescence: Whiteness and Gendered Citizenship in

American Young Adult Literature, 1904–1951" (PhD diss., University of Michigan, 2016), 70–71 and 98.
6 Mathiews, "Blowing Out the Boys' Brains," 653.
7 Akira Iriye, *Cultural Internationalism and World Order* (Baltimore, MD: Johns Hopkins University Press, 1997), here 27. See also Christopher McKnight Nichols, *Promise and Peril: America at the Dawn of a Global Age* (Cambridge, MA: Harvard University Press, 2011); Glenda Sluga, *Internationalism in the Age of Nationalism* (Philadelphia: University of Pennsylvania Press, 2013); Emily S. Rosenberg, *Spreading the American Dream: American Economic and Cultural Expansion, 1890–1945* (New York: Hill and Wang, 1982), 108–121. Some scholars have examined the issue from a youth-oriented perspective. See Julia L. Mickenberg, *Learning from the Left: Children's Literature, the Cold War, and Radical Politics in the United States* (New York: Oxford University Press, 2006). Competing forms of internationalist thought, such as Pan-Asianism or the Comintern, may also have produced their own children's literature, but such sources fall outside the scope of this book.
8 George A. Coe, "Youth and Peace," *Scribner's* 78, no. 1 (July 1925): 8–13, quoted at 9; "Disarmament of the mind" in Talya Zemach-Bersin, "Imperial Pedagogies: Education for American Globalism, 1898–1950" (PhD diss., Yale University, 2015), 140. For contrary currents in the era's youth literature and "ludic imperialism," see Caroline Lieffers, "Empires of Play and Publicity in G.P. Putnam's 'Boys' Books by Boys,'" *Diplomatic History* 43, no. 1 (January 2019): 31–56. On Progressive racism and nativism, see Marilyn Lake and Henry Reynolds, *Drawing the Global Colour Line: White Men's Countries and the International Challenge of Racial Equality* (New York: Cambridge University Press, 2008).
9 Warren G. Harding, "The Return to Normalcy," *Address to the Home Market Club of Boston*, May 14, 1920. On the era's broader debate over foreign policy, see Brooke L. Blower, "From Isolationism to Neutrality: A New Framework for Understanding American Political Culture, 1919–1941," *Diplomatic History* 38, no. 2 (April 2014): 345–376. The push toward internationalism in early twentieth-century children's literature has received some recent scholarly attention. See Diana Selig, *Americans All: The Cultural Gifts Movement* (Cambridge, MA: Harvard University Press, 2008); Gary D. Schmidt, *Making Americans: Children's Literature from 1930–1960* (Iowa City: University of Iowa Press, 2013); Megan Threlkeld, "Education for *Pax Americana*: The Limits of Internationalism in Progressive Era Peace Education," *History of Education Quarterly* 57, no. 4 (November 2017): 515–541; Jani L. Barker, "'A really big theme': Americanization and World Peace-Internationalism and/as Nationalism in Lucy Fitch Perkins's Twins Series," in Karen Sands-O'Connor and Marietta Frank, eds., *Internationalism in Children's Series* (New York, 2014), 76–94; Marietta A. Frank, "'A bit of life actually lived in a foreign land': Internationalism as World Friendship in Children's Series," in ibid., 96–106; Kristine Alexander, "The Girl Guide Movement and Imperial Internationalism during the 1920s and 1930s," *Journal of the History of Childhood and*

*Youth* 2, no. 1 (Winter 2009): 37–63; Warren Kuehl and Lynn K. Dunn, *Keeping the Covenant: American Internationalists and the League of Nations, 1920–1939* (Kent, OH: Kent State University Press, 1997), 64–75; Andrew McNally, "Empire Imaginary: International Understanding and Progressive Education in the United States" (PhD diss., University of Minnesota, 2017); and Zemach-Bersin, "Imperial Pedagogies." The interwar era also saw socialists and communists publish internationally minded youth literature. See Paul C. Mishler, *Raising Reds: The Young Pioneers, Radical Summer Camps, and Communist Political Culture in the United States* (New York: Columbia University Press, 1999), 109–130. There is a vibrant historiography covering anti-imperialism, but it has not engaged much with children's literature. See Ian Tyrrell and Jay Sexton, eds., *Empire's Twin: U.S. Anti-imperialism from the Founding Era to the Age of Terrorism* (Ithaca, NY: Cornell University Press, 2015).

10  Julia Colman et al., *The Child's Anti-Slavery Book: Containing a Few Words about American Slave Children, and Stories of Slave-Life* (New York: Carlton and Porter, 1859). The Student Volunteer Movement is discussed in Andrew Preston, *Sword of the Spirit, Shield of Faith: Religion in American War and Diplomacy* (New York: Knopf, 2012), 175–197. Another important precursor to the Progressive-era internationals included some of the more factually minded nineteenth-century children's series that featured travel. These include Jacob Abbott's *Rollo* books, Hezekiah Butterworth's *Zigzag Journeys* series, and Thomas Knox's *Boy Travellers* volumes. The early development of such periodicals is described in Karen Li Miller, "The White Child's Burden: Managing the Self and Money in Nineteenth Century Children's Missionary Periodicals," *American Periodicals* 22, no. 2 (2012): 139–157.

11  The single best treatment of the relationship between early American imperialism and Christianity is Emily Conroy-Krutz, *Christian Imperialism: Converting the World in the Early American Republic* (Ithaca, NY: Cornell University Press, 2015). On missionaries, internationalism, and the debate over imperialism, see David Hollinger, *Protestants Abroad: How Missionaries Tried to Change the World but Changed America* (Princeton, NJ: Princeton University Press, 2017); Michael G. Thompson, *For God and Globe: Christian Internationalism in the United States Between the Great War and the Cold War* (Ithaca, NY: Cornell University Press, 2015); and Ian Tyrrell, *Reforming the World: The Creation of America's Moral Empire* (Princeton, NJ: Princeton University Press, 2010).

12  Lucy W. Peabody, "Why Is Everyland?" *Everyland* 12, no. 3 (1922): 1; "Good Things for Everyland Readers," *Everyland: A World Friendship Magazine for Boys and Girls* 7, no. 1 (1916); Fanny L. Kollock, "Everyland and Every Child," *Everyland*, 7, no. 1 (1916): 28–29. Early missionary children's literature is described in Karen Sánchez-Eppler, "Raising Empires Like Children: Race, Nation, and Religious Education," *American Literary History* 8, no. 3 (1996): 399–425, and Allison Giffen and Robin L. Cadwallader, eds., *Saving the World: Girlhood and Evangelicalism in Nineteenth-Century Literature* (New York: Routledge, 2018). On the genesis of

*Everyland*, see McNally, "Empire Imaginary," and Charles Vernon Vickrey, *The Young People's Missionary Movement* (New York: YPMM Press, 1906).

13 Examples of epistolary exchange can be found, for example, in "My Little Gipsy Children," *Everyland* 5, no. 3 (1914): 162–163; "The Postman from Germany" and "A Letter from Porto Rico," 4, no. 2 (1913): 86–87; or "Stories and Letters from Indian Boys and Girls," *Everyland* 5, no. 4 (1914): 224–233. Christian internationalism described in Thompson, *For God and Globe*.

14 A. Hyatt Verrill, "Beche, the Carib Boy," 42–43, 61, and Elizabeth Gurnee Anderson, "Ana Julia, the Venezuelan Mountain Child," 53–55 in *Everyland* 7, no. 9 (1916); Helen Murphy, "Natchez, the Brown Boy of Guam," *Everyland* 7, no. 4 (1916): 108–111, 121; Arthur P. Shepherd, "Missionary or Pirate!" *Everyland* 12, no. 1 (1922): 2. To practice the cultivation of cultural relativism, the magazine often suggested games and activities that involved American children assuming the identities of foreigners and playfully mocking US customs. See, for example, Ruth Horton, "Who Is Queer?" *Everyland* 5, no. 2 (1914): 87.

15 "Miss Gulliver's Travels," 12, no. 1 (1922): 25–26. This last point is echoed by Zemach-Bersin, "Imperial Pedagogies," 110.

16 "Broadening of sympathies" quoted in *Everyland* 12, no. 1 (1922): 66. Tessie Gross quoted in *Everyland*, 7, no. 3 (1916), title page. Play described in "Everyland Exchange," 12, no. 1 (1922): 30, and see also Lisaide Colloque, "What Everyland Almost Forgot," *Everyland* 5, no. 3 (1914): 159–161, which describes a game where children dressed in the costumes of the world and practiced greeting one another in the proper local fashion. Selig, *Americans All*, 76–77, describes efforts to "play-act" and dramatize foreign cultures as an important component of the cultural gifts movement. On the era's resurgent white nationalism, see Linda Gordon, *The Second Coming of the KKK: The Ku Klux Klan of the 1920s and the American Political Tradition* (New York: Liveright, 2017).

17 A 1912 *Everyland* (vol. 4, no. 1) circular, for example, mentions a meager subscriber list of only 13,700 individuals and institutions. Syndicate series fiction, by comparison, sold into the millions altogether. On the evangelical case for empire, see Susan K. Harris, *God's Arbiters: Americans and the Philippines, 1898–1902* (New York: Oxford University Press, 2011).

18 For a few examples, see Lt. Howard Payson, *The Boy Scouts on Belgian Battlefields* (New York: Hurst & Co., 1915); Ensign Robert L. Drake, *The Boy Allies with the Flying Squadron, or the Naval Raiders of the Great War* (New York: A. L. Burt, 1915); Clair W. Hayes, *The Boy Allies in the Balkan Campaign, or the Struggle to Save a Nation* (New York: A. L. Burt, 1916); H. I. Hancock, *The Invasion of the United States; or, Uncle Sam's Boys at the Capture of Boston* (Philadelphia: Henry Altemus, 1916); Gordon Stuart, *The Boy Scouts of the Air on the French Front* (Chicago: Reilly & Lee, 1918).

19 Descriptions of youth wartime mobilization are located in Mischa Honeck, "Playing on Uncle Sam's Team: American Childhoods During World War I," *Journal of the Gilded Age and Progressive Era* 17, no. 4 (October 2018): 677–690.

20 Andrews quoted in Honeck, "Playing on Uncle Sam's Team," 679, and Threlkeld, "Education for *Pax Americana*," 523. On the American School Peace League, see Susan Zeiger, "The Schoolhouse vs. the Armory: U.S. Teachers and the Campaign against Militarism in the Schools, 1914–1918," *Journal of Women's History* 15, no. 2 (Summer 2003): 150–179.

21 Quote and WWI controversy over toys in Gary Cross, *Kids' Stuff: Toys and the Changing World of American Childhood* (Cambridge, MA: Harvard University Press, 1997), 110–113. "Stone axe of war" in H. C. Engelbrecht, *Revolt Against War* (New York: Dodd, Mead, & Co., 1937), ix. Leopold and Loeb in Paula S. Fass, *Kidnapped: Child Abduction in America* (New York: Oxford University Press, 1997), 89. On the broader domestic political climate during WWI, see David M. Kennedy, *Over Here: The First World War and American Society*, rev. ed. (New York: Oxford University Press, 2004). Textbooks and world citizenship in Susan Schulten, *The Geographical Imagination in America, 1880–1950* (Chicago: University of Chicago Press, 2001), 125.

22 "Hate war" quoted in Zeiger, "The Schoolhouse vs. the Armory," 160. *Parents* magazine quoted in Diana Selig, "World Friendship: Children, Parents, and Peace Education in America Between the Wars," in James Marten, ed., *Children and War: A Historical Anthology* (New York: New York University Press, 2002), 135; "League of Nations" in Zemach-Bersin, "Imperial Ideologies," 127. The "cultural gifts" movement is detailed in Selig, *Americans All*.

23 Blake quoted in Zeiger, "The Schoolhouse vs. the Armory," 154.

24 On the connections between feminism, women's rights, anti-imperialism, and the peace movement, see Harriet Hyman Alonso, *Peace as a Women's Issue: A History of the U.S. Movement for World Peace and Women's Rights* (Syracuse, NY: Syracuse University Press, 1993); Leila J. Rupp, "Constructing Internationalism: The Case of Transnational Women's Organizations, 1888–1945," *American Historical Review* 99, no. 5 (1994): 1571–1600; and Allison L. Schneider, *Suffragists in an Imperial Age: U.S. Expansion and the Woman Question, 1870–1929* (New York: Oxford University Press, 2008). Balch, Addams, the WILPF, and the "fetish of force" are discussed in Nichols, *Promise and Peril*, 273–320.

25 On "imperial" textbooks, see Clif Stratton, *Education for Empire: American Schools, Race, and the Paths of Good Citizenship* (Berkeley: University of California Press, 2016). Turn-of-the-century fears of feminization described in Gail Bederman, *Manliness and Civilization: A Cultural History of Gender and Race in the United States, 1880–1917* (Chicago: University of Chicago Press, 1995).

26 Quotes from McGerr, *A Fierce Discontent*, 80 and 107, and Selig, *Americans All*, 39.

27 Lucy Fitch Perkins, "'The Twins'—Their Origin," *Elementary English Review* 13, no. 5 (May 1936): 169; Eleanor Ellis Perkins, *Eve Among the Puritans: A Biography of Lucy Fitch Perkins* (Boston: Houghton Mifflin, 1956), 226; Stanley J. Kunitz and Howard Haycraft, eds., "Lucy Fitch Perkins," *The Junior Book of Authors* (New York: Wilson, 1935). A short but insightful overview of Perkins's life and work can be found in Claudia Mills, "Toward Global Community: The Twins Series of

Lucy Fitch Perkins," *Children's Literature Association Quarterly* 18, no. 1 (Spring 1993): 4–9. An earlier expression of Perkins's themes can be found in Lulu Maude Chance, *Little Folks of Many Lands* (Boston: Ginn & Company, 1904).

28  Perkins quoted in *The Italian Twins* (Boston: Houghton Mifflin, 1920), appendix. On the theme of world friendship in Perkins's work, see Barker, "'A really big theme,'" 76–94, and Karen Dillon, "'The heft of both countries in your fists': Lucy Fitch Perkins's Foreign Twins as Cultural Goodwill Ambassadors," *Children's Literature* 39 (2011): 85–106. The "fictive travel movement" is described in Kristin L. Hoganson, *Consumers' Imperium: The Global Production of American Domesticity, 1865–1920* (Chapel Hill: UNC Press, 2007).

29  Lucy Fitch Perkins, *The Japanese Twins* (Boston: Houghton Mifflin, 1912), 5; Perkins, *The Mexican Twins* (Boston: Houghton Mifflin, 1915), preface and appendix; Perkins, *The Chinese Twins* (Boston: Houghton Mifflin, 1935), 11. Perkins fan quoted in Dillon, "'The heft of both countries in your fists,'" 96. The prejudicial nature of the era's mainstream children's literature is described in J. Frederick MacDonald, "'The Foreigner' in Juvenile Series Fiction, 1900–1945," *Journal of Popular Culture* 8 (1974): 534–548, here 534, and Paul Deane, *Mirrors of American Culture: Children's Fiction Series in the Twentieth Century* (Metuchen, NJ: Scarecrow Press, 1991), 104–127. On the exclusion laws and their rationale, see Erika Lee, *At America's Gates: Chinese Immigration during the Exclusion Era, 1882–1943* (Chapel Hill: UNC Press, 2003).

30  On Gypsies, see Lucy Fitch Perkins, *The Spanish Twins* (Boston: Houghton Mifflin, 1934), 38 or *The Irish Twins* (Boston: Houghton Mifflin, 1913), 61. Germans, unsurprisingly, are the villains in *The Belgian Twins* (1917) and *The French Twins* (1918), both of which are set during World War I. Lucy Fitch Perkins, *The Eskimo Twins* (Boston: Houghton Mifflin, 1914), 91–95; Perkins, *The Pickaninny Twins* (Boston: Houghton Mifflin, 1931). On the limitations of Perkins's books, see Barker, "'A really big theme,'" 85–91. Langston Hughes quoted in Julia L. Mickenberg, "Children's Novels," in Leonard Cassuto et al., eds., *Cambridge History of the American Novel* (New York: Cambridge University Press, 2011): 868–869.

31  *Chicago Tribune* and League of Nations quoted in Perkins, *Eve Among the Puritans*, x and 226; Perkins, "'The Twins'—Their Origin," 193. The League of Nations itself was innovative for its many child-centered programs. See Dominique Marshall, "The Construction of Children as an Object of International Relations: The Declaration of Children's Rights and the Child Welfare Committee of the League of Nations, 1900–1924," *International Journal of Children's Rights* 7, no. 2 (1999): 103–147, and Kenneth Osborne, "Creating the 'International Mind': The League of Nations Attempts to Reform History Teaching, 1920–1939," *History of Education Quarterly* 56, no. 2 (May 2016): 213–240.

32  Very little biographical information about Mary Hazelton Wade currently exists, but a nice overview of her life and literary output is Tanfer Emin Tunc, "Manifest Destiny's Child: Mary Hazelton Blanchard Wade and the Literature of American Empire," *Children's Literature in Education* 48, no. 3 (2017): 245–261.

33   Mary Hazelton Wade, *Our Little Hawaiian Cousin* (Boston: L.C. Page, 1902), v–vi; Wade, *Our Little Cuban Cousin* (Boston: L.C. Page, 1902), v–vi.
34   Mary Hazelton Wade, *Our Little Philippine Cousin* (Boston: L.C. Page, 1902), vi; Eva Cannon Brooks, *Our Little Argentine Cousin* (Boston: L.C. Page, 1910), viii–ix; Wade, *Our Little Porto Rican Cousin* (Boston: L.C. Page, 1902), 21–22. The transformative power of American-led educational efforts is also discussed in H. Lee M. Pike, *Our Little Panama Cousin* (Boston: L.C. Page, 1906), 116–118. On the importance of education to Progressive imperialism, see Sarah Steinbock-Pratt, *Educating the Empire: American Teachers and Contested Colonization in the Philippines* (Cambridge: Cambridge University Press, 2019). On the currents of imperialism and racialism running through the globalist movement, see Zemach-Bersin, "Imperial Ideologies," 49, 100, 108–110.
35   Mary Hazelton Wade, *Our Little Brown Cousin* (Boston: L.C. Page, 1901), v–vi. "Same great family" in Mary Hazelton Wade, *Our Little African Cousin* (Boston: L.C. Page, 1902), v.
36   Wade, *Our Little Brown Cousin*, v–vi, 9, 14, 16–19; Wade, *Our Little Siamese Cousin* (Boston: L.C. Page, 1903), 110; Wade, *Our Little Swiss Cousin* (Boston: L.C. Page, 1903), 38–39.
37   H. Lee M. Pike, *Our Little Korean Cousin* (Boston: L.C. Page, 1905), 1–2; Mary F. Nixon-Roulet, *Our Little Alaskan Cousin* (Boston: L.C. Page, 1907), 7; Wade, *Our Little Siamese Cousin*, 21–22, 30; Blanche McManus, *Our Little Arabian Cousin* (Boston: L.C. Page, 1907), vi, 9.
38   Wade, *Our Little Brown Cousin*, 20–21; Wade, *Our Little Turkish Cousin* (Boston: L.C. Page, 1904), vi; Wade, *Our Little Porto Rican Cousin*, v–vi and 14; Wade, *Our Little African Cousin*, v–vi.
39   Wade, *Our Little Porto Rican Cousin*, 51; Wade, *Our Little Armenian Cousin* (Boston: L.C. Page, 1905); Wade, *Our Little Siamese Cousin*, 14 and 100; Nixon-Roulet, *Our Little Alaskan Cousin*, 28–29; Mary Hazelton Wade, *Our Little Jewish Cousin* (Boston: L.C. Page, 1904). McGerr notes a broader Progressive faith in the malleability of human beings and thus their capacity to change for the better in *A Fierce Discontent*, 80–81.
40   Mary Hazelton Wade, *Our Little Italian Cousin* (Boston: L.C. Page, 1903), v–vi; Blanche McManus, *Our Little Hindu Cousin* (Boston: L.C. Page, 1907), vi.
41   Eva Cannon Brooks, *Our Little Argentine Cousin* (Boston: L.C. Page, 1910), 117–118; Pike, *Our Little Korean Cousin*, viii; Mary Hazelton Wade, *Our Little Japanese Cousin* (Boston: L.C. Page, 1901), 66. Immigration, it should be noted, was its own form of foreign relations, particularly during a period of such a massive influx of foreign-born individuals. On that point, see Donna R. Gabaccia, *Foreign Relations: American Immigration in Global Perspective* (Princeton, NJ: Princeton University Press, 2012), and Matthew Frye Jacobson, *Barbarian Virtues: The United States Encounters Foreign Peoples at Home and Abroad, 1876–1917* (New York: Hill and Wang, 2000).
42   Mary Hazelton Wade, *Our Little Indian Cousin* (Boston: L.C. Page, 1901), 32.

43  Lofting quoted in Sands-O'Connor and Frank, eds., *Internationalism in Children's Series*, 6–7. See, for example, Etta Blaisdell McDonald, *Colette in France* (Boston: Little, Brown, 1914) and McDonald, *Chandra in India* (Boston: Little, Brown, 1916); R. Talbot Kelly, *Burma: Peeps at Many Lands* (London: Adam and Charles Black, 1908); Yan Phou Lee, *When I Was a Boy in China* (Boston: Lothrop, 1903); Marietta Ambrosi, *When I Was a Girl in Italy* (Boston: Lothrop, Lee & Shepard, 1906); George Demetrios, *When I Was a Boy in Greece* (Boston: Lothrop, Lee & Shepard, 1913). Virginia Olcott, *Adventures in Italy: The Story of Beppo and Lucia* (New York: Grosset & Dunlap, 1953), preface. A comprehensive overview of this internationalist children's literature can be found in Melanie A. Kimball, "Seeing the World from Main Street: Early Twentieth Century Juvenile Collections about Life in Other Lands," *Library Trends* 60, no. 4 (Spring 2012): 675–693.
44  This critique is articulated in Selig, *Americans All*, 14, and Threlkeld, "Education for *Pax Americana*," 515, 531. On the reductionist stereotypes and "clichéd predictability" proffered by the likes of Lucy Fitch Perkins, see Mills, "Toward Global Community," 5.
45  Alternative forms like Black radicalism (Marcus Garvey's United Negro Improvement Association is probably most relevant) are discussed in Steven Hahn, *A Nation Under Our Feet: Black Political Struggles in the Rural South from Slavery to the Great Migration* (Cambridge, MA: Harvard University Press, 2003). On leftist or Marxist internationalism, see Michael Denning, *The Cultural Front: The Laboring of American Culture in the Twentieth Century* (New York: Verso, 1997), and Julia L. Mickenberg, *Learning from the Left: Children's Literature, the Cold War, and Radical Politics in the United States* (New York: Oxford University Press, 2006). Iriye contrasts "liberal" and "socialist" internationalism in *Cultural Internationalism and World Order*, 33–34.
46  Zeiger, "The Schoolhouse vs. the Armory," 162.
47  An overview of the era's push toward the institutionalization of youth can be found in David I. Macleod, *Building Character in the American Boy: The Boy Scouts, YMCA, and Their Forerunners, 1870–1920* (Madison: University of Wisconsin Press, 1983).
48  Girl Scouts quoted in *Scouting for Girls: Official Handbook of the Girl Scouts* (New York: Girl Scouts, 1927), 8. On the Boy Scouts, Girl Scouts, and global affairs, see Mischa Honeck, *Our Frontier is the World: The Boy Scouts in the Age of American Ascendancy* (Ithaca, NY: Cornell University Press, 2018); Benjamin Jordan, *Modern Manhood and the Boy Scouts of America: Citizenship, Race, and the Environment, 1910–1930* (Chapel Hill: UNC Press, 2016); Susan A. Miller, *Growing Girls: The Natural Origins of Girls' Organizations in America* (New Brunswick, NJ: Rutgers University Press, 2007); Marcia Chatelain, "International Sisterhood: Cold War Girl Scouts Encounter the World," *Diplomatic History* 38, no. 2 (April 2014): 261–270; Kristine Alexander, *Guiding Modern Girls: Girlhood, Empire, and Internationalism in the 1920s and 1930s* (Vancouver: UBC Press, 2017).

49 Liisa Malkki, "Children, Humanity, and the Infantilization of Peace," in Ilana Feldman and Miriam Ticktin, eds., *In the Name of Humanity: The Government of Threat and Care* (Durham, NC: Duke University Press, 2010), 58–85. Important insights along these lines are also located in Honeck, *Our Frontier Is the World*, esp. 1–18; Karen Dubinsky, "Children, Ideology, and Iconography: How Babies Rule the World," *Journal of the History of Childhood and Youth* 5, no. 1 (Winter 2012): 5–13; Helen Brocklehurst, *Who's Afraid of Children?: Children, Conflict, and International Relations* (London: Routledge, 2006); Emily S. Rosenberg, "Rescuing Women and Children," *Journal of American History* 89, no. 2 (September 2002): 456–465; and Erica Burman, "Innocents Abroad: Western Fantasies of Childhood and the Iconography of Emergencies," *Disasters* 18, no. 3 (October 1994): 238–253. There were important precedents set here by the League of Nations. See Dominique Marshall, "The Formation of Childhood as an Object of International Relations: The Child Welfare Committee and the Declaration of Children's Rights of the League of Nations," *International Journal of Children's Rights* 7, no. 2 (1999): 103–147.

50 Dominique Marshall, "Children's Rights and Children's Action in International Relief and Domestic Welfare: The Work of Herbert Hoover Between 1914–1950," *Journal of the History of Childhood and Youth* 1, no. 3 (Fall 2008): 351–388, here 358; Julia F. Irwin, *Making the World Safe: The American Red Cross and a Nation's Humanitarian Awakening* (New York: Oxford University Press, 2013), here 169. See also Julia F. Irwin, "Teaching 'Americanism with a World Perspective': The Junior Red Cross in the U.S. Schools from 1917 to the 1920s," *History of Education Quarterly* 53, no. 3 (August 2013): 255–279.

51 Children's International Summer Villages and other such internationalist initiatives described in McNally, "Empire Imaginary." Student exchange programs are discussed in Iriye, *Cultural Internationalism and World Order*, 72–76. Pedagogical journals from the era also regularly advised teachers on how to promote international goodwill among the world's youth. See, for example, Ruth A. Barnes, "Developing International-Mindedness in Junior High School," *English Journal* 22 no. 6 (June 1933): 476–481. "International Alcoves" and clubs are described in Kuehl and Dunn, *Keeping the Covenant*, 65.

52 Heber Reece Harper, *What European and American Students Think on International Problems: A Contemporary Study of the World-Mindedness of University Students* (New York: Columbia University Press, 1931), 39. Paula Fass discusses internationalism among the era's college-aged youth in *The Damned and the Beautiful: American Youth in the 1920's* (New York: Oxford University Press, 1977), 327–361 and quoted 333. See also Britt Haas, *Fighting Authoritarianism: American Youth Activism in the 1930s* (New York: Fordham University Press, 2018), which (in part) charts the internationalist ethos of organizations like the American Youth Congress and the American Student Union.

53 Thomas Borstelmann, *Just Like Us: The American Struggle to Understand Foreigners* (New York: Columbia University Press, 2020), x. Contemporary UNESCO

children's education programs emphasizing "world-mindedness" are one example of the longevity of these ideas. Many of the postwar era's trends toward youth internationalism are described in Sara Fieldston, "The Nursery's Iron Curtain: Children, Childhood, and the Global Cold War," *History Compass* 17, no. 3 (May 2019): 1–10.

54 "International mind" in Kuehl and Dunn, *Keeping the Covenant*, 64; H. Irving Hancock, *Uncle Sam's Boys on Field Duty; or, Winning Corporal's Chevrons* (Philadelphia: Henry Altemus, 1911), 9–11; Enrique H. Lewis, "The Chinese Conspiracy; Or, a Naval Cadet's Adventures in the Celestial Empire," *Argosy* 13, no. 462 (October 10, 1891): 87.

55 Charles M. Harvey, "The Dime Novel in American Life," *The Atlantic* 100 (July 1907): 44–45; Stratemeyer quoted in Meghan O'Rourke, "Nancy Drew's Father," *New Yorker* (November 8, 2004), 120–129.

56 Statistics cited in Marilyn S. Greenwald, *The Secret of the Hardy Boys: Leslie Mc-Farlane and the Stratemeyer Syndicate* (Athens: Ohio University Press, 2004), 39. Behaviorism in Rima D. Apple, *Perfect Motherhood: Science and Childrearing in America* (New Brunswick, NJ: Rutgers University Press, 2006).

57 "Ignoramuses" in Kuehl and Dunn, *Keeping the Covenant*, 75.

5. DOLLAR DIPLOMACY FOR THE PRICE OF A FEW NICKELS

1 William MacLeod Raine, "Men in the Raw," *Argosy* 80, no. 4 (November 1915), 673–674.

2 Ibid., 674.

3 Ibid., 674–675.

4 Ibid., 675–676 and 682–683.

5 Ibid., 746.

6 On the history of *The Argosy*, see Paul B. Ringel, *Commercializing Childhood: Children's Magazines, Urban Gentility, and the Ideal of the American Child, 1823–1918* (Amherst: University of Massachusetts Press, 2015).

7 "The Log Book," *Argosy* 83, no. 4 (November 1916): 764; John S. to *Argosy* in "The Log-Book," *Argosy* 70, no. 1 (August 1912): 240.

8 Frank Ninkovich, *The Wilsonian Century: U.S. Foreign Policy since 1900* (Chicago: University of Chicago Press, 1999), 7, notes that by 1909 the United States was the world's leading exporter. On America's expanding investments in Latin America and elsewhere, see Kristin Hoganson, *Consumers' Imperium: The Global Production of American Domesticity* (Chapel Hill: UNC Press, 2007); Emily S. Rosenberg, *Spreading the American Dream: American Economic and Cultural Expansion, 1890–1945* (New York: Hill and Wang, 1982); Thomas F. O'Brien, *The Revolutionary Mission: American Enterprise in Latin America, 1900–1945* (New York: Cambridge University Press, 1996); David M. Pletcher, *The Diplomacy of Trade and Investment: American Economic Expansion in the Hemisphere* (Columbia: University of Missouri Press, 1998); Walter Nugent, *Habits of Empire: A History of American Expansion* (New York: Alfred A. Knopf, 2008), 276–304; Jay Sexton, *The Monroe*

*Doctrine: Empire and Nation in Nineteenth-Century America* (New York: Hill and Wang, 2011), 199–239; Emily S. Rosenberg, ed., *A World Connecting, 1870–1945* (Cambridge, MA: Harvard University Press, 2012); Katherine Unterman, *Uncle Sam's Policemen: The Pursuit of Fugitives Across Borders* (Cambridge, MA: Harvard University Press, 2015); and Megan Black, *The Global Interior: Mineral Frontiers and American Power* (Cambridge, MA: Harvard University Press, 2018). On "dollar diplomacy" more specifically, see Eileen Tillman, *Dollar Diplomacy by Force: Nation-Building and Resistance in the Dominican Republic* (Chapel Hill: UNC Press, 2016); Cyrus Veeser, *A World Safe for Capitalism: Dollar Diplomacy and America's Rise to Global Power* (New York: Columbia University Press, 2002); Emily S. Rosenberg, *Financial Missionaries to the World: The Politics and Culture of Dollar Diplomacy* (Durham, NC: Duke University Press, 1999); Lars Schoultz, *Beneath the United States: A History of U.S. Policy Toward Latin America* (Cambridge, MA: Harvard University Press, 1998); Emily S. Rosenberg and Norman L. Rosenberg, "From Colonialism to Professionalism: The Public Private Dynamic in United States Foreign Financial Advising, 1898–1929," *Journal of American History* 74, no. 1 (June 1987): 59–82.

9 "Bonds and battleships" quoted in Samuel Guy Inman, "Imperialist America," *Atlantic Monthly* 134 (July 1924): 116.

10 Pulp circulation figures quoted in Jeremy Agnew, *The Age of Dimes of Pulps: A History of Sensationalist Literature, 1830–1960* (Jefferson, NC: McFarland, 2018), 3–4. Cheaply made pulp magazines were often contrasted with the "slicks": more expensive middlebrow periodicals printed on expensive glossy paper. The "transnational" nature of pulp publishing is discussed in Shanon Fitzpatrick, "Pulp Empire: Macfadden Publications, Transnational America, and the Global Popular" (PhD diss., University of California at Irvine, 2013).

11 On pulp fiction more broadly, Agnew, *The Age of Dimes of Pulps*. Anti-pulp attacks were quite common. Some notable examples include "Fiction By Volume," *New York Times* (August 28, 1935), 16, or Marcus Duffield, "The Pulps: Day Dreams for the Masses," *Vanity Fair* 40, no. 4 (June 1933): 26. On young readers and pulp fiction, see Erin A. Smith, "'The ragtag and bobtail of the fiction parade': Pulp Magazines and the Literary Marketplace," in Lydia Cushman Schurman and Deidre Johnson, eds., *Scorned Literature: Essays on the History and Criticism of Popular Mass-Produced Fiction in America* (Westport, CT: Greenwood Press, 2002): 123–145, and see also Harold Hersey, *Pulpwood Editor: The Fabulous World of Thriller Magazines Revealed by a Veteran Editor and Publisher* (New York: Stokes, 1937), 5. On "clans," Paul Mandel, "Tarzan of the Paperbacks," *Life* (November 29, 1963), 11. The term itself, "clans," played off the "Tarzan Clans of America," a popular youth club that pulp publishers operated throughout the United States. On the "proletarian" Tarzan, see Margaret Ronan, "Meanwhile, Back in the Treetops," *Practical English* (May 8, 1964), 15. None of this, of course, is to suggest that adults did not read pulp fiction. But it is necessary to recognize that adolescent Americans were arguably the genre's most avid consumers. When

one considers the fact that pulps often became the basis for radio programming among young people, the genre appears even more expansive. See J. Fred MacDonald, *Don't Touch That Dial! Radio Programming in American Life from 1920–1960* (Chicago: Nelson-Hall, 1979).

12  Volney G. Mathison, "The Golden Snake and the Singing Tiger," *Complete Story Magazine* 1, no. 5 (October 25, 1924): 96; "The Stage Driver," *Complete Story Magazine* 2, no. 5 (January 25, 1925): 144; Old Timer, "Augerin' Pen," *All Western Magazine* 1, no. 2 (January 1932): 95. Nathan Vernon Madison, *Anti-Foreign Imagery in American Pulps and Comic Books, 1920–1960* (Jefferson, NC: McFarland, 2013).

13  Olney quoted in Jay Sexton, *The Monroe Doctrine: Empire and Nation in Nineteenth-Century America* (New York: Hill and Wang, 2011), 203, and see Sexton chapters 5–6 on the late nineteenth-century emergence of a more muscular Monroe Doctrine; "canon" in Brian Loveman, *No Higher Law: American Foreign Policy and the Western Hemisphere Since 1776* (Chapel Hill: UNC Press, 2010), 191. The irony here is that Olney insisted that his statement represented an attempt to forestall a jingoistic reading of the Monroe Doctrine. He discouraged interventionism by emphasizing America's inherent stability and security, but events interceded in such a way as to sustain a more militant interpretation of Olney's words. On this point, see Robert Kagan, *Dangerous Nation: America's Foreign Policy from Its Earliest Days to the Dawn of the Twentieth Century* (New York: Vintage Books, 2006), 370–374.

14  "For Boys and 'Old Boys,'" *Popular Magazine* 1, no. 1 (November 1903): 95–96; "Log-Book," *Argosy* 73, no. 1 (August 1913): 236.

15  "Our Boys To-day," *Army and Navy Weekly* 1, no. 11 (August 28, 1897): 524; Theodore Roosevelt, *State of the Union* (December 3, 1901).

16  John Fiske, *American Political Ideas* (Boston: Houghton Mifflin, 1911), ix; Josiah Strong, *Our Country: Its Possible Future and Present Crisis* (New York: Baker and Taylor, 1885), 175; Mahan quoted in Loveman, *No Higher Law*, 152. On the nation's steadily expanding presence south of the border at this time, see Thomas Schoonover, *The United States in Central America, 1860–1911: Episodes of Social Imperialism and Imperial Rivalry in the World System* (Durham: Duke University Press, 1991).

17  Edward Stratemeyer, *Treasure Seekers of the Andes or, American Boys in Peru* (Boston: Lee and Shepard, 1907), iv–v, 138.

18  Stratemeyer, *Treasure Seekers of the Andes*, 40, 128; Bonehill, *Off for Hawaii*, 45; Ralphson, *Boy Scouts in Mexico*, 142–143; W. Crispin Sheppard, *The Rambler Club on the Texas Border* (Philadelphia: Penn, 1915), 90; Yates Stirling, Jr., *A United States Midshipman Afloat* (Philadelphia: Penn, 1908), 90–91; Wilbur Lawton, *The Dreadnought Boys Aboard a Destroyer* (New York: Hurst and Co., 1911), 219 and 228–229.

19  Edward Stratemeyer, *The Young Volcano Explorers or, American Boys in the West Indies* (Boston: Lee and Shepard, 1902), 189–194; H. Irving Hancock, *Dave Dar-*

rin's *South American Cruise; or, Two Innocent Young Naval Tools of an Infamous Conspiracy* (Philadelphia: Henry Altemus, 1919), 40–41 and 254. In suggesting as much, series fiction echoed the era's textbooks, which stressed Latin American shortcomings and argued that US assistance would be essential to the advancement of neighboring nations. See Emily S. Rosenberg, "Turning to Culture," in Gilbert M. Joseph, Catherine C. Legrand, and Ricardo D. Salvatore, eds., *Close Encounters of Empire: Writing the Cultural History of Latin American Relations* (Durham, NC: Duke University Press, 1998), 500.

20  Edgar Franklin, "Washington or—Worse?" *Argosy* 57, no. 4 (July 1908): 626, 629–630, 641–642, and Franklin, "Washington or—Worse?" *Argosy* 58, no. 3 (October 1908): 505.

21  Assistant Secretary of State Francis Wilson quoted in George Herring, *From Colony to Superpower: U.S. Foreign Relations Since 1776 (New York: Oxford University Press, 2008)*, 373. On the importance of conditioning structures to the history of capitalism, see Paul Kramer, "Embedding Capital: Political-Economic History, the United States, and the World," *Journal of the Gilded Age and Progressive Era* 15 (July 2016): 331–362.

22  Ralph Bonehill, *With Taylor on the Rio Grande* (Boston: Dana Estes, 1901), 75–76. Technocrats were depicted as heroes in stories like Walter Duranty, "Money to Burn," *Argosy* 58, no. 4 (November 1908): 612; Harold C. Burr, "In League with the Black Vultures," *Argosy* 58, no. 4 (November 1908): 761–768; William Wallace Cook, "The General's Pawn," *Argosy* 67, no. 4 (November 1911): 677–687; Roy Rockwood, *Jack North's Treasure Hunt; or, Daring Adventures in South America* (New York: World Syndicate, 1907), and Reginald Wright Kauffman, "Fangs of the Leopard," *American Boy* 104, no. 8 (August 1930): 3–6. Michael Adas refers to these tropes as "engineers' imperialism" in *Dominance by Design: Technological Imperatives and America's Civilizing Mission* (Cambridge, MA: Harvard University Press, 2006). On the Open Door trade policies these children's books often espoused, see Marc-William Palen, "The Open Door Empire," in Christopher Dietrich, ed., *A Companion to U.S. Foreign Relations: Colonial Era to the Present* (Hoboken, NJ: Wiley, 2020): 271–287.

23  Ross Kay, *The Go Ahead Boys and Simon's Mine* (New York: Barse and Hopkins, 1917), 5–6; Tom Curry, "Diamonds of Catirimani," *Wide World Adventures* 17, no. 1 (February 1930): 81–82; J. Allan Dunn, "O'Donnell's Demonstration," *Complete Story Magazine* 5, no. 3 (September 25, 1925): 3–61. On "race management," see David R. Roediger and Elizabeth D. Esch, *The Production of Difference: Race and the Management of Labor in U.S. History* (New York: Oxford University Press, 2012), and Jason M. Colby, *The Business of Empire: United Fruit, Race, and U.S. Expansion in Central America* (Ithaca, NY: Cornell University Press, 2011). Interestingly, British pulp fiction focused on Latin America often emphasized similar themes. See Ross G. Forman, "When Britons Brave Brazil: British Imperialism and the Adventure Tale in Latin America, 1850–1918," *Victorian Studies* 42, no. 3 (Spring 1999–Spring 2000): 454–487.

24  H. Irving Hancock, *The Young Engineers in Mexico; or, Fighting the Mine Swindlers* (Philadelphia: Henry Altemus, 1913), 41–46; Edward Stratemeyer, *Treasure Seekers of the Andes or, American Boys in Peru* (Boston: Lee and Shepard, 1907), iv–v, 138; Capt. Ralph Bonehill [Edward Stratemeyer], *Off for Hawaii or, The Mystery of a Great Volcano* (New York: Mershon, 1899), 3–4, 35; Edward Stratemeyer to Robert Kinkead, January 6, 1910, Outgoing Mail, NYPL SSR. On interventionism, see, for example, Captain Wilbur Lawton, *The Boy Aviators in Nicaragua or, In League with the Insurgents* (New York: Hurst, 1910). Stratemeyer and the Caribbean discussed in Karen Sands-O'Connor, "The Stratemeyer Chums Have Fun in the Caribbean: America and Empire in Children's Series," in O'Connor and Marietta A. Frank, eds., *Internationalism in Children's Series* (New York: Palgrave Macmillan, 2014): 59–75. On the very real influence of American soldiers and mercenaries in Latin America, see Lester D. Langley and Thomas Schoonover, *The Banana Men: American Mercenaries and Entrepreneurs in Central America, 1880–1930* (Lexington: University Press of Kentucky, 1995).
25  Oscar Patch Hawley, "Powell's Peculiar Projectiles," *Popular Story Magazine* 4, no. 3 (July 1905): 82–83; Kilbourne, *Army Boy in Mexico*, 223; G. Harvey Ralphson, *Boy Scouts in Mexico* (Chicago: M.A. Donohue, 1911), 142; Sheppard, *The Rambler Club on the Texas Border*, 82, 262.
26  H. Irving Hancock, *Dave Darrin at Vera Cruz; or, Fighting with the U.S. Navy in Mexico* (Philadelphia: Henry Altemus, 1914), 60; Yates Stirling, Jr., *A United States Midshipman Afloat* (Philadelphia: Penn, 1908), 157; Frank Patchin, *The Battleship Boys in the Tropics; or, Upholding the American Flag in a Honduras Revolution* (Philadelphia: Henry Altemus, 1912), 54, 184–185, and 213.
27  Lieutenant Howard Payson, *The Boy Scouts Under Fire in Mexico* (New York: A.L. Burt, 1914), 224–235. Payson was a pseudonym used by boys' book author John Henry Goldfrap. See M. P. Holsinger, "A Bully Bunch of Books: Boy Scout Series Books in American Youth Fiction, 1910–1930," *Children's Literature Association Quarterly* 14 (1989): 178–182. On America's enduring political and economic investments in Mexico during the era, see John Mason Hart, *Empire and Revolution: The Americans in Mexico since the Civil War* (Berkeley: University of California Press, 2002).
28  Malcolm Wheeler-Nicholson, "Fire and Sword," *Thrilling Adventures* 3, no. 1 (September 1932): 64; Randolph Hayes, "The Bandit's Game," *Argosy* 69, no. 1 (April 1912): 121; D. L. Crosthwait, "The Greaser," *Argosy* 69, no. 2 (May 1912): 261–262; Payson, *Boy Scouts Under Fire in Mexico*, 224–235; Hancock, *Dave Darrin at Vera Cruz*, 64. See also Robert Emmet MacAlarney, "The Guns of Doom," *Argosy* 73, no. 2 (September 1913), 418–427, and H. Irving Hancock, *Uncle Sam's Boys as Lieutenants; or, Serving Old Glory as Line Officers* (Philadelphia: Henry Altemus, 1919).
29  Fremont B. Deering, *Border Boys with the Mexican Rangers* (New York: A.L. Burt, 1911), 28, 41, 51, 124, 128, 143; Frank Fowler, *The Broncho Rider Boys with Funston at Vera Cruz; or, Upholding the Honor of the Stars and Stripes* (New York: A.L. Burt, 1916), 170; G. Harvey Ralphson, *Boy Scouts in Mexico or, On Guard with*

*Uncle Sam* (Chicago: M.A. Donohue, 1911), as quoted in Holsinger, "Bully Bunch of Books," 179. Blaine quoted in Sexton, *The Monroe Doctrine*, 183.
30  Deering, *Border Boys with the Mexican Rangers* , 143.
31  Noname [Luis Senarens], "Along the Orinoco; or, With Frank Reade, Jr., in Venezuela," *Frank Reade Library* 5, no. 130 (1892): 10–14; F. K. Scribner, "Dropping Into Mexico," *Argosy* 83, no. 1 (August 1916): 90–94; G. Harvey Ralphson, *Boy Scouts in Mexico or, On Guard with Uncle Sam* (Chicago: M.A. Donohue, 1911), as quoted in Holsinger, "Bully Bunch of Books," 179.
32  Theodore Roosevelt, "Sixth Annual Message to Congress," December 3, 1906. Anticolonial nationalism covered in Erez Manela, *The Wilsonian Moment: Self-Determination and the International Origins of Anticolonial Nationalism* (New York: Oxford University Press, 2007). Dollar diplomacy's critics are discussed in Rosenberg, *Financial Missionaries to the World*, 122–150, while *The Atlantic* is quoted in Emily S. Rosenberg, "Revisiting Dollar Diplomacy: Narratives of Money and Manliness," *Diplomatic History* 22, no. 2 (Spring 1998): 164–166.
33  John Hopper, "Deserter," *Thrilling Adventures* 2, no. 4 (August 1932): 60–61, 65–66.
34  Ibid.; George Bronson-Howard, "Norroy, Diplomatic Agent," *Popular Magazine* 3, no. 6 (April 1905): 108. Butler quoted in Hans Schmidt, *Maverick Marine: General Smedley D. Butler and the Contradictions of American Military History* (Lexington: University Press of Kentucky, 1998), 231; Knox quoted in Herring, *From Colony to Superpower*, 373. Rosenberg, *Financial Missionaries to the World*, 63–64, similarly notes that US officials appointed as customs receivers denounced indigenous opposition movements as the work of grafters or bandits.
35  "The Log-Book," *Argosy* 83, no. 3 (October 1916): 573; Patchin, *Battleship Boys in the Tropics*, 149; Lawton, *Dreadnought Boys Aboard a Destroyer*, 90–91 and 154. An older (but later abandoned) ethic of hemispheric multilateralism is described in Caitlin Fitz, *Our Sister Republics: The United States in an Age of American Revolutions* (New York: Liveright, 2016).
36  Edgard Franklin, "Americans After All," *Argosy* 85, no. 3 (June 1917): 371, 409–410.
37  Ibid.; Herring, *From Colony to Superpower*, 370 and 386; Rosenberg, *Financial Missionaries to the World*, 78. Theodore Roosevelt himself had once remarked that "If any South American State misbehaves towards any European country, let the European country spank it," quoted in Sexton, *The Monroe Doctrine*, 226. On paternalism as a guiding principle of the era's foreign relations, see Mary Renda, *Taking Haiti: Military Occupation and the Culture of U.S. Imperialism, 1915–1940* (Chapel Hill: UNC Press, 2001), quoted at 15. Representations of Latin Americans as children are discussed in John Johnson, *Latin America in Caricature* (Austin: University of Texas Press, 1980), 116–156.
38  Brooks, *Under the Allied Flags*, 321–322; Hancock, *Dave Darrin at Vera Cruz*, 21–23; G. Harvey Ralph, *Boy Scouts in Mexico or, On Guard with Uncle Sam* (Chicago: M.A. Donohue, 1911), 5. On the Panama Canal, see Lt. Howard Payson, *The Boy Scouts at the Panama Canal* (New York: A.L. Burt, 1913); Victor Appleton, *The*

*Moving Picture Boys at Panama; or, Stirring Adventures Along the Great Canal* (New York: Grosset & Dunlap, 1915); George Parsons Bradford, "The Panama Cipher," *Popular Magazine* 1, no. 2 (December 1903): 79–94.

39 Brooks, *Under the Allied Flags*, 321–322; Ralph, *Boy Scouts in Mexico*, 5; Arthur J. Burke, "The Sword of Dessalines," *Wide World Adventure Trails* 14, no. 2 (June 1929): 267–277; Tom Webb, "The Shining Blade," *Adventure* 50, no. 1 (December 10, 1924): 111, 114; Ralph Smith, "War in the Bundocks," *Wide World Adventures* 16, no. 1 (November 1929): 74–80; Steve Rankin, "The Devil Dancers," *Thrilling Adventures* 1, no. 3 (March 1932): 91–99; Frederic Nelson Litten, "'Semper Fidelis': The Story of a Hurricane and a Voodoo Threat," *American Boy* 108, no. 6 (June 1934): 20–41. On the Panama Canal, see Payson, *Boy Scouts at the Panama Canal*. Additional pulp stories set during the occupation of Haiti appear in Arthur J. Burks, *Black Medicine* (Sauk City, WI: Arkham House, 1966). The imperial character of postbellum US commercial expansion into Latin America (and elsewhere) is described in Walter LaFeber, *The New Empire: An Interpretation of American Expansion* (Ithaca, NY: Cornell University Press, 1963). On the reading habits of marines, see Renda, *Taking Haiti*, 64–65.

40 Fowler, *Broncho Rider Boys with Funston at Vera Cruz*, 254–255; Patchin, *Battleship Boys in the Tropics*, 56 and 184; Howard Payson, *The Motor Cycle Chums South of the Equator* (New York: Hurst, 1914), 242–243 and 252; Hancock, *Dave Darrin's South American Cruise*, 22, 46–47; Hancock, *Dave Darrin at Vera Cruz*, 145. Aggressive rhetoric about avenging perceived Latin American insults to the US flag became more common throughout the country following the 1891 "Baltimore Affair," wherein several Yankee sailors were killed by a Chilean mob. See Joyce S. Goldberg, *The "Baltimore" Affair* (Lincoln: University of Nebraska Press, 1986).

41 "Juan Bautista Alberdi of Argentina Warns Against the Threat of 'Monroism' to the Independence of Spanish America," in Dennis Merrill and Thomas G. Paterson, eds., *Major Problems in American Foreign Relations to 1920*, 7th ed. (New York: Cengage, 2010), 151; Francisco García Calderón, *Latin America: Its Rise and Progress* (1913), as quoted in Loveman, *No Higher Law*, 193. Fredrick B. Pike, *Hispanismo, 1898–1936: Spanish Conservatives and Liberals and Their Relations with Spanish America* (Notre Dame, IN: University of Notre Dame Press, 1971); Sandino quoted in Peter H. Smith, *The Talons of the Eagle: Latin America, the United States, and the World*, 3rd ed. (New York: Oxford University Press, 2008), 104–105.

42 Hancock, *Dave Darrin at Vera Cruz*, 157 and 256. On the myth of America's hemispheric indispensability, see Sexton, *The Monroe Doctrine*, 199–240 and Loveman, *No Higher Law*, 181–205.

43 Mark I. West, "Not to Be Circulated: The Response of Children's Librarians to Dime Novels and Series Books," *Children's Literature Association Quarterly* 10, no. 3 (Fall 1985): 137–139; Melanie A. Kimball, "Seeing the World from Main Street:

Early Twentieth Century Literature for American Youth about Life in Other Lands," *Library Trends* 60, no. 4 (Spring 2012): 675–693.

44  Charles J. L. Gilson, "Cinderface," *Frontier Stories* 5, no. 6 (March 1927): 123, and advertisement for "Cinderface" in *Frontier Stories* 5, no. 5 (February 1927): 173.

45  "Peter the Brazen" in Lee Server, *Danger Is My Business: An Illustrated History of the Fabulous Pulp Magazines* (San Francisco: Chronicle Books, 1993), 22–26 and 50; Seward Hopkins, "Live Cargo," *Argosy* 57, no. 2 (May 1908): 356; Elbert D. Wiggin, "The Lure of the Nile," *Argosy* 69, no. 3 (June 1912): 773; Henry Holt, "In the Heart of Africa," *Complete Story Magazine* 1, no. 2 (September 10, 1924): 126; Wiggin, "The Lure of the Nile," *Argosy* 69, no. 2 (May 1912): 264; Sheykh Abdullah, "'He Who Goes Fantee,'" *Argosy* 79, no. 3 (June 1915): 611–621. On this theme more broadly, see Kristin L. Hoganson and Jay Sexton, eds., *Crossing Empires: Taking U.S. History into Transimperial Terrain* (Durham, NC: Duke University Press, 2020).

46  Paul Kramer, "Empires, Exceptions, and Anglo-Saxons: Race and Rule between the British and the United States," *Journal of American History* 88, no. 4 (March 2002): 1315–1353. Anglophobia in American culture discussed in Sam W. Haynes, *Unfinished Revolution: The Early American Republic in a British World* (Charlottesville: University of Virginia Press, 2010). For stories about the French Legion, see Peter Forrest, "Legion Steel," *Thrilling Adventures* 1, no. 1 (December 1931): n.p.; Theodore Roscoe, "Foley of the Foreign Legion," *Wide World Adventures* 14, no. 3 (July 1929): 325–350; George E. Holt, "Barbary Blood," *Frontier Stories* 6, no. 2 (May 1927): 3–4.

47  L. Patrick Greene, "Death Valley," *Frontier Stories* 5, no. 4 (January 1927): 56–58; Greene, "Fetish," *Frontier Stories* 6, no. 1 (April 1927): 78–80; Curtis Mitchell, "Texas to Africa: The True Story of a Texas Puncher Who Went to Africa and Fought Some of the Bloodiest Fights That Continent Had Ever Seen," *All Western Magazine* 1, no. 1 (October 1931): 46; George Fielding Eliot, "Ordeal By Fire," *Wide World Adventures* 16, no. 3 (January 1930): 327–362. Some of these characters were probably modeled on the life of Frederick Russell Burnham, an American adventurer who traveled through Africa and served with the British during the Boer War. See Steve Kemper, *A Splendid Savage: The Restless Life of Frederick Russell Burnham* (New York: Norton, 2017). The immensely influential figure of Tarzan, who has been discussed at great length elsewhere, will not warrant much discussion here. See A. G. Hopkins, *American Empire: A Global History* (Princeton, NJ: Princeton University Press, 2018), 437–440; Gail Bederman, *Manliness & Civilization: A Cultural History of Gender and Race in the United States, 1880–1917* (Chicago: University of Chicago Press, 1995), 217–239; and Marianna Torgovnick, *Gone Primitive: Savage Intellects, Modern Lives* (Chicago: University of Chicago Press, 1990). Tarzan was, of course, revealed to be the Briton Lord Greystoke, but, Torgovnick notes, the books were written by an American and possessed American political and cultural sensibilities.

48 S.B.H. Hurst, "Quicksands of Empire," *Wide World Adventures* 14, no. 3 (July 1929): 367–385; George Fielding Eliot, "One More River to Cross," *Wide World Adventures* 15, no. 2 (September 1929): 249–263; Evan Anglesea, "Documentary Evidence," *Frontier Stories* 6, no. 1 (April 1927): 114–116.
49 L. P. Holmes, "Pride of Blood," *Wide World Adventures* 15, no. 3 (October 1929): 375–384; Nels Leroy Jorgensen, "Face," *Frontier Stories* 5, no. 5 (February 1927): 73–74; Hugh Clifford, "The Quest of the Golden Fleece," *Pioneer Tales* 5, no. 6 (February 1928): 38; Barry Scobee, "White Men Stick Together," *Adventure* 45, no. 1 (February 10, 1924): 162; Eugene Cunningham, "Breed of the Border," *All Western Magazine* 1, no. 3 (March 1932): 56. As such, pulps sometimes contrasted with classroom educators beginning to explore malleable "culture" (as opposed to immutable racial characteristics) as the principal driver of human difference. See Zoe Burkholder, *Color in the Classroom: How American Schools Taught Race, 1900–1954* (New York: Oxford University Press, 2011). On race and the making of US foreign policy more broadly, see Michael H. Hunt, *Ideology and U.S. Foreign Policy* rev. ed. (New Haven, CT: Yale University Press, 2009).
50 William H. Greene, "The Savage Strain," *Argosy* 67, no. 4 (November 1911): 745; Lothrop T. Stoddard, *The Rising Tide of Color Against White World-Supremacy* (New York: Scribner's, 1920); George W. Crichfield, *American Supremacy: The Rise and Progress of the Latin American Republics and Their Relations to the United States Under the Monroe Doctrine*, 2 vols. (New York: Brentano's, 1908), 1: 386. For the influence of "blood-units" in diplomacy, see Stuart Anderson, *Race and Rapprochement: Anglo-Saxonism and Anglo-American Relations, 1895–1904* (Rutherford, NJ: Fairleigh Dickinson University Press, 1981). On the pulps' emphasis on physicality and the "purity of the white racial body," see Fitzpatrick, "Pulp Empire," 120. Though not extensively discussed here, another important dimension to the racial politics of pulp magazines was the anti-Asian "Yellow Peril" motif. See Madison, *Anti-Foreign Imagery*, chap. 1.
51 Lothrop Stoddard, *The Revolt against Civilization* (New York: Scribner's, 1922); Malcolm Wheeler-Nicholson, "Bobrikoff's Banquet," *Wide World Adventures* 17, no. 2 (March 1930): 167–168; Peter Forrest, "The Street of Blood," *Thrilling Adventures* 1, no. 1 (December 1931): 108–109; Malcolm Wheeler-Nicholson, "The Scarlet Killer," *Thrilling Adventures* 1, no. 4 (April 1932): 6–47 and quoted at 26; John Hopper, "Panama Plot," 5, no. 2 (April 1933): 8–44. For similar themes, see also H. G. Fry, "Human Wolves," *Wide World Adventures* 15, no. 3 (October 1929): 435–447.
52 Charles J. Finger, *Tales from Silver Lands* (New York: Doubleday, 1924).
53 Stimson quoted in Walter LaFeber, *The American Age: U.S. Foreign Policy at Home and Abroad, 1750 to the Present*, 2nd ed. (New York: Norton, 1994), 359.
54 On a rising tide of economic nationalism and resistance to US financial domination in Latin America, see Loveman, *No Higher Law*, 240–241. On the anticapitalist strain of Depression-era pulps, see Agnew, *Age of Dimes and Pulps*.

55 Hull quoted in Irwin F. Gellman, *Good Neighbor Diplomacy: United States Policy in Latin America, 1933–1945* (Baltimore, MD: Johns Hopkins University Press, 1979), 51; Good Neighbor policy likewise covered (and FDR quoted) in LaFeber, *The American Age*, 375–379. On the exercise of nonmilitary "soft power" in Latin America, see Greg Grandin, *Empire's Workshop: Latin America, the United States, and the Rise of the New Imperialism* (New York: Holt, 2006).

56 Quoted in Smith, *The Talons of the Eagle*, 71. Justin Hart describes the State Department's turn toward cultural diplomacy in *Empire of Ideas: The Origins of Public Diplomacy and the Transformation of U.S. Foreign Policy* (New York: Oxford University Press, 2013). Some of this shift can also be attributed to the influence of historian Herbert Eugene Bolton and the so-called "Borderlands school," a group of scholars who consciously sought to combat the "Black Legend" emphasizing Spanish colonial cruelty. They did so, in part, by demonstrating the long history of Iberian American cultural interpenetration and Pan-American partnership. See David J. Weber, *Myth and the History of the Hispanic Southwest* (Albuquerque: University of New Mexico Press, 1987), 33–54.

57 See Paul Lopes, *Demanding Respect: The Evolution of the American Comic Book* (Philadelphia: Temple University Press, 2009), 3, who notes that "the field of pulp magazines . . . had the greatest direct influence on the structure and rules of art in the new field of comic books." "Remediation" described in Jay David Bolter and Richard Grusin, *Remediation: Understanding New Media* (Cambridge, MA: MIT Press, 1999).

## 6. COMIC BOOK COLD WAR

1 "Captain Marvel and the American Century," *Captain Marvel Adventures* no. 110 (July 1950). The relevance of this example is reaffirmed in Bradford W. Wright, *Comic Book Nation: The Transformation of Youth Culture in America* (Baltimore, MD: Johns Hopkins University Press, 2001), 56. Fawcett Comics, it should be noted, did not simply put words in Truman's mouth; the President was fond of addressing young people about their role in the Cold War. See Marilyn Holt, *Cold War Kids: Politics and Childhood in Postwar America, 1945–1960* (Lawrence: University Press of Kansas, 2014), 27.

2 Adult consternation quoted in Gary Cross, *The Cute and the Cool: Wondrous Innocence and Modern American Children's Culture* (New York: Oxford University Press, 2004), 170. Considering their cultural ubiquity, comic books have received too little attention from historians. But some of the better treatments include Wright, *Comic Book Nation*; Jean-Paul Gabilliet, *Of Comics and Men: A Cultural History of American Comic Books* (Jackson: University Press of Mississippi, 2010); Shawna Kidman, *Comic Books Incorporated: How the Business of Comics became the Business of Hollywood* (Berkeley: University of California Press, 2019); Paul Douglas Lopes, *Demanding Respect: The Evolution of the American Comic Book* (Philadelphia: Temple University Press, 2009); William W. Savage, Jr., *Comic Books and America, 1945–1954* (Norman: University of Oklahoma Press, 1990);

Chris York and Rafiel York, eds., *Comic Books and the Cold War: Essays on the Graphic Treatment of Communism, the Code and Social Concerns* (Jefferson, NC: McFarland, 2012); David Hajdu, *The Ten-Cent Plague: The Great Comic Book Scare and How It Changed America* (New York: Picador, 2008); Christopher Murray, *Champions of the Oppressed?: Superhero Comics, Popular Culture, and Propaganda in America During World War II* (New York: Hampton Press, 2011); Trischa Goodnow and James J. Kimble, eds., *The Ten-Cent War: Comic Books, Propaganda, and World War II* (Jackson: University Press of Mississippi, 2017); and Mike Benton, *The Comic Book in America* (Dallas, TX: Taylor, 1989). Data on comic book readership in Wright, *Comic Book Nation*, 58 and 155; Harvey Zorbaugh, "The Comics—There They Stand!" *Journal of Educational Sociology* 18, no. 4 (1944): 196–203; and Kidman, *Comic Books Incorporated*, 1–2. These circulation figures, moreover, do not consider the global nature of the comic book's reach. On the international impact of comics, see Paul Hirsch, "Pulp Empire: Comic Books, Culture, and U.S. Foreign Policy, 1941–1955" (PhD diss., University of California, Santa Barbara, 2013).

3   "Backyard Battleground," *Daring Confessions* no. 6 (January 1953).
4   Victoria M. Grieve, *Little Cold Warriors: American Childhood in the 1950s* (New York: Oxford University Press, 2018), 20; Josette Frank, "What's in the Comics?" *Journal of Educational Sociology* 18, no. 4 (1944): 220. On the shift to a new style of postwar imperialism, see Daniel Immerwahr, *How to Hide an Empire: A History of the Greater United States* (New York: Farrar, Straus and Giroux, 2019). On developmentalism, see David Ekbladh, *The Great American Mission: Modernization and the Construction of an American World Order* (Princeton, NJ: Princeton University Press, 2010). It should be noted that adults also read comic books, particularly servicemembers. In an effort to boost morale, the federal government even included comic books in its list of priority items to be sent to the front lines during World War II. Therefore, the genre should be seen as primarily but not exclusively the province of young people. On the importance of comics to military personnel, see Hirsch, "Pulp Empire." One of the first attempts to connect foreign policy with comic book content appeared in Ariel Dorfman and Armand Mattelart, *How to Read Donald Duck: Imperialism Ideology in the Disney Comic* (London: International General, 1975). Some broader connections between the postwar US imperium and youth culture are discussed in Denis Jonnes, *Cold War American Literature and the Rise of Youth Culture: Children of Empire* (New York: Routledge, 2015) and Michael Scheibach, *Atomic Narratives and American Youth: Coming of Age with the Atom* (Jefferson, NC: McFarland, 2003).
5   Aquaman quoted in *More Fun Comics* no. 90 (April 1943). On comics and World War II, see Wright, *Comic Book Nation*, 30–55; Michael Uslan, *America at War: The Best of DC War Comics* (New York: Simon & Schuster, 1979); David Kendall, ed., *Best War Comics* (New York: Carrol and Graf, 2007). On wartime campaigns to promote youthful patriotism, see Robert William Kirk, *Earning Their Stripes: The Mobilization of American Children in the Second World War* (New York: Peter

Lang, 1994). Neither should one discount the fact that some of the earliest comic book artists were Jewish and used the medium to symbolically fight Nazi ideology. See Arie Kaplan, *From Krakow to Krypton: Jews and Comic Books* (Philadelphia: Jewish Publication Society, 2008).

6 "Pass-along circulation" in Gabilliet, *Of Comics and Men*, 191–192. Changes to the structure and style of childhood during the 1940s covered in Steven Mintz, *Huck's Raft: A History of American Childhood* (Cambridge, MA: Harvard University Press, 2004), 254–274.

7 On the working relationship between the comic book industry and US war planners, see Paul Hirsch, "'This Is Our Enemy': The Writers' War Board and Representations of Race in Comic Books, 1942–1945," *Pacific Historical Review* 83, no. 3 (2014): 448–486. As many scholars have pointed out, Jewish comic writers and publishers hardly needed federal directives to declare their opposition to totalitarian tyranny. They were some of the first mainstream voices to announce their opposition to Nazi Germany's brutal and anti-Semitic policies. On the more thoroughly politicized nature of wartime and postwar America's youth culture, see Margaret Peacock, *Innocent Weapons: The Soviet and American Politics of Childhood in the Cold War* (Chapel Hill: UNC Press, 2014).

8 Letter from Fawcett Publishers in P. C. Hamerlinck, ed., *Fawcett Companion: The Best of FCA* (Raleigh, NC: TwoMorrows, 2001), 12.

9 Wright, *Comic Book Nation*, 57–58. Though these comic subgenres represent the bulk of the source material discussed here, they represent only a fraction of the industry's larger input. Westerns, romances, high school drama, and funny animals also circulated widely and dealt, either directly or indirectly, with Cold War themes. Given the sheer volume of material, they could not be addressed here. There is still much archival work to be done. On the latter (funny animals) and arguably most influential genre, see Daniel Immerwahr, "Ten-Cent Ideology: Donald Duck Comic Books and the U.S. Challenge to Modernization," *Modern American History* 3, no. 1 (2020): 1–26.

10 "Atomic-Age Wars," *Atom-Age Combat* (February 1953). Technological worship in, for example, "Sub Killers," *American Air Forces* no. 7 (August 1952); "On Target," *Atom-Age Combat* (February 1953); "America's Atom-Age Airplane," *Atom-Age Combat* (February 1953); "I, SAGE," *Atom-Age Combat* (February 1953). Technology and narratives of America's deserved dominance in Michael Adas, *Dominance By Design: Technological Imperatives and America's Civilizing Mission* (Cambridge, MA: Harvard University Press, 2006). America's early cultural reactions to nuclear energy are chronicled in Paul S. Boyer, *By the Bomb's Early Light: American Thought and Culture at the Dawn of the Atomic Age* (Chapel Hill: UNC Press, 1994).

11 "Atomic-Age Wars," *Atom-Age Combat* (February 1953); "Captain Marvel and the Atomic War," *Captain Marvel Adventures* no. 66 (October 1946). See also "Operation Vengeance," *Atomic War!* no. 2 (December 1952). Often, the comic would

simply state that war might break out "between the United States and another country!" See "On Target," *Atom-Age Combat* (February 1953). On Cold War internationalism, see Talya Zemach-Bersin, "Imperial Pedagogies: Education for American Globalism, 1898–1950" (PhD diss., Yale University, 2015). Early efforts at children's atomic education are discussed in JoAnne Brown, "'A is for Atom, B is for Bomb': Civil Defense in American Public Education, 1948–1963," *Journal of American History* 75, no. 1 (June 1988): 68–90.

12  On the shift to a named enemy, see "World War III Unleashed," *World War III* no. 1 (March 1953). "Will You Know What to Do?" *If an A-Bomb Falls* no. 1 (1951); "Commando Crackerjack," *Atomic War!* no. 3 (Feb. 1953); *Captain America* 76 (May 1954) and *Captain America* 77 (July 1954). An overview of the era's formal foreign relations can be found in George C. Herring, *From Colony to Superpower: U.S. Foreign Relations since 1776* (New York: Oxford University Press, 2008), 595–650.

13  "Trial by Terror," *T-Man* no. 9 (January 1953); "The Secret Weapons," *Fightin' Marines* no. 44 (November 1961); "Under Cover of Darkness," *Kent Blake of the Secret Service* no. 12 (March 1953); "He Won't Go Back!" *Battlefield* no. 11 (May 1953). On the evolving nature of eugenic discourse, see David Mitchell and Sharon Snyder, "The Eugenic Atlantic: Race, Disability, and the Making of an International Eugenic Science, 1800–1945," *Disability and Society* 18, no. 7 (2003): 843–864. On an emerging sense that the world's people were united by a desire to "be American," see Thomas Borstelmann, *Just Like Us: The American Struggle to Understand Foreigners* (New York: Columbia University Press, 2020).

14  "Greece," *Kent Blake of the Secret Service* no. 5 (January 1952); "Inside Red China," *War Comics* no. 49 (September 1957); "Red Shadow Over South America," *Spy Cases* no. 27 (December 1950); Marvel Boy quoted in York and York, eds., *Comic Books and the Cold War*, 30–31.

15  "Airlift," *War Comics* no. 40 (March 1956). Similar expression of gratitude in "The Man-Eaters!" *Spy Cases* no. 19 (October 1953). On the *Foreign Affairs* analogy, see "Trail of Doom," *Spy Cases* no. 10 (April 1952), which provided a pages-long introduction to Indo-Pakistani relations and the Kashmir question.

16  "Daredevils Only Die Once!" *T-Man* no. 11 (May 1953); South Koreans in York and York, *Comic Books and the Cold War*, 34–35; "Bloody Oil," *John Wayne Adventure Comics* no. 21 (July 1952); "The Killers of the Nile," *T-Man* no. 18 (October 1954).

17  "The Deserters to Red Doom," *T-Man* no. 26 (June 1955); "Master of Destruction," *T-Man* No. 26 (June 1955); "Behind the Iron Curtain," *T-Man* No. 32 (Feb. 1956); "The Communist Zone," *Spy Cases* no. 18 (August 1953).

18  "The Voice of Russia," *T-Man* no. 11 (May 1953); *Atomic War!* no. 4 (April 1953); "Atomic Age Wars," *Atom-Age Combat* (February 1953); "Pipeline to Peril," *T-Man* no. 9 (January 1953); "Greece," *Kent Blake of the Secret Service* no. 5 (January 1952); "The Plot to Blow Up the U.S.A.," *T-Man* no. 11 (May 1953).

19  "A Blow for Freedom," *Battlefield Action* no. 44 (November 1962); "The Commissar's Girl," *Battlefield Action* no. 46 (1957).

20 "The Man with Two Faces," *Kent Blake of the Secret Service* no. 5 (January 1952); "Assault in Armenia!" *Spy-Hunters* no. 15 (December 1951–January 1952); "Mademoiselle Mig," *American Air Forces* no. 9 (1952); "Jonathan Kent, Counterspy," *Spy and Counterspy* no. 1 (August–September 1949); "Danger Zone!" *Battlefield* no. 8 (February 1953).

21 "My Rival," *Atom-Age Combat* 1, no. 2 (January 1959). Medical text quoted in Elaine Tyler May, *Barren in the Promised Land: Childless Americans and the Pursuit of Happiness* (Cambridge, MA: Harvard University Press, 1995), 154.

22 "Backyard Battleground," *Daring Confessions* no. 5 (January 1953). Other examples quoted in Michael Barson and Steve Heller, eds., *Red Scared! The Commie Menace in Propaganda and Popular Culture* (San Francisco: Chronicle Books, 2001).

23 Think tank quoted in Ann Hulbert, *Raising America: Experts, Parents, and a Century of Advice about Children* (New York: Vintage, 2003), 244. Helen Louise Crounse [as "Joyce Jackson"], *Joyce Jackson's Guide to Dating* (Eau Claire, WI: E. M. Hale, 1957), 2. "Love IQ" tests in Michael Barson, *Agonizing Love: The Golden Era of Romance Comics* (New York: HarperCollins, 2011), 30–31 and 90–91. Romance comics more broadly in Michelle Nolan, *Love on the Racks: A History of American Romance Comics* (Jefferson, NC: McFarland, 2008). The Cold War politics of *Seventeen* in Jennifer Helgren, *American Girls and Global Responsibility: A New Relation to the World During the Early Cold War* (New Brunswick, NJ: Rutgers University Press, 2017). On the intersection between postwar domesticity, romantic deviance, and national security, see Elaine Tyler May, *Homeward Bound: American Families in the Cold War Era* (New York: Basic Books, 1988); Sharon Stephens, "Nationalism, Nuclear Policy, and Children in Cold War America," *Childhood* 4, no. 1 (1997): 103–123; Laura McEnaney, *Civil Defense Begins at Home: Militarization Meets Everyday Life in the Fifties* (Princeton, NJ: Princeton University Press, 2000); Marilyn Holt, *Cold War Kids: Politics and Childhood in Postwar America, 1945–1960* (Lawrence: University Press of Kansas, 2014); Sara Moslener, *Virgin Nation: Sexual Purity and American Adolescence* (New York: Oxford University Press, 2015).

24 "Combat Correspondence," *Two-Fisted Tales* no. 24 (November–December 1951); "Combat Correspondence," *Two-Fisted Tales* no. 22 (July–August 1951); "Letters," *G.I. Combat* no. 131 (August–September 1968); "Readers Sound Off!" *G.I. Combat* no. 118 (June–July 1966). Other women writing to war comics in "Depth Charges," *Capt. Storm* no. 18 (March–April 1967); "Letters," *G.I. Combat* no. 145 (January 1971). Not everyone wished to challenge stereotypes though. See Roberta Millard to *Star Spangled War Stories* no. 135 (October–November 1967), who argued that "a woman's place is in the home. And that includes girls."

25 "Final Decision," *Kent Blake of the Secret Service* no. 5 (January 1952); "This Is Korea," *Battle* no. 26 (February 1954). See also "What Do You Know About Korea?" *Battle Brady* no. 14 (June 1953).

26 "No Survivors," *War Comics* no. 8 (February 1952); "Why We Fight," *War Comics* no. 38 (November 1955); "Sneak Attack!" *Battle* no. 6 (January 1951); "Atrocity Story," *Battlefield* no. 2 (June 1952).

27 "Secret of the Tunnel," *American Air Forces* no. 8 (1952); "Night Attack," *Men's Adventures* no. 17 (December 1952). Similar motifs in "To the Victors!" *Battle Cry* no. 3 (September 1952). Further examples of imperiled Korean youth in "The Story of a Slaughter," *War Adventures* no. 2 (March 1952). On the political potency of imperiled children, see Karen Dubinsky, "Children, Ideology, and Iconography: How Babies Rule the World," *Journal of the History of Childhood and Youth* 5, no. 1 (Winter 2012): 5–13, and Erica Burman, "Innocents Abroad: Western Fantasies of Childhood and the Iconography of Emergencies," *Disasters* 18, no. 3 (1994): 238–253.

28 "Ransom," *The U.S. Marines in Action!* no. 3 (December 1952); "Korea . . . Where They Die," *American Air Forces* no. 7 (August 1952); "The Temple of Motang-Po," *War Comics* no. 14 (December 1952); "A Few Minutes More!" *Battlefield* no. 3 (August 1952); "Passage to Peril," *Kent Blake of the Secret Service* no. 8 (July 1952); "The Flag," *War Comics* no. 21 (September 1953). On the subject more broadly, see Christina Klein, *Cold War Orientalism: Asia in the Middlebrow Imagination, 1945–1961* (Berkeley: University of California Press, 2003).

29 "The Face of the Enemy," *War Comics* no. 8 (February 1952); "Blood!" *Battle* no. 6 (January 1951); "P.O.W." *Battle* no. 7 (March 1952); "The Good Guy," *Battle Action* no. 1 (February 1952); "Slam into Combat," *Combat Casey* no. 24 (October 1955). For "epiphanies" concerning the essential inhumanity of communists, see also "Liberation," *Battlefield* no. 2 (June 1952) and "Mission: Massacre," *Combat* no. 2 (July 1952).

30 "Kent Blake," *Kent Blake of the Secret Service* no. 14 (July 1953); "Kent Blake," *Kent Blake of the Secret Service* no. 13 (May 1953); "The Voice," *Kent Blake of the Secret Service* no. 13 (May 1953); "Nightmare at Noon," *Spy Cases* no. 7 (October 1951).

31 Second person also in "Basic Training!" *Combat Casey* no. 23 (August 1955). "Combat Correspondence," *Two-Fisted Tales* no. 27 (May–June 1952) and "Combat Correspondence," *Two-Fisted Tales* no. 22 (July–August 1951); "Combat Correspondence," *Two-Fisted Tales* no. 24 (November–December 1951). Unfortunately, no publishers appear to have retained the hundreds of thousands of fan letters they received. This brief survey of reader responses thus relies only upon the correspondence editors chose to publish. Another potential source here might be so-called fanzines, amateur comic books created by enthusiasts. But I have yet to discover an archive that collects such material in an accessible manner, at least from the time period under consideration here.

32 Letter to Iron Man quoted in Wright, *Comic Book Nation*, 223. Exchange regarding military integration in *Shock SuspenStories* no. 13 (February–March 1954) and *Shock SuspenStories* no. 15 (June–July 1954).

33 Exchange regarding military integration in *Shock SuspenStories* no. 13 (February–March 1954) and *Shock SuspenStories* no. 15 (June–July 1954). Histories of the international context for American civil rights include Mary L. Dudziak, *Cold War Civil Rights: Race and the Image of American Democracy* (Princeton, NJ: Princeton University Press, 2000), and Thomas Borstelmann, *The Cold War and the Color*

Line: *American Race Relations in the Global Arena* (Cambridge, MA: Harvard University Press, 2001).

34 First quote pulled from "Suspenstory Scribblings," *Crime SuspenStories* no. 11 (June–July 1952). All others contained in *Shock SuspenStories* no. 15 (June–July 1954); "Shock Talk," *Shock SuspenStories* no. 8 (April–May 1953). Faith Corrigan, "'Superman' Plays Librarian as Comics Go Social-Minded," *New York Times* (May 16, 1956).

35 See, for example, "The Fight for Freedom," *Battle* no. 46 (May 1956); "Your Role in the Cold War," *Battlefield Action* no. 48 (September 1962). "Shock Talk," *Shock SuspenStories* no. 8 (April–May 1953); "Kill Captain America!" *Men's Adventures* no. 28 (July 1954); "Destination: DEATH," *Kent Blake of the Secret Service* no. 5 (January 1952). Flurry of youth reporting to local police in John E. Moser, "Madmen, Morons, and Monocles: The Portrayal of the Nazis in Captain America," in Robert G. Weiner, ed., *Captain America and the Struggle of the Superhero: Critical Essays* (Jefferson, NC: McFarland, 2009), 28. Comic books and the Red Scare in Amy Kiste Nyberg, *Seal of Approval: The History of the Comics Code* (Jackson: University Press of Mississippi, 1998).

36 See Hirsch, "Pulp Empire," chap. 5; John A. Lent, ed., *Pulp Demons: International Dimensions of the Postwar Anti-Comics Campaign* (Madison, NJ: Fairleigh Dickinson University Press, 1999); and, for the French case, Richard Ivan Jobs, "Tarzan Under Attack: Youth, Comics, and Cultural Reconstruction in Postwar France," *French Historical Studies* 4 (Fall 2003): 687–725.

37 "Sadistic drivel" in Sterling North, "A National Disgrace (And a Challenge to American Parents)," *Chicago Daily News*, May 8, 1940. Comic book boycotts and burnings described in Gerard Jones, *Men of Tomorrow: Geeks, Gangsters, and the Birth of the Comic Book* (New York: Basic Books, 2004), 240–241. Anti-comic crusade in Hajdu, *Ten-Cent Plague* and Savage, *Comic Books and America*, 95–103. The broader campaign against juvenile delinquency is described in James Gilbert, *A Cycle of Outrage: America's Reaction to the Juvenile Delinquent in the 1950s* (New York: Oxford University Press, 1986).

38 "The Patriots," *Shock SuspenStories* no. 2 (December 1952); "In Gratitude," *Shock SuspenStories* no. 11 (March 1954); "KLAGG!" *Tales of Suspense* no. 21 (September 1961); "Titan, the Amphibian from Atlantis," *Tales of Suspense* no. 28 (April 1962).

39 A similar but short-lived effort at self-censorship had been attempted once before, in 1948, under the auspices of a trade group known as the Association of Comics Magazine Publishers. It failed because too few of the major publishers agreed to abide by its standards. The second attempt, in 1954, proved more successful due to increased public pressure. A copy of the later "Code of the Comics Magazine Association of America (1954)" can be found in the appendix of Gabilliet, *Of Comics and Men*, 313–316. A good capsule history of the Comics Code is Amy Kiste Nyberg's "Poisoning Children's Culture: Comics and Their Critics," in Lydia Cushman and Deidre Johnson, eds., *Scorned Literature: Essays on the History and Criticism of Popular Mass-Produced Fiction in America* (Westport, CT: Green-

wood Press, 2002): 167–186. The anti-comics crusade is discussed in Hirsch, "Pulp Empire," chapters 4–5 and John A. Lent, ed., *Pulp Demons: International Dimensions of the Postwar Anti-Comics Campaign* (Madison, NJ: Fairleigh Dickinson University Press, 1999). Paul C. Mishler, *Raising Reds: The Young Pioneers, Radical Summer Camps, and Communist Political Culture in the United States* (New York: Columbia University Press, 1999).

40   Gabilliet, *Of Comics and Men*, 313–316.
41   Laura A. Belmonte, *Selling the American Way: U.S. Propaganda and the Cold War* (Philadelphia: University of Pennsylvania Press, 2008), and Justin Hart, *Empire of Ideas: The Origins of Public Diplomacy and the Transformation of U.S. Foreign Policy* (New York: Oxford University Press, 2013). Some of the few surviving examples of the comic book propaganda circulated by the United States overseas can be found in the National Archives at College Park, MD, RG 306, Records of the US Information Agency (NARA RG 306). *Newsday* article (and Murrow quote) in NARA, RG 306, Container 16, "Master File Copies of Pamphlets and Leaflets." On the USIA's larger anticommunist campaign overseas, see Nicholas J. Cull, *The Cold War and the United States Information Agency: American Propaganda and Public Diplomacy, 1945–1989* (Cambridge: Cambridge University Press, 2008). The USIA's comic book campaign is discussed in Hirsch, "Pulp Empire," chap. 6.
42   *Secuestradores* and *Renacer* both held at the Michigan State University Comic Arts Collection; *Los Apuros de Nerón* in NARA, RG 306, Records of the US Information Agency, Container 16, Master File Copies of Pamphlets and Leaflets; *Escuela de Traidores* in RG 306, Container 21. A particularly rich collection of Alliance for Progress comics is held at NARA, RG 306, Container 16, Master File Copies of Pamphlets and Leaflets. *On to the Goal!* in NARA, RG 306, Container 16. Chinese-language example in NARA, RG 306, Container 21. Vietnamese and Grenadan examples covered in Fredrik Strömberg, *Comic Art Propaganda* (New York: St. Martin's, 2010), 78–79. Iraqi case described in Richard L. Graham, *Government Issue: Comics for the People, 1940s–2000s* (New York: Abrams Comicarts, 2011), 9. For similar themes, see Margaret Peacock, "Broadcasting Benevolence: Images of the Child in American, Soviet, and NLF Propaganda in Vietnam, 1964–1973," *Journal of the History of Childhood and Youth* 3, no. 1 (Winter 2010): 15–38. And while beyond the scope of this project, it should be noted that the United States did not stand alone in attempting to sway youth opinion overseas. The Soviet Union and its proxy states were similarly committed to circulating ideologically driven comic books.
43   Judy Kaplan and Linn Shapiro, eds., *Red Diapers: Growing Up in the Communist Left* (Urbana: University of Illinois Press, 1998); Hoover, Dulles, and "corruption of youth" quoted in *The Red Iceberg* (St. Paul, MN: Impact Publishing, 1960); *Is This Tomorrow?* (St. Paul, MN: Catechetical Guild, 1947); General Thomas S. Power, *Design for Survival* no. 1 (1968); J. B. Matthews, "The Commies Go After the Kids," *American Legion Magazine* 47, no. 6 (December 1949)– 62; *It's Time for*

*Reason, NOT Treason* (Washington, DC: Liberty Lobby, n.d.). For similar themes, see also *Socialists' Plans for Control of the USA* (Columbus, OH: State Publishing, ca. 1960). Conservative children's literature is more thoroughly discussed in Michelle Ann Abate, *Raising Your Kids Right: Children's Literature and American Political Conservatism* (New Brunswick, NJ: Rutgers University Press, 2010). Young Americans for Freedom in John A. Andrew, *The Other Side of the Sixties: Young Americans for Freedom and the Rise of Conservative Politics* (New Brunswick, NJ: Rutgers University Press, 1997).

44 "The Dirty War," *American Air Forces* no. 12 (January 1953). See also "The Powder Keg," *Spy Cases* no. 7 (Oct. 1951).

45 "Vietnam Vengeance," *Jungle War Stories* no. 1 (July–September 1962); "A Walk in the Sun," *Jungle War Stories* no. 2 (January–March 1963). See also "Lt. Hunter's Hellcats," *Our Fighting Forces* no. 106 (April 1967).

46 "Customs of Vietnam" and "The Enemy in Viet Nam" in *Jungle War Stories* no. 2 (January–March 1963); "Laos" in *Jungle War Stories* no. 3 (April–June 1963); "The Helping Hand," *Jungle War Stories* no. 5 (October–December 1963); "Iron Man," *Tales of Suspense* no. 39 (March 1963); "Iron Man vs. Gargantus," *Tales of Suspense* no. 40 (April 1963). A different depiction of the war in popular culture appears in Gregory A. Daddis, *Pulp Vietnam: War and Gender in Cold War Men's Adventure Magazines* (Cambridge: Cambridge University Press, 2020).

47 "Pop Goes the War," *Newsweek* (September 12, 1966), 66 and quoted in Wright, *Comic Book Nation*, 193.

48 Youth politicization discussed in Mintz, *Huck's Raft*, 310–334; Rebecca de Schweinitz, *If We Could Change the World: Young People and America's Long Struggle for Racial Equality* (Chapel Hill: UNC Press, 2009); and Susan Eckelmann Berghel, Sara Fieldston, and Paul M. Renfro, eds., *Growing Up America: Youth and Politics Since 1945* (Athens: University of Georgia Press, 2019).

49 "Readers Sound Off!" *Our Fighting Forces* no. 106 (April 1967); "The Firing Line," *Blazing Combat* no. 3 (April 1966); "The Firing Line," *Blazing Combat* no. 4 (July 1966). Similar sorts of arguments were simultaneously playing out in contemporary children's letters to US presidents. See Susan Eckelmann Berghel, "'Remove Our Troops from Veit Nom and Listen': Youth Diplomacy and Johnson's Vietnam War," Eckelmann Berghel et al., eds., *Growing Up America*, 36–53.

50 "The Firing Line," *Blazing Combat* no. 3 (April 1966); "The Firing Line," *Blazing Combat* no. 4 (July 1966); "Letters," *G.I. Combat* no. 134 (February–March 1969).

51 "Via Air Mail," *Star-Spangled War Stories* no. 150 (May 1970). Letter to Iron Man in Wright, *Comic Book Nation*, 241. Similar theme in "Letters," *G.I. Combat* no. 144 (October–November 1970).

52 Quoted in "Readers Sound Off!" *Our Fighting Forces* no. 107 (June 1967). This "declension narrative" echoed by Randy Duncan, Matthew J. Smith, and Paul Levitz, *The Power of Comics: History, Form, and Culture* (London: Bloomsbury, 2015), and Lopes, *Demanding Respect*, 61–74, though Kidman, *Comic Books Incor-*

*porated*, rightly points out that this was more a question of the comic's transition into new media like television and film.

53 The dawn of the "Silver Age" described in Robert Genter, "'With Great Power Comes Great Responsibility': Cold War Comics and the Birth of Marvel Comics," *Journal of Popular Culture* 40, no. 6 (2007): 953–978. On the rise of countercultural comic book heroes, see Ramzi Fawaz, *The New Mutants: Superheroes and the Radical Imagination of American Comics* (New York: NYU Press, 2016).

54 By the 1970s, only 15% of boys and 8% of girls reported regularly reading comics. See Gabilliet, *Of Comics and Men*, 205. The transition from "mass" to "direct" market described in Lopes, *Demanding Respect*, xvii–xviii and 99–103. The figures on contemporary readership are found in Kidman, *Comic Books Incorporated*, 2, though as she points out, the genre has now become a "cinematic universe" that exposes more people around the world to its characters in a year than have ever picked up and read a comic book.

EPILOGUE

1 David Perlmutter, *The Encyclopedia of American Animated Television Shows* (Lanham, MD: Rowman & Littlefield, 2018), 243–245.

2 G.I. Joe's first television appearance occurred in 1982. It was a short commercial meant to advertise a Marvel comic book (and Hasbro toys) with the same name. It received such a strong response that the idea for a syndicated series quickly took shape. See *G.I. Joe Yearbook* 1 (March 1985). On the transition to television in America, see Edward D. Berkowitz, *Mass Appeal: The Formative Age of the Movies, Radio, and T.V.* (New York: Cambridge University Press, 2010), 110–152.

3 It might also be noted that the original line of action figures, first launched in 1964, consisted of Green Berets directly associated with the Vietnam War. But by 1970, and in response to the divisiveness of the conflict, the company rebranded their toy soldiers as an "Adventure Team," who, instead of fighting in identifiable wars, were deployed on nondescript missions. For an overview of this evolution, see Kim Gittleson, "How Did GI Joe Become the World's Most Successful Boys' Toy?" *BBC News* (February 18, 2014), and Tom Engelhardt, *The End of Victory Culture: Cold War America and the Disillusioning of a Generation*, rev. ed. (New York: Basic Books, 2007), 176–178 and 282–285. One argument regarding the apolitical nature of G.I. Joe appears in Gary Cross, *Kids' Stuff: Toys and the Changing World of American Childhood* (Cambridge, MA: Harvard University Press, 1997), 204, though it should also be noted that the show's original story editor, Buzz Dixon, claims to have fought for "stories . . . that are much more rooted in the real world" and that "involve real world problems." See interview in *G.I. Joe Yearbook* 2 (March 1986).

4 "Generational disaffiliation" in Denis Jonnes, *Cold War American Literature and the Rise of Youth Culture: Children of Empire* (New York: Routledge, 2015), 37. Postmodern transformation in Anne Scott MacLeod, *American Childhood: Essays on Children's Literature of the Nineteenth and Twentieth Centuries* (Athens:

University of Georgia Press, 1994), 198–209. Youth leadership within the era's rights revolutions discussed in Gael Graham, *Young Activists: American High School Students in the Age of Protests* (DeKalb: Northern Illinois University Press, 2006); Rebecca De Schweinitz, *If We Could Change the World: Young People and America's Long Struggle for Racial Equality* (Chapel Hill: UNC Press, 2009), and Britt Haas, *Fighting Authoritarianism: American Youth Activism in the 1930s* (New York: Fordham University Press, 2018).

5   For an overview of these many developments, see Donna L. Gilton, *Multicultural and Ethnic Children's Literature in the United States* (Lanham, MD: Scarecrow Press, 2007); Julia L. Mickenberg, *Learning from the Left: Children's Literature, the Cold War, and Radical Politics in the United States* (New York: Oxford University Press, 2006); and Julia L. Mickenberg, "Children's Novels," in Leonard Cassuto et al., eds., *Cambridge History of the American Novel* (New York: Cambridge University Press, 2011), 861–878.

6   On the interplay between international relations and domestic issues at the time, see Mary L. Dudziak, *Cold War Civil Rights: Race and the Image of American Democracy* (Princeton, NJ: Princeton University Press, 2000), and Penny Von Eschen, *Race Against Empire: Black Americans and Anticolonialism, 1937–1957* (Ithaca, NY: Cornell University Press, 1997). The scholarship on contemporary Native American children's literature is voluminous, but excellent overviews can be found in Beverly Slapin and Doris Seale, *Through Indian Eyes: The Native Experience in Books for Children* (Los Angeles: University of California Press, 1998), and Clare Bradford, *Unsettling Narratives: Postcolonial Readings of Children's Literature* (Ontario: Wilfrid Laurier University Press, 2007). So too is there an extensive archive of Black children's literature. Excellent overviews include Katharine Capshaw Smith, *Children's Literature of the Harlem Renaissance* (Bloomington: Indiana University Press, 2004); Rudine Sims Bishop, *Free Within Ourselves: The Development of African American Children's Literature* (Westport, CT: Greenwood Press, 2007); and Wilma King, *African American Childhoods: Historical Perspectives from Slavery to Civil Rights* (New York: Palgrave Macmillan, 2005). On Latinx children's literature and the importance of bilingualism in particular, see Elia Michelle Lafuente, "Latino Children's Literature: An Overview," in Patricia Montilla, ed., *Latinos and American Popular Culture* (Oxford: Praeger, 2013): 273–288. When Puerto Rican author and librarian Pura Belpré wrote *Perez y Martina* (New York: Viking, 1932), it was the first Spanish-language children's book published by a mainstream press; Belpré later wrote several more children's books detailing Puerto Rican folklore. On the Puerto Rican case more broadly, see Marilisa Jiménez-García, "Every Child Is Born a Poet: The Puerto Rican Narrative within American Children's Culture" (PhD diss., University of Florida, 2012). Chamorro children's books include Bonnie Mitchell, *Coconuts for Candy* (Agat, GU: BB Mitchell, 1972); Marsha D. Akau, *Endless Summer: An Adventure Story of Guam* (New York: Vantage Press, 1976); Diane Chambers, *The Adventures of Carmen and the Wishing Stone* (Guam: Taro Patch, 1987); and Evelyn Flores,

*Dolphin Day* (Agat, GU: Green Island Publishers, 1988). On the Asian American experience, see Michael M. Levy, *Portrayal of Southeast Asian Refugees in Recent American Children's Books* (Lewiston, NY: E. Mellen, 2000) and Ymitri Mathison, *Growing Up Asian American in Young Adult Fiction* (Jackson: University Press of Mississippi, 2018). There are, of course, myriad scholarly works covering postcolonial literature, but to my knowledge (and most unfortunately), there has yet to appear a single comprehensive study of "colonized" children's authors "talking back" to the American empire. Something along those lines, however, is hinted at in Raphael Dalleo, *American Imperialism's Undead: The Occupation of Haiti and the Rise of Caribbean Anticolonialism* (Charlottesville: University of Virginia Press, 2016), who notes that the American protectorate inspired a 1932 collaboration between Langston Hughes and Arna Bontemps, *Popo and Fifina: Children of Haiti*, as well as Hughes's later children's book, *The First Book of the West Indies*.

7   Nancy Larrick, "The All-White World of Children's Books," *Saturday Review* (September 11, 1965), 63–66 and 84–85. Black intellectuals (among other nonwhite thinkers), of course, had long noticed the stereotypes people like Larrick suddenly "discovered" in the 1960s. Publishing statistics found in Gilton, *Multicultural and Ethnic Children's Literature*, 95. On lingering biases within the industry, see Philip Nel, *Was the Cat in the Hat Black?: The Hidden Racism of Children's Literature, and the Need for Diverse Books* (New York: Oxford University Press, 2017), and Naomi Lesley, *Fictions of Integration: American Children's Literature and the Legacies of* Brown v. Board of Education (New York: Routledge, 2017).

8   Adrian Wooldridge, "Henty's Heroes," *The Economist* (December 9, 1999); Rod Dreher, "Benedict Option Kids' Libraries," *American Conservative* (July 23, 2019). See also Meghan O'Rourke, "Nancy Drew's Father: The Fiction Factory of Edward Stratemeyer," *New Yorker* (November 8, 2004): 120–129, and Deirdre H. McMahon, "'Quick, Ethel, Your Rifle!': Portable Britishness and Flexible Gender Roles in G. A. Henty's Books for Boys," *Studies in the Novel* 42, nos. 1 and 2 (Spring and Summer 2010): 154–172. On conservative childrearing more generally, see Michelle Ann Abate, *Raising Your Kids Right: Children's Literature and American Political Conservatism* (New Brunswick, NJ: Rutgers University Press, 2010).

9   Elizabeth Evans, *Understanding Engagement in Transmedia Culture* (New York: Routledge, 2020); Carrie Lynn Reinhard, *Fractured Fandoms: Contentious Communication in Fan Communities* (Lanham, MD: Lexington Books, 2018); Paul Booth, *Playing Fans: Negotiating Fandom in the Digital Age* (Iowa City: University of Iowa Press, 2015); danah boyd, *It's Complicated: The Social Lives of Networked Teens* (New Haven, CT: Yale University Press, 2014); Philip M. Napoli, *Audience Evolution: New Technologies and the Transformation of Media Audiences* (New York: Columbia University Press, 2011).

10  On Marvel movies and US empire, see Peter J. Bruno, "Infinity Wars: Post 9/11 Superhero Films and American Empire" (MA thesis, City University of New York, 2019), and Matthew Alford, *Reel Power: Hollywood Cinema and American Supremacy* (New York: Pluto Books, 2010). Online gaming and military recruit-

ment in Jordan Uhl, "The US Military Is Using Online Gaming to Recruit Teens," *The Nation*, July 15, 2020, www.thenation.com; Engelhardt, *The End of Victory Culture*; and on diminishing US power, see also Natasha Zaretsky, *No Direction Home: The American Family and the Fear of National Decline, 1968–1980* (Chapel Hill: UNC Press, 2007); Daniel J. Sargent, *A Superpower Transformed: The Remaking of American Foreign Relations in the 1970s* (New York: Oxford University Press, 2015); William O. Walker, *The Rise and Decline of the American Century* (Ithaca, NY: Cornell University Press, 2018); Victor Bulmer-Thomas, *Empire in Retreat: The Past, Present, and Future of the United States* (New Haven, CT: Yale University Press, 2018).

11 On the reach of today's American empire, see Daniel Immerwahr, *How to Hide an Empire: A History of the Greater United States* (New York: Farrar, Straus and Giroux, 2019), especially chapters 21 and 22. "Politics of childhood" in Anita Casavantes Bradford, "'La Niña Adorada del Mundo Socialista': The Politics of Childhood and U.S.-Cuba-USSR Relations, 1959–1962," *Diplomatic History* 40, no. 2 (April 2016): 298–299.

12 The unaccountability of the foreign policy establishment and a need for greater public investment in diplomacy is discussed in Michael H. Hunt, *Ideology and U.S. Foreign Policy*, rev. ed. (New Haven, CT: Yale University Press, 2009), 180–182 and 193–194.

# INDEX

Page numbers in *italics* indicate illustrations.

Abbott, Jacob, 270m10
abolitionism in early children's literature, 123–24
Adams, William Taylor (Oliver Optic), 61, 179
Africans/Black Americans: amateur newspapers and, 103–4, 114–15; anti-imperialism/internationalism and, 136–37, 142, 275n45; as authors of children's literature, 228, 295–96n6; Korean War in comics and, 213; *Pickaninny Twins*, 136; pulp periodicals set in Africa, 159, 179–81, 284n47
Aguinaldo, Emilio, 256n19
Alcott, Louisa May, 36–37; *Little Women*, amateur newspaper in, 91, 262n5
Alexie, Sherman, 252n51
Alger, Horatio, 61, 254n11, 255n12
Alliance for Progress, 216, 293n42
*Amateur Journal*, 99
amateur newspapers, 16–17, 89–118; agency of children expressed through, 92–95, 107–13; anti-imperialism and internationalism in, 99–101, 115–18; availability and popularity of, 89–90, 92–94; circulation and audience, 109–10, 265n32; conflicts between/attacks by adult printing establishments, 91–92; decline in popularity of, 106, 265n32, 267–68n54; "the Dom," 90–91, 101, 114, 118; foreign and global relations in, 101–6, 266n38; girls creating, 91, 262n3, 262n5; homogeneity (white middle-class male) of creators, 90–91, 106, 262n3; NAPA and regional APAs, 90, 105, 114–15, 267nn50–51; parental/adult concerns about, 117, 267n50, 267n52; racial minorities as child readers and producers of, 91, 99–101, 114–15, 262n3; racism in, 89, 91, 92–98, 102–3, 112, 114–15; school newspapers and, 268n54; serialized fiction fans' interest in, 188; settler colonial project and storytelling in, 95–101, 111–13; status quo ante, child acceptance of, 113–15; toy or tabletop presses, 38–39, 88, 90, 93, 106, 262n3; variety of content, topics, and styles, 90–91, 92; on Western themes, frontier concerns, and Native Americans, 89, 94–101, 116–17, 263–64n19. *See also* gender, in amateur newspapers
Amateur Press Associations (APAs), regional, 90
America First, 190
*American Air Forces* comic, 205–6
*American Boy* magazine, 5, 37, 59, 63
American Century, concept of, 1–2, 19, 188, 217
American Field Service, 149
American Friends Service Committee, 150
American Indians. *See* Native Americans/Indians
American Legion, 217
American School Peace League, 129
Andrews, Fannie Fern, 129, 145

299

anti-imperialism and internationalism, 17, 119–53; agency of children and, 152; alternative forms of, 145, 259n7, 275n45; in amateur newspapers, 99–101, 115–18; children's organizations and, 128–29, 146–51, 149; Christian and missionary literature preceding, 123–28; in comic books, 213; Doctor Doolittle books (Lofting), 144; immigration, treatment of, 123, 126–27, 135, 274n41; letter and gift exchanges between US and foreign children, publications encouraging, 125–26; liberal authors, post-Vietnam dominance of, 6, 7–10, 146, 227–28, 242n26; limitations and shortcomings of children's literature of, 136–37, 138–40, 145–46; *Little Cousin* books (Wade), 133, 137–44; pacifism and, 122, 123, 129–34, 137, 149, 150; Progressives and, 120–23, 128–33, 137–39, 143–46, 150–52; pulp periodicals versus, 152–53, 159–60, 171–72, 185–87; race/racism and, 121–23, 131, 136–37, 142, 228; reader responses/participation/reaction, 137, 146, 150, 271n17; rewriting children's literature, 130–33; rights revolutions of 1960s/1970s and, 227–30; serialized fiction and, 88, 119–22, 260–61n58; shift away from militarized Indian policy, in dime novels and Westerns, 47–54, 52, 251n47, 252n51; success, evaluating, 150–53; travelogues for children preceding, 270n10; "Twins" books (Perkins), 133–37, 135, 143, 144; Vietnam War, responses to, 218–23, 226–27; World's Children, Children of Other Lands, Peeps at Many Lands, and Little People Everywhere series, 144; WWI and, 122, 128–30, 144, 145, 147, 148. *See also* gender, in anti-imperial/internationalist literature
Appleton, Victor, 83–84
Aquaman, 192
*The Argosy/Golden Argosy* (periodical), 28, 29, 37, 103, 156, 158
*Army and Navy Weekly*, 31–32, 160
Army Boy series, 76–78
Association of Comics Magazine Publishers, 292n39
*The Atlantic*, 171, 197

*Atom Age Combat*, 202
"atomic age" and comic books, 194–96, 199, 213

*Baltimore Sun*, 175
Barrows, William, Twelve Nights in the Hunter's Camp, 28–29
Batman and Robin, 192, 194
Battle comics, 210–11
*Battlefield* comic, 205
Beadle, Erastus and Irwin, 24, 25, 39–40
Belpré, Pura, *Perez y Martina*, 296n6
Berlin Blockade and Airlift, 195, 197
Bernstein, Robin, 236n6
Beveridge, Albert, 59, 93, 94
Black Americans. *See* Africans/Black Americans
Black radicalism, 275n45
Blaine, James G., 170
Blake, Katherine Devereux, 131
Bolton, Herbert Eugene, 286n56
Bontemps, Arna, 297n6
Border Boys series, 170
Borderlands school, 286n56
Borneo, 182
Boxer Rebellion, 56, 76–77
Boy Pioneers, 251n47
Boy Scouts, 119, 129, 130, 147, 149, 169, 192, 251n47
*Boy Travellers* series, 270n10
"Boyology," 64
boys. *See specific entries at* gender
*Boys' and Girls' Journal*, 42
*The Boys' Best Weekly*, 35
*Boy's Life*, 63–64
*The Boys' Own*, 42
British empire: in American pulp periodicals, 159, 180–83, 185; children's literature of, 61, 235n4, 238–39n12, 255n12; Latin America, British pulp fiction focused on, 280n23
British Guiana, 182
Bryan, William Jennings, 174
Bud Dajo, Philippines, American military atrocities at, 78
Buffalo Bill, 31, 32, 33, 53
*Buffalo Bill's Stories*, 32, 33

Bureau of Indian Affairs agents, 28, 97
Bureau of Needy Children, 148
Burnett, Frances Hodgson, *Little Lord Fauntleroy*, 256n16
Burnham, Frederick Russell, 284n47
Butler, Smedley, 172
Butterworth, Hezekiah, 179, 270n10

Calamity Jane, 250n41
Camp Fire Girls, 149, 192
Canby, Harry, 80
Captain America, 190, *191*, 194, 196
*Captain Marvel Adventures*, 188, 193
Caribbean. *See* Latin America and Caribbean
Carlisle School, 99
Carnegie Endowment for International Peace, 129, 150
Carson, Kit, 42
Castro, Fidel, 215, 216
Catechetical Guild, *Is This Tomorrow?*, 217
Catholics and Catholicism, 127, 150, 217
Census Bureau, "closure" of frontier by, 38, 102
Central America. *See* Latin America and Caribbean
Century of the Child, 1–2
Charlton Comics, 211, 220
cheap fiction, 13–15, *14*, 23–24, 241–42n24. *See also specific types*
*Chicago Tribune*, 137
"child," defined, 237n9, 261n2
child-authored works: dime novel-style stories and Westerns, 21–22, 23, 38–47, 53–54; girls and gender in, 40–42, 44–47; modern production of, 230–31; Native Americans/Indians in, 39–42, 250n37. *See also* amateur newspapers
childhood/adolescence as distinct developmental phase, 2, 3, 11, 265n34
Children of Other Lands books, 144
Children's Bureau, 120, 148
Children's International Summer Villages, 149
children's libraries, 7, 120–21, 131
children's literature in the American Century, 1–19; American Century and Century of the Child, mutual reinforcement of, 1–2, 11–13, 188; cheap fiction as source material for, 13–15, *14*, 23–24, 241–42n24; between Civil War and Vietnam War, 2, 10, 11–12; colonized other, children as, 239n13, 240n19; dangers of ignoring imperialism/foreign affairs in current literature, 230–32; deconstruction of imperial narratives and, 10; defining "child," 237n9, 261n2; defining "empire" and "imperial," 235–36n4; distinct developmental phase, childhood/adolescence regarded as, 2, 3, 11, 265n34; imperial consciousness in American children, efforts to instill, 2–7, *7*, 9–10; liberal authors, post-Vietnam dominance of, 6, 7–10, 146, 227–28, 242n26; modern resurgence of imperialist/conservative literature, 18, 229–30; reader responses/participation/reaction, 6–10, 239–40nn14–15 (*see also* reader responses/participation/reaction); television, rise and dominance of, 18, 190, 223, 225–27, 227; white boys as main audience for, 5–6, 15 (*see also* gender; race/racism). *See also* amateur newspapers; anti-imperialism and internationalism; comic books and Cold War; dime novels and Westerns; pulp periodicals; serialized fiction
*Children's Missionary Fund*, 124
children's organizations, 128–29, 146–51, *149*, 192. *See also specific organizations by name*
*Children's Work for Children*, 124
*The Child's Anti-Slavery Book*, 124
China and Chinese: in amateur newspapers, 102–3, 107, 114, 116; anti-imperialism/internationalism and, 144–45; in comic books, 195–97, 206–7, 216, 218; in dime novels and Westerns, 32; in pulp periodicals, 179; in serialized fiction, 56, 76–77
Christian children's literature, 123–28, 151
CIA, 214, 215
circulation numbers: amateur newspapers, 261n2; for cheap versus quality material, 13; of children's works generally, 5; comic books, 192, 217, 220, 223, 271n17, 287n2; dime novels and Westerns, 44; pulp periodicals, 184, 278n10; serialized fiction, 62, 85, 255n14

Civil War, 11, 14, 23–24, 107, 193, 216, 225
Clarke, Herbert, 114–15
Cold War. *See* comic books and Cold War
colonialism. *See* children's literature in the American Century; *specific colonized peoples and nations*
comic books and Cold War, 18, 188–223; adult readership, 287n4; American way of life, promoting, 196; anti-imperialism and internationalism in, 213; in "atomic age," 194–96, 199, 213; communist infiltration of comics industry, fears about, 211–14; conservative movements producing, 216–18; decline of, 190, 219–23, 295n54; dime novels compared, 212; government-produced comics, 214–18, 215, 293nn41–42; Korean War, 196, 198, 204–10, 213, 218; military force, justifying use of, 204–7; parental/adult concerns about, 188, 190, 211–14; popularity of, 188–89, 201, 295n54; pulp periodicals turning into, 187, 188, 286n57; race/racism and, 196, 197, 206–7, 209–10, 213, 219, 222–23; reader responses/participation/reaction, 204, 208–11, 220–22, 291n31; romantic plots and interludes, 200–204, 210; silver age of comics, 222–23; Vietnam War and, 189, 190, 216, 218–23; in WWII, 190–94, 191, 205, 216, 287n4, 288n7. *See also* gender, in comic books
Comics Code of 1954, 213–14, 220
Committee on Public Information (CPI), 128
communism. *See* Marxism/socialism/communism
compulsory education laws, 107, 128, 146, 192
Comstock, Anthony, 51, 120
Conan the Barbarian, 158
Conrad, Joseph, *Heart of Darkness*, 180
conservative movements: comic books produced by, 216–18; modern resurgence of imperialist/conservative literature, 18, 229–30
Crockett, Davy, 102
Cuba and Cubans, 12, 16, 226; in amateur newspapers, 105–6; anti-imperialist/internationalist children's literature and, 139; comic books for, 215, 216; in *Little Cousin* books, 139; Platt Amendment, 185–86; pulp periodicals and, 168, 186; in serialized fiction, 57, 62, 63, 68, 70–72, 74, 79, 85–86. *See also* War of 1898
cultural gifts movement, 17
cultural internationalism movement, 122

*Daring Confessions*, 202
Darrow, Clarence, 130
DC comics, 18, 189, 222
Deering, Fremont B., 170
Dell Comics, 220
Depression Era, 146, 184–88, 252n50
didactic children's literature, 11, 31, 74, 146, 156, 227, 240n20, 244n6, 260–61n58
dime novels and Westerns, 16, 21–54; advertisements in, 31; amateur newspapers denouncing, 116, 117; boys as primary audience for, 24, 244n5; child-authored works, 21–22, 23, 38–47, 53–54; comic books compared, 212; federal agents and pacifists, scornful treatment of, 28; parental/adult concerns about, 14, 24, 36–38, 47, 49, 51–53, 52, 60–61, 248n26, 252n52, 254n11; pulp periodicals' direct descent from, 158; rape discourse in, 25, 27–28, 45–46; reader responses/participation/reaction, 22–24, 26, 31–38, 53–54, 247n19; reading clubs for, 43; "respectable" children's periodicals, collapse of, 247n7; rise in availability and popularity, 13–15, 14, 23–24; serialized fiction compared, 56, 57, 60–61, 67, 119, 253n3; settler colonial project and storytelling, 22, 23–31, 25, 46–47 243n2. *See also* gender, in dime novels and Westerns; Native Americans/Indians
Disney films, 102, 186
Dixon, Franklin W., 16
Doctor Doolittle books (Lofting), 144
dollar diplomacy, 17, 157, 159, 162–67, 172–73, 186
"the Dom." *See* amateur newspapers
Don Sturdy series, 82–83, 86
Drago Doctrine, 174
Dreiser, Theodore, 80–81
Dulles, Allen, 217

INDEX | 303

East Germany, 200
EC (Entertaining Comics), 18, 189, 204, 210, 212–14
education. *See* schooling and education
Egypt, 198
empire, children's literature on. *See* children's literature in the American Century
Erdrich, Louise, 252n51
*Escuela de Traidores*, 216
*The Eskimo Twins*, 136
eugenics and race theory, 183, 196, 288n13
European Relief Council, 148
evangelical doctrine, 123–28, 151
*Everyland* (magazine), 124–26, 271n14, 271nn16–17
exceptionalism, 19, 126, 139, 181, 227
expansionism. *See* manifest destiny and expansionist rhetoric
*Los Expoliadores*, 215, 216
exterminationism, 27, 52, 56, 72, 94, 95, 96, 98, 112, 114, 123, 168, 261n1

"Fairy Tale Wars," 268–69n5
fan mail. *See* reader responses/participation/reaction
Fawcett Publishers, 188, 195
FBI, 213
Fiction Wars, 60, 158
Filipinos. *See* Philippines and Filipinos; US-Philippine War
Finger, Charles, *Tales from Silver Lands*, 184
First World War. *See* World War I
Fiske, John, 161
flag, veneration of, 56, 64, 65, 74, 75, 78, 79, 176–77, 213, 283n40
the Flash, 194
*Foreign Affairs* (magazine), 197
foreign relations, children's literature on. *See* children's literature in the American Century
4-H, 192
Fraternal Order of Police, 217
French Foreign Legion, 180, 218
frontier. *See* dime novels and Westerns; settler colonial project and storytelling; Western and frontier concerns

*Frontier Series*, 24–26, 25
Future Farmers of America, 192

Gaines, William, 212
Gardner, Erle Stanley, and Perry Mason stories, 158
gender: infiltration by girls of genres aimed at boys, 5, 6; manliness, concerns over, 5, 63–68, 117, 132, 200, 229, 256n16; "new girls" and New Women, 47, 138, 250–51n42; school culture, girls' experience of freedom of, 248n25, 265n34; white boys as intended audience for imperialist literature, 5–6, 24; women's suffrage and feminist movements, 131, 138, 267n51, 271n24. *See also* rape discourse
gender, in amateur newspapers: childhood restrictions to compared by adolescents to gender restrictions, 107–8; girls, amateur newspapers created by, 91, 262n3, 262n5, 267n51; manliness, concerns over, 117; production, white male middle-class domination of, 90–91, 106, 262n3; status quo ante, child acceptance of, 114, 267n51
gender, in anti-imperial/internationalist literature: involvement of female writers and educators, 122, 129, 131–32; manliness, concerns over, 132; "Twins" books aimed at both boys and girls, 134
gender, in comic books: femmes fatales, 200–202; manliness, concerns over, 200; passive/traditional gender roles, 202, 203–4, 290n24; popularity with girl readers, 188–89, 203–4, 295n54; rape discourse, 200; romantic plots, 200–204, 210
gender, in dime novels and Westerns: in child-authored stories, 40–42, 44–47; dime romance fiction for girls, 45, 250n38; girl readers, 32–33, 34–36; girl writers, 44–47, 250n38, 250n41; rape discourse in settler colonial narratives, 25, 27–28, 45–46; women as authors of, 44, 50, 250n41
gender, in pulp periodicals: lower-class female readership, association with, 158; rape discourse, 154–55

gender, in serialized fiction: Chinese characters and treatment of ladies, 77; defeminization of Native women, 72–73; feminization of colonized races, 68; girls, series written for, 83, 84, 260n53; girls' responses to, 83–84; manliness, concerns over, 63–68, 256n16; miscegenation, discouragement of, 73, 257n31; rape discourse, 72–73
general disaffiliation, 226–27
German-American Bund, 190
Germans, portrayals of, 128, 136
G.I. Joe (TV cartoon series and toy), 225–26, 295nn2–3
Gilded Age, 22, 23, 54, 60, 89, 94, 103, 107, 111, 117, 124, 243n2
Girl Scouts, 129, 147, 149, 192
girls. See specific entries at gender
Golden Argosy/The Argosy (periodical), 28, 29, 37, 103, 156, 158
Good Neighbor Policy, 185–86
Grant, Madison, 183
Great War. See World War I
Greeley, Horace, 37, 92, 94, 263n16
Green Lantern, 194
Grenada, 225
Guam, 125, 161, 228
Gypsies, portrayals of, 136

Haggard, H. Rider, and Allan Quatermain stories, 61
Haiti, 159, 176, 185, 283n39
Hall, G. Stanley, 64, 113, 256n16
Hancock, H. Irving, 170
Hand, Harry, 100–101
Harding, Warren, 123, 183
Hardy Boys series, 16, 55, 61, 185
Harlem Renaissance, 136–37
Hawaii and Hawaiians, 105, 126, 138
Hawthorne, Nathaniel, 262n3
*Heathen Children's Friend*, 124
Henty, G. A., 61, 229, 255n12
Hersey, Harold, 158
Hispanics: as authors of children's literature, 228, 296–97n6. See also Latin America and Caribbean; specific Latin countries
Hitler, Adolf, 190, *191*
Honduras, 159, 168

Honeck, Mischa, 236n6, 239n14
Hoover, Herbert, 148, 185
Hoover, J. Edgar, 217
House Un-American Activities Committee (HUAC), 212
Hughes, Langston, 136–37, 297n6
Hull, Cordell, 185

immigration, 3, 17, 91, 92, 102–3, 107, 123, 126–27, 135, 183, 230, 274n41
imperialist children's literature. *See* children's literature in the American Century
*Indian Stories*, 50
Indians. *See* Native Americans/Indians
informal imperialism and American investment capital, 257n33
Ingraham, Prentiss, *The Boy Guide*, 25
Intercollegiate Liberal League, 150
International Good-Will Day, 149
internationalism. *See* anti-imperialism and internationalism
Iraqis, comic books for, 216
Iron Man, 209, 219–20, 222

Jackson, Helen Hunt, *Century of Dishonor*, 49
*The Japanese Twins*, 135–36
Jews: as comic book artists, 288n5, 288n7; *Our Little Jewish Cousin*, 142
John Birch Society, 217
*John Wayne Adventure Comics*, 198
Johnson, Lyndon, 218
Junior Red Cross, 128–29, 148, 149, 192
juvenile delinquency, 92, 129, 146, 192, 212, 252n52, 292n37

Kay, Ross, 166
Kearney, Denis, 116
Keene, Carolyn, 16
Kefauver, Estes, 211–12
Kennedy, John F., 218
Key, Ellen, 1
Kilburne, C. E. (Charles), 76, 258n36
Know-Nothing. *See* nativism
Knox, Thomas, 270n10
Knox, Philander, 173
Korea, Koreans, and Korean War, 196, 198, 204–10, 213, 218

Ku Klux Klan and Kiddie Klavern youth outreach groups, 127, 142
Kurtzman, Harvey, 212

Larrick, Nancy, 229
Latin America and Caribbean: British pulp fiction focused on, 280n23; in comic books, 214–16, *215*; Good Neighbor Policy in, 185–86; Monroe Doctrine and Roosevelt Corollary, 18, 56, 157, 159, 170, 172, 173, *175*, 279n13; pulp periodicals and, 17, 157, 161–63, 165–68, 173–78, *175*, 185–86; serialized fiction and, 74, 160–61. *See also specific countries and conflicts*
L.C. Page & Company, 133, 138
League for a Durable Peace, 149
League of Nations, 123, 137, 150, 151, 273n31, 276n49
Leopold, Nathan, 130
Liberty Lobby, 217
Liberty Toy Company, 130
*Little Cousin* books (Mary Hazelton Wade), 133, 137–44
Little People Everywhere series (McDonald and Dalrymple), 144
Loeb, Richard, 130
Lofting, Hugh, 144
London, Jack, 59
Luce, Henry, 1, 19, 188

*MAD* magazine, 214
Mahan, Alfred Thayer, 161
USS *Maine*, 85, 106
manifest destiny and expansionist rhetoric: in amateur newspapers, 59, 94, 97, 104, 106, 110, 112, 113; anti-imperialism/internationalism and, 122–24, 128, 153; in dime novels and Westerns, 22, 28–31, 36, 39, 54; introduced through children's literature, 2, 6, 8, 10–13, 16, 18, 19; public rejection of, 227; pulp periodicals and, 160–65; in serialized fiction, 59, 73, 80, 88
manliness, concerns over, 5, 63–68, 117, 132, 200, 229, 256n16
Mao Zedong, 196
Marshall Plan, 199
Marvel Boy, 197

Marvel comics/cinematic universe, 18, 189, 219, 231, 295n2
Marxism/socialism/communism: anti-imperialist/internationalist children's literature and, 145, 269n7, 270n9; *G. I. Joe* not mentioning, 226; House Un-American Activities Committee (HUAC), 212; pulp periodicals and, 158, 183–84; Red Scares, 145, 183, 211, 213, 218; Russian Revolution, 145, 183–84; Vietnam War, 18, 189, 190, 216, 218–23. *See also* comic books and Cold War
Mathiews, Franklin K., 119–21
McDonald, Etta Blaisdell, 144
McKinley, William, 68–69, 139
Mexican Revolution, 56, 155–56, 157, 168–70
*The Mexican Twins*, 135, 136, 178
Mexico and Mexicans, 97, 104, 159, 162, 166–71, 176, 178, 182, 216
Middle East, 198, 216, 225
Millenialism, 123
mind control, 198, 208
missionary literature, 123–28
Monroe Doctrine, 18, 56, 157, 159, 170, 172, 173, *175*, 279n13
Moro War, 78
Munro, George, 24
Murrow, Edward R., 216
muscular Christianity, 66

Nancy Drew series, 16, 55, 61, 185
National Amateur Press Association (NAPA), 90, 105, 114–15, 267nn50–51
National Catholic Welfare Council, 149–50
National Council of Churches, 149–50
National Student Committee for the Limitation of Armaments, 150
National Student Forum, 150
National Youth Administration, 148
Native Americans/Indians: amateur newspapers, as subjects of, 89, 94–101, 116–17, 263–64n19; amateur newspapers, Indian child readers and producers of, 91, 99–101; in anti-imperialist/internationalist children's literature, 138, 143–44; as authors of children's literature, 228, 296n6; Bureau of Indian Affairs agents, low opinions of, 28, 97;

Native Americans/Indians (*cont.*)
in child-authored stories, 39–42, 250n37; children's accounts of actual encounters with, 32–33; exterminationism, 27, 52, 94, 95, 96, 98, 112, 168, 261n1; "indigenous texts," Native American reading of dime novels as, 252n51; "noble savage" motif, 28–29, 98; *Our Little Indian Cousin*, 138, 143–44; Peace Policy and education initiatives, 47–54, 98–101; in settler colonial narratives, 23–31, 25, 39–40; shift away from militarized Indian policy, 47–54, 52, 251n47, 252n51; "soft" settler colonialism regarding, 123; vanishing Indian trope, 28–29, 47, 96
nativism, 17, 18, 69, 85, 91, 102–3, 116, 117, 121, 122, 125, 142, 228; Know Nothing, 102
"new girls" and New Women, 47, 138, 250–51n42
*The New Student*, 150
*New York Times*, 90, 114, 115, 211
Newbery Medal, 184
*Newsday*, 214
*Newsweek*, 220
Nicaragua, 172, 175, 185, 197
"noble savage" motif, 28–29, 98
Norris, Frank, 59
nuclear weapons and comic books, 194–96, 199, 213

Office of War Information, 192
Old Glory series, 56, 62, 65–66, 69, 71, 86, 255n14
"Old Pard," 32, 34, 43
Olney, Richard, 159, 279n13
*On to the Goal!* comic, 216
Open Door trade policies, 280n22
orphan trains, 248n26
*Our Little Cousin* books (Mary Hazelton Wade), 133, 137–44

pacifism: anti-imperialism/internationalism and, 122, 123, 129–34, 137, 149, 150; dime novels and Westerns, scornful treatment in, 28
Pan-Africanism, 145
Panama Canal, 105, 157, 176, 184

Pan-American Conference (1933), 185
Pan-American Day, 186
Pan-Asianism, 259n7
panic of 1893, 60
parental/adult concerns: about amateur newspapers, 117, 267n50, 267n52; about comic books, 188, 190, 211–14; about dime novels and Westerns, 14, 24, 36–38, 47, 49, 51–53, 52, 60–61, 248n26, 252n52, 254n11; about juvenile delinquency, 92, 129, 146, 192, 212, 252n52, 292n37; about serialized fiction, 83, 119–22, 268n2
Parenthood in a Free Nation, 203
*Parents* magazine, 131, 133
pass-along effect, 85, 192
Payson, Howard (John Henry Goldfrap), 168–69, 281n27
Pearl Harbor, 190
Peeps at Many Lands series, 144
Perkins, Lucy Fitch, 133–37, 135, 143, 144, 145, 148, 151
Peru, 161–62, 186, 214
Philippines and Filipinos, 16, 226; in amateur newspapers, 105–6; as authors of children's literature, 228; Boy Scouts and Girl Scouts, 147; in *Little Cousin* books, 139; in pulp periodicals, 168; in serialized fiction, 56, 57, 63, 64, 66–74, 71, 77–79, 86; in "Twin" books, 136. See also US-Philippine War
*Pickaninny Twins*, 136
Pioneer series, 253n3
Platt Amendment, 185–86
Pomeroy, Jesse (the "Boston Boy Fiend"), 53, 252n52
Pratt, Richard Henry, 99
Progressives and Progressive Era: amateur newspapers and, 111, 118; anti-imperialism/internationalism and, 17, 120–23, 128–33, 137–39, 143–46, 150–52; dime novels/Westerns and, 22, 23, 47, 50, 251n44
Protestant evangelical doctrine, 123–28, 151
Protestant work ethic, 66–67, 70, 162
*Publisher's Weekly*, 189
*Puck* (magazine), 52

Puerto Rico and Puerto Ricans, 56, 142, 147, 161, 163, 228, 296–97n6
pulp periodicals, 17–18, 154–87; anti-imperialism/internationalism versus, 152–53, 159–60, 171–72, 185–87; British empire, American characters in, 159, 180–83; comic books, turning into, 187, 188, 286n57; Depression and shifts in federal policy affecting tone of, 184–87; dime novels, direct descent from, 158; dollar diplomacy and, 17, 157, 159, 162–67, 172–73, 186; expansionist rhetoric, changing nature of, 160–65; global reach beyond Western hemisphere, 178–84; Latin America and Caribbean as backdrop for, 17, 157, 161–63, 165–68, 173–78, *175*, 185–86; on military interventions, 167–78, *175*; paternalist rhetoric of, 174, *175*, 178, 282n37; race/racism in, 159, 161–74, *175*, 176, 179–83, 285nn49–50; reader responses to/participation in/reaction against, 156, 158–60; rise and development of, 154–60; youth readership of, 158, 278–79n11. *See also* gender, in pulp periodicals

Quality comics, 18, 189

race theory and eugenics, 183, 196, 288n13
race/racism: abolitionism in early children's literature, 123–24; in amateur newspapers, 89, 91, 92–98, 102–3, 112, 114–15; anti-imperialism/internationalism and, 121–23, 131, 136–37, 142, 228; authors of children's literature, racial minorities as, 228–29, 296–97n6; comic books in Cold War and, 196, 197, 206–7, 209–10, 213, 219, 222–23; in dime novels and Westerns, 39 (*see also* Native Americans/Indians); extermina-tionism, 27, 52, 56, 72, 94, 95, 96, 98, 112, 114, 123, 168, 261n1; imperialism and racism as mutual reinforcers, 5–6; Ku Klux Klan and Kiddie Klavern youth outreach groups, 127, 142; paternalist rhetoric of pulp periodicals towards non-whites, 174, *175*, 178, 282n37; post-Vietnam rise in authors of color, 18; Progressives and, 122; in pulp periodicals, 159, 161–74, *175*, 176, 179–83, 285nn49–50; rights revolutions of 1960s/1970s and, 228; in serialized fiction, 56, 62–63, 68–73, *71*, 76–79, 82, 85, 86, 121–22; in settler colonial narratives, 29–31, 246n13; slavery, adolescent comparisons of childhood restrictions to, 107–8; white supremacy, 29, 73, 103, 115, 182–84, 228. *See also specific nations, nationalities, and racial/ethnic groups*
racial minorities as child readers: amateur newspapers, Black and Indian children as readers/producers of, 91, 99–101, 114–15, 262n3; Harlem Renaissance and, 136–37; texts produced for/about, 15, 228, 229, 242n26
rape discourse: in comic books, 200; in pulp periodicals, 154–55; in serialized fiction, 72–73; in settler colonial narratives/dime novels/Westerns, 25, 27–28, 45–46
Rauschenbusch, Walter, 132–33
reader responses/participation/reaction, 6–10, 239–40nn14–15; to anti-imperialist/internationalist texts, 137, 146, 150; to comic books, 204, 208–11, 220–22, 291n31; to dime novels and Westerns, 22–24, 26, 31–38, 53–54, 247n19; to pulp periodicals, 156, 158–60; to serialized fiction, 55, 57–58, 62, 80–88, 259n46; Stratemeyer and, 55, 57–58, 81–85, 87–88, 167, 259n46
Reagan, Ronald, 216, 226
Red Cross, 128–29, 148, *149*, 192
Red Scares, 145, 183, 211, 213, 218
Reid, Captain Mayne, 61
remediation, 187
rights revolutions of 1960s/1970s, 227–30
Rolt-Wheeler, Francis, *The Boy with the U.S. Indians*, 48–49
Roosevelt, Franklin Delano, 185–86
Roosevelt, Theodore, 59, 63, 68, 73, 117, 133, 157, 160, 172, 186, 256n15, 282n37
Roosevelt Corollary, 56, 157
Rover Boys series, 55, 81–82
Russell brothers (Old Glory series), 62, 66–73, *71*, 76, 82, 86
Russian Revolution, 145, 183–84
Russia/Soviet Union. *See* Marxism/socialism/communism

*Saludos Amigos* (Disney film), 186
Sandino, Augusto, 178
*Saturday Evening Post*, 183
schooling and education: compulsory education laws, 107, 128, 146, 192; girls' experience of freedom of, 248n25, 265n34; school newspapers, 268n54; textbooks, 244n6, 253n4, 272n25, 280n19
Second World War. *See* World War II
*Los Secuestradores*, 216
"sensational" fiction. *See* dime novels and Westerns
serialized fiction, 16, 55–88; anti-imperialism/internationalism and, 88, 119–22, 260–61n58; authors of, 55–56, 61; dime novels and Westerns compared, 56, 57, 60–61, 67, 119, 253n3; foreign relations, focus on, 56–57, 253–54n5; manliness, concerns over, 63–68; parental/adult concerns about, 83, 119–22, 268n2; racism in, 56, 62–63, 68–73, 71, 76–79, 82, 85, 86, 121–22; reader responses to/participation in/reaction against, 55, 57–58, 62, 80–88, 259n46; rehabilitative power of Americanism, focus on, 73–79, 75; rise and development of, 59–63; strenuous lives and adventures of boy heroes of, 61–62, 63–68, 74–76; US-Philippine War and, 16, 56, 62, 64, 66, 67, 68, 256n19; values and morals reinforced by, 66–68; War of 1898 and, 54, 56, 58, 61, 62, 64, 66, 68, 74, 75, 82, 85–86, 128, 258n33; Western series, 253n3, 255n12; WWI in, 128. *See also* gender, in serialized fiction; Stratemeyer, Edward, and Stratemeyer Syndicate
settler colonial project and storytelling: in amateur newspapers, 95–101, 111–13; in dime novels and Westerns, 22, 23–31, 25, 46–47 243n2; "soft" versions of, 123
The Shadow, 158
Sherman, William Tecumseh, 261n1
*Shock SuspenStories*, 212
Siberia, 184
slavery: abolitionism in early children's literature, 123–24; adolescent comparisons of childhood restrictions to, 107–8
"slicks," 278n10

socialism. *See* Marxism/socialism/communism
South Africa, 181
Soviet Union. *See* Marxism/socialism/communism; Russian Revolution
Spain and Spaniards, 68, 74, 79, 86, 139, 286n56
Spanish-American War. *See* War of 1898
Sprague, William C., 59
*St. Nicholas* (magazine), 50, 51, 117
Starry Flag Series, 74
Stephens, Ann S., *Malaeska*, 44, 250n41
Stimson, Henry, 185
Stoddard, Lothrop, 183
Strategic Defensive Initiative, 226
Stratemeyer, Edward, and Stratemeyer Syndicate, 16, 55–58; Alger and, 254n11; anti-imperialist/internationalist children's literature and, 119, 121–22, 126, 137, 139; competitors of, 73–74, 76, 77; conservative interest in works of, 229; Depression era affecting, 185; girls, series written for, 83, 84, 260n53; imperialist intentions of, 55–58, 121–22, 126; Latin American focus, shift to, 160–62; portrait of Stratemeyer, 58; race/racism and, 68–73; reader responses and fan mail, use of, 55, 57–58, 81–85, 87–88, 167, 259n46; rise/development of serialized fiction and, 61–63; on Theodore Roosevelt, 256n15; strenuous lives and adventures of boy heroes of, 61–62, 63–68; on textbooks, 253n4; "Twin" books compared, 134; Western series, 253n3. *See also specific series, e.g.* Old Glory series
"strenuous life" dogma, 63, 66, 256n15
Strong, Josiah, *Our Country*, 107, 161
Student Volunteer Movement, 124, 270n10
Superman, 192, 194

*Tales from the Crypt*, 212
*Tales of Suspense*, 212
Tarzan, 158, 181, 278n11, 284n27
television, rise and dominance of, 18, 190, 223, 225–27, 227
Teller Amendment, 68
*The Three Caballeros* (Disney film), 186

*Thrilling Adventures* series, 164
*Time* magazine, 1
Tom Swift series, 61
Tousey, Frank, 24
toy or tabletop presses, 38–39, 88, 90, 93, 106, 262n3
travelogues for children, 179, 270n10
Truman, Harry, 188, 193, 286n1
Turner, Frederick Jackson, 31, 113
"Twins" books (Lucy Fitch Perkins), 133–37, 135, 143, 144

Ukraine, 183–84
*Uncle Sam's Boys in the Philippines*, 78–79
Uncle Sam's Boys series, 170
United States Book Company (USBC), 60
United States Food Administration, 129
United States Information Agency (USIA), 214, 216, 293n41
US-Philippine War, 16, 56, 62, 64, 66, 67, 68, 139, 160, 256n19

vanishing Indian trope, 28–29, 47, 96
Venezuela, 126, 166, 171, 271n14
Vietnam War, 18, 189, 190, 216, 218–23, 226–27, 230, 295n3
Vietnamese American authors of children's literature, 228
Voice of America, 199
voting age, child proposals to lower, 108–9

Wade, Mary Hazelton, 137–44, 145, 148, 151
*War Comics*, 207
War of 1898: amateur newspapers and, 105; USS *Maine*, 85, 106; pulp periodicals and, 157, 160; serialized fiction and, 54, 56, 58, 61, 62, 64, 66, 68, 74, 75, 82, 85–86, 128, 258n33
War on Terror, 216, 230
Washington, George, 148
Wayne, John, 198, 230
Wertham, Fredric, 212
Western and frontier concerns: amateur newspapers, Western and frontier themes in, 89, 94–101, 116–17, 263–64n19; Census Bureau, "closure" of frontier by, 38, 102; Cold War- and Disney-inspired revival of, 102; fading of interest in, 101–2; pulp periodicals, 154–56; in serialized fiction, 253n3, 255n12. *See also* dime novels and Westerns; settler colonial project and storytelling
*Western Weekly*, 28
White House Conference on Children and Youth, 148
white supremacy, 29, 73, 103, 115, 182–84, 228. *See also* race/racism
Wide Awakes, 107
*Wide World Adventures*, 167
Wilder, Laura Ingalls, Little House on the Prairie series, 252n50
Wilson, Woodrow, 129, 168
Winfield, Arthur (pseudonym for Edward Stratemeyer), 55, 81
*Winnetka Graded Book List*, 121, 255n14
Women's Peace Party, 149
Woodcraft Indians, 251n47
Workingmen's Party, 116
World Court, 150
World War I, 17, 122, 128–30, 144, 145, 147, 148
World War II, 151, 187, 188, 190–94, *191*, 205, 216, 287n4, 288n7
World's Children series (Virginia Olcott), 144
Wounded Knee Massacre, 47
Writers' War Board, 193

"Yellow Peril," 76, 135, 258n36, 285n50
*Young America*, 32
*Young Americans Abroad*, 179
Young Americans for Freedom, 217
*Young Aspirant* (amateur newspaper), 116
Young Men's and Young Women's Christian Associations (YMCA/YWCA), 129, 192
Young People's Missionary Movement, 124

*Zigzag Journeys* series, 179, 270n10
Zorro, 158

ABOUT THE AUTHOR

BRIAN ROULEAU is Associate Professor of History at Texas A&M University. He is the author of *With Sails Whitening Every Sea: Mariners and the Making of an American Maritime Empire*.

www.ingramcontent.com/pod-product-compliance
Lightning Source LLC
Chambersburg PA
CBHW030636150426
42811CB00077B/2160/J